AF862209

Cultural Economics & the Creative Economy

Series Editors
Erwin Dekker, Erasmus University Rotterdam, Rotterdam
The Netherlands
Andrej Srakar, University of Ljubljana, Ljubljana, Slovenia
Michael Rushton, Indiana University, Bloomington, USA

This series aims to provide original and societally relevant perspectives on the modern creative economy from the perspective of cultural economics broadly understood. In the past decades it is increasingly realized that value in the economy is realized in the creative industries and the more traditional cultural sectors. This series will aim to shed light on how value is created and realized and how the creative economy shapes the broader economy. We believe that trends in the creative economy are often a sign of things to come in the broader economy, this is true for the way in which work is organized, how innovation happens, how entrepreneurs act and the relevance of cities in the modern economy.

The series will provide a collection of works of leading cultural economists on theoretical and empirical topics. It will cover the field in its most broad sense and focus on the current open problems and topics in cultural economics, covering micro, macro end methodological aspects.

Carolina Dalla Chiesa · Anders Rykkja
Editors

Cultural Funding and Financing

A Guide to New and Traditional Models in Arts and Culture

palgrave
macmillan

Editors
Carolina Dalla Chiesa
Department of Arts and Culture Studies
Erasmus University Rotterdam
Rotterdam, Zuid-Holland, The Netherlands

Anders Rykkja
School of Arts, English and Languages
Queen's University Belfast
Belfast, UK

ISSN 2662-4478 ISSN 2662-4486 (electronic)
Cultural Economics & the Creative Economy
ISBN 978-3-031-96695-8 ISBN 978-3-031-96696-5 (eBook)
https://doi.org/10.1007/978-3-031-96696-5

This work was supported by Queen's University Belfast and Erasmus Universiteit Rotterdam.

© The Editor(s) (if applicable) and The Author(s) 2026. This book is an open access publication.

Open Access This book is licensed under the terms of the Creative Commons Attribution 4.0 International License (http://creativecommons.org/licenses/by/4.0/), which permits use, sharing, adaptation, distribution and reproduction in any medium or format, as long as you give appropriate credit to the original author(s) and the source, provide a link to the Creative Commons license and indicate if changes were made.
The images or other third party material in this book are included in the book's Creative Commons license, unless indicated otherwise in a credit line to the material. If material is not included in the book's Creative Commons license and your intended use is not permitted by statutory regulation or exceeds the permitted use, you will need to obtain permission directly from the copyright holder.
The use of general descriptive names, registered names, trademarks, service marks, etc. in this publication does not imply, even in the absence of a specific statement, that such names are exempt from the relevant protective laws and regulations and therefore free for general use.
The publisher, the authors and the editors are safe to assume that the advice and information in this book are believed to be true and accurate at the date of publication. Neither the publisher nor the authors or the editors give a warranty, expressed or implied, with respect to the material contained herein or for any errors or omissions that may have been made. The publisher remains neutral with regard to jurisdictional claims in published maps and institutional affiliations.

This Palgrave Macmillan imprint is published by the registered company Springer Nature Switzerland AG
The registered company address is: Gewerbestrasse 11, 6330 Cham, Switzerland

If disposing of this product, please recycle the paper.

Acknowledgements

The editors are grateful for receiving a joint library grant for open access publication from Erasmus University Rotterdam and Queen's University Belfast.

We would like to thank all the authors for contributing their time and excellent work. The excellent support provided by our editor Ellie Duncan and Supraja Yegnaram made a huge difference in terms of getting the book you are reading ready for publication. The process would not have been as smooth without your input and guidance.

Anders would like to thank Rebecca Clarke, his colleagues Dr Ali FitzGibbon and Dr Kim Marie Spence, and Dr Kurt Taroff, Professor Maeve McCusker, Professor Paul Stapleton, Denise Toner, Áine Egan and the rest of the leadership of the School of Arts, English and Languages at Queen's University Belfast, for their timely and generous support of the publication of this volume. Furthermore, he would like to thank the UiA Crowdfunding Research Center (in particular, Professor Rotem Shneor and Dr Prince Baah-Peprah), Ziaul Haque Munim, Lars Julius Halvorsen, Daniel Nordgård, and Stein Bjelland.

At last, for his part, a shout out to Torgeir Gullaksen, who more than any person he knows understands the importance of the role of funding and financing in the production of artistic works and cultural experiences.

Carolina would like to share thanks to Voordekunst, in the Netherlands, for their openness to welcoming researchers to discuss new forms of funding for the arts, and her colleagues at the Arts and Culture Department of Erasmus University Rotterdam for valuable discussions, especially in the context of the research cluster "Values in the Creative Economy" (ViCE).

Finally, the editors would like to thank Hans Abbing, Erwin Dekker, Lluís Bonet, Maria O'Brien, and Dylan Thompson for their time and invaluable help with peer reviews.

Competing Interests Anders Rykkja acknowledges the receipt of a grant from the Research Council of Norway [301291] that helped fund work undertaken as one of the editors of this volume.

Praise for *Cultural Funding and Financing*

"This timely and impressive book gives contemporary academic and multidisciplinary insights into the complex topic of funding and financing of art and culture, with contributions from 21 leading scholars in the field. It covers a broad range of funding opportunities, from traditional funding models to new and fully digital models, leveraged by new technologies. I highly recommend the book for scholars as well as practitioners in the cultural and creative sectors."

—Trine Bille, *Professor of Cultural Economics, Copenhagen Business School, Denmark*

"This timely collection of essays by a number of distinguished contributors will fill a significant gap in the cultural economics literature. The volume will provide essential guidance to artists, cultural organisations and policy makers in their efforts to deal with rapid changes in the arts funding landscape in the contemporary world."

—Professor David Throsby, *Distinguished Professor of Economics, Macquarie Business School, Macquarie University, Australia*

"*Cultural Funding and Financing* is a timely and ambitious volume that offers one of the most comprehensive examinations to date of how artists and cultural organizations access resources in a rapidly evolving landscape. What makes this book stand out is its insistence on bridging traditional and emerging models—philanthropy, public subsidy, crowd-funding, online patronage, and more—while resisting simplistic narratives of innovation or decline. The editors bring together a remarkable range of scholars who ground their chapters in conceptual clarity, empirical rigor, and an interdisciplinary sensibility that reflects the real complexity of cultural production today. For researchers, policymakers, and practitioners alike, this collection is an indispensable guide to the shifting terrain of cultural finance."

—Joanna Woronkowicz, *Associate Professor, O'Neill School of Public and Environmental Affairs, Indiana University, US*

Contents

Notes on Contributors

Aline Albertelli is a researcher and practitioner specializing in cultural policy, creative entrepreneurship, and innovative governance models for the cultural sector. Her work explores how creative practices intersect with public and private sectors to foster sustainable and participatory cultural ecosystems. At KEA, she has contributed to research, project management, and policy studies supporting cultural and creative industries across Europe. She also serves as the Community Manager of*b.creative*, a global network of creative entrepreneurs. Holding an MA in Cultural Economics and Entrepreneurship, she actively engages in academia, co-authoring research that bridges theory and practice in cultural innovation.

Lluís Bonet is Professor in the Department of Economics and Director of the Cultural Management Program at the University of Barcelona. His main fields of research are cultural policy, cultural economics and arts management. Lluís has been a research fellow at MIT and the University of Montpellier and a guest lecturer in over 50 different countries. In 2023, he received the ENCATC award for outstanding contribution for his exceptional scholarship and sustained contributions to cultural management and policy education and research.

François Colbert Carmelle and Remi-Marcoux Chair in Arts Management, Codirector, Master of Management in International Arts Management, HEC Montréal. He is among top scholars in arts marketing having published close to 200 works and being one of the most cited authors in his discipline. He is Founding Editor of the International Journal of Arts Management and the AIMAC Conference. He also is the author of "Marketing Culture and the Arts" published in 16 languages. In 2002, he was awarded the Order of Canada for his many achievements and unique contributions in developing the field of arts management. Professor Colbert was given the honorary title of "International Master" by the Chinese Ministry of Science and Technology in 2018.

Carolina Dalla Chiesa is Assistant Professor of Cultural Economics (Arts & Culture Department - Erasmus University Rotterdam in the Netherlands). She is trained as a cultural economist and cultural anthropologist. Her research focuses on the economics of funding models for the arts and culture post-digitalization, crowdfunding, amateur economy, and economic-sociological theories applied to cultural markets. She was awarded Best PhD Thesis (2021) by EGSSH, Erasmus University Rotterdam, and currently chairs the Research Cluster "Values in the Creative Economy" at the Erasmus School of History, Culture and Communication.

Sophia Gaenssle holds her PhD from Ilmenau University of Technology, where she is an affiliated Senior Researcher. She specializes in digital, entertainment, and media markets, bringing extensive expertise in social media creators and stardom. With a background in economics, her research focuses on analysing creative industries from an economic and predominantly empirical perspective. Currently, she works as a data scientist at LEG Thüringen, contributing to trend analyses and foresight research.

Manel González-Piñero is Professor of Economics and Innovation at the University of Barcelona (UB) and ESMUC, the Official Music College of Catalonia, and co-directs the Summer School in Management of Creativity (HEC Montréal-UB). He is the Director of Innovation at the Health Research and Innovation Institute of the Universitat Politècnica de Catalunya (UPC) and co-founder of XartecSALUT, a health tech innovation network. Manel supports social impact initiatives, collaborating with programs such as Ship2B, SINAPSIS for live arts, and Mobile World Capital. He holds a PhD in Economics, an MBA, and degrees in Business Administration and English Philology.

Alice Demattos Guimarães (PhD) is a Brazilian cultural-urban economist, graduated in economics from the Federal University of Minas

Gerais. She holds a masters in Global Markets and Local Creativity as an Erasmus Mundus fellow between the University of Glasgow, Universitat de Barcelona, and Erasmus University of Rotterdam. She has worked as a researcher in the field of urban development correlated to the cultural sector, with a focus on museums and performance arts. Recently, she completed her PhD in Responsible Innovation and Regional Development at the Western Norway University of Applied Sciences (HVL), as part of the international CROWDCUL project on crowdfunding in the cultural sector. Her dissertation investigated the promises and tensions of cultural-creative crowdfunding across diverse contexts.

Christian Handke is Associate Professor (with*ius promovendi)* of Cultural Economics at Erasmus University Rotterdam. His research interests include the economics of creative industries, innovation and creativity, copyright, and text and data mining. He is associated editor of the Journal of Cultural Economics and co-editor of the Review of Economic Research on Copyright Issues. He has been consulting for the European Commission, the National Academies of the Sciences (USA), the Federal German Ministry of Justice, the UK Intellectual Property Office, Industry Canada, and the World Intellectual Property Organization, among others.

Wojciech Hardy is Assistant Professor at the Faculty of Economic Sciences, University of Warsaw. His research focuses on technological change, digitisation and their effects on various aspects of everyday life, including labour and cultural consumption in the context of attention economics, digital intermediaries and algorithms. Wojciech acts as the co-leader of the Association for Cultural Economics Poland (ACEP) and is the coordinator of the DELab's Research Lab on Digitization in the Cultural and Creative Sectors.

Sigrid Hemels is Full Professor of Tax Law at Erasmus University Rotterdam School of Law, the Netherlands, State Councillor in the Advisory Division of the Dutch Council of State, affiliated with Lund University School of Economics and Management, Sweden and International Fellow in the 2024–2025 Theme Digitax at the Pufendorf Institute for Advanced Studies, Lund University.

Sigbjørn Hjelmbrekke holds a PhD from Erasmus University, Rotterdam, in cultural economics, on the topic of music streaming services. He teaches economics and research methods at the University of South-Eastern Norway. His main research interests are within welfare economics and industrial organization, applied to the cultural sector or more generally.

Elisabetta Lazzaro (PhD in Economics) is Full Professor of Creative and Cultural Industries Management, and Head of the Arts & Creative Ecosystems research & innovation cluster at the Business School for the Creative Industries, University for the Creative Arts, UK. She has a track record of 80+ publications in international peer-reviewed journals, books and policy reports on the economics, business and policy of arts markets, cultural heritage, creative industries and digital innovation, cultural participation, entrepreneurship, sustainable business models and financing in culture and creative industries. Prof. Lazzaro is the recipient of 50+ research grants, the advisor of major organisations in the cultural and creative sectors, and an invited keynote speaker worldwide.

Ellen Loots is Associate Professor of Cultural Economics at the Erasmus School of History, Culture & Communication (ESHCC), Erasmus University Rotterdam. Her research interests include cultural, creative, and circular entrepreneurship. She studies (collaborative) business models and (alternative) forms of finance and funding in the arts and cultural and creative industries.

Natalia Maehle is Professor at the HVL Business School, Western Norway University of Applied Sciences. She is doing teaching and research in the field of responsible innovation and entrepreneurship, digital economy, crowdfunding, marketing, and consumer behavior. Prof. Maehle is a crowdfunding expert, and a member of the Editorial board at the Journal of Alternative Finance. She has an excellent track record of publications in the highly-ranked international peer-reviewed journals and is a regular presenter at international conferences.

Anna Mignosa (PhD) is Associate Professor at the University of Catania (Italy) and works also at Erasmus University Rotterdam (the Netherlands). Her research interests focus on economics of cultural heritage and cultural policies, economics of performing arts, economics of craft, and the relationship between culture and development. She is co-editor of the Handbook on the Economics of cultural heritage (Edward Elgar, 2013), the Economic Analysis of Craft (Palgrave, 2019) and Teaching Cultural Economics (Edward Elgar, 2020). Anna continues to bridge her academic research in cultural economics with practical experience by actively engaging in both grassroots and institutional cultural and creative projects.

Douglas Noonan is Professor at the O'Neill School at IU Indianapolis. His research focuses on a variety of policy and economics issues related to the cultural affairs, urban environments, neighbourhood dynamics, and quality-of-life. His research has been sponsored by a variety of organizations (e.g., National Science Foundation, Environmental Protection Agency, Lincoln Institute of Land Policy, National Endowment for the Arts) on topics like policy adoption, environmental risks, energy, air quality, spatial modelling, green urban revitalizations, and cultural economics. He is currently the co-editor-in-chief of the Journal of Cultural Economics, co-founder and Faculty Director IU Center for Cultural Affairs, and co-director of the Arts, Entrepreneurship, and Innovation Lab.

Marek Prokůpek is Associate Professor of Strategic Arts Management at KEDGE Arts School, KEDGE Business School in France. Prior to that, he worked as a Postdoctoral Fellow at LabEx ICCA (Industries Culturelles et Création Artistique) in Paris and as Assistant Professor in Arts Management at Prague University in Economics and Business, where he obtained PhD in 2017. Marek's research focuses on innovative business models of arts and cultural organizations and their financing strategies and the role of ethics in museum fundraising. Since January 2025, Marek has held the role of Associate Editor for the Arts Governance section of the International Journal of Arts Management.

Anders Rykkja is Lecturer in Arts and Cultural Industries Management at Queen's University Belfast. His research interests include cultural entrepreneurship, platform economics, crowdfunding, the music business and management of cultural and creative organisations. He collaborates with the University of Agder's (Norway) Crowdfunding Research Centre and was the coordinator of Knowledge Works, a Norwegian Ministry of Culture sponsored research centre on the cultural and creative industries. Anders formerly worked over twenty years in artist management, concert and festival production, artistic programming, and home entertainment. He has handled programming for European Capitals of Culture and been secretary general of the Norwegian Festival Association.

Rotem Shneor is Full Professor of entrepreneurship at the University of Agder's School of Business and Law in Norway and leads its Alternative Finance Research Center. Currently, he serves as editor-in-chief of the Journal of Alternative Finance (ALF). Earlier, he has co-founded the Norwegian Crowdfunding Association, served as an affiliate researcher at the Cambridge University Center for Alternative Finance, and has overseen the publication of high-impact industry reports. He has published extensively in leading academic journals, including JBR, DSS, ERD, ISBJ, IR, IJEB&R, EM, ECRA, BH, VC, TECHIS, IJEI, and others; as well as contributed chapters to several edited volumes. He is also lead editor and author of a popular book on Advances in Crowdfunding Research and Practice.

Helleke van den Braber is Professor of Cultural Value, Patronage and Society at Utrecht University, The Netherlands. She publishes and teaches the dynamics and cultural function of post-Romantic arts patronage, focusing on contemporary and historical exchange patterns between artists or cultural institutions and their patrons.

Yosha Wijngaarden is Assistant Professor of Media and Creative Industries at the Erasmus School of History, Culture & Communication (ESHCC), Erasmus University Rotterdam. She is the academic coordinator of the MA Media and Creative Industries, and co-chair of the research cluster Music, Industry, Culture & Society (MICS). Her research interests include work practices, innovations, inequality and earnings in the cultural and creative industries.

List of Figures

Chapter 7

Chapter 8

Chapter 9

Chapter 11

Chapter 12

Chapter 17

List of Tables

Chapter 15

Chapter 16

CHAPTER 1

Introduction

Carolina Dalla Chiesa and Anders Rykkja

1 Preamble

Artists and creators entering cultural[1] markets in the current post-digital environment may have more options to access funding and finance to sustain their work than was the case in the past. Let us examine a hypothetical example.

Consider the case of an independent musician. Our artist, who has yet to sign a recording contract, is working with a manager to build a career in their local market. To achieve artistic recognition and financial stability, the artist must build a fan base of dedicated followers. The idea is that over time these followers convert to become paying fans. Success, however, is not given. The market the artist will be entering and competing within is already overcrowded. The manager suggests that an efficient strategy to garner attention under these circumstances is for

C. Dalla Chiesa (✉)
Erasmus University Rotterdam, Rotterdam, The Netherlands
e-mail: c.dallachiesa@eshcc.eur.nl

A. Rykkja
Queen's University Belfast, Belfast, Northern Ireland, UK
e-mail: a.rykkja@qub.ac.uk

© The Author(s) 2026

C. Dalla Chiesa and A. Rykkja (eds.), *Cultural Funding and Financing*, Cultural Economics & the Creative Economy,
https://doi.org/10.1007/978-3-031-96696-5_1

the artist to produce and post music-related content on social media platforms, such as TikTok, Instagram, and YouTube, at regular intervals while working on the music.

Next to that, out hypothetical manager suggests doing a crowdfunding campaign. While artists may dislike the sales-like features that this (not so new) practice offers[2], the funding would cover some of the considerable costs of recording a debut album. Moreover, the adoption of crowdfunding may enable the artist to expand their follower base by tapping into the participatory features and community-building logics of this model.

Let's suppose that the campaign is a success. Our musician will then record an album as a first step up the ladder towards a professional career. Releasing the album for general distribution involves partnering with an online distribution aggregator for streaming platforms (e.g. DistroKid) while making music available on Bandcamp and SoundCloud. The artist decides to use these platforms because of their reputation and proven track records of helping similar bands and performers reach legions of niche fans outside their local market. The idea is that these fans, once converted, reciprocate by providing backing either financially through the purchase of songs and albums or endorsements or through appreciations via comments and likes to generate attention.

A further possibility to increment financial support is if our imaginary artist convinces a number of existing (or new) fans to support him/her/they on Patreon (or other patronage-based platforms). The platform, premised on a recurring subscription model (also called 'subscription crowdfunding') offers a monthly income in exchange for access to music and content behind a paywall. The yield may at first be relatively low, considering that each subscriber only pays a couple of dollars or euros a month, but it may stabilise at higher levels over time if the number of subscribers grows.

Now, let us presume that these initial forays into online positioning and attention-grabbing are successful. Our hypothetical musician can then use the momentum to explore new avenues. One evident option is to perform concerts and sell merchandise. Another possibility is to apply for public funding. Reaching this stage means that the number of available alternative options increases, as the range of novel and traditional models that can be appropriated expands.

The culmination of this process may be that our artist and manager are confronted with a *make-or-buy* decision. They can continue working independently, or they can sign with intermediaries (e.g. producers, labels, publishers, and agents). If they decide to contract the services of an intermediary, benefits apply in that these stakeholders take over some of the administrative and practical obligations, thereby reducing the transaction costs involved in production and distribution. Examples include the logistics of touring and concert promotion, the collection and distribution of royalties, the acquisition of public and private funding to develop the artistic project, or the coordination and implementation of social media marketing strategies. If they choose to continue as an independent team (a true Do it Yourself (DIY) strategy), there is still the third option to broker agreements with some but not all the intermediaries. In most cases, however, the task of searching for multiple-funding-sources does not end with these make-or-buy decisions. Artists reaching this stage in their career progressions will most likely continue optimising a proprietary path towards funding their work until reaching an ideal combination that provides necessary financial sustainability.

* * *

This story is illustrative of why we decided to embark on the journey towards compiling the present volume. It is also a fairly accurate example of some of the ways in which artists explore the contemporary funding and financing landscapes.

We could have told a different version of the same story by changing the characters and context. (a) Our account could have been an exemplification of the way in which independent video game producers combine the use of different types of digital platforms to capture attention and generate revenue (Gonzalez-Piñero & Rykkja, this volume). (b) It could have been a report about how fans, creators and influencers use social media to monetise content production (Gaenssle, this volume). (c) A third variation could have been a story similar to how the producers of the New Zealand-based film Boy (2010) successfully combined direct and indirect public funding with income from distribution deals and crowdfunding to launch the feature in the USA (Ferrer-Roca, 2015). Another scenario may be a story informed by current research (Elkins & Fry, 2022). about the experiences of street performers and buskers migrating to digital platforms for donations We could also, with ease, expand the scope and scale of our examples beyond emerging artists or independent production. Our illustrations could have explored (d) how established museums and other cultural organisations combine the use of corporate philanthropy (Colbert, this volume) with individual donations via online platform mechanisms (Lazzarro, this volume), or (e) the rise of public–private partnerships financing initiatives with clear public good attributes (see Mannino & Mignosa, 2017). (f) Historical examples could be conveyed as well to illustrate how patronage has been and still is a force to be reckoned in the arts (see van den Braber, this volume) ranging from typically known examples—like the Medici's famous role in sponsoring the flourishing of the arts in Renaissance Florence—to more contemporary, digital-based, patronage (see Hardy, this volume). In a nutshell, each chapter in this book will show a difference facet of funding and financing with its particular focus on either novel or traditional forms.

However, we chose the story of an independent musician navigating the path to establishing a viable music project as our initial anecdotal account. We chose this narrative because it is representative of the circumstances and conditions faced by many artists and independent cultural producers. In other words, we purposefully deviated from a tale based around well-known examples. Our choice was motivated by wanting to highlight how a majority of artists, creators and organisations producing culture fund their work and careers through the use of different digital and non-digital financing models.

Let's move on. It is possible to argue that nothing is new in the world of cultural funding and financing. Our musician's pursuit of money, attention and fandom is by no means unique. Throughout history, artists have always needed to approach a range of different actors and institutions for funding, such as the church, royals and nobility, public authorities, commissioners, and wealthy patrons (Whitaker & Grannemann, 2019; Williams, 1981). We can trace the origins of these patronage expressions, at minimum, back to ancient Rome (Veyne, 1990). Beginning in Renaissance Italy in the fifteenth century, privileges by decree to protect the right to print books paved a subsequent and complementary path for the introduction of copyright regulations of varying forms and lengths to protect a right to remuneration (Kretschmer et al., 2010). Throughout the twentieth century, systemic cultural policy interventions, such as the establishment of national arts councils (for example, the Arts Council in the UK) or programmes (the Federal Art Project in the United States in 1935), represent models of public support that help fund the projects or work of artists and organisations (Wyszomirski, 2004) with varying justifications about the reasons for redirecting citizens tax contributions to arts funding (Rushton, 2023). In addition to appropriating some or all these tools and opportunities, artists also resorted to markets and other exchange formats to trade art for money or in-kind contributions. As such, there is ample evidence to suggest that the mixed use of varying parts of sources of patronage, other forms of private support, state funding, royalty remuneration and earned income is the norm rather than the exception.

All in all, we cannot claim that the current situation illustrates the practice of blending traditional and modern approaches to funding and financing in the Cultural and Creative Sectors and Industries (CCSI). What we do argue—and this goes back to the question of *why* we need this volume—is that these funding and financing models are currently evolving. Digitalisation and the emergence of platform-based business models are, on the one hand, a major shift explaining these developments. On the other hand, these changes result from non-existent or inadequate access to sufficient funding, a situation faced by many artists and organisations in the CCSI, either because demand for funding is higher than before or because access to typical sources is diminished. We will further clarify our thinking around these advances in the following two sub-sections.

Context Part 1

Fifteen years ago, cultural budgets[3] allocated to governmental agencies for redistribution started to decrease after the financial crisis in 2008 (Bonet & Donato, 2011). The impact of the contractions is that many countries still struggle with providing the same level of pre-crisis provision and access to funding (Bonet, this volume). In some cases, the reasons can be explained by the persistence of cuts in public funding resulting from the adoption of policies of austerity (Ashton, 2022). In other cases, explanations point towards the way funding to bail out the CCSI was managed after a more recent crisis, namely, COVID-19. For example, research conducted within the EU reveals that economic interventions prioritised supporting larger national institutions over support towards the much more numerous self-employed artists and independent producer organisations (Betzler et al., 2021; Daniels, 2023; Hylland et al., 2022; Lamonica & Isernia, 2021). This adds to an already long list of reports and research providing evidence of artists and organisations across subsectors of the CSSI that find access to funding difficult (IDEA Consult,

2013; Khlystova et al., 2022; Klamer et al., 2006). A final development is the concurrent transformation whereby governments are shifting parts of their interventions from being direct co-financers of projects (Schuster, 1989) to public–private cost-sharing alternatives (Saz-Carranza & Longo, 2012; Albertelli & Mignosa, this volume) and the use of matching grants (Dalla Chiesa et al., this volume).

As a consequence, this first context is characterised by the combined effects of a diminished access to public funding, growth in for-profit cultural activities, and the impact of COVID-19 on the financial capacity of the CCSI (FitzGibbon & Tsioulaki, 2022; Khlystova et al., 2022; Pratt, 2020). This indicates that public funding—either through direct grants and subsidies or indirectly through tax rebates and incentives (Hemels, this volume)—could do with a fix and update, especially towards entertaining more mixed-model options (Dalla Chiesa et al., 2025). We may therefore as a result of major economic crises (Srakar & Čopič, 2012) and the proliferation of dispersed mechanisms of participation, consumption and production through online platforms (Waldfogel, 2017) experience an increase in redistribution of authority and distributed funding strategies as models evolve. The emergence of crowdfunding (see Noonan, this volume) is likely one of the many examples of how digitalisation enabled new funding avenues, especially for niche creators and yet-unknown projects seeking market and non-market validation. In the next subsection, we focus on the latter outcomes to help understand the expansion of more diverse funding and financing models.

Context Part 2

The impact of digitalisation, in particular the lowering of production costs and the underlying shift in business models from sales of products to access via service provision (Dubois & Westar, 2021), has brought an increase in the number of self-producing creators and independent producers competing for attention and revenue in cultural markets. Evidence shows that our post-digital context is marked by the emergence of a diversity of specialised markets, independent productions, audiences and suppliers compared with the preceding pre-digital period (Napoli, 2016). This fragmentation also leads to a widening gap between high- and low-earners, a change that is difficult to reconcile with the initial promises of a long-tail model intended to provide funding and finance for producing and distributing niche products. In most cases, digitalisation has instead appeared to accentuate the persistence of so-called 'superstar effects' (Rosen, 1981). The result is a challenging, competitive and complex environment. The formation of quality criteria and income generation increasingly rely on commentary and attention built through social media following. Major organisations and established artists typically justify their work based on conventional criteria of autonomy, excellence, and aesthetics. For a legion of niche creators, emerging artists, and organisations, the path to financial sustainability is rather challenging, as they do not have resources, networks, or a following to substantiate such claims.

In and of itself, this is simply evidence of current times and thus historically contingent on technological change. However, it is important to consider a few matters of concern, such as (a) the often inability of artists and cultural organisations to quickly adjust to such changes and incorporate new practices. (b) It may also reveal more blurred lines between artistic and non-artistic expressions (see Abbing, 2022, for a more detailed analysis of contemporary changes in how we define 'arts' and 'culture'), something which challenges the roles of governments intervening in support of contemporary cultural production (Rykkja & Bonet, 2023).

Having both contexts in mind, we compiled this volume at a time when stakeholders (including artists, cultural and creative organisations, governments, and intermediaries at the subsectoral level) are in a state of quandary. They either struggle to adapt traditional practices to the current post-digital context and acknowledge the emergence of new financing methods. Or they embrace these developments and new tools without critically reflecting on their limitations and capacity to exacerbate existing inequalities of access to funding across the CCSI. These are the rationales behind our objectives and goals.

2 The Goals

A few premises thus support the publication of this edited volume. On the one hand, there is a need for new thinking and innovation around public funding models among scholars (Loots et al., 2022) that can help inform the work of governments (Mazzucato et al., 2025). On the other hand, there is a need to understand how to integrate the range of new platform-based options (Part II) with what we call 'traditional' funding and financing models: direct or indirect public funding, sponsorship, philanthropy, patronage in the classic sense and copyright (Part I). These issues, alongside our reflections in the preceding section, constitute the background and the rationale we draw upon to formulate the objectives and aims of the book.

As it is not always obvious how to separate between 'public' and 'private' goals in funding the arts and culture (cf. Srakar & Čopič, 2012), or to make distinctions between niche and commercial cultures (Cowen, 2000), we find it more straightforward to focus on the *means* to acquire funding, or what we call the various funding and financing models. With this aim, we want to better understand the diverse sets of tools and practices related to accessing funding and finance available to 'make art', 'create' and 'build a career' for and within the CCSI. This edited volume thus focuses on exploring, discussing and understanding the *diverse funding and financing landscape*, with a special emphasis on developments post-digitalisation. The work offered in this book is largely conceptual, driven by the intent to describe, rather than prescribe, past and present developments in the making and distribution of the arts and culture.

To expand our thinking, we want to address three concerns. The *first* concern is the necessity of providing basic understanding regarding what is known about both *traditional* (we also recognise them as 'core' models to avoid a historical dispute around what is modern and what is traditional) and *emerging* funding and financing models post-digitalisation and how they advance on each other. A *second* concern is informed by the need to understand how a variety of entrepreneurially orientated artists and institutions[4] may combine the use of different funding and financing models to access resources for the production and dissemination of culture as well as the difficulties they encounter in adopting these (Borin et al., 2018; see also Shneor, this volume, on barriers related to using investment-based models in the arts). Our *final* matter of concern is a return to the justifications for why we advocate for a greater focus on funding and financing models or, in other words, a discussion about the ways to access the *means of cultural production* that needs to be at the centre of how we make various art forms available to the public. As Guimarães and Maehle (this volume) demonstrate in a prolific case study, the way in which funding happens greatly determines how art is accessed by the public, with varying degrees of public (bottom-up) participation.

The aforementioned concerns have been the basis for selecting and commissioning individual chapters of this book. For each of them, we asked authors to consolidate our current knowledge of funding and financing alternatives and to further expand on research agendas from a theoretical and empirical perspective. Some of the questions guiding authors are: How are cultural activities funded or financed? Are the chosen models premised on valuation by experts and/or crowd coordination? Does the collaboration with platforms or intermediary organisations enable creativity? Which funding sources are typically involved in this process? Can we identify differences in uptake and use between industries? Are the fund seekers for-profit enterprises, or are their missions aligned with contributing to the public good? Depending on the answers to these and similar questions, the funding process may involve contributions from public or private entities, crowdfunding with or without match-funding, complementary revenue from intermediary producer firms, personal savings, earned income, philanthropic donations from private sponsors, online and offline patronage, trusts, and foundations. As the subtitle states (A Guide to New and Traditional Models of Funding), our aim is to support readers in learning or discovering more about what we consider to be the essential models supporting cultural production in the CCSI. We hope to do this by also providing numerous examples reflecting current practice (without necessarily aiming to be exhaustive, see the section on Limitations).

Before we delve into the chapters' details, we introduce some of the theoretical approaches we have identified while searching for literature on funding and financing models and our interpretations about the use of key terminologies from an interdisciplinary perspective. We do that in order to avoid overly essentialist views about funding being a simple matter of money allocation, or, on the other hand, a representation of societal morals. We wish to remain in between as we understand that the act of funding the arts or seeking means to finance is **both** a financial fact about project goals and money allocation, and a representation of morals, meaning and symbols that money conveys.

3 A Note on the Literature: Objective, Pragmatic and Critical Approaches

Our search for literature is premised on a belief that an interdisciplinary programme is needed to realise the outlined ambitions of describing and explaining the current obstacles and issues related to access to funding and financing in the CCSI. What does such a perspective look like? Our readings have led us to identify three distinct approaches: the objectivist view, which we argue emphasises an agnostic approach towards analysis of economic structures, tools, and models to interpret cultural markets; the pragmatic view, which concentrates on the behaviour of artists and their choice of entrepreneurial strategies to overcome difficulties in accessing funding or finance; and the critical view, which addresses systemic inequalities and ideological critiques around the way funding and financing the arts and culture is organised.

The first perspective, which we refer to as the *objective* view, considers funding and financing as integral components of the process of producing and consuming culture, thereby making them part of an objective economic analysis. An intentionally proclaimed objective view tends to focus on the facts (causes and consequences) that structure the CCSI the way they are. The economic processes that constitute arts and culture as markets can thus be studied, provided some considerations are given to ensure that models (Throsby, 2008) do reflect how the arts and culture constitute a particular case, different from other sectors of the economy (Baumol & Bowen, 1965).

To provide some examples of this perspective,[5] a typical microeconomic justification for public grants and subsidies lies in the natural monopolist model applied to the arts (Throsby, 1994). Firms operating a natural monopolist model face high fixed costs and increasing returns to scale. At the same time, pricing at the marginal cost for expensive performing arts products would result in a loss, where the difference is covered by a subsidy that allows pricing at the break-even level for greater welfare (Throsby & Withers, 1979). An example of the objective view applied to the digital world is the perspective that information goods also have high fixed costs but virtually zero marginal reproduction costs (Shapiro & Varian, 2000). Coupled with the high switching costs and network effects characteristic of platform economies, market concentration prevails in the hands of a few firms that are not threatened by *contestability* (the threat of new entrants keeping prices and firm behaviour in check). In the absence of regulation, in the long run, the rewarding structure of the creative sectors might unveil some worrying consequences, especially for creators whose bargaining power is diminished along with their individual rewards for creation (Towse, 2025).

The second perspective we highlight is the *pragmatic* view. The approach sees access to funding as an integral part of the set of contextual particularities in the CCS that artists, self-employed freelancers, and other cultural workers face when trying to position themselves in artistic labour markets (Abbing, 2022; Menger, 1999). The singularity of this perspective is the mix of a heterodox take on the entrepreneurship phenomenon, with some consensus that these forms of labour, seen through lenses of entrepreneurship (cf. Feder & Woronkowicz, 2022), violate multiple assumptions of what is considered the classic approach of studying entrepreneurial behaviour and perspectives of entrepreneurship as a practice (cf. Loots, 2023; Shane & Venkataraman, 2000). These forms of entrepreneurship could be seen as the outcome of creating something' that works in specific contexts through, for example, improvisation; trial and error (cf. the appropriation of the concept of bricolage from anthropology, see Baker & Nelson, 2005); hustling for access to resources (Steedman & Brydges, 2023); understanding valuation regimes (Dekker, 2015); or as a result of interactions in creative circles and co-creative communities (Dekker & Morea, 2023; Morea & Dalla Chiesa, 2024). The idea of pragmatism here refers to research describing and explaining justifications, relationality, and actual forms of exchange with the use of both qualitative and quantitative methodologies. More than giving an empirical state-of-the-art, the pragmatic approach can also make use of historical approaches to understand social dynamics around everyday justifications, critiques, and practices (cf. Boltanski & Thévenot, 1991).

The third perspective we identify is the critical view on funding and financing models. This approach makes a case that the problems with access to money are caused by a willed (and unwanted) subordination of cultural value to economic value (cf. Flew et al., 2019, for a discussion). The root cause is claimed as the *privatisation* of arts and funding (Alexander, 2018), which was driven in many countries by the introduction of a rhetoric situating the arts as a part of the creative industries to legitimise continuous government support (Bell & Oakley, 2015; O'Brien, 2014). The outcome was that support for traditional arts and heritage became unbalanced, favouring the commercial side of these industries, where arts and culture were less important (Banks & Hesmondhalgh, 2009). This shift also resulted in a concentration on knowledge-based goods, treating arts and culture as inputs rather than outputs (Garnham, 2005). The idea conveyed by this literature is the need for a reckoning with the misconception that arts and culture require private investment to thrive when what is required is a rethink in terms of how government support is provided. This is because many forms of production, distribution and consumption of culture are either unviable within industrial frameworks of economic production (O'Connor, 2024) or because market conditions make public funding of production and supply a necessity (see Rushton, 2023, for a detailed look at why arts funding is morally justified).

Although our overview is compact and, to a certain extent, arbitrary, we contend that these perspectives differ from one another in important ways and have their own strength and weaknesses as theoretical traditions. Yet, we have not nudged scholars to choose one perspective or another, but rather encouraged them to follow their own preferences, theories and methods when it comes to discussing funding and financing models. Our hope is that the choice of deciding to compile the volume without adhering to a specific theoretical framework may contribute to more connections across these perspectives, thereby showing a path towards building interdisciplinarity (of theories and methods). This sometimes (meaning not always) happens. More efforts can be made, of course, which explains why we underscore such an approach.

4 Terminology: Models, Mechanisms, and Tools Versus Funding or Financing

Across the literatures we reviewed, actions, processes and schemes for obtaining funding or financing goes by different names. The cultural crowdfunding literature uses for example *mechanism* (Loots et al., 2023), *method* (Mollick, 2014), and *tool* (Demattos Guimarães et al., 2024) to describe and explain a similar phenomenon. Upon reflection, we decided as editors to adopt the term *model* because it signifies an encompassing set of contextualised relationships through which individual parts connect to generate specific outcomes.

Our rationale is simple and, in part, effective because it relies on exclusion. The term mechanism refers to a structure of interrelated parts that produces specific effects or causal relationships. For example, in the social sciences, the transmission of values through education is a mechanism by which individuals normalise their behaviours. The term tool, on the other hand, refers to parts that make such mechanisms function properly. On social media, for example, users interact with one another via tools such as comments, likes and messages. The term method is intrinsic to discussions about methodology. It can refer to both a technique for collecting and processing information and the epistemological approach that a humanist scholar or social scientist uses to address empirical phenomena; in other words, a process or specific way of producing knowledge about something. Then, we turn to the term *model*, which can be conceptualised as an abstraction about specific phenomena using concepts to analyse social reality and sometimes predict behaviour.

A caveat is that the use of models throughout the volume is inconsistent. This is because the rationales for preferring models came to us in hindsight. Therefore, the contributing authors were free to use whichever term they preferred. Some, including one of us (Dalla Chiesa, this volume), use 'mechanisms' because the analysis focuses on the effects of using specific schemes and devices. Others prefer 'tool' as a term because the focus shifts to questions of human negotiations, tweaking of expectations/conventions, contexts and real-life operations. In some cases, 'methods' is chosen as a descriptor for a process of doing something in a particular way. The term 'model' can however encompass the effects of mechanisms, the tools of human agency, and the procedural steps of a method as part of its functionality. We therefore chose to use this term in the book title as it is abstract enough to include the goals of the various scholars contributing to the volume.

The second matter of concern is the need to clarify the terms 'funding' and 'financing.' From our perspective, the interchangeability of financing and funding is similar to the polysemic use of tools, mechanisms, methods, and models in academic literature. A special issue in the Journal of Cultural Economics (2022) also uses financing and funding interchangeably, which raises the question of why we repeat both terms when referring to ways in which creators access various revenue sources. It is worth discussing whether and how these terms need to be differentiated.

In Klamer et al. (2006), for example, funding and financing represent the same rationale, whereby a certain amount of money is granted to cultural institutions through markets, governments, or civil society. No further literature in the arts and cultural domains made a similarly clear distinction, which then leads us to other academic disciplines, namely, development economics. For Fay et al. (2021), funding is fundamentally a cash-flow issue (i.e. where the money for the *xyz* project comes from), whereas financing refers to the arrangements by which the funds are made available; hence, the broad strategies employed to generate revenues from various mechanisms. Moreover, Keenan et al. (2019) say that 'Funding can be defined as the direct payment made by often local, public, and/or private actors for the purposes of investing in preparation for a future project. Financing includes the utilisation of market-based instruments that may or may not utilise third-party funding to leverage what is otherwise underwritten to be an independently feasible project investment'. UNDP (2017) sees funding as '…transferring resources from a financial contributor to a recipient…', while financing is the question of '…structuring different financial flows to achieve a common result'.

These examples of categorical distinctions between funding and financing offer the requisite sensitivity to understanding the trade-offs in either funding or financing investments. From this perspective, funding would represent a focused application of money directed to a specific goal, typical of a grant or subsidy, while financing would refer to a broader revenue model— i.e. how various sources are combined—to generate financial sustainability on a larger scale. Simply put, funding is a source, while financing is the question of how to manage and pay for the use of one of multiple sources from an economic perspective.

While this distinction is not always necessary, for the purposes of this edited volume, it is useful for differentiating between the mechanisms used to grant money or in-kind resources and those used to generate revenues from typical market transactions. In this way, we would think of streaming models (see Hjelmbrekke, this volume) as a way to finance cultural production via royalty payments due to the exploitation of copyrights (see Handke, this volume) and philanthropic donations to arts institutions (see Colbert, this volume) as a form of external funding for the organisation, without any promise that this will provide a steady and lasting source of income for them.

5 Limitations

The volume is not a handbook. This means that the individual chapters cannot make any claims to serve as the authoritative literature guide on funding and financing culture. It also implies that there will be limitations in terms of coverage. While the text is comprehensive, providing both conceptual analysis and examples of traditional and some new models of funding and financing, we limit our focus to available funding and financing models. Available means models (again, encompassing tools, methods, and mechanisms) that are unlikely to change due to hype, new fads and fashions. When we say *unlikely*, we mean that we are interested in the variations of funding options around the *normal curve*. NFTs, for example, will not feature prominently as tools used as part of models, except when it comes to addressing the value of blockchain (see Lazzarro, this volume; Handke, this volume), as these are not funding models in themselves and seem to constitute a digital hype (Diadkov, 2024). We are thus not interested in the next big thing in terms of funding but rather in taking stock of the past and present to understand future avenues better.

Second, this edited volume is not dedicated to fundraising. It consequently provides little advice on the best ways for managers and entrepreneurs to access funding or finance, which would require a more prescriptive approach. While this topic is extremely prolific in the arts and culture (see for example Alexander & Murphy, 2022; Turrini & Voss, 2020; Pecoraro et al., 2023), we understand that our contribution lies in zooming out of fundraising as a management practice in favour of mapping funding and financing alternatives from a broader interdisciplinary perspective. When we discuss fundraising, we do it with the concern that some financing models come with a challenge around the ethics of funding sources (Prokupek, this volume).

Third, other scholarship is quite successful in highlighting the brute fact that much public funding for the arts often favours the well off and indulges the preferences of the highly educated and culturally socialised elites (Rushton, 2023). It is not our intention to either dispute or extend this perspective (however, see Bonet, this volume), but rather to recognise the value of more popularised forms of cultural content, descended from so-called high art, shared via social media, online platforms, and other channels that have contributed to commodifying and desacralising the arts from their canon (Cowen, 2000). These often exist outside the realm of state-induced funding mechanisms, thus having a life of their own, enabled by online-based financing models. Individual chapters in Part II describe and analyse the use and potential of some of these models, including their efficiency and effectiveness. They adopt a more descriptive, theory-driven approach and therefore do not focus overtly on the impact of such models on inequality in its various forms. These are important considerations that would constitute the project of another publication focused on this matter.

Having said that, we believe that the offer of new or revised conceptual foundations may trigger future (much needed) empirical research into funding and financing models in markets across the CCSI. One of our hopes is that the insights fellow students and academics may gain from reading the volume are ideas for research addressing evident practical issues a range of people and organisations in the CCS are faced with in terms of accessing resources to produce, exhibit and in other ways disseminate their work.

6 The Structure of This Book

To explore the topic, we invited selected contributors to present and interpret their understanding of a particular funding and financing model for creators, organisations or artists operating in cultural markets. Throughout the introductory chapter, we have already outlined several of these contributions, giving the reader a sense of the book's direction.

This book is structured into three main sections. Part I, called 'Core Funding and Financing Models', outlines the central funding and financing models we consider: direct public funding, indirect tax incentives, private sponsorship, patronage, and royalties distributed through copyrights.

We start Part I with perhaps the most widely regarded source of public funding and financing for the arts, namely, direct forms of state support structured via direct funding and supported on cultural policymaking rationale. Lluis Bonet explores the complexities of direct government contributions to culture, focusing on the efficiency, legitimacy, financial mechanisms and international spending levels. The chapter highlights how public funding reflects government values and priorities while addressing economic, social, and political justifications for investing in cultural initiatives. The author discusses various forms of government intervention, emphasising the importance of a supportive regulatory environment and efficient administrative structures to enhance cultural funding. By analysing disparities in cultural spending across different countries, the chapter underscores the need for comprehensive data and a nuanced understanding of the nexus between the context wherein cultural policies are implemented and the effectiveness and efficiency of public support for the arts and heritage. The chapter ultimately advocates for the careful consideration of funding and financing models to ensure equitable and sustainable cultural investment.

Following up on the differences between direct and indirect funding models, we invite Sigrid Hemels to explore the mechanisms of indirect arts subsidies. This chapter discusses the role of tax incentives as a funding model for the arts and culture sector, emphasising their potential as a policy instrument to enhance financial sustainability. It highlights the complexities and ethical considerations surrounding tax incentives, including issues of fairness and the risks associated with *philanthrocapitalism*, where wealthy individuals influence public funding decisions through tax-deductible donations. The chapter outlines various forms of tax incentives, their effectiveness, and the need for careful evaluation and accountability. By examining the dynamics of tax incentives within different cultural contexts, particularly in Europe, the author argues for a balanced approach that considers both the financial and ethical implications of funding the arts, ultimately advocating for policies and tools that promote transparency and equity.

In sequence, we invite Helleke van den Braber to discuss the main theoretical and empirical aspects of patronage from a historical perspective. This chapter explores the evolving dynamics of gift exchange between artists and private patrons, emphasising the resurgence of arts patronage in Europe influenced by established philanthropic traditions from the USA. It discusses the shift from traditional patronage to modern, long-term relationships where artists seek sustainable support from individual benefactors. The author examines the historical context of both pre- and post-Romantic patronage, highlighting key aspects such as patronage dynamics, reciprocity, negotiation strategies and the balance between gift and transaction. By analysing contemporary examples of patronage, the chapter illustrates how artists and patrons navigate their relationships, aiming for mutual benefits while also addressing the ethical implications of these exchanges. The discussion emphasises the importance of understanding the complexities of modern patronage practices and their historical roots in shaping the current landscape of arts funding.

François Colbert subsequently examines the role of philanthropic fundraising and sponsorship within the arts marketing framework, specifically in the North American context. It discusses how cultural organisations rely on private donations and sponsorships to supplement government support, particularly as public funding has become increasingly limited. The author outlines the dynamics of the donor journey, emphasising factors such as motivations, trust, loyalty and the importance of aligning sponsors with the artistic mission of the organisation. Through a detailed analysis of the sponsorship market, the chapter highlights the necessity for cultural organisations to understand donor preferences and establish mutually beneficial relationships. Additionally, it explores innovative financing models outside traditional frameworks, advocating for a strategic approach to arts funding that enhances both financial sustainability and community engagement.

We finish Part I with a quintessential contribution on the workings of copyrights and royalties' distribution in the arts and culture (particularly illustrated with the music industries) by Christian Handke. This chapter examines the critical role of copyright in supporting creators within the CCSI, particularly in the context of digitalisation. It discusses the complexities and challenges associated with copyright systems, including collective rights management, user-generated content and the influence of platforms and artificial intelligence. The author identifies a paradox for creators: while digitalisation allows for more collaborative value creation with users, these outputs also require stronger protections against the dominance of commercial platforms that control much of the copyright landscape. The chapter emphasises the need for a balanced approach to copyright policy that allows for flexibility in creator-user interactions while ensuring robust defences for creator interests. Ultimately, it advocates for a reformed copyright system that can adapt to the evolving digital environment, supporting creators without sacrificing their rights or financial sustainability. Handke also highlights the importance of non-monetary benefits to creators, as contractual agreements often incorporate in-kind contributions to them.

Part II, called 'Extended (Digital-Based) Funding and Financing Models', moves on to more contemporary, all-digital funding and financing models, which may or may not have enabled greater levels of public participation through decentralised models on online platforms. In this section, we examine what we consider some of the key digital funding or financing models operated by artists or, more broadly, cultural content-creators: reward-based crowdfunding, investment-based crowdfunding, matchfunding, online patronage, social media monetisation with user-generated content, and, lastly, the emergence of the streaming model, illustrated by the case of recorded music.

This section starts with Douglas Noonan's analysis of the benefits and constraints of crowdfunding for the arts and culture. This chapter explores the evolution of reward-based crowdfunding in the CCSI post Mollick's seminal article (2014), focusing on data from Kickstarter projects. It highlights significant trends, including the rise of tabletop games and the decline of traditional categories like film and music. The author emphasises how crowdfunding serves as a market research tool, enabling creators to learn and build reputations rather than just providing funding. The dynamics of crowdfunding are examined in relation to broader market influences, including the role of niche audiences and the challenges faced by creators. The chapter argues that while crowdfunding can offer financial support, its primary value lies in its informational advantages to creators and backers, and it calls for further research to understand its impact on the creative economy better.

In a prolific analysis of the barriers of online investment and equity options for artists, Rotem Shneor discusses the reluctance of artists to adopt investment crowdfunding as a fundraising mechanism, despite its potential for generating larger financial returns compared to non-investment models. It introduces the Fear-Prejudice-Ignorance (FPI) framework, which identifies three main mental barriers that hinder artists from embracing investment crowdfunding: fear of failure, prejudice against commercial activities, and ignorance of the crowdfunding process. The chapter further explores the origins and implications of these barriers and suggests strategies to mitigate them, such as education, match funding schemes and functional integration of services. Ultimately, it aims to provide insights into improving artists' engagement with investment crowdfunding and enhancing their financial opportunities in the CCSI.

Carolina Dalla Chiesa, Ellen Loots and Yosha Wijngaarden elaborate a conceptual framework to understand matchfunding in the chapter titled 'Matching Money in the Arts and Culture' which distinguishes between online and offline models. The chapter elaborates the argument that matchfunding serves as a strategic mechanism where financial contributions from various sources, such as government and private funders, are intentionally combined to incentivise further donations. The chapter discusses the historical reliance of cultural organisations on diverse funding sources, emphasising the emergence of online crowdfunding platforms as innovative intermediaries that facilitate matchfunding. By leveraging these platforms, organisations can enhance their fundraising efforts while addressing funding gaps typically encountered in the CCSI. The authors also highlight this funding model's potential benefits and challenges, including issues of equity, access, and the implications of shifting decision-making power from centralised authorities to the crowd (and how it implies a shift in cultural policymaking) and the potential of this model to reduce transaction costs. Ultimately, the chapter contributes to understanding how matchfunding can reshape funding dynamics within the cultural ecosystem.

Advancing on other forms of dispersed online financial support for the arts, Wojciech Hardy discusses the emergence of online crowd-patronage as a new model for financing creative work, highlighting its unique features and potential benefits for artists. It explains how these platforms enable direct financial support from niche audiences to creators, providing a more stable income compared to traditional funding methods. The author categorises the main types of online patronage, such as subscription-based models and tipping systems, and explores the dynamics and contexts in which these platforms operate. The chapter emphasises the inclusivity of crowd-patronage, allowing not just established artists but also emerging creators to connect with supporters and build sustainable income streams. Lastly, it identifies gaps in current research on crowd-patronage, suggesting areas for future inquiry to understand better its impact on the creative workforce and the cultural landscape.

As many contemporary creators in the cultural and creative sectors use social media to share or monetise on creative content distribution, we welcomed the contribution of Sophia Gaenssle on User-Generated Content via social media and the processes of monetising via online platforms. Her chapter delves into the various remuneration mechanisms that social media creators utilise to monetise their content and art, addressing two main questions: how do these creators earn income, and what implications does this have for financing cultural production, particularly in the core arts? It outlines both direct payment methods, such as ad revenue sharing, subscriptions, and tipping systems, as well as indirect income sources through brand partnerships and affiliate marketing. The chapter highlights the evolving landscape of digital cultural production, emphasising that while social media platforms have democratised content creation, they also introduce challenges related to algorithmic biases and market dynamics that may favour established creators over emerging talent. Ultimately, it suggests that social media is reshaping traditional funding models in the arts, prioritising commercial and engagement-driven content while opening new avenues for creative expression and income generation.

The last chapter of this section delves into the details of the streaming model by Sigbjørn Hjelmbrekke, who uses recorded music as a case study to illustrate its mechanisms. This chapter analyses the evolution of music streaming as a financing model for the music industry, highlighting the transition from ownership-based sales to subscription-based access. It discusses the benefits and challenges associated with streaming services, including how they alter the distribution of revenues among artists, rights holders, and platforms. The author differentiates between various revenue-sharing models, such as the pro rata and user-centric approaches and examines their implications for artists of different popularity levels. The chapter also addresses issues like the precarious nature of creative labour, the impact of streaming on earnings, and crowd-patronage's role in providing creators more stable income.

Part III, called 'Case-Studies and Illustrations', presents a few selected case-based examples that either expand on previous sections or provide in-depth examinations of a specific sector. We select cases that explore, in sequence, museum-based exploration of digital tools, public–private partnerships in the heritage sector, fundraising practices of cultural institutions, video game monetisation strategies and, lastly, an in-depth study of a community-based crowdfunding project.

This section starts with Elisabetta Lazzaro's overview of the digitally based mechanisms museums use to generate new forms of funding. The chapter examines the innovative funding and financing models that museums and cultural heritage institutions adopt in response to traditional financial challenges. It highlights how digital technologies, including crowdfunding, contactless donations, digital payments and tokenised rewards, are transforming the funding landscape for these institutions. The author discusses various case studies, particularly focusing on smaller museums, to illustrate how these models can foster community engagement and enhance financial sustainability. Additionally, it explores the implications of adopting these digital funding tools, emphasising the importance of inclusivity and collaboration in expanding audiences and building loyalty. The chapter concludes by addressing the challenges and opportunities arising from these new financial models, suggesting areas for future research in cultural funding and financing.

Further, we advance on novel partnership potentials to leverage funding options to the CCSI using the case of Public–Private-Partnerships (PPPs) as a governance model in a chapter written by Aline Albertelli and Anna Mignosa. This chapter analyses the role of PPPs as alternative financing mechanisms for the cultural sector, particularly in museums and heritage management. It discusses the evolution of cultural policy and governance, highlighting how the reduction of direct government intervention has led to increased private sector involvement through PPPs. By examining case studies from Italy and Brazil, the chapter illustrates how these partnerships can address financial challenges faced by cultural institutions while fostering community engagement and participation. The authors emphasise that while PPPs offer potential benefits, such as improved efficiency and resource allocation, they also present power dynamics and transparency challenges. Ultimately, the chapter argues that PPPs represent a viable alternative to traditional public funding, enabling cultural institutions to enhance their sustainability and relevance in contemporary society.

Still in line with unveiling an analysis of arts funding in cultural institutions, Marek Prokupek develops an in-depth case study on the ethical complexities and dynamics of philanthropy in arts funding, particularly through the lens of the National Portrait Gallery's decision to reject a significant donation from the Sackler Trust due to its association with the opioid crisis. It discusses how cultural institutions are increasingly scrutinised for their funding sources and the ethical implications of accepting donations from controversial entities. The chapter highlights the growing influence of activist movements advocating for transparency and accountability in philanthropy, as well as the need for robust ethical frameworks in donor evaluations. By examining the tensions between financial necessity and public accountability, the author emphasise the importance of aligning funding practices with institutional values and social responsibility, ultimately advocating for a shift towards more ethical and equitable philanthropic practices in the arts.

Manel González-Piñero and Anders Rykkja shift the focus to video games and Catalonia (Spain) in a contribution that explores how independent video game development studios navigate the evolving landscape of monetisation within the creative industries. Two case studies provide insights into the balancing acts of small creative firms in maintain creative autonomy and financial sustainability. Findings highlight the importance of emerging technologies, community-driven engagement, and adaptive monetisation models, based on 'platform internal' (e.g. premium sales of games) 'platform external' (e.g. crowdfunding and the sales of merchandise.) and other means, such as work-for-hire and co-creation and production with their communities of followers. The research shows how these strategies not only enhance financial sustainability but also foster creative autonomy. A contribution for practitioners is offering a roadmap for other independent studios facing similar challenges.

Our edited volume ends with a hopeful contribution by Alice Demattos Guimarães and Natalia Maehle on the concept of creating value in the cultural sector through crowdfunding and collaborative efforts engaging audiences, emphasising the importance of co-creation and co-production in arts and culture. It highlights how digitalisation has transformed community engagement, enabling diverse groups to collectively contribute to cultural projects. Using a case study of the OVO—Formation and Transformation Orchestra in Brazil, the authors illustrate how this orchestra utilises crowdfunding and crowd-patronage to support its activities while fostering socio-economic resilience and enhancing community-rooted artistic values. The chapter argues that by leveraging digital platforms, cultural projects can not only secure funding but also facilitate meaningful participation and engagement among artists, backers and communities, thereby reshaping traditional funding dynamics. With this, we want to reinforce the collective character of some funding alternatives in that they resemble communities of artists (Becker, 1982), now revamped by new digital technologies, and empowered by crowdsourcing.

7 A Short Conclusion: Funding and Financing as Spin-Offs?

This volume contains numerous examples that highlight how digital funding and financing models introduce new ways to reorganise the matchmaking process between those who receive money (or in-kind contributions) and those who provide them. What we should remember, however, is that most of these models, in one way or another, are spin-offs that combine different forms, tools and practices, sometimes drawing on the reach of modern technology. For example, a streaming model consists of a monetary reward model, made possible by the institutional infrastructures of copyrights and the development of digital apps. Digital matchfunding, to give a second example, arguably combines the crowdfunding model with direct public funding for the arts into a single mechanism. Online patronage is yet another example whereby technology amplifies the efficiency of traditional forms of patronage, notably the subscription list format. In general, we believe that creating new ways to fund and finance projects means bringing together various sources into unique or specific models, which mix different funding and financing tools. Some of these emerging models, in particular crowdfunding, have served as cushions for moments of crisis and enabled numerous artists and organisations in the CCSI to weather the impacts of austerity measures and reductions in grant availability.

One penultimate observation is that the relatively under-discussed issue of funding and financing models is likely influenced by path dependency.[6] The adoption or rejection of certain models in different geographic contexts may be partially explained by whether adoption is incentivised. This is not always the case. One reason for lack of adoption could therefore be the perceived threat to the position of stakeholders and the continuity of institutional order these models represent because they are premised on bottom-up or community-based logics. A major barrier in relation to progress is the lack of acceptance for the condition that novel ways of combining funding and financing tools with either public, private or civil society origins involve a redistribution of decision power furthermore, a lack of incentives equates a lack of uptake. The combined impact of sectorial resistance and incentives leads to stagnation. A solution could be to frame the process as a matter of creating new tools to enable cultural production and consumption through monetary or in-kind support, rather than a complete upheaval of funding and financing models per se. Going forward, perhaps a more fruitful discussion could focus on how all available alternatives complement or substitute each other, which types of cultural products they apply to, and under what conditions; this topic deserves its own agenda due to the diversification of funding alternatives.

Finally, we made this book project envisioning the work of researchers looking for a 'guide' on how to explore the variety of monetary and non-monetary available sources. A guide gives some directions, points to potential outcomes, and hopefully helps someone reach their end goals. A guide, however, does not always give clear-cut answers when acting as a facilitator of knowledge and communication. For our purposes, we see this work fitting in a less strict view where we understand the complexities of the topic but avoid giving right-or-wrong binary directions. We would like to see our work as helping to share knowledge by bringing together and compiling the work of distinguished scholars on an important topic: the acquisition of resources needed for creation, production, distribution, and consumption of arts and culture.

It is therefore our hope this volume serves scholars and practitioners seeking academic support for their ideas, future projects, and empirical avenues. On a more personal level, we hope that the contributions you are about to read provide interesting insights about a more forward-looking funding landscape and contribute to unveiling the latest avenues available to research on funding and financing of the arts.

Notes

1. In this edited volume, we often use the term "culture" more broadly than "arts" to encompass non-core artistic products and refer to a complex web of creators related or not to purely artistic endeavours. To facilitate our understanding, the term "CCS" is used to generally represent the cultural and creative sectors with a special focus on artistic and core cultural production.
2. The first dedicated crowdfunding platform, ArtisShare, launched in 2001. It was also the year that the band Marillion used their website to fund the recording and production of their album Anoraknophobia. These two events, along with Marillion's initial crowdfunding campaign in 1997 to finance a North American tour, are widely considered as the parting shots for using crowdfunding as a funding tool.
3. When it comes to government spending on cultural services, investments have been decreasing and represent, on average, 1.2% of total spending across the OECD (OECD, 2022).
4. Individuals and organisations across the CCSI are becoming more entrepreneurial (Peterson, 2018). This tendency is corroborated by studies that detail how self-employment in the creative economy is the norm rather than the exception (Woronkowicz & Noonan, 2019). While we agree that these working conditions do not equate to all artists becoming entrepreneurs, it implies that analysing questions of how to access funding or finance should consider the perspective that many artists or micro-organisations (<10 employees) may act as entrepreneurs by necessity (see Galloway & Levie, 2001;

Stanworth & Stanworth, 1997 for an explanation of the concept) and do so, often reluctantly (Haynes & Marshall, 2018).

5. Scholars adopting the objective view are less worried with why we came to value the arts as we do from a socio-cultural and historical perspective, but more concerned with unveiling the empirics around the past, present and future of market and non-market exchanges in the arts and its consequences for economic organisation (see Blaug, 2001, for a detailed discussion of its methodological underpinnings).
6. Path dependency is a term that emerged in the institutional economics literature of Douglas North (1990) and was elaborated in the field of cultural economics when it comes to assessing the provenance of artworks, regional development, and evolutionary perspectives on cultural production; thus, it is a context- and place-based perspective.

References

Abbing, H. (2022). *The Economies of Serious and Popular Art: How They Diverged and Reunited*. Palgrave Macmillan.

Alexander, V. D. (2018). Heteronomy in the Arts Field: State Funding and British Arts Organizations. *The British Journal of Sociology, 69*(1), 23–43.

Alexander, V. D., & Murphy, O. (2022). Fundraising in the Arts. In C. Devereaux (Ed.), *Managing the Arts and Culture* (pp. 60–93). Routledge.

Ashton, D. (2022). Funding Arts and Culture: Everyday Experiences and Organisational Portfolio Precarity. *European Journal of Cultural Studies, 26*(3), 388–407.

Baker, T., & Nelson, R. E. (2005). Creating Something from Nothing: Resource Construction Through Entrepreneurial Bricolage. *Administrative Science Quarterly, 50*(3), 329–366.

Banks, M., & Hesmondhalgh, D. (2009). Looking for Work in Creative Industries Policy. *International Journal of Cultural Policy, 15*(4), 415–430.

Banks, M., & O'Connor, J. (2021). "A Plague Upon Your Howling": Art and Culture in the Viral Emergency. *Cultural Trends, 30*(1), 3–18.

Baumol, W. J., & Bowen, W. G. (1965). On the Performing Arts: The Anatomy of Their Economic Problems. *The American Economic Review, 55*(1/2), 495–502.

Becker, H. S. (1982). *Art Worlds*. University of California Press.

Bell, D., & Oakley, K. (2015). *Cultural Policy*. Routledge.

Betzler, D., Loots, E., Prokůpek, M., Marques, L., & Grafenauer, P. (2021). COVID-19 and the Arts and Cultural Sectors: Investigating Countries' Contextual Factors and Early Policy Measures. *International Journal of Cultural Policy, 27*(6), 796–814.

Blaug, M. (2001). Where Are We Now On Cultural Economics. *Journal of Economic Surveys, 15*, 123–143.

Boltanski, L., & Thévenot, L. (1991). *On Justification*. Princeton University Press.

Bonet, L., & Donato, F. (2011). The Financial Crisis and Its Impact on the Current Models of Governance and Management of the Cultural Sector in Europe. *ENCATC Journal of Cultural Management and Policy, 1*(1), 4–11.

Borin, E., Donato, F., & Sinapi, C. (2018). Financial Sustainability of Small- and Medium-Sized Enterprises in the Cultural and Creative Sector: The Role of Funding. In I. E., H. Pechlaner, & E. Borin (Eds.), *Entrepreneurship in Culture and Creative Industries: Perspectives from Companies and Regions* (pp. 45–62). Springer International Publishing.

Caves, R. (2000). *Creative Industries: Contracts Between Art and Commerce*. Harvard University Press.

Čopič, V., Inkei, P., Kangas, A., & Srakar, A. (2013). *Trends in Public Funding for Culture in the EU*. European Union, EENC Report.

Cowen, T. (2000). *In Praise of Commercial Culture*. Harvard University Press.

Cunningham, S., & Flew, T. (2019). Introduction to a Research Agenda for Creative Industries. In S. Cunningham & T. Flew (Eds.), *A Research Agenda for Creative Industries* (pp. 1–21). Edward Elgar Publishing.

Dalla Chiesa, C., Loots, E., Brandelli Bucco, G., & Wijngaarden, Y. (2025). Matchfunding Momentum: The Effect of Institutional Funding on the Success of Crowdfunded Cultural and Creative Projects. *Journal of Alternative Finance*, 0(0).

Daniel, R. (2023). *Global Crisis and the Creative Industries: Analysing the Impact of the COVID-19 Pandemic*. Routledge.

Diadkov, M. (2024). Understanding the Past to Anticipate Tomorrow. *Forbes*. https://www.forbes.com/councils/forbesbusinesscouncil/2024/04/22/nfts-in-2024-understanding-the-past-to-anticipate-tomorrow/

Dekker, E. (2015). Two Approaches to Study the Value of Art and Culture, and the Emergence of a Third. *Journal of Cultural Economics, 39*, 309–326.

Dekker, E., & Morea, V. (2023). *Realizing the Values of Art*. Springer.

Demattos Guimarães, A., Maehle, N., & Bonet, L. (2024). The Relational Forms of Cultural-Creative Crowdfunding: A Typology of Practices Through Mapping Platforms in Europe and Latin America. *Poetics, 105*, Article 101913.

Dubois, L.-E., & Weststar, J. (2022). Games-as-a-Service: Conflicted Identities on the New Front-line of Video Game Development. *New Media & Society, 24*(10), 2332–2353.

Eikhof, D. R., & Haunschild, A. (2006). Lifestyle Meets Market: Bohemian Entrepreneurs in Creative Industries. *Creativity and Innovation Management, 15*, 234–241.

Elkins, M., & Fry, T. R. (2022). Beyond the Realm of Cash: Street Performers and Payments in the Online World. *Journal of Cultural Economics, 46*(2), 231–248.

Ferrer-Roca, N. (2015). Multi-platform Funding Strategies for Bottom-tier Films in Small Domestic Media Markets: Boy (2010) as a New Zealand Case Study. *Journal of Media Business Studies, 12*(4), 224–237.

Fay, M., Martimort, D., & Straub, S. (2021). Funding and Financing Infrastructure: The Joint-use of Public and Private Finance. *Journal of Development Economics*. 150.

Feder, T., & Woronkowicz, J. (2022). Reluctantly Independent: Motivations for Self-employed Artistic Work. *Journal of Cultural Economics*, 1–19.

FitzGibbon, A., & Tsioulakis, I. (2022). Making it Up: Adaptive Approaches to Bringing Freelance Cultural Work to a Cultural Ecologies Discourse. *European Urban and Regional Studies, 29*(4), 461–478.

Flew, T., Cunningham, S., & Flew, T. (2019). A Research Agenda for Creative Industries. In Chapter 4: *Creative Industries: Between Cultural Economics and Cultural Studies*. Edward Elgar Publishing.

Hylland, O. M., Mira, B., Katarina, L. G., Christian, H., Arturo, R. M., Kate, O., Jaka, P., & Uzelac, A. (2022). Pandemic Cultural Policy. A Comparative Perspective on Covid-19 Measures and their Effect on Cultural Policies in Europe. *International Journal of Cultural Policy, 30*(1), 81–100.

Galloway, L., & Levie, J. (2001). *Global Entrepreneurship Monitor.* Scotland University of Strathclyde, Glasgow, Issue.

Garnham, N. (2005). From Cultural to Creative Industries. *International Journal of Cultural Policy, 11*(1), 15–29.

Granger, B., Stanworth, J., & Stanworth, C. (1995). Self-employment Career Dynamics: The Case of Unemployment Push'in UK Book Publishing. *Work, Employment and Society, 9*(3), 499–516.

Haynes, J., & Marshall, L. (2018). Reluctant Entrepreneurs: Musicians and Entrepreneurship in the 'New' Music Industry. *The British Journal of Sociology, 69*(2), 459–482.

IDEA consult. (2013). Survey on Access to Finance for Cultural and Creative Sectors: Evaluate the Financial Gap of Different Cultural and Creative Sectors to Support the Impact Assessment of the Creative Europe Programme. E. C. Brussels.

Keenan, J. M., Chu, E., & Peterson, J. (2019). From Funding to Financing: Perspectives Shaping a Research Agenda for Investment in Urban Climate Adaptation. *International Journal of Urban Sustainable Development, 11*(3), 297–308.

Khlystova, O., Kalyuzhnova, Y., & Belitski, M. (2022). The Impact of the COVID-19 Pandemic on the Creative Industries: A Literature Review and Future Research Agenda. *Journal of Business Research, 139*, 1192–1210.

Klamer, A., Petrova, L., & Mignosa, A. (2006). *Financing the Arts and Culture in the European Union.* European Parliament. Committee on Culture and Education.

Kretschmer, M., Bently, L., & Deazley, R. (2010). In Deazley, R, Kretschmer, M., & Bently, L. (Eds.), *Privilege and Property: Essays on the History of Copyright.* Open Book Publishers.

Lamonica, A. G., & Isernia, P. (2021). The COVID-19 Pandemic and Cultural Industries in the EU and in the United KINGDOM: A Perfect Storm. In E. Salvador, T. Navarrete, & A. Srakar (Eds.), *Cultural Industries and the Covid-19 Pandemic* (pp. 11–26). Routledge.

Loots, E. (2023). Entrepreneurship Research in Cultural and Creative Industries: Identifying Key Ingredients of a 'Hodgepodge.' In I. Hill, S. R. S. T. A. Elias, S. Dobson, & P. Jones (Eds.), *Creative (and Cultural) Industry Entrepreneurship in the 21st Century* (pp. 17–30). Emerald Publishing Limited.

Loots, E., Betzler, D., Bille, T., Borowiecki, K. J., & Lee, B. (2022). New Forms of Finance and Funding in the Cultural and Creative Industries. Introduction to the Special Issue. *Journal of Cultural Economics, 46*(2), 205–230.

Mazzucato, M., O'Connor, J., & Bennett, T. (2025). The Art of the Public: Cultural Economy and Cultural Policy. *Journal of Cultural Economy*, 1–14.

Menger, P.-M. (1999). Artistic Labor Markets and Careers. *Annual Review of Sociology, 25*(1), 541–574.

Morea, V., & Dalla Chiesa, C. (2024). Scratching the Surface of Urban Change: Art Collectives as Public Entrepreneurs. *International Small Business Journal, 42*(1), 67–89.

Napoli, P. (2016). Requiem for the Long Tail: Towards a Political Economy of Content Aggregation and Fragmentation. *International Journal of Media & Cultural Politics, 12*(3), 341–356.

North, D. C. (1990). *Institutions, Institutional Change and Economic Performance*. Cambridge University Press.

Mangset, P. (2020). The End of Cultural Policy?1. *International Journal of Cultural Policy, 26*(3), 398–411. https://doi.org/10.1080/10286632.2018.1500560

Mangset, P., Heian, M. T., Kleppe, B., & Løyland, K. (2018). Why Are Artists Getting Poorer? About the Reproduction of Low Income Among Artists. *International Journal of Cultural Policy, 24*(4), 539–558.

Mannino, F., & Mignosa, A. (2017). Public Private Partnership for the Enhancement of Cultural Heritage: The Case of the Benedictine Monastery of Catania. In Ateca-Amestoy, V., Ginsburgh, V., Mazza, I., O'Hagan, J., Prieto-Rodriguez, J. (Eds.), *Enhancing Participation in the Arts in the* EU. Springer.

Mollick, E. (2014). The Dynamics of Crowdfunding: An Exploratory Study. *Journal of Business Venturing, 29*(1), 1–16.

O'Brien, D. (2014). *Cultural Policy: Management, Value and Modernity in the Creative Industries*. Routledge.

O'Connor, J. (2024). *Culture is Not an Industry: Reclaiming Art and Culture for the Common Good.* Manchester University Press.

Pecoraro, F., Turrini, A., & Volpe, M. (2023). *Fundraising for the Arts.* Bocconi University Press.

Peters, J., & Roose, H. (2020). From Starving Artist to Entrepreneur. Justificatory Pluralism in Visual Artists' Grant Proposals. *British Journal of Sociology, 71*, 952–969.

Peterson, M. (2018). Cultural Entrepreneurship: Unlocking Potential through Value Creation University of Exeter. *Exeter.* https://ore.exeter.ac.uk/repository/handle/10871/34526

Pratt, A. C. (2020). A Research Agenda for Cultural Economics. *Journal of Cultural Economics, 44*(1), 185–187.

Potts, J., & Cunningham, S. (2008). Four Models of the Creative Industries. *International Journal of Cultural Policy, 14*(3), 233–247.

Rykkja, A., & Bonet, L. (2023). Government Matching of Cultural Crowdfunding: An Exploratory Comparative Analysis of the Spanish and Swedish Cases. *Debats, 8*, 249–273.

Rushton, M. (2023). *The Moral Foundations of Public Funding for the Arts.* Springer Nature.

Saz-Carranza, A., & Longo, F. (2012). Managing Competing Institutional Logics in Public-Private Joint Ventures. *Public Management Review, 14*(3), 331–357.

Schuster, J. M. D. (1989). Government Leverage of Private Support: Matching Grants and the Problem with New Money. In M. J. Wyszomirski & P. Clubb (Eds.), *The Cost of Culture: Patterns and Prospects of Private Arts Patronage.* ACA Books.

Shane, S., & Venkataraman, S. (2000). The Promise of Entrepreneurship as a Field of Research. *Academy of Management Review, 25*(1), 217–226.

Shapiro, K., & Varian, H. (2000). *Information Rules.* Harvard Business School.

Srakar, A., & Čopič, V. (2012). Private Investments, Public Values: A Value-Based Approach to Argumenting for Public Support to the Arts. *Cultural Trends, 21*(3), 227–237.

Stanworth, C., & Stanworth, J. (1997). Reluctant Entrepreneurs and their Clients: The Case of Selfemployed Freelance Workers in the British Book Publishing Industry. *International Small Business Journal, 16*(1), 58–73.

Steedman, R., & Brydges, T. (2023). Hustling in the Creative Industries: Narratives and Work Practices of Female Filmmakers and Fashion Designers. *Gender, Work & Organization, 30*(3), 793–809.

Swords, J. (2017). Crowd-Patronage-Intermediaries, Geographies and Relationships in Patronage Networks. *Poetics, 64*, 63–73.

Thornton, P. H., Ocasio, W., & Lounsbury, M. (2013). *The Institutional Logics Perspective: A New Approach to Culture, Structure and Process*. Oxford Academic.

Throsby, D., & Withers, G. (1979). *The Economics of the Performing Arts*. Edward Arnold.

Throsby, D. (1994). The Production and Consumption of the Arts: A View of Cultural Economics. *Journal of Economic Literature, 32*(1), 1–29.

Throsby, D. (2000). *Economics and Culture*. Cambridge University Press.

Throsby, D. (2008). Modelling the Cultural Industries. *International Journal of Cultural Policy, 14*(3), 217–232.

Throsby, D., & Zednik, A. (2011). Multiple Job-Holding and Artistic Careers: Some Empirical Evidence. *Cultural Trends, 20*(1), 9–24.

Towse, R. (2025). Economics of Platforms, Copyrights and Regulation in the Creative Industries. *Review of Economic Research on Copyright Issues, 21*, 29–46.

Turrini, A., & Voss, Z. (2020) Strategic Fundraising in the Arts: The Mistake of Selling. In Addis, M., & Rurale, A. (Eds.), *Managing the Cultural Business: Avoiding Mistakes, Finding Success* (pp 280–311). Routledge.

UNDP. (2017). Funding to Financing UNDAF Companion Guidance. https://unsdg.un.org/resources/funding-financing-undaf-companion-guidance

van Haaften-Schick, L., Whitaker, A. From the Artist's Contract to the blockchain Ledger: New Forms of Artists' Funding Using Equity and Resale Royalties. *Journal of Cultural Economics, 46*, 287–315.

Velthuis, O. (2005) *Talking Prices: Symbolic Meanings of Prices on the Market for Contemporary Art*. Princeton University Press.

Veyne, P. (1990). *Bread and Circuses: Historical Sociology and Political Pluralism*. Penguin Press.

Waldfogel, J. (2017). How Digitization Has Created a Golden Age of Music, Movies, Books, and Television. *Journal of Economic Perspectives, 31*(3), 195–214.

Weber, D. (2000). Culture or Commerce? Symbolic Boundaries in French and American Book Publishing. In M. Lamont & L. Thévenot (Eds.), *Rethinking Comparative Cultural Sociology* (pp. 127–147). Cambridge University Press.
Williams, R. (1981). *Culture*. Fontana Paperbacks.
Whitaker, A., & Grannemann, H. (2019). Artists' Royalties and Performers' Equity: A Ground-Up Approach to Social Impact Investment in Creative Fields. *Cultural Management: Science and Education, 3*(2), 33–52.
Woronkowicz, J., & Noonan, D. S. (2019). Who Goes Freelance? The Determinants of Self-employment for Artists. *Entrepreneurship Theory and Practice, 43*(4), 651–672.
Wyszomirski, M. (2004). From Public Support for the Arts to Cultural Policy. *Review of Policy Research, 21*, 469–484.

Open Access This chapter is licensed under the terms of the Creative Commons Attribution 4.0 International License (http://creativecommons.org/licenses/by/4.0/), which permits use, sharing, adaptation, distribution and reproduction in any medium or format, as long as you give appropriate credit to the original author(s) and the source, provide a link to the Creative Commons license and indicate if changes were made.

The images or other third party material in this chapter are included in the chapter's Creative Commons license, unless indicated otherwise in a credit line to the material. If material is not included in the chapter's Creative Commons license and your intended use is not permitted by statutory regulation or exceeds the permitted use, you will need to obtain permission directly from the copyright holder.

PART I

Core Funding and Financing Models

CHAPTER 2

Direct Government Contribution to Culture: Legitimacy, Financial Mechanisms and Level of Spending Compared Internationally

Lluís Bonet

1 Introduction

The model of public funding of arts and heritage cannot be dissociated from cultural policy itself. Public funding of the arts makes transparent and explicit the values and objectives of government policy, its priorities, decision-making patterns and administrative organization (Klamer et al., 2007). A careful reading of public budgets and their subsequent liquidation often provides much more information about a political strategy than the rhetoric of political speeches in parliament or in the media. Alongside funding, having a good regulatory framework, that is general (administrative, commercial, labour or tax) as well as sector specific (e.g. protection of cultural heritage, single book price, etc.) in its orientation is a key condition for providing order and legal security for various national systems of cultural production. Besides, the oversight of government policy and

L. Bonet (✉)
University of Barcelona, Barcelona, Spain
e-mail: lbonet@ub.edu

© The Author(s) 2026

C. Dalla Chiesa and A. Rykkja (eds.), *Cultural Funding and Financing*, Cultural Economics & the Creative Economy,
https://doi.org/10.1007/978-3-031-96696-5_2

the regulatory framework need good mechanisms of information, incentive, inspection and sanction. These issues also require funding and an efficient administrative structure. In practice, the different instruments are interconnected. For example, improving the employment situation of artists, a hot topic because of the pandemic, not only requires a favourable legislative framework but also direct funding and better social security coverage.

In any case, of the set of government instruments supporting culture, only some are specifically financial instruments with budgetary implications, such as public spending or the granting of tax benefits. Due to their direct impact on the market and its suppliers, both mechanisms capture a large part of the interest of citizens and cultural agents. Some key questions arise in this context. What are the main forms of government intervention in the cultural sphere? What role does the public sector play in the general funding of arts and culture? Which artistic sectors, heritage areas or types of activity receive greater attention and funding from the different government agencies with an impact on life, production and cultural experience? There are no unique answers to these questions on an international scale, since they depend fundamentally on the political culture, the social recognition of culture and the forms of public intervention in the economy of each analysed country. This fact explains the focus and even the implicit biases that researchers interested in the topic have. As Mark Schuster points out, in the United States research objectives tend to concentrate on justifying government support because scholars do their work in a context where the dominant beliefs and assumptions centre around ideas that cultural affairs are primarily a private responsibility (Schuster, 1994). This apriorism changes when the person analysing comes from another context.

Most of the conceptual reflection and empirical studies on government funding of culture have been carried out from a Western perspective, in a context dominated by liberal democracies and market economies. Several issues have merited attention from researchers who have studied the subject. Economic analyses have examined how the decline in productivity of labour-intensive activities has compelled public financing systems to fund the provision of cultural public goods and merit goods, in accordance with societal values. (Baumol & Bowen, 1966; Throsby, 1992). The limited redistributive effects have also been studied in terms of socioeconomic equity (Bennett et al., 2009; Bourdieu and Darbel, 1969), and territorial distribution between populated areas and peripheral or rural regions (Schuster, 1990; Ponzini, 2016). Another relevant aspect has been the international comparison between the different intervention models, the volume of the contribution per capita and by subsectors and the preferential use of certain mechanisms, via direct provision, subsidy, matching-grant or tax benefits (Cummings & Schuster, 1989; Klamer et al., 2007). In any case, the choice of the issues analysed is influenced by the desire to complement or provide a critical look at pre-existing academic contributions, the productive and social conditions of the cultural subsectors and the models of government intervention existing in the respective countries. And in some cases, also the desire to influence the public debate with solid academic arguments in dialogue with the interests of the lobbying action of cultural stakeholders.[1]

This chapter focuses on the analysis of government spending, explaining its evolution and the different justifications that legitimize the public policies that support it. Despite the scarcity of comparable data on an international scale, which predominantly focus on developed countries, attempts are made to explain the ways in which the various existing financial mechanisms are operationalized, as well as what are some of the prevailing managerial models. The available sources are not homogeneous with respect to the items included under the generic name of culture. The OECD and Eurostat data used in this work encompass the set of expenditures from the broad chapter of recreation, culture and religion. Other more specific works only consider cultural services, encompassing under this term support for the arts and cultural heritage. In the area of communication, a very important item corresponds to the maintenance of public radio and television services, whose support mechanisms would deserve a separate chapter. It is not within the scope of this text to discuss which is the best definition of the term culture,[2] since what is intended is to present a broad and as far as possible comparative view about government spending on culture on an international scale.

2 Arguments Justifying Government Support for Culture

Why are there so many differences regarding the volume of financial resources per capita or related to GDP invested in supporting culture at international level, but also between different cities and regions within the same country? Why are some cultural activities and subsectors favoured over others? What is the link between the financing mechanisms used and the political and organizational models prevailing in the different countries? To answer these questions, it is necessary to analyse first the arguments used to justify government intervention and the consequent financial investment in culture.

In the Western world, since the establishment of the modern state, it was basically the need to consolidate nation-states and to have an educated workforce that was the motivation that drove national elites and governments to fund cultural institutions, from museums to arts schools and theatres. Obviously, the arguments and strategies implemented change depending on the ideology in government, as a diversity of alternatives can be offered, from radical libertarian to fascist or communist totalitarianism, passing through different liberal or social democratic visions. The first, defended today for example by Donald Trump in the USA or Javier Milei in Argentina aims to dismantle the liberal democratic substratum. This policy of dismantling the cultural action of the state should not be confused with the totalitarian strategy of fascism or communism based on strong control by the state, the party and the official unions (Bonet & Zamorano, 2020).

In Western democracies, cultural policies developed since the second half of the twentieth century have been driven by liberal and social democratic ideologies. If these policies in the nineteenth century focused on the protection and enhancement of cultural heritage and support for artistic education and public reading, they have after the second world war expanded (Poirrier, 2010). In a first development through incorporating support for artistic excellence and cultural democratization. Thereafter, its evolution took a further turn towards the end of the century by adding support for cultural and creative industries and more horizontal mechanisms of cultural democracy. The premise of the model, whose international dissemination was backed by the Council of Europe and UNESCO, was justified by a combination of mixed public economics and philosophical arguments (Throsby, 2010).

In the liberal tradition there are various views, from those who only accept government intervention to preserve cultural heritage and the legacy of artistic manifestations for future generations, to those who also defend the government action when it complements citizen education or innovation capacity due to culture spillover effects; all this under the principles of transparency, reasonableness and neutrality of government intervention (Rushton, 2000). In countries such the United States, indirect financial mechanisms such as tax benefits or incentives for private action have been preferred to direct spending, because the latter was considered less efficient, clientelist and not transparent enough. In Western Europe and other democratic countries, under the "welfare state" model, promoted by both Christian Democratic, Conservative and Social Democratic governments, the state's ambit of action encompasses not only educational, health or social policies but also cultural policies.

The economic arguments used in both cases, with nuances more or less favourable to government funding of culture, can be summarized in three main factors: (a) efficiency, (b) equity and (c) protection of cultural production and national heritage in international trade context.

The analysis of economic efficiency in the arts has focused on market failure as a mechanism to solve the issue of providing the socially optimal amount of cultural goods as a way to satisfy demand that aligns with the set of preferences of the citizens (Rushton, 2022). This is because some cultural services are public goods, meaning products that once provided to their audience are non-rival (any extra user does not diminish the benefits to anyone else enjoying the good) and non-exclusive (there is no practical way to keep people from enjoying the good). The reason why public goods are not efficiently supplied by the market comes from the fact that these products entail a cost but there is no easy way for the supplier to collect revenue (Schuster, 1994). Examples of public goods would be heritage landscapes and monuments, historical archives, free-to-air terrestrial broadcasting or outdoor public art since the fact of enjoying them does not prevent others from being able to do so.

Other cultural goods and services, such as live shows, arts education or independent movie production, can be considered merit goods. In this case, the economic argument is that whenever social benefits exceed private benefits, a good will be underproduced, unless additional non-market resources can be incorporated into the production of the good. Thus, despite not being pure public goods, merit goods nevertheless deserve government support since they generate positive external benefits and economic spillovers, similarly to public goods. That is to say, the increase in people who benefit from the provision of these goods thanks to government support, implies a social benefit higher than the private benefit that would be obtained by the smaller number of users who could acquire it at market price.

In the case of the performing arts the increase over time in the cost of the live show, given its growing differential in terms of labour productivity with respect to most economic activities, generates a growing deficit known as "cost disease" (Baumol & Bowen, 1966). Since it only satisfies the preferences of the few who can afford exclusionary prices, alternative means of financing are necessary to ensure its survival. To the extent that the serious arts could be considered merit goods in certain contexts, the deficit could be covered by public or philanthropic support, supplemented by exchange in terms of prestige value or access to specific audiences that interest business sponsors.

Promoting creation and access to the arts generates long-term benefits, as does having a good education system and platforms that foster innovation, greater economic development and greater social well-being. Additionally, the spillover effect spreads to other sectors, such as tourism. Given that private capital markets do not work sufficiently efficiently when it comes to long-term impact investments, subsidising the generation of these externalities is particularly important both because of the length of artistic productions and the high risk of independent cultural production. Additionally, the great difficulty in remunerating the effort involved in creating new artistic styles, meaningful experiences, new functionalities and formats, or even better governance and management models, plays a significant role (Bonet, 2025). Given that most innovations in the field of culture are the result of open innovation processes, copyright and intellectual property rights do not tend to cover the uncertain investment in innovation made by creators and cultural institutions.

In summary, the argument goes that left in the exclusive hands of the market, most of these outcomes would not exist or would be due to the exclusive privilege of a minority. However, not everyone takes this position, as exemplified by the scepticism of public choice economists regarding the remedial abilities of governments: "The lack of correspondence between the prescriptions derived from welfare economics and the widespread intervention of governments in arts provision is the signal given to public choice economists, like the author, that attempts to rectify market failure may be frustrated by 'government failure'" (Peacock, 2000 p. 190). Nonetheless beyond this innate scepticism of some, the key question resides in how cultural services with governmental support are provided, since as discussed below there are different models of ownership and management, a fact that conditions their efficiency.

Another aspect to consider is the ability of public spending and tax benefit mechanisms to encourage private investment or leverage private philanthropy towards the arts and heritage (Brooks, 1999). Furthermore, the possibility of a regulatory framework that generates specific taxes to nurture support funds for certain activities, or that forces large companies to invest in cultural production, as would be the case of broadcasting in the financing of cinema (Fiorini, 2023).

Alongside the problem of efficiency is the more philosophical question of equity, the second key factor previously noted. In principle, subsidizing the cost of goods that generate externalities by making their acquisition cheaper redistributes the benefit among people with lower purchasing power. The problem appears when the type of subsidized goods is only of interest to people with a certain type of cultural capital and high levels of education, who belong to middle and upper social classes (Bennett et al., 2009; Bourdieu and Darbel, 1969). In addition, if the officials who decide what is subsidized share the values of these social groups, the equitable intention is denatured, and abuse by rent seekers can occur (Peacock, 2000). Governments therefore need to consider the socioeconomic principle of equity, such as the redistributive effect, when designing and implementing interventions as a way to avoid this pernicious effect.

On the other hand, the impact in terms of territorial distribution between populated areas and peripheral or rural regions is much more promising (Ponzini, 2016; Schuster, 1990). Market dynamics tend to centralize the provision of cultural services in large cities and in affluent neighbourhoods and regions. Government cultural action, particularly in countries where local administrations have the resources and competences, compensates and redistributes much better than the market. There is still nevertheless much to learn about institutional inequities in the arts. Conventional wisdom may not reflect empirical realities, and it is necessary to incorporate redistribution by large cultural organizations towards their stakeholders, often professionals with low incomes, to fully understand the redistributive capacity of the arts with respect to the financing of non-artistic activities (Chen & Noonan, 2023).

Another aspect to consider is the dissociation between the individual's preference when acting as a consumer or as a citizen, a phenomenon that can be analysed using contingent valuation methodologies (Bille, 2024). As a citizen, someone can defend the need to have in their city libraries, schools and artistic residences, theatre or jazz seasons, as well as civic centres for young people or the elderly, without personally using any of these services. Likewise, citizens can vote for politicians who defend local or national culture and heritage, especially when their own cultural and linguistic identity and expressions are perceived to be threatened by homogenization processes. Homogenization is here connected to globalization and the goals of businesses that want to reach more people while cutting costs, as well as to political groups that want to reduce ethnic or regional differences that go against their control.

Not all artistic expressions or all heritage manifestations evoke the same level of social consensus, and therefore their financing with public resources is justified. A study comparing the recipients of philanthropic donations in the USA and the UK found that in the former case it was the large professional arts institutions that benefited the most, while in the latter it was much more modest activities and institutions (Baumol & Bowen, 1966). The reason given was that in the UK, since public administrations subsidized large orchestras, museums and performing arts companies to a much greater extent, citizens could allocate their donations to more semi-professional amateur activities. It should be noted, however, that the activities deserving public funding evolve as societies and their values change. In increasingly culturally diverse societies, the "median voter" argument weakens, because the expressions to be promoted and the heritage to be protected are diversifying, as is the requirement to make the various cultural policy paradigms more participatory (Bonet & Négrier, 2018). In general, the more engaged contemporary art generates more suspicion than the more established cultural heritage, although this depends on the dominant ideology. In countries such as the USA, controversial art has been one of the factors that has questioned and reduced the budget of arts support agencies (Rushton, 2000). A series of surveys conducted between 1990 and 2016 show how proposals to substantially reduce public funding of the arts were not well-aligned with public opinion, including among Republican party voters (Jacobsmeier, 2020).

The third and last economic argument is related to the protection of cultural production and national heritage in international trade context. There are two quite different types of international trade restrictions usually invoked (Mas-Colell, 1999). The first is the "cultural exception" claim, an appeal for the legitimacy of import restriction measures based on the cultural nature of the goods or services concerned. The second restriction is peculiar to national cultural heritage, affecting not on the import, but on the export of heritage artifacts. To understand the first, it is necessary to differentiate between the protection of national cultural production and the protection of the production of national culture. In the first case, in the light of imperfect and strategic competition, it is necessary to consider the possible advantages of strategic competitive moves and, on the other, the political-economic realities of rent-seeking. In the second case, it can be argued the existence of network externalities that could generate a failure in the transmission to the market of a demand that actually exists. The differential economies of scale in cultural production depending on the size of the market explains why small countries have to resort more to direct support for the national cultural industry than larger countries, as can be seen in the financing of films in Europe (Fioroni, 2023). Finally, the restriction on cultural heritage exports is due to the asymmetry of purchasing power between communities and countries, sometimes accentuated by an unequal colonial relationship, allowing collectors with resources to buy heritage assets from other countries, without flow in the opposite direction. In both cases, the issue of national identity is particularly important for the support of culture in smaller market and weaker countries (Schuster, 1994).

Intertwined with the previous political arguments, from a pragmatic point of view the following explanatory factors stand out:

(a) Electoral benefit: certain politicians start from the presumption that the electorate will positively welcome public spending on culture. This presumption has been proven empirically true at a local scale in Spain. Parties in power that increase their spending on culture in the year before municipal elections have a greater probability of winning the electoral contest (Sanjuan et al., 2020). The results would probably be different in a country where cultural activities were perceived as elitist and at the service of free riders.

(b) Lobbying capacity of powerful stakeholders: cultural operators who are better organized, with more resources and who know the implications of the various existing support strategies can better influence public policies, favouring the arguments, the implementation of the instruments and the financial resources that benefit them better.

(c) Use of economic and social impact studies to justify cultural action: many cultural institutions commission impact studies, methodologically not always accurate enough, to justify the economic and social return of government spending on culture. Beyond the long-term evidence of the positive externalities that culture can generate (Bille, 2024), its abuse must be avoided. On the other hand, it should be borne in mind that other activities, such as sport, can generate greater impacts.

(d) Instrumental use of culture in the service of other public policies: cultural diplomacy, territorial branding or urban renewal strategies use cultural expressions and services to achieve their specific objectives. In all these cases both parties' benefit, as it generates employment, income and additional cultural activity.

Throughout the history of mankind, the support of public authorities for culture did not respond to the search for the general interest, but certain artistic and cultural expressions, as well as heritage, have been instrumentally used to serve the interests of powerful people. In most cases, the contribution was sought in terms of prestige or for the enjoyment obtained by the prince and his court. Also, because the iconography developed or the cultivation of the language of the dominant groups (and the marginalization of other unwanted iconographies and languages) allowed the strategy of the powerful to be legitimized. A text that clearly explicitly states this strategy can be found in the "Mémoires de Louis XIV pour l'instruction du Dauphin" written at the end of the seventeenth century. This mixture of interests has not completely disappeared today, as can be seen in most of the arguments used to legitimize support for and allocate public resources to culture. However, in liberal democratic societies what fundamentally legitimizes public intervention is its character as a public good and merit good.

Totalitarian regimes follow very similar interests, even though arts education and artistic and sporting achievements are considered beneficial for the people and the country. Education and culture are uniformizing and propagandistic instruments. It is not surprising that these regimes devote a lot of resources to cultural action. Countries with illiberal populist governments pursue similar goals although instead of being radically suppressed, dissent is marginalized, and discriminatory criteria for the distribution of subsidies are followed with the aim of favouring demonstrations and ideologically similar clienteles (Bonet & Zamorano, 2020).

3 Government Spending on Culture on an International Scale

The public sector has three major complementary economic mechanisms to respond to the funding needs of culture: direct support through public spending, indirect contribution through tax benefits to individuals, third sector entities and companies and market regulation mechanisms that incentive public–private cooperation and alternative sources of funding. Other chapters in this book explain government policy through tax benefits and other sources of finance, while the focus of this chapter is public spending. It should be noted, however, that most countries use all three mechanisms in different proportions to a greater or lesser extent (Čopič et al., 2013). For this reason, the comparative analysis of public policies must evaluate the impact and interdependence of the existing financing mechanisms, as well as their individualized and aggregated effect on the cultural sector.

As noted, very little information is available on a global scale about government spending on culture. The UNESCO Institute for Statistics collects information focused on Sustainable Development Goal (SDG) indicators. The 11.4.1 indicator collects information on the expenditure on the protection of the cultural and natural heritage of those countries that have answered their questionnaire. Although this information is partial, it provides a first approximation of the great differences that exist between countries and regions. The difference in spending per capita at purchasing power parity between countries and regions is very large.

> The results for the 57 countries for which data are available from 2018 to 2021 show that the range of values for public expenditure on heritage for developing countries is significantly less compared to developed countries. As a result, the median public expenditure on heritage preservation for European countries reporting was 72.9 PPP$ -constant 2017 USD- per capita, compared to a median of less than 15.0$ for other regions: 12.5 PPP$ for Northern Africa and Western Asia, 10.5 PPP$ per capita for Latin America and the Caribbean, 4.6 PPP$ for Eastern and South-Eastern Asia and less than for 1.0 PPP$ for sub-Saharan Africa. (UNESCO Institute for Statistics, 2023)

To understand the investment effort of each country in culture, it is useful to analyse the proportion of public expenditure on total government expenditure, as well as its evolution over time. This indicator allows knowing the degree of priority given to culture compared to other public policies such as education or health. If we take as an indicator the proportion represented in the year 2022 by spending on "recreation, culture and religion" on the total government budget collected by the OECD, we find very noticeable differences, both between European countries and outside the Old Continent. A group of small states such as Iceland, Estonia, Hungary, Latvia or Lithuania dedicate more than 2% of their budget to the cultural field. At the other end and below 0.6% of the total budget, are countries such as Greece, Italy, the United Kingdom, Colombia or Japan. As already mentioned, public spending is only one of the means of a government policy, and in countries like the United Kingdom and especially the USA, tax benefits play a very important role by encouraging private spending on culture.

During the quarter of a century between 1998 and 2022, there are countries that reduce the contribution to culture with respect to total expenditure, including local, state and central government. Nevertheless, as can be seen in the upper-left part of Fig. 1, those with the name in brown had a contribution of more than 1% in the last year analysed, with exceptional cases such as Iceland and Estonia above 2%. In the lower part in red, there are countries where the weight loss of the contribution to culture during the last twenty-five years leads them to dedicate in the year 2022 less than 1% of their total government budget. Among these are countries that have suffered severe budget crises such as Colombia or Romania, where the weight of culture has been reduced by almost 3%.

The financial crisis of 2008 legitimized the cuts to achieve balanced budgets and greater fiscal discipline. However, the fragmentation of cultural policy left arts and culture funding vulnerable to further cuts, forcing a rethinking of the values and arguments needed to protect it (Husson, 2013). In some countries, such as Greece, Portugal, Ireland, Spain or Italy, it had a devastating impact on the sustainability of many cultural entities and projects, mainly in the independent sector (Bonet & Donato, 2011). Many of these countries have partially recovered the previous budgetary situation without, however, reaching the pre-crisis level of financing. Other large countries in prolonged recession and with higher private co-financing, such as the United Kingdom or Japan, have also been reducing their contribution to culture.

On the right of Fig. 1, there are countries that have seen increased government contribution to culture in the long period 1998–2022, despite the financial and the pandemic crisis. Beyond countries such as

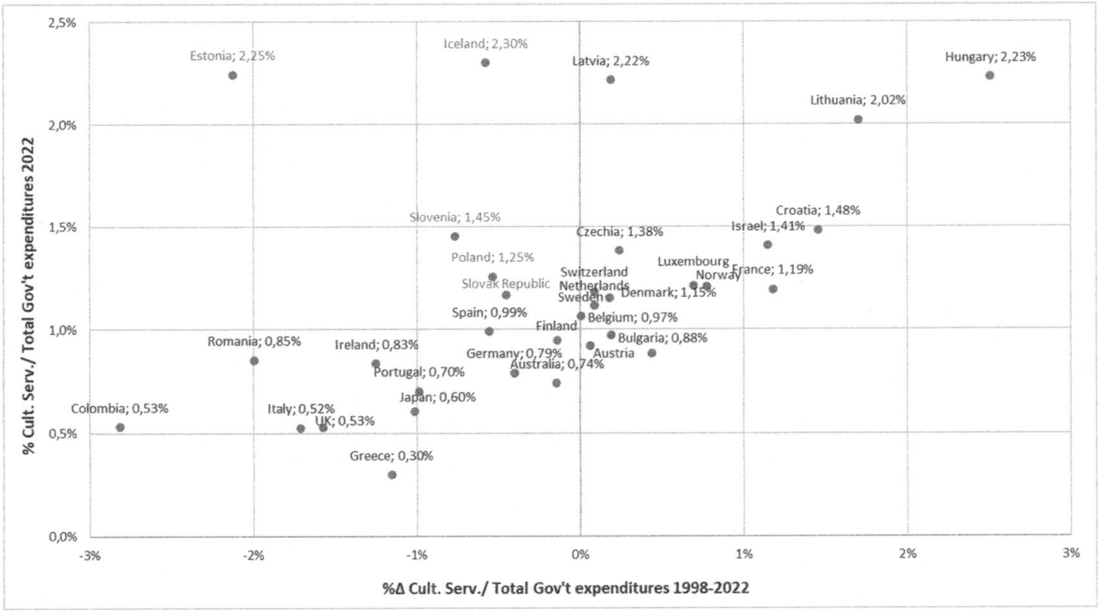

Fig. 1 Proportion of 'recreation, culture and religion' expenditure to total Gov't expenditure 2022, and increase of this proportion over the period 1998–2022 (*Note* Sourced from OECD Data Explorer, own elaboration)

France, Israel, Croatia or Lithuania which have increased their relative contribution above 1%, the case of Hungary stands out, which has almost increased the weight of culture by 2.5%, placing it at 2.23% of its total budget.

Most Western countries saw government funding for culture grow during the second half of the twentieth century, as cultural policies and government departments of culture were established. However, few historical series are available that allow us to evaluate the main trends that explain this evolution beyond individual countries. In Israel, for example, the analysis of the variations in public expenditure in the field of performing arts over a period of 48 years shows that the trends in funding are associated with changes in level of education and income of the population, as well as ethnic composition (Feder & Katz-Gerro, 2012). In countries like France, supporting culture is considered an essential mission of the state (Masclet de Barbarin, 2012), accepted without criticism by most citizens, which explains why even in periods of crisis its level of funding has been maintained.

In the USA, direct arts subsidies first became a federal venture in the early years of the New Deal (1933–1934), but from the end of the Second World War until 1965 when the NEA was stablished, federal arts subsidies were only ad hoc (Brooks, 2004). The contribution in constant dollars only grew during the first fifteen years. After that, they decreased up until the end of the century. Slowly, but with large differences between them, the states and local administrations have offset the marginal contribution of direct spending in the USA arts support system: between 2000 and 2020, the aggregate funding for the arts increased by almost 17% (Stubbs & Mullaney-Loss, 2021).

In contrast, China's "government acts as an authoriser, a service, a guide, and a supervisor in the cultural sphere" (Wang, 2006, as reported by Tu & Tao, 2017), making it the sector's primary contributor. With the reforms of 2004 and 2005, and the construction of service-orientation government, per capita public cultural spending increased from 10.23 yuan in 2005 to 49.67 yuan in 2015, and the ratio of public cultural spending in GDP rose to 0.082% from 2005 to 2015.

In the case of Latin America and the Caribbean region, we only have, as Table 2.1 shows, partial data on the level of willingness that different governments have in supporting culture. In the case of Colombia, the data does not match with the OECD monitor ones. In any case, the region follows the rule that central government of smaller countries contribute more than big ones, although in the case of the federal states of Brazil and Argentina, the contribution of states and municipalities is much more important than those of the central government (Table 1).

On a local scale, the resources used by municipalities to strengthen their prestige and promote the quality of life of their citizens through culture show great differences from city to city within the same country. Notwithstanding, in a study on the weight of public funding in the cultural promotion of 16 large international metropolises, a high correlation is observed between the proportion of public resources and the political culture of each country (Tokbaeva, 2018). In Stockholm, as well as in Shanghai and Shenzhen, the entire investment is made with direct public resources. The proportion in four other major European cities surveyed (Amsterdam, Brussels, Paris and Rome) is just over 90%. However, in Toronto, London, Seoul, the level of direct public funding reduces to two thirds of the total amount. On the other hand, in Toronto, London or Seul it represents around two thirds of the total, in Los

Table 1 Estimation of the share of cultural budgets in relation to total government budgets in Latin-American and the Caribbean countries, 2018*

Country	*Ministry of culture (or equivalent) %*	*Other central gov't departments*	*Regional and local governments*
Brazil	0.07	n.d	0.48%
Paraguay	0.07	n.d	n.d
Argentina	0.18	0.52%	0.45%
Colombia	0.19	0.05%	n.d
Ecuador	0.22	n.d	n.d
Mexico	0.24	0.08%	n.d
Jamaica	0.26	n.d	n.d
Chile	0.35	0.42%	n.d
Dominican Rep	0.36	n.d	n.d
Peru	0.38	n.d	n.d
Panama	0.42	n.d	n.d
Uruguay	0.56	n.d	n.d
Trinidad & Tobago	0.69	n.d	n.d
Costa Rica	0.79	n.d	n.d

Note Sourced from Lobos, Lopez and Gribnicow (2021). Own elaboration

* The results of the three columns cannot be aggregated given the lack of data in some countries, which when they exist can be tied subsidies and that the value on which the share is calculated corresponds to the total budget of each level of government, therefore on different bases

Angeles and Tokyo over 50%, in San Francisco 35%, and in the exceptional case of New York the public contribution only represents 26% of the available resources.

To internationally compare the fiscal effort and the weight of the public sector supporting culture, two complementary indicators are used: government spending on culture per inhabitant and total government spending respectively in relation to GDP. The differences between countries can be very significant in both indicators, not only given the different level of economic development but also because of very heterogeneous political cultures. In the European Union case, a region that shares a quite similar political culture, the differences can be much greater than one might expect. Thus, the weight of total public expenditure in relation to the total GDP of each country varies between 21.2% in the case of the Republic of Ireland and 58.3% in the case of France, with an EU average of 45.1%. If this happens at the level of the European Union, made up of countries that share a similar regulatory framework, the gap widens on a global scale, because alongside highly interventionist countries there are others where the role of the public sector and its investment in the cultural sphere is much smaller, in some cases residual.

Expenditure per capita also shows great differences, with Luxembourg contributing €637 per inhabitant, while Greece allocates only €31, with an EU average of €189. The differences between countries are explained by the combination of factors such as the different economic situation, the weight of the public sector in the economy, the role traditionally given to culture, as well as the number and volume of activity of public cultural facilities. In order to try to see it visually in Fig. 2, the European countries that transited during the last decade of the twentieth century from planned economies to market economies have been marked in red, the Mediterranean countries in blue, in black the north-western countries.

Another relevant aspect is the distribution of expenditure by government level, as shown in Fig. 3. In the case of Europe, there is an inverse relationship between the size of the country and the decentralization of spending. Countries of very small size, such as Cyprus or Malta, are not likely to decentralize spending. Iceland is an exception. Slightly larger countries, such as Bulgaria, Hungary or Ireland, follow the same parameter due to political tradition or a lack of trust with the local administration. A rather surprising case is the Italian one, since the concentration of expenditure at the central level contrasts with the rich dynamism and strong identity of its cities and regions. On the other hand,

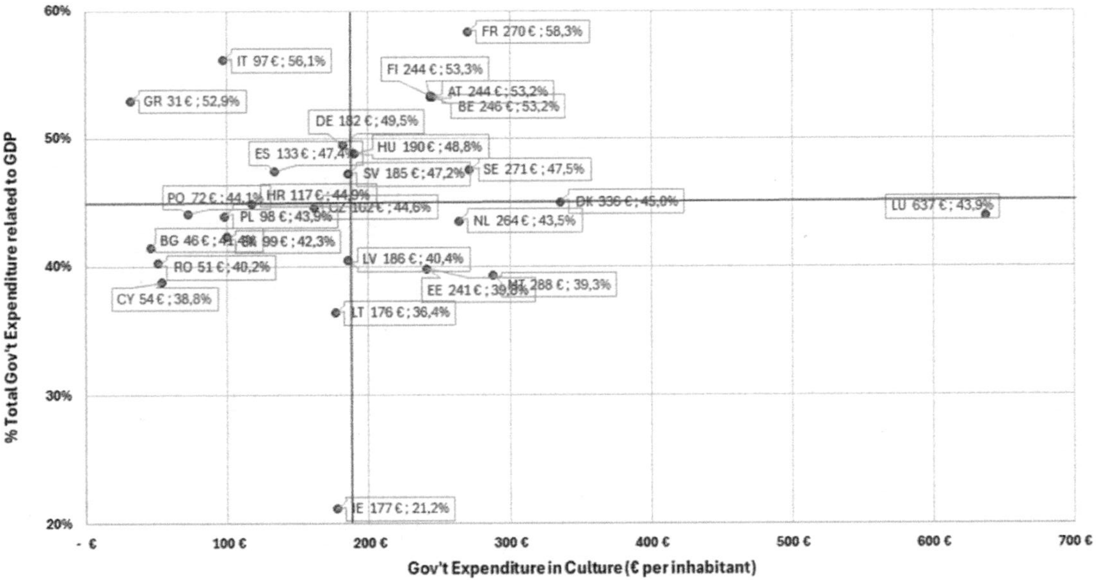

Fig. 2 Government expenditure in recreation, culture and religion per capita related to % of total government expenditure to GDP of EU countries (2022) in OECE countries with available data (*Note* Source is Eurostat. Own elaboration)

in federal or assimilated countries (Germany, Belgium, Spain, Switzerland and to a lesser extent Austria) or with strong local autonomy (France, the Netherlands, Poland or Romania) the central government has a much more marginal role. Outside of Europe, the situation is similar in the federal countries of Anglo-Saxon culture (Australia, Canada or the USA) and in Latin America (specially in Argentina and Brazil) but not at local level (Lobos et al., 2021), except for some big metropolises.

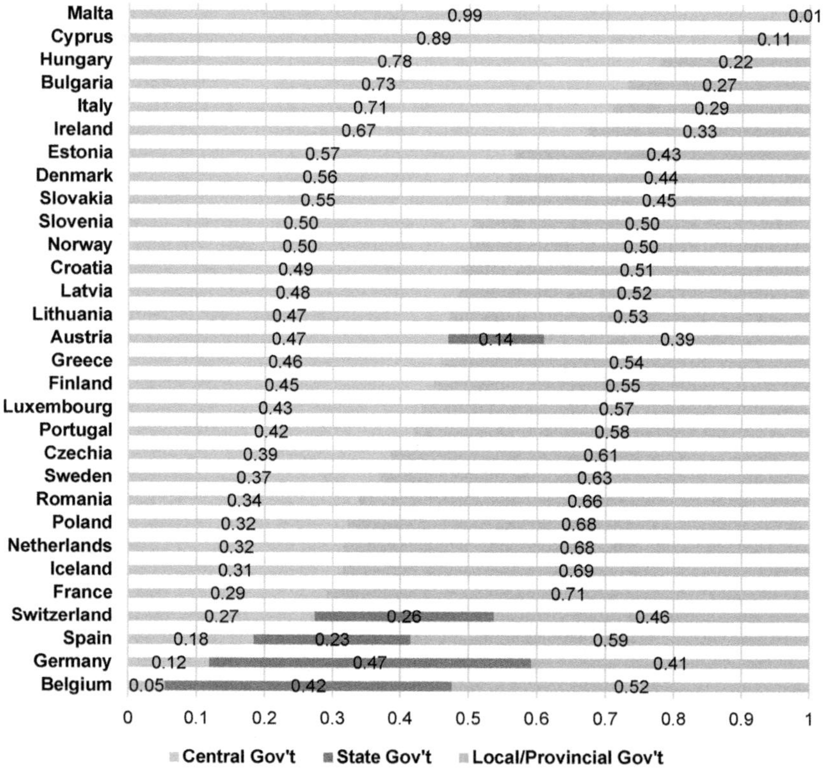

Fig. 3 Distribution by levels of government of public expenditure of European Countries on recreation, culture & religion, 2022 (*Note* Source is OECD Data Explorer. Own elaboration)

4 Management and Financing Mechanisms for the Arts and Heritage

The financing of cultural events and production through public expenditure is carried out through three main mechanisms: (a) the direct, indirect or outsourced provision of public cultural goods or services; (b) the acquisition of cultural products from private operators; and (c) current or capital transfers to professionals and cultural institutions external to the public sector. The combination and relative weight of these four financing mechanisms depend on the one hand, on the tradition and evolution of the management models of public services in each country, and in particular on the level of development of its welfare state; and, on the other hand, of the respective promotion policies for activities of general interest and the productive fabric and domestic non-profit entities. Both aspects cannot be separated from the political, democratic or authoritarian framework established in each country.

Public Provision

There are three ways of carrying out the public provision of cultural goods or services by the administration, its equipment and publicly owned projects: direct provision, indirect provision and outsourced management (Bonet & Négrier, 2020). When the ownership and management of a cultural facility is carried out directly by the administration and its staff we will talk about direct provision, while when the entity in charge has a different legal status from the government entity from which the resources come (for example, when it is managed by a public foundation or consortium, or another level of administration) we will talk about indirect public provision. A very common alternative to these two models is outsourced management through competitive public bidding. In this case, the operators who win the competition, mostly profit-making or non-profit private entities, undertake to provide the service in exchange for a government contribution that covers the estimated financial deficit; in return, they must stick to the programming and public price policy established in the competition program contract.

In most continental European and Latin American countries, the provision of cultural services by the public administration is the most common mechanism and concentrates a large part of the government budget allocated to culture. The larger the network of cultural centres, museums, libraries, archives or publicly owned theatres in a certain territory, as well as their level of activities, the higher this budget will be. In Latin American countries, the number of publicly owned facilities is much lower than in Europe, but the size and number of employees of large national theatres or museums can be extremely large (Almeida & Halty, 2024; Saravia, 1993). In this region, central banks play a prominent role, as they treasure large collections and, not being at the mercy of political ups and downs or recurring budget crises, they are one of the most stable heritage institutions in the respective countries.

In the case of Anglo-Saxon countries, the direct provision is less since many cultural projects are either delegated to independent quasi-governmental entities, with a specific budget allocation, or are managed directly by non-profit entities. However, with the implementation of models of new public management, many countries have developed hybrid management and financing models. In countries in transition from planned economies, the abrupt change to a market economy during the 1990s generated a dual system: one part consisting of large venues and ensembles totally subsidized by the state and one part independent sector operating with funding from very small grants. In other European countries, such as Italy, for example, mixed public–private models of management were developed. Evidence, however, shows that these only operate well in large audience venues (Dalle Nogare & Bertacchini, 2015).

Acquisition of Cultural Products and Services from Private Operators

The second mechanism of government funding in culture is the acquisition of products or services from private operators. There are multiple ways to do it: purchase of artwork; acquisition of cultural heritage from individuals or using the preferential right of withdrawal in public auctions; order or purchase of publications and other supports to nurture libraries; payment of copyright, interpretation or reproduction as well as the use of all types of digital resources; ticket subscription for shows to be represented in theatres and festivals; or hiring professionals or companies to develop projects or provide cultural services to the public sector. Another form of government procurement is spending vouchers for young people or other vulnerable groups for the purchase of cultural products, which not only aim to encourage cultural consumption but also increase the sales of local suppliers.

The more developed a cultural policy is, the more resources are fed to the private cultural sector through the acquisition of its products and services by different government entities. The multiplier and strengthening capacity of the domestic cultural fabric of this public expenditure when it is well oriented can be important.

Current or Capital Transfers to Professionals and Cultural Institutions External to the Public Sector

The main financing mechanism via transfer to professionals, organizations and cultural companies is the public subsidy. This can be for current expenses or for capital investment (for example, repair or restoration of heritage buildings or acquisition of machinery and technology). In both cases, they can be nominative, automatic or competitive transfers. In the first case, the receiving entity and the value of the transfer are recorded in the public budget, and it tends to favour unquestionable institutions and projects, well rooted in the respective territory. In the second case, the funding is transferred based on a pre-established formula based on objective indicators such as the turnover volume, or the number of inhabitants. In the third case, the administration opens a public call, with specific objectives and requirements, with the aim of guaranteeing transparency and equal opportunities. They usually tend to be transfers of a smaller unit amount than registered ones. There are also other ways of transferring resources to the cultural sector, such as prizes or the administration of a remunerative public concession.

A complex and little-analysed issue is financial transfers beyond the borders of the administrative territory. First, because the boundaries between cultural development cooperation and the promotion of international cultural relations, both from the point of view of cultural diplomacy and from the support to domestic cultural production internationalization, are quite confusing. Secondly, because much of the cultural development cooperation transfers resources to entities of very different jurisdictions, from companies or national institutions with cooperation projects, to the finalist entities receiving the aid in the recipient country, or to mixed consortia, with the complexities inherent in these processes. Thirdly, because many of the aid programs are designed with a Western mentality without considering environments of great resource and legal insecurity, and the multiple obstacles that hinder local cultural development: the absence of infrastructure, material, skills, organization and regulation; ultimately, lack of political will and in some cases even audience will (Mefe, 2004). In a context of great informality that does not go well with the transparency requirements of donor agencies, most cultural projects move forward thanks to the commitment, passion, perseverance and inventiveness of the actors involved.

Refundable and Guarantee Funds

Some countries have developed more sophisticated financial instruments to support cultural business initiatives. It can be used directly from a government service or agency or through a public financial institution or private financial entities in agreement with government agencies. In general, they consist of returnable public contributions, even though in the case of bankruptcy the responsibilities are reduced, since they are accompanied by guaranteed mechanisms to reduce the risk of both the cultural agents and the financial entities that participate in the process.

A first mixed instrument is repayable contributions. It consists of a public contribution in the form of co-financing, in the double modality of subsidy plus loan. The return of the aid is made within a period adjusted to the financial needs of the project and considering the success or failure of the proposal. The aim is to allow the cultural entrepreneur to have liquidity to start his business project. A second type consists of returnable funds, participatory loans to emerging cultural companies or start-ups. Support is given in the initial phases of long-term business projects without involving the entry of any outside partner, nor any dilution of the company's ownership structure. A third source of financing is loans for fixed and current assets. Most of these instruments are usually supplemented with a guarantee fund from the public support bodies to reduce the requirements for guarantees by the participating financial institutions. The guaranty can be generalized to other areas, such as for example to reduce or even cancel the cost of insurance in the case of international exhibitions.

Other Financial Support Funds and Mechanisms

The origin of the financial resources made available to culture by the state can come from general tax revenues or from specific taxes that feed sectoral funds, such as the funds for the promotion of audiovisual production, the independent performing arts sector, the publishing industry or the preservation of national monuments. These funds are fed by taxes on box office revenue, billing or the volume of sales of reprographic, reproduction and printing equipment, as well as part of the tax collection from the national lottery or gambling. While in the fund of cinematography there is a transfer from the most successful productions, often foreign, towards the independent production; in the case of the lottery, the popular classes and gambling addicts end up financing infrastructure and cultural productions for cultivated audiences. These mechanisms, criticized from fiscal orthodoxy for contravening both the principle of unity, the principle of budgetary sincerity, the principle of budgetary universality and the principle of non-allocation of revenue which results from it (Masclet de Barbarin, 2012), have the advantage of giving long-term stability to vulnerable cultural sectors.

Another critical aspect to consider is the efficiency and impact of the different existing mechanisms. In the audiovisual field, where the European Audiovisual Observatory has been describing and evaluating the different ways of supporting the sector for years, it is observed that public support (direct public funding + production incentives) is vital for the financing of films in Europe, representing around half of total financial investment (Fioroni, 2023). Despite being the primary source of financing for European fiction feature films, direct public funding has been steadily declining in recent years, making up only 24% of the total financing volume in 2020, down from 29.4% in 2016. In contrast, the share of production incentives increased significantly from 9.6% of total financing in 2016 to 17.8% in 2020. Nevertheless, the average budgets and financing structures in individual European countries can differ significantly from the aggregated pan European figures, given that the prominence of direct public funding is negatively correlated with market size: 58.5% in the case of small markets (countries will less of 10 million admissions per year) while it drops to 19.8% in large film production markets (countries with more of 50 million admissions, like Germany, France, the UK or Italy).

5 Conclusions

Most of the data and academic literature on government funding culture corresponds to countries with high levels of development, mostly in North America and Europe. Many of these countries have a long tradition of intervening politically to defend the interests of culture and legitimize the reasons that justify the funding of this singular economic sector in front of other economic and political agents and ultimately in front of taxpayers. The dominant context in most of these countries, with liberal democracies, developed welfare systems and a rich framework of instruments to implement public policies, determines the approach and interpretation carried out by most academics who have treated the subject. With respect to other regions, the case of Latin America and the Caribbean is interesting because it raises similar questions from the perspective of countries with less economic development (Lobos, Lopez & Gribnicow, 2021). The limitation of comparable data on a global scale conditions the present chapter.

The value of public resources available depends on: a) the operating deficits of existing cultural ensembles and venues, a network created by wealthy countries that believe on the value of arts and heritage, b) the lobbying capacity of artists, their associations and cultural companies; and c) the perceived instrumental utility (prestige, clientele, attraction of other businesses) that elected politicians and government institutions obtain. Since the political cost of closing a venue is quite high—especially when it is government owned—and its operating costs are increasing (Baumol & Bowen, 1966), since the 1990s attempts have been made to find more efficient management mechanisms, seeking co-financing and incorporating models of private management. However, as seen in the data presented, there are quite few large budget reductions in developed countries.

The observation of the cultural policy strategies of several countries shows that the greater the availability of resources, long-term political stability and degree of public–private interaction, the more sophisticated and varied are the financial mechanisms made available to the sector. This fact makes strategies better suited to the inherent diversity of cultural subsectors and to a heterogeneity of circumstances, from the business needs of the cultural industries to those of the non-profit world or the manifestations of traditional culture.

Conversely, in middle-income countries in Latin America or Asia, the volume of public resources allocated to arts and heritage, as well as the complexity of the instruments made available for cultural policy, are very scarce. There may be a few large public facilities in the capital city or the main metropolises of the country, with a lot of staff and resources at their disposal. Projects of the elites for the elites, trying to replicate the most outstanding projects of the most developed countries. Next to it, a voluntary independent sector subject to clientelist subsidy systems or very poorly endowed is languishing.

In countries with authoritarian regimes, cultural policy and its funding is at the instrumental service of propaganda and the loyalty of elites or party members. In these cases, the preferred mechanism is direct government spending, although mixed mechanisms of sponsorship by politically close business groups are also not uncommon.

In Europe, one of the leading sectors in proposing imaginative alternatives and due to its ability to lobby is the audiovisual sector. Instruments such as support for international co-production or refundable and guarantee funds, were initially tested in support of cinema to later be implemented in the publishing field or the performing arts. In any case, the proportion of direct government resources invested in the operation of the various networks of museums, libraries and other public facilities takes the lion's share. However, the distribution of responsibilities between levels of government is key to discerning the different types of institutions and projects that are supported. In general, the closer the financial decision-making centre is to the event, activity or cultural institution, the more funding it receives (Bonet & Négrier, 2020). That is why it is not surprising that in countries with autonomous local or regional administrations with sufficient economic resources, the proportion of them allocated to culture is generally higher than the proportion allocated by the respective central administrations.[3] At the same time, countries of small size or with minoritized languages and cultural expressions tend to devote more resources to their revitalization and safeguarding.

A key issue is who decides and under what criteria government spending on culture is distributed. While with tax benefits, the individual or institutional taxpayer decides (the one who generates more income or expenditure, and therefore benefits more from the tax reduction), with direct expenditure it depends on the organizational model and the procedures of the cultural policy. In countries where government intervention is direct, the decision is in the hands of governmental officials and elected politicians, members of ad hoc appointed expert committees and programmers and curators of government-funded cultural facilities. In the countries based on the arm's length system, the power of the civil servant disappears, since it is the members of the committees, usually independent experts in each subject, as well as the programmers and curators who make the decisions based on criteria pre-established by the highest officials of Arts Councils or equivalent institutions. In both cases, most of them are people belonging to the cultural elite, experts with high levels of education who have similar criteria on concepts such as excellence, quality, educational value or social impact (Abbing, 2022).

There is still a long way to go to obtain detailed information on the mechanisms and value of direct government financial support for culture on a global scale. This is an area where cooperation between researchers from different regions is needed to obtain information, agree on standards that allow comparison and contextualize it in the respective political cultures and institutional frameworks. Likewise, it is necessary to delve deeper into the different approaches that allow critical legitimization of government support, from technical, geographical, and ideological perspectives. Finally, the impact of digitalization and AI will need to be incorporated into the analysis of cultural financing, as these entail a paradigm shift in the mechanisms for supporting creativity, cultural expressions and the preservation and enhancement of cultural heritage.

Competing Interests The writing of this chapter was supported by a grant from the Research Council of Norway [301291].

Notes

1. Some of the published research dealing with these topics has been funded by Arts councils or government departments of culture (i.e. National Endowment for the Arts or the Canada Council), as well as by sector advocacy organizations such as the American Council for the Arts.
2. An excellent introduction could be found in one of the first attempts to compare internationally the different ways to support the arts (Schuster, 1985).
3. Compendium of Cultural Policies & Trends. *Share of spending on culture by level of government (2011–2017)* https://www.culturalpolicies.net/statistics-comparisons/statistics/funding/#1563453131381-77d52055-b082

References

Abbing, H. (2022). *The Economies of Serious and Popular Art*. Palgrave Macmillan.

Almeida, F., & Halty, G. (2024). *Gestión Grandes Teatros Iberoamericanos*. Montevideo.

Baumol, W. J., & Bowen, W. G. (1966). *Performing Arts: the Economic Dilemma*. Twentieth Century Fund.

Bennett, T., et al. (2009). *Culture, Class, Distinction*. Routledge.

Bille, T. (2024). The Values of Cultural Goods and Cultural Capital Externalities: State of the Art and Future Research Prospects. *Journal of Cultural Economics, 48*(3), 347–365.

Bonet, L. (2025). Driving Innovation in Cultural Management. In Cogliandro Beyens, G. (Ed.), *Evolution of Cultural Management and Policy in Europe*. ENCATC Advances in Cultural Management and Policy Book Series, Routledge.

Bonet, L., & Donato, F. (2011). The Financial Crisis and Its Impact on the Current Models of Governance and Management of the Cultural Sector in Europe. *Encatc Journal of Cultural Management and Policy, 1*, 4–11.

Bonet, L., & Négrier, E. (2018). The Participative Turn in Cultural Policy: Paradigms, Models, Contexts. *Poetics, 66*, 64–73.

Bonet, L., & Négrier, E. (2020). La politique culturelle à l'épreuve de l'agence. Essai de combinaison d'approche principal agent et stakeholder (PA&S). *Pyramides, revue du Centre d'Études et de Recherches en Administration Publique*, 30 bis: 285–303.

Bonet, L., & Zamorano, M. M. (2020). Cultural Policies in Illiberal Democracies: A Conceptual Framework Based on the Polish and Hungarian Government Experiences. *International Journal of Cultural Policy, 27*(5), 559–573.

Bourdieu, P., & Darbel, A. (1969). *L'amour de l'art: Les musées d'art européens et leur public*. Éditions de Minuit.

Brooks, A. C. (1999). Do Public Subsidies Leverage Private Philanthropy for the Arts? Empirical Evidence on Symphony Orchestras. *Nonprofit and Voluntary Sector Quarterly, 28*(1), 32–45.

Brooks, A. C. (2004). In Search of True Public Arts Support. *Public Budgeting & Finance*.

Chen, W., & Noonan, D. (2023). Sharing the Stage: Exploring Inequities in Resources for the Arts Across Funding Institutions. *American Behavioral Scientist*, 1–27.

Compendium of Cultural Policies & Trends. https://www.culturalpolicies.net/

Čopič, V., Inkei, P., Kangas, A., & Srakar, A. (2013). *Trends in Public Funding for Culture in the EU*. EENC Report.

Cummings, M. C., & Schuster, J. M. D. (Eds.). (1989). *Who's to Pay for the Arts? The International Search for Models of Arts Support*. American Council for the Arts.

Dalle Nogare, C., & Bertacchini, E. (2015). Emerging Modes of Public Cultural Spending: Direct Support Through Production Delegation. *Poetics, 49*, 5–19.

Feder, T., & Katz-Gerro, T. (2012). Who Benefits from Public Funding of the Performing Arts? Comparing the Art Provision and the Hegemony-Distinction Approaches. *Poetics, 40*, 359–381.

Fioroni, M. (2023). *Fiction Film Financing in Europe: Overview and Trends 2016–2020*. European Audiovisual Observatory.

Husson, J.-F. (2013). Une approche sociopolitique du financement de la culture. In H. Pauliat (Ed.), *Culture et politiques publiques culturelles en Europe : Quelles valeurs à préserver en temps de crise ?* (pp. 111–126). Presses universitaires de Limoges.

Jacobsmeier, M. L. (2020). Public Opinion on Government Funding of the Arts in the United States: Demographic and Political Factors. *International Journal of Cultural Policy, 27*(4), 463–484.

Klamer, A., Petrova, L., & Mignosa, A. (2007). Funding the Arts and Culture in the EU. *Journal of Cultural Economics, 5*(4), 1–6.

Lobos, S., Lopez, V., & Gribnicow, A. (2021). *Public Funding for Culture and Creativity in Latin America and the Caribbean*. Inter-American Development Bank.

Mas-Colell, A. (1999). Should Cultural Goods Be Treated Differently? *Journal of Cultural Economics, 23*, 87–93.

Masclet de Barbarin, M. (2012). *Le double visage du financement public de la culture en France*. Hal-00879601.

Mefe, T. (2004). Financement de la culture au Cameroun: Soutien aux actions, absence d'infrastructures. *Africultures, 60*(3), 19–25.

Peacock, A. (2000). Public Financing of the Arts in England. *Fiscal Studies, 21*(2), 171–205.

Poirrier, Ph. (dir.). (2010). *La culture comme politique publique. Essais d'histoire compare*. La Documentation française.

Ponzini, D. (2016). Introduction: Crisis and renewal of contemporary planning. *European Planning Studies, 27*(7), 1237–1245.

Rushton, M. (2000). Public Funding of Controversial Art. *Journal of Cultural Economics, 24*, 267–282.

Rushton, M. (2022). *The Economic Approach to Public Funding for the Arts*. Indiana University working paper.

Sanjuan, J., Rausell, P., Coll, V., & Abeledo, R. (2020). Mayors, Using Cultural Expenditure in an Opportunistic Way Improves the Chances of Re-election, But Do Not Do It: Revisiting Political Budget Cycles. *Sustainability, 12*, 9095.

Saravia, E. (1993). Le financement de la culture en période de récession. Réflexions à propos de l'Amérique latine. *Revue françoise d'administration publique*, 65(janvier-mars): 119–127.

Schuster, J. M. D. (1985). *Supporting the Arts: An International Comparative Study. Canada, Federal Republic of Germany, France, Italy, Great Britain, Netherlands, Sweden, United States*. National Endowment for the Arts.

Schuster, J. M. D. (1990). Correlates of State Arts Support: The Geographic Distribution of Organizations, Artists, and Participation. In D. B. Pankratz & V. B. Morris (Eds.), *The Future of the Arts: Public Policy and arts Research* (pp. 81–104). Praeger.

Schuster, J. M. D. (1994). Arguing for Government Support of the Arts: an American View. In O. Robison, R. Freeman, R., & C. A. Riley II (Eds.), *The Arts in the World Economy* (pp. 42–55). University Press of New England.

Stubbs, R., & Mullaney-Loss, P. (2021). *Public Funding for Arts and Culture in 2020*. GIA. https://www.giarts.org/publicfunding-arts-and-culture-2020

Tokbaeva, D. (2018). How Culture Is Financed in Worlds Cities: A Comparative Analysis of Public Funding, Private Giving and New Funding Models in 15 Cities from Los Angeles to Shanghai. *Journal of Creative Industries and Cultural Studies, 2*, 120–122.

Throsby, D. (2010). *The Economics of Cultural Policy*. Cambridge University Press.

Tu, B., & Tao, X. (2017). Impact on Public Cultural Spending: The Perspective of Institutional Change in Government Cultural. *Open Journal of Political Science, 7*(July 3), 335–344.

UNESCO Institute for Statistics. (2023). *Global Trends in Reporting Data for Cultural and Natural Heritage* https://uis.unesco.org/en/news/global-trends-reporting-data-cultural-natural-heritage

Wang, J. G. (2006). New concept of government cultural function. *Social Science Forum, 1*, 98–101.

Open Access This chapter is licensed under the terms of the Creative Commons Attribution 4.0 International License (http://creativecommons.org/licenses/by/4.0/), which permits use, sharing, adaptation, distribution and reproduction in any medium or format, as long as you give appropriate credit to the original author(s) and the source, provide a link to the Creative Commons license and indicate if changes were made.

The images or other third party material in this chapter are included in the chapter's Creative Commons license, unless indicated otherwise in a credit line to the material. If material is not included in the chapter's Creative Commons license and your intended use is not permitted by statutory regulation or exceeds the permitted use, you will need to obtain permission directly from the copyright holder.

CHAPTER 3

Funding the Arts and Culture Through Tax Incentives

Sigrid Hemels

1 Introduction

Governments can apply several instruments to achieve policy goals, including cultural policy goals. Such instruments include:

1. Legislative obligations and prohibitions, for example, on a minimal number of school hours spent on music classes or a prohibition of using animals in performances;
2. Information campaigns and nudging, for example, a governmental campaign to stimulate museum visits or buying art;
3. Fines or levies, for example, a fine on making art that does not suit the government or a luxury tax on (certain) works of art;
4. Subsidies:

S. Hemels (✉)
Erasmus University Rotterdam School of Law, Rotterdam, The Netherlands
e-mail: hemels@law.eur.nl

© The Author(s) 2026

C. Dalla Chiesa and A. Rykkja (eds.), *Cultural Funding and Financing*, Cultural Economics & the Creative Economy,
https://doi.org/10.1007/978-3-031-96696-5_3

- Direct subsidies, e.g. direct transfers of funds from the government to the arts, for example, subsidies and grants for museums and theatres;
- Tax incentives: provisions in tax law that indirectly support the arts. Examples are tax benefits for (cultural) giving and reduced value-added tax (VAT) rates for theatre tickets and art sold by artists.

These instruments are complementary. For a given policy goal, a government can consider either of these instruments or a combination of instruments. Governments experiment with these instruments which leads to innovations that sometimes are successful and sometimes not. At times, governments also use these instruments to obtain a competitive advantage. If successful, other countries may follow suit. This might lead to a crowding out of private investments if the government takes over by, for example, providing direct subsidies and/or tax incentives. In an ideal situation, a government would pick the instrument or combination of instruments that suits the goal pursued best at the least cost for society. However, because of, for example, successful lobbying, this might not always be the case. This chapter discusses tax incentives as a policy instrument for cultural funding.[1] In Sect. 2, the concept of tax incentives is defined. In Sect. 3, some basic rules and principles that apply to tax incentives are briefly discussed. Section 4 analyses various benefits and drawbacks of funding culture with tax incentives. The chapter ends with a conclusion in Sect. 5. Throughout the chapter, various examples of tax incentives for the arts and culture are discussed. Because of the background of the author, the emphasis is on examples from the Netherlands and the European Union (EU).

This chapter applies the traditional methodology for tax law research, the legal doctrinal research method. This is based on research of literature, legislation and case law. Given that the law is all about norms, this means that this chapter might be perceived as being more normative than the reader might be used to in social science research.

2 The Tax Incentive Concept

The Organisation for Economic Co-operation and Development (OECD, 2010) defined tax incentives as provisions of tax law, regulation or practices that reduce or postpone revenue for a comparatively narrow population of taxpayers relative to a benchmark tax. Tax incentives can take various forms. Examples are exemptions from the tax base or from the definition of taxable subject, specific income deductions, tax credits and reduced rates. Also, tax incentives can be found in almost any kind of tax law and can be aimed at almost any kind of policy aim. Tax incentives vary widely between countries and may be very country-specific. Sometimes, they may seem more generally applied, but on a closer look, superficially similar tax incentives, such as for philanthropic giving, may still be different in the legally very relevant details. This reflects the fact that there is not one tax system in the world but that each country, even in the EU, has its own specific tax system. A country's tax system, in turn, reflects the preferences of a country at a certain moment of time, for example, regarding the role of the government in a society.

There are many different ways of categorising tax incentives. One possibility is a categorisation based on the beneficiary. For example, the Global Leaders Institute for Arts Innovation (2024) distinguishes artist-based, place-based; and industry-based incentives; Hemels and Goto (2017) distinguish museums and cultural heritage; the audiovisual industry; the art market; copyright; and artists, OECD (2020) distinguishes tax incentives for philanthropic entities; giving; and cross-border philanthropy in all OECD member countries and Del Federico et al. (2021) combine a country-specific overview with a categorisation of beneficiaries (cultural heritage owners; patrons; museums and nonprofits; art cities; and international investors) and the EU VAT Directive[2] gives a categorisation of supplies and services that may qualify for a reduced VAT rate (for an overview of those rates in the various EU countries I refer to European Commission, 2024). However, other categorisations are possible as well, such as based on the policy aim, the law in which incentives are included, or the form they have. As this chapter is not meant to provide a comprehensive overview of existing tax incentives, it does not include such categorisation. A reader who is interested in such an overview is referred to other sources, including the aforementioned.

A tax incentive reduces the tax income of the government. Introducing a tax incentive means that the government must either reduce other spending (direct subsidies or tax incentives), increase the tax burden on other taxpayers, or increase government lending, which means shifting the burden to future generations. In that respect, a tax incentive does not differ from a direct subsidy. Tax incentives are not a 'free lunch' but a cost to the government that must be weighed against alternative, possibly more effective and efficient, policy and spending options, including direct subsidies (Grapperhaus, 1971, p. 6).

3 Underlying Rules and Principles

As tax incentives are part of tax legislation, they are bound to the legal rules and principles underlying that legislation. These are not only moral rules but also hard legal rules. Such rules are embedded in national constitutions, international treaties and, in the EU, EU law that supersedes national legislation. Governments must obey these rules and courts make sure that they do. Such rules restrict the policy freedom to apply tax incentives. In order for tax incentives to be effective, governments must also take into account economic 'rules' that might not be imposed by law books and courts but will have an impact on the actual effect of any policy measure, including tax incentives.

Equity-Efficiency Trade-Off

Two universal principles to be considered in relation to tax law, including when analysing tax incentives, are the (legal) principle of equity and the (economic) principle of efficiency. There is always a trade-off between the two, as no tax measure can be both perfectly equitable and perfectly efficient. The most equitable tax, which taxes everyone exactly according to their personal circumstances, is rather inefficient and thus not feasible given that the main function of taxation is to obtain a budget for government expenditures. Conversely, the most efficient taxes, such as a poll tax, where every taxpayer pays the same amount of tax, are not very equitable. Tax legislation is, for that reason, a compromise between those two principles.

How the two principles are weighed is a political decision that has different outcomes across countries and in time, depending on dominant political preferences. The same applies to using tax legislation for ancillary functions next to the budgetary function. Most countries also use tax law as a policy instrument, for example, to redistribute wealth and encourage or discourage certain behaviour. Using tax incentives as a policy instrument to increase funding for the arts and culture is an example of this instrumental use of taxation.

EU Law

In the EU, governments must make sure that support (whether through subsidies or tax incentives) does not infringe state aid rules (Articles 107–109 of the Treaty on the Functioning of the EU, TFEU). Granting aid through state resources which distorts or threatens to distort competition by favouring certain undertakings or the production of certain goods is prohibited. Several forms of state aid are allowed. This includes aid not exceeding €200,000 over any period of three fiscal years per undertaking (de minimis aid).[3] This helps when incentives are specifically aimed at self-employed artists or small-scale cultural institutions.

Furthermore, aid to promote culture and heritage conservation is allowed where such aid does not affect trading conditions and competition in the EU to an extent that is contrary to the common interest (Article 107(3)(d) TFEU). Notification to and approval of the European Commission is necessary before member states can introduce such aid.

The General Block Exemption Regulation (GBER)[4] provides that if certain requirements are met, several categories of aid with an incentive effect are exempt from the notification obligation. This includes aid for culture and heritage conservation. Article 53(2) GBER stipulates for which cultural purposes and activities the aid may be granted. This includes, amongst others, museums, archives, libraries, theatres, concert halls, film heritage institutions, tangible and intangible cultural heritage, cultural events and education, music and literature. Investment and operating aid are covered as long as the eligible costs (as defined in Article 53 GBER) remain below the notification thresholds stipulated in article 4(1)(z) GBER. Article 54 GBER provides for the requirements for audiovisual works. Member states must ensure that this aid supports cultural products. Aid for film studio infrastructure is not eligible, and the aid may not be reserved exclusively for nationals. Activities with a predominantly commercial character are also not covered by the GBER. This includes, amongst others, press and magazines (written or electronic), fashion, design and video games. However, commercially difficult films, such as in minority languages or low-budget films and documentaries, may be covered (Articles 2 (140) and 53 GBER). In 2023, the EU

Council invited the European Commission to support and stimulate the competitiveness and independence of European videogame companies through a review of the application of state aid rules, in particular, where appropriate, within the framework of a revision of the GBER.[5] Despite lobbying efforts of the industry (see, for example, European Games Developer Federation, 2024), up to the time of writing, such an amendment has not been made.

EU Member States must also respect the fundamental freedoms enshrined in the TFEU: the free movement of citizens, goods, workers, services, capital and the freedom of establishment (articles 18, 45, 49, 56 and 63 TFEU). The purpose of these freedoms is the creation of an internal market, a market without internal borders or import and export restrictions. This means, for example, that EU Member States cannot support national artists by introducing a higher tax on sales of works of foreign artists.

4 Benefits and Drawbacks of Funding Culture with Tax Incentives

Many tax experts have reservations about tax incentives. Some of their arguments against these provisions apply to direct subsidies as well, but others are more specific to tax incentives. The OECD (2010) stipulated various theoretical and practical allegations against tax incentives in general. OECD (2020) specifically discussed arguments in favour and against tax incentives for philanthropy. In addition, non-tax experts have also expressed their reservations, especially on the question of whether tax incentives that promote (cultural) giving are aligned with democratic values. Tax incentives may, however, also be effective in obtaining certain policy goals. In this section, various drawbacks and benefits of tax incentives for the arts and culture are analysed. These include notions of democracy, fairness, efficiency and effectiveness.

Democracy

Tax incentives for philanthropic giving are a specific category of tax incentives. These are of particular financial importance for cultural institutions, such as museums, especially in the US, but also, although possibly to a lesser extent, in many other countries (O'Hagan, 2011).

In the past 10 years or so, tax incentives for philanthropic (including cultural) giving have been criticised as being undemocratic (Vallely, 2020). This criticism is related to the more general discussion that emerged in the US (and is still predominantly a US discussion; see Haydon et al., 2021, pp. 356, 363, 370) but later spread to other countries on so-called 'philanthrocaptalism'. On the other hand, such tax incentives may also have the opposite effect of strengthening a democratic society in which not only the government decides on, for example, which art(forms) deserve support. Both arguments are discussed below.

Philanthrocaptalism

Originally, philanthrocapitalism was used as a relatively positive term. According to Bishop (2013, p. 474), he minted it in 2006 in The Economist (Bishop, 2006). In Bishop and Green (2008), philanthrocapitalism, philanthropy using big-business-style strategies, such as applied by Bill Gates, was seen as a force for societal change 'in a climate resistant to government spending on social causes'. Bishop and Green (2008) considered philanthrocapitalism a more efficient and effective alternative to traditional large-scale grant-making philanthropy. Some drawbacks were addressed, but on balance the weighing was positive. In 2013, Bishop explained: 'The determining feature of philanthrocapitalism is not, as its critics suggest, a determination to replace traditional grant-making or the democratic process of civil society with so-called market-based solutions, but rather its laser-like focus on achieving "impact"'. (Bishop, 2013, p. 477).

Nevertheless, the term philanthrocapitalism gained a predominantly negative connotation (Haydon et al., 2021), not only in mainstream media but also in academic articles (for example, McGoey et al., 2018). Haydon et al. (2021, p. 359) note in their comprehensive analysis of the academic discourse on the topic that academic articles were published by a small set of mainly negative authors, that the studies were non-empirical and that critical conceptions appeared largely limited to surface-level debate. The critical accounts emphasised philanthrocapitalism as a mode of governance—a means of agenda setting and policy creation by the ultra-rich. Reich (2018) was of the opinion that rich philanthropists are a threat to democracy as they set priorities and agendas without any form of control.

Haydon et al. (2021, p. 354) observed that the critics of philanthrocapitalism argue that by embracing neoliberal ideals, philanthrocapitalism entrenches and accentuates wealth and power inequalities. Philanthro-capitalism, in this sense, was regarded in mainstream media as asserting the primacy of the capitalist ideology in all sectors, including the civil society space, where philanthropists receive board memberships of, for example, cultural institutions, in return for generous gifts resulting in no longer the state, but 'the rich' deciding on 'what is good for the people' (Alibhai-Brown, 2021). When, during the 2019 World Economic Forum, the Dutch historian Rutger Bregman was asked for solutions to rising inequality and social unrest, he replied: 'The answer is very simple. Just stop talking about philanthropy. And start talking about taxes... Taxes, taxes, taxes. All the rest is bullshit'. (Guardian News, 2019).

Next to this dichotomy between pursuing goals through tax-funded government policies that are decided on by democratic rules and preferences on the one hand and by privately funded philanthropy that is decided by using individual preferences (which includes personal (possibly political) interests) on the other, a relation was also made with tax incentives for philanthropic giving. Critics perceived it as being undemocratic that rich people were steering through their gifts, but also that they were partly using government money for this by reducing their tax burden by tax-deductible philanthropic giving (Vallely, 2020). Through the tax incentive, they are steering money, that is, in part government money, in the direction they prefer without—as is claimed—democratic checks and balances (Bosma & Muskens, 2019).

However, according to Haydon et al. (2021, p. 359), the discussion would benefit from greater nuance. In their view, critical conceptions in the academic discourse appear to be largely limited to surface-level debates without engaging theoretically with the concept. In addition, even though the debate had a very strong US focus and participation, its conclusions are in the popular debate often transplanted to continental Europe. This transplant often happens without acknowledging the differences between US funding of the cultural sector and the dominant government funding model in most continental European countries. For example, Bosma and Muskens (2019) used US examples to come to conclusions about the Netherlands. However, as was pointed out by Hiltrop (2019) and Dijkgraaf (2019) there are important differences between the US and a continental European country such as the Netherlands.

Hiltrop (2019) noted that in the Netherlands philanthropic organisations must meet strict requirements before they can receive tax-deductible gifts. In my view, this is not really different from the situation in the US. US tax law also includes requirements that philanthropic organisations must meet. It seems, however, that in the debate on philanthrocapitalism, these democratic checks and balances on what qualifies as a philanthropic organisation and a philanthropic gift have not been given enough attention. For example, Dutch philanthropic organisations must not only pursue the public benefit for at least 90%, they are also obliged to publish information on a website, including their annual accounts, the composition of the board and an activity report.

In addition, in continental European countries such as the Netherlands, cultural organisations are still dominantly funded by the government. Dijkgraaf (2019) observed that in the Netherlands private gifts are not an alternative for government funding, as private donations do not amount to more than 2% of the total government budget. Notwithstanding private patronage, the government, or rather: the taxpayer, is still the major donor in countries such as the Netherlands. Boards of Dutch cultural organisations are not hijacked by large donors. Cultural governance requirements would also not allow this, as is evidenced by principle 3, the independency principle, of the 2019 Dutch Cultural Governance Code (Cultuur + Ondernemen, 2020).

This mixing of US arguments in a European continental context might be prevented if more emphasis were put on government contributions to the cultural sector in Europe. In addition, it could be for the benefit of cultural organisations if they would give more credit to the government and taxpayers as their major donors. A beautiful example is the *Wirtschafts Universität Wien*. The entrance of the library- and conference building of this Viennese business university features a big plaque thanking all Austrian citizens as their tax contributions enabled the building of the campus. Such an acknowledgement puts claims that rich citizens are buying their way into cultural organisations in a more continental European perspective and makes clear that US research or sentiments cannot be transplanted directly. By not including this more European perspective, cultural (and other charitable) organisations run the risk that US rhetoric influences the European political debate. In addition, the debate seems to be focused on a few well-known individuals and foundations, such as the Bill & Melinda Gates Foundation. Haydon et al. (2021, p. 371) observed that this foundation is unlikely to be representative of all philanthrocapitalist individuals and institutions.

Co-Deciding Citizens

It seems that the critique on having citizens co-deciding on the allocation of a very small part of government expenditures through tax incentives for philanthropic giving (within the boundaries set by government regulations) implies that the government always knows better and that only the government of the day should decide what activities are for the public benefit and, more specifically, which cultural activities deserve support and which do not.

This raises the question of why the government should have a monopoly on what is and what is not for the public benefit. Dijkgraaf (2019) observed that in an ideal world, the government would take care of all public benefits, but in reality, the government often turns out to be unreliable, also because of changing political winds. He noted that not only rich philanthropists but also governments may at times be capricious, untransparent, shortsighted and, of course, political. Furthermore, he added that even if the government follows the preferences of the majority, this may lead to imbalances. He gave the example of a society in which 51% of the population does not like classical music and therefore abolishes all subsidies for orchestras: is that just bad luck for the 49% of lovers of classical music? This happened in the Netherlands in the fall of 2024 when the government, which included several populistic parties, wanted to raise the VAT rate on entrance tickets for museums, theatres, concert halls and on books and newspapers as of 2026, but not on cinema tickets and amusement parks.[6]

In Dijkgraaf's view, philanthropists can bring stability by softening the effects of government policy or the free market. Furthermore, specific, risky or avant-garde art might not (yet) be supported by the government but may be supported by individual philanthropists. Philanthropy may also correct the government. Allowing for philanthropy suits a pluriform society in which there is room for opposing and minority opinions and in which it is not just the government that, for example, decides what is 'good' art. Philanthropy and incentivising philanthropic giving by tax incentives may support this and thus be suitable, next to, not instead of, direct subsidies in a democratic society.

Relation with the Roles in an Economic Transaction

From an economic point of view, four roles can be distinguished in an economic transaction: the payer, the beneficiary, the one caring for the product or service and the decision-maker. These roles vary depending on whether a transaction takes place in the market sphere, the government sphere or the philanthropic sphere. This may have important implications as will be discussed below.

Market

In a market transaction, the four roles are usually combined in one person. If I care about a particular painting and I decide I want to have it, I pay for it and I then benefit from obtaining it. In a pure market transaction, the consumer has the decision power. The producer, the artist or the cultural institution takes into account the preferences of consumers and produces for them. The drawback of the market model is that some products might not be produced or only in low quantities as consumers might not (yet) be interested or perceive them as being too expensive. Examples are avant-garde forms of art, certain opera performances and arthouse films.

Government

Because of the perceived underproduction of certain cultural products as a result of market outcomes, governments have decided to interfere in markets for culture. In continental Europe, many cultural institutions are mainly funded by direct subsidies from local or national governments. Many governments also fund cultural institutions indirectly by granting tax incentives for cultural giving. An example is the deductibility of gifts.

These different forms of government grants have different effects from a policy point of view. The effects that are intended by the policy must be taken into account when deciding on the most suitable policy instrument. To make this analysis, three parties must be distinguished. First, all taxpayers (those who pay) pay the taxes that enable the government to provide for direct grants or tax incentives. Art enthusiasts (those who care) are a subgroup of the group of all taxpayers. The second party is the government, which makes the rules both for direct and indirect incentives and selects the eligible cultural institutions (those who decide). A subgroup might be advisory boards or special agencies of the government that decide or advise on eligibility. The third party consists of the cultural institutions that the government wants to support (those who benefit).

Where in a market transaction the four roles are united in one person, these are spread over different parties when a direct subsidy is involved. All taxpayers pay for the product, but the decision is made by the government or a government agency. The art enthusiasts who care about the product are only a subgroup of all taxpayers, and the beneficiaries of the subsidy might be an even smaller group. There is no direct financial relation between cultural institutions and art enthusiasts. The preferences of the public are not necessarily of relevance for funding. The government or a governmental agency decides which cultural institutions get what amount of money, and all taxpayers have to fund this. Art enthusiasts are not given a responsibility for sustaining the arts. This might have the effect that cultural institutions focus on the government and their advisory bodies and forget about the preferences of the public. The result may be elite art that is only aimed at a small group of insiders. According to Mourato and Mazzanti (2002, p. 63), relying only on experts' judgement may be dangerous, leading to improper allocation of resources, arbitrariness, lobbying pressures for funding and paternalism.

The alternative for expert decisions, top-down decisions by politicians and bureaucrats, also has drawbacks. The decision process may lack transparency, there is much room for lobbying and favouritism, prestige projects may stand a better chance, and it may have the effect of encouraging 'state art' where the state attempts to impose its taste on the creative industries and artists conform to the tastes of politicians to obtain funds (Van de Ploeg, 2002, p. 355). In both cases not necessarily the preferences of the public prevail, but those of the decision-makers, experts, politicians or bureaucrats.

Philanthropy

The starting point with a tax incentive for private donations is the bottom-up decision of the art enthusiast (those who care) to make a donation, for example of 100. Because of the incentive scheme, the art enthusiast gets a tax incentive, for example, a deduction for income tax purposes of 30%. Only this deduction, 30 in the example, rather than the whole gift, has to be funded by all taxpayers. Therefore, the role of the payer is not fully imposed on all taxpayers; they only have to fund the incentive (30 in the example). The other part (70) is paid for by the art enthusiasts: those who decide on the funding and care about the product or service. Those who benefit are probably, but not necessarily, part of this group, but the beneficiaries can be a much broader group, for example, students with low income who now can afford to attend a play for which the ticket price is below cost, because of private donations making up for the difference.

The effect of using a tax incentive instead of a direct subsidy is twofold. First, unlike the situation with a direct subsidy, cultural institutions have to take into account the preferences of their public and create a bond with them to attract donations. Where the initiative for a direct subsidy lies with the government, with a tax incentive the public, the art enthusiasts, have the initiative in granting money. The second effect of using a tax incentive instead of a direct subsidy is that all taxpayers only have to pay part of the costs. The other part is financed by the art enthusiasts.

The reason why many governments support philanthropic giving through tax incentives may be found in the so-called public policy rationale for tax incentives for philanthropic organisations. This entails that philanthropic organisations take tasks upon themselves that would otherwise have to be provided by the government (Hopkins, 2011, p. 13). As this means less costs for the government, part of that benefit is passed on through tax incentives. The US House Committee on Ways and Means formulated this rationale as follows in 1939:

> The exemption from taxation of money or property devoted to charitable and other purposes is based upon the theory that the government is compensated for the loss of revenue by its relief from the financial burden which would otherwise have to be met by appropriations from public funds, and by the benefits resulting from the promotion of general welfare.[7]

Similarly, the German Federal Fiscal Court (*Bundesfinanzhof*) held in 1966 that as the promotion of philanthropic purposes is one of the domestic political tasks of a modern state, the government can also try to encourage citizens' willingness to make sacrifices through tax measures.[8]

Effects of Tax Incentives for Giving to Culture

Private gifts to culture may have the following effects:

1. Broadening of the financial base of cultural and heritage institutions: an additional source of income next to government subsidies, leading to more funding.
2. Strengthening the financial base of cultural institutions: gifts from private individuals are usually less sensitive to political and economic changes, provided cultural institutions have created a bond with the art enthusiasts;
3. Strengthening the social base of cultural institutions: private gifts provide an opportunity to create and foster a bond with the public.

Therefore, if policy objects include that cultural institutions take notice of the preferences of the public, create a bond between art enthusiasts and cultural institutions, broaden and strengthen the financial and social base of cultural institutions and/or reduce the costs of all taxpayers of the government support, a tax incentive such as a gift deduction may be more effective as a policy instrument than a direct subsidy.

This does not mean that all direct subsidies for cultural institutions must be replaced by tax incentives. For certain costs, such as security, heating, accounts and other exploitation costs, it can be difficult to attract private funds. Governments are usually willing to fund such base costs of selected cultural institutions by direct subsidies. Furthermore, a government may deem it important to fund certain art forms that are recognised by experts but not yet by the public. In that case, a direct subsidy could be the most effective instrument.

Direct subsidies are, therefore, not necessarily better or worse than tax incentives (or the other way around). These instruments can simply serve different policy objects.

Fairness

In the discussion on tax incentives for (cultural) giving, the claim is made that such incentives mainly benefit the rich (Vallely, 2020). Whether this is indeed the case partly depends on the design of the incentive. If it is a deduction from taxable income in an income tax system with a progressive tax rate (e.g. a tax rate that increases as taxable income increases), such as, for example, in the USA, the UK, Germany and Japan, someone in a higher tax bracket will benefit more than someone in a lower tax bracket who gave exactly the same amount. Surrey and McDaniel (1985, p. 87) called this the 'upside-down effect' of tax incentives.

However, this upside-down effect can be neutralised in various ways. One example is allowing gift deductions against one fixed rate that is not linked to the amount of income. This is the case in the Netherlands, where individuals can only deduct their gifts against a fixed personal income tax rate of 37.48% (2025 rate), where the highest income tax rate is 49.5%. Another option is not to allow an income deduction ('allowance') but a deduction from the tax paid, a tax credit. In such cases, usually, a percentage of the gift can be deducted from the tax due, as is the case, for example, in France and Canada. In this system, the benefit from the same amount of charitable giving is exactly the same for a high-income and a low-income earner. Another option is the system of tax assignment that is applied in, for example, Italy and several Eastern European countries such as Hungary, Lithuania, Poland, Romania and Slovakia (Nährlich, 2013, p. 26). In such a system, taxpayers may assign a percentage of the tax due to (usually specific) charities. These solutions all solve the upside-down effect.

Another example of a tax incentive that is controversial because of fairness considerations is the Irish tax exemption for artists (Irish Tax and Customs, 2023). Since 1969, Ireland has provided for a tax exemption for income artists earn from their artistic works. These must be original and creative works generally recognised as having cultural or artistic merit, such as books, plays, musical compositions, paintings and sculptures. Before 2006, a full exemption applied to such income, meaning that also millionaire pop stars, football players and politicians with income from bestseller *memoires*, did not pay tax on such income. This attracted foreign artists, such as English pop artist Lisa Stansfield, Scottish author Irvine Welsh and French author Michel Houellebecq. Their move to Ireland meant they could enjoy this tax exemption (Chrisafis, 2005). However, in the aftermath of the 2007–2013 financial and economic crisis that hit Ireland hard, the exemption was reduced in various stages and is now limited to € 50,000. Apparently, this was not enough for some foreign artists and many of them, including Stansfield, Welsh and Houellebecq, left Ireland. Furthermore, because of EU rules, Ireland could no longer require the artist to live in Ireland. Since then, qualifying income taxable in Ireland from artists living in another EU or European Economic Area member state also benefits from the exemption.

Even with the cap, one can raise the question of whether it is fair that someone with € 50,000 income from artistic works does not have to pay tax, whereas someone with the same income from work as a teacher, nurse or fireman has to pay tax (unless she writes a bestseller). This exemption of which a small number of artists have a big personal benefit but of which the costs are spread out over a very large group of taxpayers, is a typical example of an incentive for which there is a strong and powerful lobby. Every time when the exemption was under threat, immediately an effective lobby started to work, managing to save the exemption to some degree (Carabini, 2010). This was for the benefit of those with income from artistic works (no matter whether they are recognised as artists or not) but at the cost of all Irish taxpayers.

Efficiency and Effectiveness

An important condition for tax incentives to be effective is that they target price-elastic activities. This means that the reduction in price, because of the tax incentive, changes the behaviour of taxpayers. For example, from research in various countries it has become clear that philanthropic giving is, to a certain extent, price elastic (Adena, 2021). This means that tax incentives that make it cheaper to give may have a stimulating effect on gifts. However, it is not always easy to measure price (in)elasticity, especially not beforehand when the policy is being made.

Targeting Tax Incentives

The better targeted (and thus more equitable and effective) a tax incentive is, the more complicated it will be, both for the tax administration to execute and for taxpayers to make use of it. On the other hand, simple incentives that are easy to execute will usually have a broad scope and are difficult to target in special groups. This reduces the effectiveness and efficiency of these tax incentives. An example is a reduced VAT rate for theatre performances as is allowed by the EU VAT Directive. First, the definition of a theatre performance has to be established. This might not be as straightforward as it seems. For VAT, objectively—from the point of view of the average consumer—similar products and services must be treated the same. This led the Dutch Supreme Court to the decision that having cultural content is not a requirement for the reduced VAT rate for performances. For that reason, a peep show qualified as a theatre performance as it entailed a performance on a stage which a certain amount of people could attend after paying an entrance fee.[9] The same definition problem applies to other products that can both be cultural or commercial, such as photographs (Hemels, 2020).

Not only can a reduced VAT rate apply to a much wider range of products than might be desirable from a cultural policy point of view, but such tax incentive also applies to all consumers. This includes consumers with high incomes and consumers who are insensitive to the ticket price. This might not suit the objective of the government policy. It is much easier to target a direct subsidy to certain products, producers or consumers. This may be done, for example, by using discount cards for low-income consumers such as students and subsidies for specific performances. In such cases, a tax incentive is more expensive than a direct subsidy and could lead to a waste of government resources.

It is not always impossible to target tax incentives. For example, France provides for a deduction for companies that acquire artworks from living artists and put them on permanent display at a location generally accessible to the public or employees, such as a museum or a company's entrance foyer. Not only contemporary artists but also their dealers benefit indirectly from this tax incentive. It gives artists the opportunity to sell their work and enables them to build a reputation. Furthermore, it enables the public to get acquainted with modern art. France grants a similar tax incentive to companies that buy musical instruments and give them on loan to musicians. This tax incentive enables talented artists to play valuable instruments to the benefit of both the musician and the audience. Dealers of old instruments and manufacturers of new instruments also indirectly benefit because the incentive reduces the costs of these instruments.

Another well-targeted tax incentive is the option that various countries, including France, the UK, the Netherlands, Ireland, Belgium, Italy and Spain, offer to pay certain taxes (usually inheritance tax, but, for example, in Ireland and Italy also other taxes) with eminent cultural heritage or works of art (Hemels, 2021). This incentive allows countries to act quickly when an eminent work of art might leave the country. Not all art and cultural heritage qualifies for this incentive. Specific requirements are applied, usually by expert committees, to assess the eminence of the work.

Unpredictability of the Costs of Tax Incentives

If a government opts for a tax incentive instead of a direct subsidy, estimations must be made on effects and costs. It is much more difficult to allocate a maximum budget to ('cap') a tax incentive than to allocate a specific amount of funds to a direct subsidy. Usually, tax incentives are 'open-ended', which means that anyone who qualifies for the tax incentive may make use of it until it is abolished. Therefore, it is difficult to predict the costs of a tax incentive before the policy is introduced.

Usually, the estimation of the costs of a tax incentive is based on the amount by which tax revenue is reduced because of the introduction of a tax incentive. Often, it is assumed that behaviour of taxpayers and revenue from other taxes will be unchanged. This is understandable, as it is very difficult to estimate and include behavioural change as a variable in the calculation, but it also makes the estimation less realistic (Kraan, 2004,

p. 137). Not only will taxpayers often change their behaviour in reaction to a tax incentive, but usually such change is the intention of the tax incentive. Without a behavioural change, the incentive would not be effective and, by default, not be efficient either. However, Kraan (2004, p. 137) also mentions that many governments seem to assume that the accuracy that might be gained by using a more realistic method which does include behavioural effects, is generally not worth the effort. It is difficult to predict and calculate behavioural effects without introducing many variables in the equation.

Accountability

As at the time of their introduction, less than perfect estimations must be made about the costs and effects of tax incentives, it is important that tax incentives are accounted for and evaluated properly to establish whether the policy reached its goal (was effective) at the lowest costs (was efficient). Unfortunately, in general, tax incentives have the drawback that, compared with direct subsidies, there is less information and less democratic control on these expenditures than on direct subsidies. Usually, direct subsidies are accounted for in the annual government budget, which has to be adopted by parliament. As tax incentives reduce government income, these are only implicitly reflected in the budget in the estimated amount of tax income. Tax incentives are not explicitly nor specifically accounted for as an expenditure. This makes it difficult to weigh direct expenditures against tax incentives. It also means a lesser degree of budgetary control on tax incentives and complicates control of the lawfulness and effectiveness of expenditures.

To get a better grip on tax incentives, since the 1960s, several countries have started to account for these incentives in tax expenditure reports. The content and the status of these reports vary widely. In many countries, parliament does not have to vote on these overviews or discuss these in connection with the direct expenditure budget. Tax incentives are, therefore, often still not accounted for and budgeted for in the same way as direct subsidies.

This relative invisibility of tax incentives makes it even more important to evaluate their effectiveness and efficiency on a regular basis. In addition, some countries use so-called sunset legislation when introducing a tax incentive. Sunset legislation automatically expires after a certain period (for example, five years) unless explicitly renewed or extended. This is the reverse of the practice in which tax incentives exist indefinitely unless explicitly abolished. Sunset legislation is often applied in the US.

A regular evaluation of tax incentives or sunset legislation is not a guarantee that ineffective or inefficient tax incentives will be abolished. Decisions on tax incentives are often highly political and influenced by lobby groups. This is especially the case when the beneficiaries each have a high benefit and are a small, well-organised group with good access to policymakers. As the costs of the tax incentive are spread out over a large group of anonymous taxpayers, they are usually unaware that they bear the cost of this privilege for a small group and do not protest against it. If members of parliament do not sufficiently take into account the interests of this silent majority and are susceptible to the lobbying of these small, powerful groups, existing ineffective or inefficient tax incentives may remain in place.

5 Conclusion

Tax incentives are not inherently better or worse than other policy instruments such as spending programs, regulation and information campaigns. Policy objects should determine the most effective and efficient instrument in a certain situation. With respect to cultural policy goals, tax incentives may have the benefit over direct subsidies in that they are a direct and efficient way to take into account the preferences of the public. However, this also means that the government shares its decision-making with citizens, including wealthier citizens. Whether this is desirable or not is a political question. In answering this question, one must take care of not transplanting US experiences to, for example, continental European countries with a very different cultural funding mix. In any case, tax incentives must be democratically controlled, accounted for and evaluated in the same way as direct spending programs. As this is currently not always the case, tax incentives are, in that respect, inferior to direct subsidies and should be applied with care.

Notes

1. For an extensive discussion of tax incentives for cultural heritage, culture and the creative industries, including in different countries, see Hemels and Goto (2017) and Del Federico et al. (2021).

2. Council Directive 2006/112/EC of 28 November 2006 on the common system of value added tax, Annex III, sub 7 (consolidated version of 1 January 2024).
3. Commission Regulation (EU) No 1407/2013 of 18 December 2013 on the application of Articles 107 and 108 of the TFEU to de minimis aid.
4. Commission Regulation (EU) No 651/2014 of 17 June 2014 declaring certain categories of aid compatible with the internal market in application of Articles 107 and 108 of the Treaty (consolidated version of 1 July 2023).
5. Council conclusions on Enhancing the cultural and creative dimension of the European video games. Sector (C/2023/1345), *Official Journal of the European Union* 30 November 2023.
6. Wijziging van enkele belastingwetten en enige andere wetten (Belastingplan, 2025), Kamerstukken II, 2024–2025, 36.602, no. 2. As a result of pressure from Parliament (more specifically a motion that was adopted by the Second Chamber of Parliament (Kamerstukken II, 2024–2025, 36.602, nr. 140) and the threat of the First Chamber of Parliament to reject the whole Tax Plan 2025), the government proposed, in September 2025, to raise the income tax to avoid this raise of the VAT rate in 2026.
7. H. Rep. No. 1860, 75th Cong., 3d Sess, 19 (1939).
8. Bundesfinanzhof, Urt. v. 11.11.1966, Az.: VI R 45/66.
9. Hoge Raad 5 December 2008, 43908, ECLI:NL:HR:2008:BB0678.

References

Adena, M. (2021). Tax-price Elasticity of Charitable Donations—Evidence from the German Taxpayer Panel. In H. Peter, B. Werlen, G. Lideikyte Huber (Eds.), *The Routledge Handbook of Taxation and Philanthropy* (pp. 219–235). Routledge.

Alibhai-Brown, Y. (2021, October 26). From Mark Zuckerberg to the Sackler Family, Beware the Rise of the 'Philanthrocapitalists'. *iNews*. https://inews.co.uk/opinion/mark-zuckerberg-sackler-family-beware-philanthrocapitalists-1267469

Bishop, M. (2006, February 25). The Business of Giving. *The Economist*. https://www.economist.com/special-report/2006/02/25/the-business-of-giving

Bishop, M. (2013). Philanthrocapitalism: Solving Public Problems Through Private Means. *Social Research, 80*(2), 473–490.

Bishop, M., & Green, M. (2008). *Philanthrocapitalism: How the Rich Can Save the World*. Bloomsbury Press.

Bosma, M. & Muskens, R. (2019, February 2). Foute filantropen bedreigen de democratie. *NRC Handelsblad*. https://www.nrc.nl/nieuws/2019/02/01/foute-filantropen-bedreigen-de-democratie-a3652633

Carabini, S. (2010). Mistake to Abolish Artists Tax Exemption. *Liberty Online*. https://siptucommunicationsdepartment.newsweaver.ie/libertyonline/1giugzb4xsy?a=1&p=48331407&t=22917195

Chrisafis, A. (2005, June 18). Ireland May Abandon Tax Exemption Scheme for Creative Writers. *The Guardian*. https://www.theguardian.com/uk/2005/jun/18/booksnews.artsnews

Cultuur+Ondernemen (2020, 24 November). *Cultural Governance Code 2019*. Cultuur-Ondernemen. https://www.cultuur-ondernemen.nl/governance-code-cultuur/toolkit/english

Del Federico, L., Hemels, S. J. C., Rozas, J.-A., & Giorgi, S. (Eds.). (2021). *Taxation and Cultural Heritage*. IBFD.

Dijkgraaf, R. (2019, March 8). Foute filantropie en goede goede doelen. *NRC Handelsblad*. https://www.nrc.nl/nieuws/2019/03/08/foute-filantropie-en-goede-goede-doelen-a3952604

European Commission. (2024). *Taxes in Europe Database v4. VAT Search*. https://ec.europa.eu/taxation_customs/tedb/#/vat-search

European Games Developer Federation. (2024). *EGDF European Parliament Election Manifesto: Enabling Digital Growth in the EU*. https://www.egdf.eu/egdf-european-parliament-election-manifesto/

Global Leaders Institute for Arts Innovation. (2024). *Tax Incentives for Culture: A Global Tool for Supporting the Arts*. https://www.globalleadersinstitute.org/blog-post/tax-incentives-for-culture-a-global-tool-for-supporting-the-arts/

Grapperhaus, F. H. M. (1971). Vooruitblik op het belastingrecht. *Tributen aan het recht* (pp. 3–19). Kluwer.

Guardian News. (2019, January 30). *Rutger Bregman Tells Davos to Talk About Tax: 'This Is Not Rocket Science'* [Video]. YouTube. https://www.youtube.com/watch?v=P8ijiLqfXP0

Haydon, S., Jung, T., & Russell, S. (2021). 'You've Been Framed': A Critical Review of Academic Discourse on Philanthrocapitalism. *International Journal of Management Reviews, 23*(3), 353–375.

Hemels, S. J. C., & Goto, K. (Eds.). (2017). *Tax Incentives for the Creative Industries*. Springer.
Hemels, S. J. C. (2020). Say Cheese! Photographs and the Definition of Works of Art for VAT Purposes. *FIRE Journal, 2020*(1), 1–18.
Hemels, S. J. C. (2021). Paying Taxes with Cultural heritage or Rather an Exemption Upon Inheritance? In L. Del Federico, Hemels, S. J. C., J-A Rozas, & S. Giorgi (Eds.), *Taxation and Cultural Heritage*. IBFD.
Hiltrop, M. (2019, February 6). Filantropen zijn niet heilig, wel nuttig. *NRC Handelsblad*. https://www.nrc.nl/nieuws/2019/02/05/filantropen-zijn-niet-heilig-wel-nuttig-a3652967
Hopkins, B. R. (2011). *The Law of Tax-Exempt Organizations*. Wiley.
Irish Tax and Customs. (2023, April 25). *Artists' Exemption*. https://www.revenue.ie/en/personal-tax-credits-reliefs-and-exemptions/income-and-employment/artists-exemption/index.aspx
Kraan, D-J. (2004). Off-budget and Tax Expenditures. *OECD Journal on Budgeting, 4*(1), 121–142. https://www.oecd-ilibrary.org/governance/off-budget-and-tax-expenditures_budget-v4-art6-en
McGoey, L., Thiel, D., & West, R. (2018). Philanthrocapitalism and Crimes of the Powerful. *Politix, 121*(1), 29–54.
Mourato, S., & Mazzanti, M. (2002). Economic Valuation of Cultural Heritage: Evidence and Prospects. In M. De la Torre (ed.), *Assessing the Values of Cultural Heritage* (pp. 51–73). The Getty Conservation Institute.
Nährlich, S. (2013). Percentage Philanthropy. Selbstbestimmte Steuerzuweisungen an Ge-meinnützige. *Stiftung & Sponsoring, 16*(4), 26–27.
OECD. (2010). *Tax Expenditures in OECD Countries*. OECD Publishing. https://doi.org/10.1787/9789264076907-en
OECD. (2020). *Taxation and Philanthropy*, OECD Tax Policy Studies, No. 27. OECD Publishing. https://doi.org/10.1787/df434a77-en
O'Hagan, J. (2011). Tax Concessions. In R. Towse (Ed.), *A Handbook of Cultural Economics* (2nd ed., pp. 408–412). Edward Elgar.
Reich, R. (2018). *Just Giving: Why Philanthropy Is Failing Democracy and How It Can Do Better*. Princeton University Press.
Surrey, S. S., & McDaniel, P. R. (1985). *Tax Expenditures*. Harvard University Press.
Vallely, P. (2020, September 8). How Philanthropy Benefits the Super-Rich. *The Guardian*. https://www.theguardian.com/society/2020/sep/08/how-philanthropy-benefits-the-super-rich
Van der Ploeg, R. (2002). In Art We Trust. *De Economist, 150*(4), 333–362.

Open Access This chapter is licensed under the terms of the Creative Commons Attribution 4.0 International License (http://creativecommons.org/licenses/by/4.0/), which permits use, sharing, adaptation, distribution and reproduction in any medium or format, as long as you give appropriate credit to the original author(s) and the source, provide a link to the Creative Commons license and indicate if changes were made.

The images or other third party material in this chapter are included in the chapter's Creative Commons license, unless indicated otherwise in a credit line to the material. If material is not included in the chapter's Creative Commons license and your intended use is not permitted by statutory regulation or exceeds the permitted use, you will need to obtain permission directly from the copyright holder.

CHAPTER 4

Philanthropic Fundraising and Sponsorship: The Arts Marketing Perspective on Financing Cultural Projects Based in the North American Context

François Colbert

1 Introduction

From a marketing perspective, seeking sponsorships or soliciting donations from individuals is a marketing operation in which the soliciting company must first determine the interests of donors and sponsors.

There is no point in soliciting a potential donor to support a dance company if the latter's area of interest is health or education. Donations are, first and foremost, a matter of the heart. This is because the potential donor has a passion for a type of art he or she will want to help. Some patrons are unconditional lovers of sculpture or classical music. Their support will tend towards these types of organisations and little

F. Colbert (✉)
HEC Montreal, Montréal, QC, Canada
e-mail: francois.colbert@hec.ca

© The Author(s) 2026

C. Dalla Chiesa and A. Rykkja (eds.), *Cultural Funding and Financing*, Cultural Economics & the Creative Economy,
https://doi.org/10.1007/978-3-031-96696-5_4

towards other fields. It is up to the marketing department, or marketing-related personnel, to know and explore the preferences of this "market" so as not to waste time soliciting someone who isn't interested in our product.

In the same way, the search for sponsorship obeys certain rules. The sponsor pursues financial and market objectives when associating itself with a cause. The discussion becomes a business relationship. The arts company has a product to sell, and the sponsor has business objectives to achieve. The two must come together for an association to be made. Here again, it is the marketing's role to bridge the gap between the sponsor's needs and the company's desires. A theatre or a museum doesn't have to accept everything the sponsor wants in return for a sponsorship. Like any business discussion, an agreement must be reached that is satisfactory to both parties otherwise there can be no deal.

In the US, the private sector and individuals heavily support artistic companies. The same can be said for Canada, to a lesser degree. Donations and sponsorship are two segments of a market that are important for the financial health of an artistic company.

The first part of the chapter will deal with conceptual aspects of donations and sponsorships. The second part gives a glimpse of the Canadian situation and provides examples of innovative ways of financing the arts other than government involvement or box office revenues.

2 Marketing the Arts

Marketing for a non-profit arts company differs from that of a private company that must generate profits for its shareholders. In the first case, the entire marketing strategy revolves around the artistic proposition. In this sense, it is the artistic director, the museum curator or the visual artist who determines what product will be offered. The rest of the organisation serves the company's mission, and the task of marketing is to find the right customers, in sufficient quantity, at the right time for the performance or visit. The product is given to him/her and marketing can neither change it nor ask the artist to modify it to please the public. This is a so-called "product" orientation. On the contrary, a private company asks the consumer what they want and organises itself to give them the product they seek while making a profit. We will then speak of a "market" orientation.

Furthermore, the consumer market is not the only one targeted by a cultural organisation. It also seeks grants from governments, it looks for partners (co-producers, media support), and it solicits donations and sponsorships. This donation or sponsorship requested must offer benefits to the person in return for their donation or to a company in return for their sponsorship. In marketing terms, a product is defined as "a set of benefits perceived by the consumer" (Colbert & Ravanas, 2018). The search for private financing necessarily involves offering benefits to potential donors or sponsors. All of these benefits will be the product offered, and potential donors will form a market, that of donations, while sponsors will form the sponsorship market. Effective marketing to any of these markets requires knowledge of the behaviour of these "consumers".

3 The Donor as Consumers: An Incentive-Based Framework

We have already said that giving to charity—and the arts are considered as such, is a matter of the heart. However, several elements constitute the donor's journey in his action of giving or giving back. Figure 1 illustrates some of the elements that make up the donor behaviour model.

Initially, the person must be interested in the art form and be sensitive to a donation proposal. The donor will not necessarily be a supporter of the company in question. He or she may never have had the opportunity to see the productions it offers. But he/she will be one of the people who love this art form and who is inclined to make a monetary contribution.

We can distinguish two forms of donations: the exchange relationship and the communal relationship (Wiggins & Rapp, 2010). In the first case, the person will expect to receive something in exchange for their donation, usually under the form of a mention either in the house program

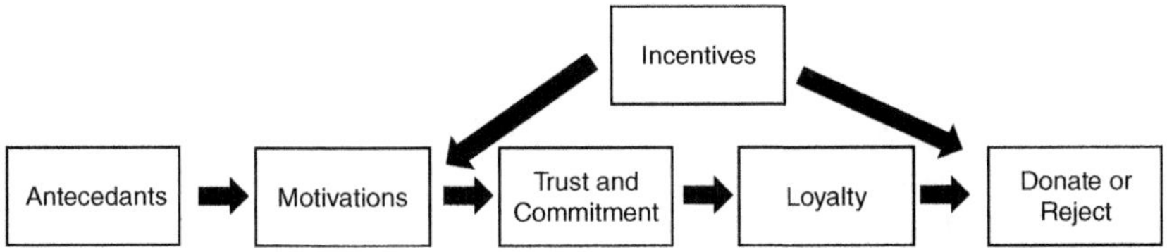

Fig. 1 The path to donation

or in some form of publicity. We are here at the level of the transaction which benefits both parties. In the second case, the person wants to help the other party and does not condition their help on receiving compensation, even if it exists. Thus, some people do not want their donation to be known, often for fear of being solicited by a host of other organisations, or for other reasons. They will insist that their name not appear in the list of donors.

Motivations and Preferences

If the choice of a cause to which to donate comes from a personal preference, other motivations come into play in this process of giving. One of them, which is very strong, is that of the norm of social responsibility (Barnes, 2011). This is true both in Canada and in the US and is linked to the Protestant ethic that says, "if you are wealthy, it is because God loves you, but you must give back to your community". In the US, after the American Revolution, the citizens rejected the model of a federal state imposing its decisions. They opted for a model where it is up to the community to decide what is good for it. This is particularly true for the education, health and culture sectors. These three sectors are therefore seen as a local responsibility and it is the citizens, locally, who must decide whether we should build a school or create a symphony orchestra or even build a hospital. Citizens have long understood the notion that it is their responsibility to give back to their community according to their financial means. This primary desire of not wanting the federal government to get involved at the local level, at the same time as this sense of being responsible for the vitality of one's community, explains the little federal aid for the performing arts or museums in the United States. That is why the income of the majority of cultural companies is based on the sale of tickets and other products (i.e. parking, shops, etc.) and on donations and/or sponsorships. Ticket sales and donations/sponsorships each represent approximately 50% of company revenues. This is also the reason why being a member of the board of directors of an artistic company involves not only giving your time but also financially supporting the company. The more prestigious the company, the higher the financial contribution required. So, just to become a member of the board of directors of a large company, one must sign a check for several tens of thousands of dollars and contribute to the annual collection, oneself as an individual, as well as the company to which one belongs.

Beyond a sense of cultural, normative or moral responsibility, other factors contribute to encouraging people to give. These factors are either intrinsic or extrinsic to the individual. Intrinsic motivation to give to culture is generally linked to the satisfaction of doing something good and useful to the community. Extrinsic motivation can be of two types, either in tangible form such as a receipt for tax purposes, or in intangible form such as praise, recognition, or grades (Wiggins & Rapp, 2010). This extrinsic motivation therefore comes from the prestige given by the fact of having contributed to a recognised company (prestige motivations), or from the image that the donor wants to project of himself in society (image motivations, or self-signalling), or by the status that one receives from its peers (status-based motivations), or to respond to the social norm which requires contributions to the well-being of the community to which they belong (social motivations).

The amount of the donation will therefore be linked to household income. But it is important to notice that usually the majority of donors are people who send small amounts and are not necessarily rich.

Moderating Effects

Any company must cultivate its donors to ensure that they repeat their donation from one year to the next and even increase this donation over the years. Moreover, it is often said that becoming a donor to a company first involves purchasing a ticket for a show, then the next step is to take out a subscription and then transform this subscriber into a donor. This may initially be for a small amount; what is important at first is not the amount of the donation but the commitment of the person to the company. The amount of the donation may increase over the years as this person feels more and more involved. The loyalty of the regular donors leads them to feel committed to the company at the same time as they grant it trust.

Note that receiving a tax receipt to reduce one's taxes is a secondary motivator; the receipt is not the main reason for donating. It should be understood that this tax reduction applies to the percentage taxed on marginal income. Thus, if the marginal tax rate is 40%, the person only recovers 40% of the amount paid. It still costs 60% to the donor.

The relationship of trust between the donor and the company is built over time, as is the commitment to it. This notion of time, and the secondary notion of tax incentives, influence the degree of loyalty towards the company (moderating effect).

Trusts and Commitment

A company that wants to retain its buyers will want to build a relationship of trust with them so that they feel committed to their products. Trust allows to maintain a long-term relationship with the donor. A company that builds a high level of trust helps reduce the uncertainty of the relationship and the risk of being disappointed (Barra et al., 2018). In an artistic company, this trust comes from the assurance that the coming season will be as interesting as the previous ones, encouraging the consumer to resubscribe and maintain or even increase their level of donations. The person will feel involved in the relationship with the company and will want to maintain it. It will be both, an emotional sense of closeness, and a desire to maintain this relationship. One must therefore have confidence in the company to be a long-term donor and have developed an emotional connection with it. A high level of trust and commitment will lead to donor loyalty. The pride of feeling part of the company will also be an element that will lead to this loyalty.

Loyalty

In marketing, we often use the definition of loyalty proposed by Oliver (1999, p. 34): "a deeply held commitment to re-buy or re-patronise a preferred product/service consistently in the future, thereby causing repetitive same-brand or same-brand set purchasing, despite situational influences and marketing efforts to have the potential to cause switching behaviour".

The level of donor loyalty is conditioned by his/her confidence in the organisation and sense of commitment as we saw in the previous section. This trust and commitment lead to a positive attitude towards that organisation and a desire or willingness to contribute again. These three levels of loyalty are called cognitive loyalty (knowing the organisation), affective loyalty (appreciating the organisation), and behavioural loyalty (deciding to renew your donation) (Barra et al., 2018).

Incentives to Donate or Re-donate

While pride will positively influence the decision to donate, it is gratitude that will determine the amount of the donation, and this gratitude comes from the feeling of affiliation with the organisation whether the donation is recognised or not (Paramita et al., 2020). Note that the length of time as a donor and the tax incentives also have an influence on the decision to donate and the amount of the donation.

Another influencing factor on willingness to donate (or subscribe again) is tolerance for disappointment. The cumulative effect of the satisfaction that the consumer feels towards a company which presented him with seasons that he appreciated will build a tolerance for disappointment if one of the productions does not meet his expectations (Obaidalahe et al., 2017) This tolerance will come from accepting that a work may not suit the person, thus somehow placing the blame on the person himself, or that the rest of the season is so interesting that it erases a less good evening.

4 The Sponsor in Search of Its Market

Fundraising is part of what could be called the private market. The other aspect of this market is sponsorship. The sponsor uses this way to reach its own market by investing part of its advertising budget to support a cultural company. This is what can be defined as "indirect marketing". The sponsor and the sponsee enter into a business relationship, and the objective is to arrive at a partnership that is beneficial for both parties.

The Sponsees Point of View

The audience of performing arts companies as well as museum visitors can be considered a niche market for a potential sponsor. These are an educated clientele who generally benefit from higher-than-average incomes. As a result, the sponsor can position its brand as offering a sophisticated product. Also, as a general rule, it is a group of patrons with a strong level of commitment and loyalty who appreciate the support that sponsors offer to an art form that they cherish (Olson, 2010).

Of course, audiences in the arts are not as large as what you find at major sporting or other types of events. However, their advantage is one of strategic positioning for the sponsoring companies. It allows them to communicate more effectively with sophisticated potential customers. The diversity of audiences that the arts reach is also an asset. Each cultural company reaches a defined audience. Some have a very sophisticated or traditional image (e.g., opera, classical music, art museum), while others have anare avant-garde driven (e.g., contemporary art museum or contemporary dance company). Unlike sports which require a winner and a loser and provoke one-dimensional emotions (a fight for victory), the arts offer a wider range of subjects and a wider palette of emotions.

That being said, the artistic companies can and must choose with whom they want to do business. The sponsorship market is one of establishing a business relationship between the sponsor and the sponsee. Sponsorship provides the potential sponsor with access to a sophisticated market segment. The sponsee must choose the sponsor who fits with the artistic vision of the company. There must be congruence between the two partners. The artistic company is free to accept or not the terms requested by the sponsor. When both parties agree, a profitable business relationship can develop for everyone involved.

Sense Making

Arts managers must seek to understand the potential sponsor and how they can align with the artistic vision of the company. The sponsor is pursuing marketing goals by partnering with the company, and all employees of the artistic company must understand this relationship. "A pitch to the sponsor must, therefore, be crafted with everyone's understanding in mind. The more that arts managers (and board members) listen, the more likely they are to see, communicate, act on, and benefit from the opportunities that can exist in a sponsorship" (Daellenbach et al., 2016).

The Sponsor's Point of View

For the sponsor too, there must be a fit with the company that it is about to sponsor. The greater this fit, the more successful the sponsorship will be, not only from a marketing point of view but also in terms of establishing this profitable business relationship for both parties.

From a marketing perspective, not only is the notion of fit important, but the perceived sincerity of the sponsorship also matters. Usually, a sponsor wants to sell a product, hence the evaluation of the sponsorship will be measured by the rate of increase in sales. Choosing a company in the field of arts is not the most appropriate decision if the increase in sales is the utmost objective; sponsoring a sporting event may lead to better or immediate results. The notion of the authenticity of the business relationship perceived by the visitor or spectator will bear better fruit. People's positive attitude towards the art they consume may transfer to the advertised product if the sponsor is seen as genuinely wanting to support the art company or museum for example (Cornwell & Kwon, 2020). It should be noted that the effects of sponsorship may persist for up to a year despite the fact that the customer may, in the meantime, be exposed to promotional campaigns from other brands (Simmons & Becker-Olsen, 2006).

For the sponsor, accompanying the sponsorship with a broader marketing campaign will have a beneficial effect on attitude towards the brand, recognition of the brand and the long-term effect on the spectator's memory (DeGaris et al., 2017).

In the particular case of a venue that holds several different art forms, it is important spectators are satisfied with the venue because this satisfaction or dissatisfaction will affect the attitude towards the sponsor and even the intention to buy its product (MicheliniI et al., 2017). Hence the importance for the venue to take care of customer service; a bad service to the client from the venue will affect all partners.

Type of Sponsor and Fit of the Sponsorship

The consumer's evaluation of the sponsorship will not be the same depending on whether the sponsor is a private company, a Crown corporation or a government department. The most appreciated sponsorships by patrons are those associated with private companies, followed by Crown corporations and government ministries or departments, respectively (Colbert et al., 2005).

There is also a difference between sponsoring a high art versus popular art company. If the sponsorship effort is clearly commercial in nature (selling the product), it is preferable for the sponsor to choose a popular art organisation. On the contrary, if the intention to sell is more subtle in the sense that we only want to generate goodwill, then high art is the appropriate market (Carrillat et al., 2008).

Ambush Marketing

"Ambush marketing is a contentious practice whereby brands communicate an association with an event without being an official sponsor" (Weeks et al., 2017). An ambush common practice is for companies that are not one of the sponsors of an event to advertise in relation to the event—such as, for example, congratulating the organisation that organises this event. The idea here is to attach its campaign to the event to gain visibility or goodwill. This may have the effect of reducing the visibility effect of the main sponsor. To counter this attack, the sponsor can include increased recall of sponsor cues or communicate a distinctly unique attribute like sponsor exclusivity. This can help improve recall for the sponsor brand and reduce recall for the ambush brand. Note that the danger of the customer confusing the sponsor and the ambusher is much greater when the product of the latter is congruent with the event (a musical instrument seller at a music festival, for example). Reminding viewers that the sponsor has secured exclusivity or is the exclusive sponsor of the event helps the viewer distance the sponsor's product from that of the ambusher and reinforces the brand by more closely associating it with the event.

A sponsor may attempt to prevent ambusher activity through legal means, but this may be counterproductive if these actions generate controversy that could be harmful to the sponsor.

5 The North American Private Sector Involvement in the Arts

To understand how the model exists in different countries, one must look back at the history of a particular country. In North America, three traditions exist according to events taking place 200 years ago. French Canada (the province of Quebec) model was borrowed from France, while in English Canada it is the British model of Arts Council that prevailed. As we saw before, the United States decided, after the American Revolution of 1765, "not to have a king again" and thus stated that education, health and culture were the responsibility of the community, not the federal government. It's worth noting that the great concert halls and cultural organisations in the US all began as closed organisations serving only those who funded them. It was only later that the general public was admitted, and these organisations became not-for-profit corporations (Accominotti et al., 2018).

The Canadian Model: English Canada Versus French Canada or the French Model Versus the British Model

When it comes to funding cultural organisations, one of Canada's particularities is that the country can be seen as a conjunction of various models. Indeed, Canada borrowed from each of three systems: France, England and the United States. It's worth remembering that Canada was originally French before becoming British after France was defeated by the English in 1760. The French-speaking province of Quebec followed the French model, creating a Ministry of Cultural Affairs in 1963. English-speaking Canada followed the British tradition, creating the Canada Council for the Arts in 1957. English-speaking Canada also borrowed from the American model of philanthropy, being itself Protestant in tradition. However, arts and culture do not appear in the wording of the Canadian constitution written in 1867. It is therefore an area that a province like Quebec claims to have jurisdiction over. The federal government has always refrained from directly creating its own Ministry of Culture, so as not to create a constitutional squabble. It has, however, intervened, first by setting up a Department of Communications (communications are under federal jurisdiction), then by renaming it the Department of Canadian Heritage, which includes a whole series of divisions, including sport, the state museums in Ottawa, the Canada Council for the Arts, Telefilm Canada, etc., and programs such as festival support. The provinces refrained from begrudging because the cultural community welcomed the new money from the government of Canada and would not have sided with the provinces in a cockfight between the provinces and the federal government. Québec, for its part, created a *Conseil des Arts et des Lettres du Québec* in 1992 under pressure from the cultural community, which envied the independence from politicians of a structure like the Canada Council for the Arts. By creating this council, Quebec, like Canada, became an entity that borrowed from both the French and British models. This is because most of the Canadian provinces have both a Ministry of Culture and an Arts Council. The same can be said at the municipal level. Most of the larger cities have a division of culture along with a municipal art council.

The American Model, Its Application to the Canadian Model: Similarities and Differences Between French Canada Versus English Canada or Catholic Versus Protestant

Since the early 1980s, various levels of government in Canada have encouraged cultural companies to turn to patronage and sponsorship to boost their revenues. Indeed, the financial problems of these governments were serious, and the means to help a fast-growing sector were becoming increasingly scarce. Anecdotally, in the province of Quebec, until the 1980s, an artistic company that received a donation could have the amount of that donation subtracted from the grant it received from the provincial government. Obviously, this did not encourage the solicitation of private support. It was during the financial crisis of the 1980s that cash-strapped politicians changed their policy and forced cultural companies to find new funds by soliciting businesses and individuals. This was no easy task. First of all, there was a distrust on the part of the Quebec cultural community that, when a company supported a theatre, it would try to dictate artistic policy. This did not happen in practice. The second difficulty was the absence of a tradition of philanthropic contributions by individuals and companies in the province. Not only did the leaders of artistic companies (especially the small ones) not know how to raise funds, but they also had to find arguments to convince potential patrons and sponsors who were not used to be solicited. English Canada, on the other hand, had adopted the American method early on and could already count on a good pool of donors and sponsors. That said, after 40 years of effort, the level of private support in Quebec is beginning to be substantial.

A quick aside to explain a fundamental difference between English Canada and French Canada (mostly Quebec) when it comes to sponsorship. This difference lies, surprisingly, in the religion observed in the two parts of Canada. English Canada has a Protestant religious tradition—as does the United States, where being rich guarantees a place in heaven, since "if you're rich, it's because God loves you." To do this, however, you have to give back to the community. This is a powerful incentive to contribute to charitable causes. On the other hand, Catholic tradition preaches that "it's harder for a rich man to get into heaven than for a camel to go through the eye of a needle". The stranglehold, not to say the iron gauntlet, of the Catholic Church, which controlled just about every aspect of Quebec citizens' lives until the 1960s, discouraged its flock from pursuing industrial careers. For the majority of the population, education stopped after elementary school; for the 1% of the population going to university, the ideal choice was either to enter religious orders, medicine, or the notary's office. This likely explains why the number of wealthy people was much lower in Quebec than in English Canada and why the donation market was very small, except for church donations, which were compulsory. Fortunately, it was with the 'Quiet Revolution' of the 1960s that a modern state of Quebec was formed, where the church was excluded from managing the schools and hospital systems. The school system was thus modernised, enrolment in universities flourished, and new business schools were created, enabling the development of a modern, more well-educated society ready to meet the challenges of the modern world. Speaking of business schools, HEC Montréal was created in 1907 by the Montréal Chamber of Commerce against the will of the Catholic Church, who feared losing its influence over his followers. HEC Montréal then became the first business school to be born in Canada.

In Canada, ticket sales, subsidies and the private sector are the three main sources of funding. In the province of Quebec, statistics for the performing arts in 2020 were as follows: main activities (box office) 38.3%, private sector 12.6%, subsidies 49.1%.

The Role of Private Sector Involvement (Donations and Sponsorships) in the Marketing Strategy of Cultural Organisations

Western countries are struggling to fulfil their core missions, and many complain that their governments are neglecting the arts sector. For an economy to flourish and the arts sector to develop, a number of favourable economic factors are typically required. These include a growing population, growing income and leisure time. In the 1960s–1970s, all these factors were in the green, and demand for the arts grew exponentially. In fact, after the Second World War, Canada's population was growing by 5–6% a year, working hours were falling steadily, and wages were rising. Getting a university degree became an objective for a large part of the population, leading to exponential growth in demand for goods and services, including, of course, arts and culture. On the other hand, the supply side of the equation was also growing. There was room on the market for more theatre, classical music and museums. Schools of theatre, music, etc. were founded in droves. But this golden age is over. To take Canada as an example, since the 1990s, the population has been growing slowly, the workweek has stopped shrinking, and wages are stagnant. Meanwhile, our art schools continue to produce more and more talented young people year after year, looking for a place in a slow-growing market. Unable to find employment with existing companies, many decide to set up their own groups, thus contributing to the overcrowding of the sector and the pressure on governments and the private sector for donations and sponsorships.

To compensate for the difficulty of obtaining public or private support, new models have been tried out in various countries. These could be described as hybrid models, for which Battilana and Lee (2014) give the following definition: Hybrid organizations are the activities, structures, processes and meanings by which organisations make sense of and combine aspects of multiple organisational forms.

In this final section of the chapter, we will explore two models that work to the benefit of artists and cultural organisations, the case of cooperatives and the case of not-for-profit companies backed up by a private enterprise. We will then finish with the description of a unique model of a bank for the cultural sector that was created the government of the province of Quebec.

Cooperatives

In Canada, there are a number of different ways of supporting the arts. The transformation of buildings into not-for-profit entities is one example. Toronto's ArtScape is an non-profit-organisation (NPO) that owns buildings in various parts of the city where it rents studios to artists at below-market costs. These buildings were acquired with public assistance and also with donations from patrons. This arrangement is similar to that of housing cooperatives, which offer low-cost apartments to the underprivileged. Another slightly different example is Espace Belgo in Montreal. Here, the owner of a downtown building rents space to artists or art galleries at a very low price. In the case of Espace Belgo, however, it's not certain that this arrangement will continue after the owner's death, as his children may want to reclaim the building, whose value has obviously risen sharply over the years, given its prime downtown location.

Another similar initiative is "Building 303" project, an ambitious acquisition and renovation project to preserve the history of an important place for the 2SLGBTQIA+ artist community. Initiated by Kim Sanh

Châu, an artist and art manager of Montréal, this building makes it a creative space accessible to marginalised artists and emerging practices. In addition to creative spaces, from the ideation, it included affordable housing specially designed for artists. In fact, this will be the first accommodation for dance artists in residence in Canada.

A Not-for-Profit Organization (NPO) Backed by a Commercial Enterprise

There are several examples of models where one or more commercial enterprises are attached to an NPO. Let's look at four such models.

In the United States, public subsidies are rare. Donors, on the other hand, are generous. That said, organisations have to be inventive to make ends meet. The New Jersey Performing Arts Centre can count on a source of revenue that comes from land they own adjacent to the arts complex. The land is leased to a developer who has constructed a building with shops on the first floor and apartments above. For a fee, retail customers have access to the centre's parking lot during daytime hours, while spectators use it at night. The centre's latest financial statements show $9.1 million in other earned income, representing 15.5% of the organisation's total income.

Another example comes from Colombia in Latin America. Group Paramo is a company that organises some twenty musical events, mostly in Bogotá but also in Cali and Medellín. With no government support whatsoever, the group is profitable enough to offer one of its two music festivals with free admission. By this, the owners want to help bring the country's musical culture to as many people as possible by removing the price barrier. The group's profit-making companies, therefore, subsidise the NPO. It is interesting to note this group has been recently acquired by an American multibillionaire company called Live Nation.

China offers another example of cross-financing between for-profit companies and NPOs. In 2000, the Chinese government encouraged the creation of business clusters. The idea was to create entities made up of commercial companies and NPOs, with the commercial companies supporting the NPOs. In 2012, there were already 2,102 performing arts companies grouped into 46 conglomerates. This industrial organisation is described as the "dual track system".

One example of a cluster is the Beijing Performance and Arts, or BPA in China (Lin & Colbert, 2022). BPA comprises a total of 19 commercial enterprises and nine NPOs. The commercial enterprises include entities such as an advertising company, sports companies and media companies (e.g. a TV network). It also includes the operation of the National Stadium, which hosts various sporting events and shows. The National Stadium is China's largest cultural asset and the BPA's most valuable asset. It is located on the site of the Olympic Games, along with the Bird's Nest (the arena for Olympic competitions) and the Water Cube (swimming competitions). This area is highly emblematic in China. Another BPA entity is the Beijing Film Company. This cinema chain has annual revenues of over one billion yuan and a 30% market share in Beijing. Although the company does not produce films, it acts as an investor in the production.

The nine performing arts companies (NPOs) are not required to make a profit. They are to pursue both social and economic benefits for the community. The other 19 companies have profit as their primary objective and must financially support the other nine NPOs. These nine NPO's are: Beijing Children's Art Theatre, Beijing Dance Drama & Opera Theatre, China National Acrobatic Troupe, China Puppet Art Theatre, Beijing Folk Arts Troupe, Beijing Chinese Traditional Orchestra, China Pingju Opera, Beijing Hebei Bangzi Opera, Beijing Quju Opera.

Each year, the managers of these 28 companies present a financial plan with objectives to be achieved. For the 19 for-profit companies, this means showing a reasonable profit, and for the 9 NPOs, reaching a percentage of self-financing.

In Montreal, there are two very successful groups, both nationally and internationally known. They are *Groupe Spectra* and *Groupe Rozon*. The former presents the well-known *Montreal International Jazz Festival* and the latter the *Juste For Laughs*. Both festivals were launched in the mid-1980s with a single organisation, the festival itself as an NPO. The organisers soon realised that certain operations linked to the festival could be highly profitable, such as filming and then selling those shows internationally. They, therefore, created associated, for-profit companies to take charge of these other operations. This structure enabled the NPO to obtain government subsidies not available to for-profit companies, while the latter could apply for subsidies for some of their activities, such as video recordings, which were not available to NPOs. The model was so successful that promoters were able to resell their brands to multinational entertainment companies (*Evenko/Live Nation*). Note that this hybrid model differs from traditional models. The latter's for-profit commercial entities are there to help the NPOs, whereas the former's model sees the

NPOs as the springboards for successful commercial operations. This is not without a certain amount of grumbling from the cultural community, who see these groups swallowing up substantial public subsidies that don't go to the not-for-profit players in the arts.

A Unique Bank Model: Société de développement des entreprises culturelles (SODEC)[1]

In the 80s, the Quebec government created a corporation to support for-profit enterprises in the cultural industries: audio-visual, notably cinema, books and publishing, arts and crafts, and the music and entertainment industry. SODEC acts as a bank to support projects that traditional banks would find too risky; in addition to providing low-interest loans, it can take an equity stake; it can also award grants, notably to help producers take part in international trade fairs or promote their products.

As stated on its website, SODEC pursues objectives aimed at supporting the development and stabilisation of businesses, structuring areas of activity, creating conditions that encourage marketing and exports, promote business networking activities.

This para-governmental organisation plays an important role in supporting the industry in a French-speaking market that is, after all, very small: 9 million francophone inhabitants, compared with a North American population of some 400 million English speakers.

6 Conclusion

Over the years, Canada has adopted three major funding models: government, box office and private sector (donations and sponsorships). In French Canada, the tradition of patronage for the arts practically did not exist before the 1980s. Cultural organisations have had to learn how to solicit funds from private companies. Soliciting donors means establishing an emotional relationship between the company and the donor. Soliciting a sponsorship involves entering into a business relationship with the sponsor. Cultivating a donor base involves a series of steps that lead from the first donation to a stronger donor involvement and are guided by more than just the possibility of a tax deduction. Sponsorship and marketing, in general, are important to ensure the financial capabilities of cultural companies. Is this despite their geographical base? We suggest in that sense, both European Union and North American models, although different, require cultural organisations to look outside for opportunities and not simply depend on government funds. Thus, this chapter contribute to understanding ways to go about sponsorship and marketing vis-à-vis the need for culture's financial sustainability.

Note

1. The acronyme means "Société de développement des entreprises culturelles (Society for the Development of the Cultural Enterprises).

References

Accominotti, F., Storer, A., & Khan, S. R. (2018). How Cultural Capital Emerged in Gilded Age America: Musical Purification and Cross-Class Inclusion at the New York Philharmonic. *American Journal of Sociology, 123*(6), 1743–1783.

Barnes, M. L. (2011). "Music to Our Ears": Understanding Why Canadians Donate to Arts and Cultural Organizations. *International Journal of Nonprofit and Voluntary Sector Marketing, 16*, 115–126.

Barra, C., Pressgrove, G., & Torres, E. (2018). Trust and Commitment in the Formation of Donor Loyalty. *The Service Industries Journal, 38*(5–6), 360–377.

Battilana, J., & Lee, M. (2014). Advancing Research on Hybrid Organizing—Insights from the Study of Social Enterprises. *The Academy of Management Annals, 8*(1), 397–441.

Carrillat, F. A., d'Astous, A., & Colbert, F. (2008). The Effectiveness of Art Venue Sponsorship: An Attribution Perspective. *Journal of Sponsorship, 1*(3), 274–285.

Colbert, F., d'Astous, A., & Parmentier, M. A. (2005). Consumer Perceptions of Sponsorship in the Arts: A Canadian Perspective. *International Journal of Cultural Policy, 11*(2), 215–228.

Colbert, F., & Ravanas, P. (2018). *Marketing the Arts*. Carmelle and Rémi-Marcoux Chair in Arts Management. Montréal. Canada.

Cornwell, T. B., & Kwon, Y. (2020). Sponsorship-Linked Marketing: Research Surpluses and Shortages. *Journal of the Academy of Marketing Science, 48*, 607–629.

Daellenbach, K., Zander, L., & Thirkell, P. (2016). A Sensemaking Perspective on Arts Sponsorship Decisions. *Arts and the Market, 6*(1), 68–87.

DeGaris, L., Hee Kwak, D., & McDaniel, S.R. (2017). Modeling the Effects of Sponsorship-Linked Marketing: When Does Memory Matter? *Journal of Promotion Management, 23*(2), 320–339.

Lin, Y., & Colbert, F. (2022). Value Creation of Performing Arts: Dual System of Governance of the Beijing Performance and Arts Group. *International Journal of Arts Management, 25*(1), 106–111.

MicheliniI, L., Iasevoli, G., & Theodoraki, E. (2017). Event Venue Satisfaction and Its Impact on Sponsorship Outcomes. *Event Management, 21*, 319–331.

New Jersey Performing Arts Centre, Reports and Financials—NJPAC.

Obaidalahe, Z., Salerno, F., & Colbert, F. (2017). Subscribers's Overall Evaluation of a Multi-Experience Cultural Service, Tolerence for Disapointment and Sustenable Loyalty. *International Journal of Arts Management, 20*(1), 21–30.

Oliver, R. L. (1999). Whence consumer loyalty? *Journal of Marketing, 63*(4_suppl1), 33–44. https://doi.org/10.1177/00222429990634s105. (Original work published 1999).

Olson, E. L. (2010). Does Sponsorship Work in the Same Way in Different Sponsorship Contexts? *European Journal of Marketing, 44*(1–2), 180–199.

Paramita, W., Septianto, F., & Tjiptono, F. (2020). The Distinct Effects of Gratitude and Pride on Donation Choice and Amount. *Journal of Retailing and Consumer Services, 53*, 1–10.

Simmons, C. J., & Becker-Olsen, K. L. (2006). Achieving Marketing Objectives Through Social Sponsorships. *Journal of Marketing, 70*, 154–169.

van Teunenbroek, C., Dalla Chiesa, C., & Hesse, L. (2023). The Contribution of Crowdfunding for Philanthropy: A Review and Theoretical Framework of Reward- and Donation-Based Crowdfunding. *Journal of Philanthropy and Marketing, 28*(3), 1–15.

Weeks, C. S., O'Connor, P. J., & Martin, B. A. S. (2017). When Ambush Marketing Is Beneficial to Sponsorship Awareness: Creating Sponsor Distinctiveness Using Exclusivity and Brand Juxtaposition. *Journal of Marketing Management, 33*(15–16), 1256–1280.

Wiggins, J., & Rapp, A. (2010). A More Comprehensive Understanding and Measure of Customer Helping Behaviors. *Journal of Business Research, 63*(8), 787–792.

Open Access This chapter is licensed under the terms of the Creative Commons Attribution 4.0 International License (http://creativecommons.org/licenses/by/4.0/), which permits use, sharing, adaptation, distribution and reproduction in any medium or format, as long as you give appropriate credit to the original author(s) and the source, provide a link to the Creative Commons license and indicate if changes were made.

The images or other third party material in this chapter are included in the chapter's Creative Commons license, unless indicated otherwise in a credit line to the material. If material is not included in the chapter's Creative Commons license and your intended use is not permitted by statutory regulation or exceeds the permitted use, you will need to obtain permission directly from the copyright holder.

CHAPTER 5

Patronage in the Arts: Theories and Contemporary Challenges

Helleke van den Braber

1 Introduction

The issue of gift exchange between individual artists and private patrons has gained new relevance over the last decades, as the cultural sector in many European countries—following philanthropic traditions already firmly established in the USA—works towards building a renewed tradition of arts patronage. For artists, engaging with private supporters has yet again become a—still relatively marginal—'third way' to make money, alongside entering in market-oriented exchanges and applying for government support. Individual artists across the globe are experimenting with building ties with private donors, finding ways to engage not just with groups of funders, but with individual benefactors too. With them they seek to build one-on-one ties that—unlike most crowdfunding initiatives—are not focused on short-term or project-based support, but aimed at long-term, sustainable and personal backing for their work and careers.[1] Benefactors support artists by giving money or grants, providing

H. van den Braber (✉)
Utrecht University, Utrecht, The Netherlands
e-mail: h.m.vandenbraber@uu.nl

© The Author(s) 2026

C. Dalla Chiesa and A. Rykkja (eds.), *Cultural Funding and Financing*,
Cultural Economics & the Creative Economy,
https://doi.org/10.1007/978-3-031-96696-5_5

workspace or time, giving access to their networks, or through implicit or explicit approval, moral support or encouragement. Patrons, unlike investors or collectors, are not in it to benefit financially. In this respect, the patronage system is very different from the for-profit investments associated with some forms of reward-based crowdfunding. Although Bourdieu (1998) and Brewer (2018) have rightly pointed out that even in arts patronage the altruistic gift does not exist, the donations that patrons offer to artists are charitable in intent, ostensibly aimed at facilitating the artist's work, at encouraging their artistic development, or at fostering the arts in general (Balfe, 1993, p. 3; van den Braber, 2021, p. 16). Yet the role of patron does bring invaluable quid pro quos. Donations to artists serve as catalysts for cycles of sustained, reciprocal gift-giving that provide patrons with important, yet often exclusively symbolic or non-material rewards and benefits (Komter, 2007).

While artists, on their part, *are* mostly in it to benefit financially, they usually take care to frame their requests for support as essentially disinterested, intended to benefit not them personally but to help enhance the quality of their artistic work, help them make important contributions to the art discipline or genre they are practising, or promote the arts in general (van den Braber, 2024, p. 15). Importantly, for them, too, the sustained exchange of gifts with their patrons tends to yield not just money but vital social, symbolic and other non-material rewards as well. Worldwide current examples of this type of sustained, one-on-one exchange include a contemporary visual artist engaged in a long-term gift relationship with a patron/collector of his work[2] (2021), a performance artist individually funded by a rich theatre enthusiast[3] (2024), three literary authors sustained by two wealthy readers of their work (2024),[4] two individual donors closely collaborating with a film maker in the creation of a film documentary as part of a bigger commitment to patronage (2022)[5] and—a little longer ago—two examples of pop bands bankrolled long-term by an individual well-heeled fan (2000 and 2014).[6] All these artists and patrons are—whether aware of it or not—modern representatives of a long-standing tradition.

In this chapter, I will first give a brief overview of the history of both pre- and post-Romantic arts patronage, before exploring ways of researching patronage exchange. I will do so by highlighting four key aspects, providing a brief synthesis of related conceptual and theoretical arguments for each. One key concept is the issue of *patronage dynamics*. What are the exchange patterns of one-on-one relationships? How—and why—do both parties work at creating a balance of power? This question is taken up further in key issue 2, that of ***exchange and reciprocality***. What is it, exactly, that is exchanged between patrons and artists? How to evaluate what both parties put in and get out of their alliance? What role does the artwork (the object, performance, production, thought or vision created by the artist and enabled by the donor) and its autonomy play in their game of give and take? Another key concept is the issue of ***negotiation***. What have been the negotiation strategies open to artists throughout history? And which 'gift modes' allow them, according to gift theory, to stake out their position? A last key aspect is that of ***gift versus transactionality***. How can artists navigate between the demands of the market economy and those of the gift economy?

It is important to emphasize that for such a large and historically influential cultural practice, remarkably little theorizing has been done. While research on contemporary entrepreneurship and funding models is mostly done in marketing and communication studies, cultural economics or sociology of the arts, most historical patronage research has been undertaken—often independently and without reference to each other's fields—by social historians (Gaehtgens & Schieder, 1998; Kocka & Frey, 1998) and by generations of literary historians, music historians and art historians (Gold, 1982; Kempers, 1992; Chimènes, 2004; Reist, 2022; Tyler, 2017 to name but a few). Their important work has yielded indispensable insights into the nature and context of patronage interaction in past centuries but is mostly based on isolated case studies and tends to be mainly descriptive in nature (Swords, 2017, p. 65). Research attempting to draw conceptual lines between historical and contemporary (one-on-one) patronage practice is very rare. A happy exception is the important work of art historian Jonathan Nelsen and economist Richard Zeckhauser on Renaissance patronage patterns (2008, 2024). A number of social scientists have also considered the subject in its historical dimensions. Some incisively but only briefly (Brewer, 2018); some more extensively (Becker, 1982; Bourdieu, 1986, 1998; Zolberg, 1982). Patronage researchers looking for conceptual models would do well to consult the work of anthropological gift theorists (Gouldner, 1960; Komter, 2005, 2007), gift economists (Kolm, 2008; Velthuis, 2019) or philanthropy researchers (Bekkers & Wiepking, 2011). Their fields—although not focused on historical continuities nor on the arts—pay close and useful attention to the motives of donors and recipients in gift practices.

2 Pre-Romantic Patronage History (Before 1800/1850)

Historically, the term 'arts patronage' has referred broadly to the provision of private funds for creating, organizing or promoting arts and culture by monarchs, church leaders, nobles, wealthy merchants or other representatives of powerful, well-positioned groups (Gaehtgens & Schieder, 1998; Nelson & Zeckhauser, 2008). Artists hold important cultural capital that has historically made it very attractive for patrons to associate with them: they have the ability to create the kind of art that had the power to establish or boost the patron's reputation. In this arrangement, it was typically the patrons who pulled the strings. From late Middle Ages and Renaissance onwards, they were in a position to offer artists commissions or positions at their courts or households, to (partly) determine the style, theme or iconography of their work, and to either accept or reject the dedications or requests artists directed at them (Green, 2019).

Entering into patronage relationships with artists cost money and was not intended to yield economic benefits. Crucially, it enabled patrons to come forward as munificent art promotors, generous and selfless. As a form of 'socially coded gift-giving' (Smith, 2012, p. 54), it brought them strong social and reputational benefits: the strategic display of their relationship with important artists and of their high-quality work enhanced their reputation, helped represent their power, and allowed them to impress friend and foe alike. Yet it was vitally important to conceal these benefits and frame their position as essentially noble and selfless. Smith (2012, p. 54) asserts that pre-Romantic patronage is 'a tacitly coercive and vitally interested process predicated on a fiction that it is free and disinterested'. For many patronage researchers, this intriguing difference between the *practice* and the *representation* of the patronage process makes it such a fascinating and rewarding research topic.

Artists tried to capitalize on this difference by catering both to their benefactor's need to pull the strings in the relationship, and to their wish for public acclaim. In the literary and musical domain, for instance, authors and composers vied for the support of patrons by publicly dedicating their work to an intended benefactor (Green, 2019, p. 2) or by praising and flattering them in the prologue (Tingle, 2020, p. 191). Another strategy was to showcase gratitude and deference in a special, public poem of praise, either before securing their support or afterwards (Tingle, 2020, p. 94). In visual arts, celebrated artists allowed their patrons to signal both their wealth and their refinement by creating prominent, beautifully decorated private chapels in major churches—prime locations that would be visited by the general public as well as by their patron's peers (Nelson & Zeckhauser, 2008, pp. 113–114).

This arrangement highly favoured patrons but presented them also with significant risks. As benefactors, they were precariously dependent on the artists they supported. The art works that were created under their patronage could misrepresent them, be of lower quality than expected, or be delivered late or not at all. The public dedication of mediocre compositions, paintings or texts to their name could be unsolicited or unwelcome. The upkeep of the relationship could require much more or much higher donations than they expected. Or, and this was the greatest risk, the work created under their protection could backfire or offend, and provoke criticism, ridicule or resistance from the very audience they had intended to dazzle and impress (Nelson & Zeckhauser, 2024, p. 35).

Prominent examples of these pre-Romantic patronage dynamics include fourteenth-century royal Anne of Bohemia using her resources and status to patronize the author Chaucer in order to influence her commemoration during and after her own lifetime (Tingle, 2020, p. 173), well-connected Dutch female author Maria Margaretha van Akerlaecken publicly dedicating her works to powerful patrons within the Dutch Republic and abroad—sometimes successfully (Geerdink, 2020, p. 353), and sixteenth-century members of the Medici family signalling the importance of their clan and impressing the Florentine urban elite through the commissioning of works by the best artists of their day (Nelson & Zeckhauser, 2008, pp. 48–49).

3 Post-Romantic Patronage History (After 1800/1850)

Meanwhile, artists' attitudes were changing. Over time, especially after 1800, they began to perceive of the patronage system as oppressive and restrictive as well as supporting and enabling. At the same time, as the power of the church and nobility declined and a commercial market for the arts developed, engaging with a patron became less of a necessity and more of a choice. In the wake of new, Romantic notions of self-awareness, value and autonomy, artists were no longer content with catering to the wishes of a patron; they started to feel that patrons should cater to their wishes instead (Baumol & Baumol, 2002, p. 167). Patronage, as an essentially premodern form of social exchange, had to create new reciprocities if it were not to seem at odds with the modern world (Rainey, 1998, p. 74).

To that end, artists now entered into forms of long-term gift exchange with those well-connected bourgeois lovers of art that they felt were sympathetic to their work and understanding of their artistic mission, carefully selecting the benefactors they chose to engage with (Chimènes, 2004, p. 9; Epstein, 2022, p. 6; Gaehtgens & Schieder, 1998, pp. 13–16; Zolberg, 1982, p. 2). To avoid outdated association with the coercive powerplay of earlier patronage discourses, they sought their benefactors no longer among the very rich or powerful. Instead, they recruited them from the small circle of well-heeled bourgeois art connoisseurs and art lovers that not only frequented their shows, concerts, poetry readings or performances, but also showed a committed love of and belief in the kind of art they and their fellow artists were creating (Kocka & Frey, 1998, p. 84). This type of patron was typically motivated *not* by broader social acclaim, but by a desire to be part of—and acknowledged by—the networks their *protégés* moved in, and to be viewed as a credible enabler of their artistic vision. For artist, the patron's belief in the value of their work became a vital prerequisite. To maintain their credibility, they needed their patrons to be invested in their work without threatening its autonomy. Patrons were expected to offer financial benefits, be their champion and defender, and open up their networks within and outside of the art world (Epstein, 2022; p. 71; Rainey, 1998, p. 34; Wexler, 1997, p. 3). The strategic display of their relationships with these well-heeled insider/connoisseur type of patrons solved artist's financial problems without damaging their legitimacy. It enhanced their reputation in the art world and—crucially—helped them to impress fellow artists, critics, dealers, publishers, impresarios and other art world insiders (Epstein, 2022, p. 19).

Working in a market system made artists less dependent on private support, and this new independence, and a new insistence on non-negotiable artistic autonomy, meant that artists gradually imposed new demands and conditions on their patrons (Balfe, 1993, pp. 306–307; van den Braber, 2021, p. 33). Post-Romantic patrons had to abandon the tactics of tacit coercion of their predecessors. They could no longer treat artists as passive and dependent recipients of top-down commissions and support but needed to approach them as an equal partner in a balanced, reciprocal interaction (Gaehtgens & Schieder, 1998, p. 84). Another condition was that patrons could still take the initiative,[7] and still reap important social and reputational benefits from the arrangement, but were expected to absolutely respect the autonomy of the artist's work. It also remained essential to appear selfless and disinterested—which means that researchers of post-Romantic patronage should remain very alert to the continuing gap between patronage practice and the representation of that practice to the outside world.

While negotiating these and other unwritten rules and conditions, artists and their benefactors carefully and gradually searched for new balance and new reciprocity. Negotiations were by no means without a struggle. Prominent examples of this dynamic include the carefully coded, precarious interactions between French composers, performers and bourgeois music connoisseurs in the Paris salons of the 1880s (Chimènes, 2004), the tentative negotiations between the quietly rebellious Dutch visual artist Gerard Bilders and his meddlesome patron Johannes Kneppelhout around 1880 (Bilders, 2008; van den Braber, 2019); the fraught exchanges between British theatre visionary Edward Gordon Craig and over twenty different European admirers of his work (van den Braber, 2017b, p. 133), and the new modes of authorship European and American modernist writers discovered through their relationship with patron-collectors (Rainey, 1998, pp. 5–6). By the beginning of the twentieth century these new, post-Romantic patronage dynamics had emerged fully, shaping how artists and benefactors could (and could not) balance their relationship—not only in their own time, but, as will be argued below, to this day.

4 Key Aspects

Key Aspect 1: The Issue of Patronage Dynamics

To analyse these patronage dynamics, it is useful to start from a very basic diagram that helps conceptualize the interaction patterns of one-on-one relationships (Fig. 1).

One-on-one patronage relationships always have the production or presentation of an artwork at their centre. The artwork (a painting, a poem, an installation, an exhibition or a performance) enables and

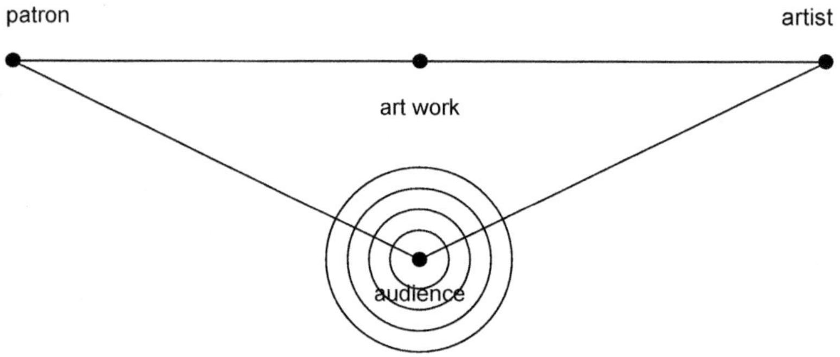

Fig. 1 Basic one-on-one patronage dynamics (*Note* Based on van den Braber [2021, p. 21; 2024, p. 20])

mediates the relationship, but may also polarize, confuse or complicate the exchange (van den Braber, 2021, 2024). Characteristic of patronage exchange is that both parties tend to feel not only responsible *for*, but also a sense of personal ownership *of* what is created between them as a result of their exchange. With artists, this sense of ownership flows logically from their position as the art work's creator; with patrons, it is strongly related to their awareness that without their support, the art works would not have been created at all, or would look or sound different (Becker, 1982, p. 91).

The historical outlines above have made clear that patrons and artist have, across the ages, felt that they can add value to their relationship by making it somehow *visible*. Performing their alliance to an audience symbolically consolidates the relationship and allows both parties to establish or perpetuate their status by signalling their cultural and symbolic capital to their peer groups or networks. This audience, big or small, has the important role of assessing, evaluating and (de)legitimizing the patronage exchange, and to assign (or withdraw) value from the patron, the artist or the artwork accordingly. Without this audience valuation the symbolic gain of patronage exchanges would be smaller, and the alliance less profitable to both patron and artist. When analysing any patronage relationship, it is vital to carefully consider to which audience—big or small—the relationship would be (or would have been, in historical contexts) observable and appreciable, and—different question—towards which audience patron and artist would most want to showcase either the

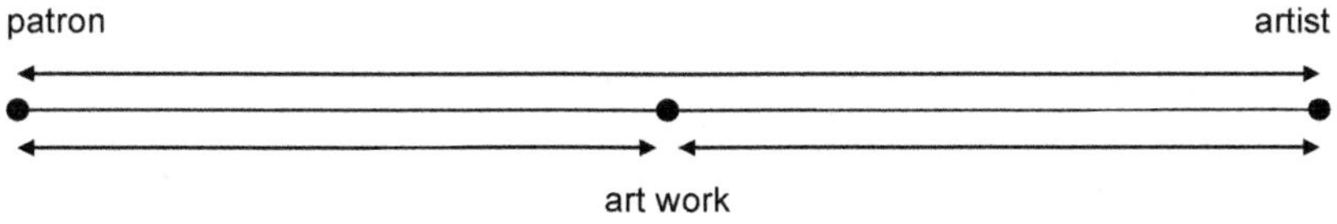

Fig. 2 Full patronage dynamics (*Note* Based on van den Braber [2021, p. 27, following Nelson & Zeckhauser, 2008, p. 17])

relationship or the resulting art works. Nelson and Zeckhauser (2008, p. 17) have argued that patronage dynamics should not be analysed as *binary* (involving patron and artist only) but as *triangular* (involving patron, artist, and audience) (Fig. 2).

The audience circles increasing in size indicate that the audience evaluating the exchange may consist of small peer groups, of wider networks, of society as a whole, or even of future audiences—appreciatively or dismissively looking back upon the exchange (and the resulting art works) in later centuries.

Superficially, the power balance in patronage relationships seems clear enough: the patron donates, and the artist accepts the gift—a form of one-way traffic. However, patronage relationships can only sustainably function if every gift (provided by the patron) is eventually followed by a reciprocal gift (offered by the artist—further elaboration of this exchange below). This pattern of reciprocation is then repeated, and these recurrent cycles of exchange help develop a relationship in which both parties feel, over time, that they benefit roughly equally (Gouldner, 1960). Striking a careful balance is important: the two parties both pursue their own material or symbolic benefit and strive for the continuation and consolidation of the relationship (Komter, 2005, p. 24). Whoever operates too opportunistically or egotistically may achieve the first, but not the second goal; conversely, those who invest too much in the advantages of the other party risk endangering their own benefits. Analysis of historical exchange patterns shows that artists and patrons involved in stable and successful patronage relationships know how to balance these two goals (Hyde, 2007, pp. x–xi; Nelson & Zeckhauser, 2008, p. 37; van den Braber, 2017a, p. 45). The third party—the audience—then assesses whether they feel that the exchange is fair and balanced and does sufficient justice to the position and status of both artist and patron. This is by no means a given.

Audiences (including critics) tend to be very censorious of those relationships that they perceive to be somehow unbalanced, especially those in which privileges seem divided unequally or claimed too explicitly. Hence the recent negative media coverage of American patron/collector Stefan Simchowitz's support of a number of individual visual artists. Critics felt that connoisseur Simchowitz, dubbed the "patron Satan" of the art world by the *New York Times*, may have favoured his protégés, but has also bullied and manipulated them, turning his generosity into a "fatal attraction for young, penniless artists whom he lured into Faustian bargains" (Ruiz, 2021; Westall, 2021).[8] We have seen that new, unwritten rules came to apply to patronage after Romanticism, and this patron violated one of them: Simchowitz clearly failed to treat his protégés as equal partners in a balanced and fair relationship, as had become the norm after 1850. In The Netherlands, controversy arose when pop patron Jan 't Hoen demanded a far-reaching say in the line-up and output of esteemed rock band Wild Romance, in exchange for major donations to the band, adding up to over 200.000 euro. This relationship, critics felt, favoured the patron way too much and did insufficient justice to the status and position of the recipient (De Grefte, 2024).[9] Here another important post-Romantic patronage rule was broken far from rigorously respecting the autonomy of the artist's work, this patron—inappropriately, many felt—put the band's autonomy under severe pressure, claiming undue involvement in the process of creation and asserting influence over the band's oeuvre (van den Braber & Hueting, 2018).

Key Aspect 2. The Issue of Reciprocity

We have seen that fostering and maintaining patronage relationships requires engaging in complex, repeated cycles of exchange. In post-Romantic times—to put it in Bourdieusian terms (Bourdieu, 1986)—patronage involves, in a joint and reciprocal effort, the shift of economic capital (money), social capital (connectivity) and valuation (consecration) from patron to artist, and cultural capital (and its attendant signals of cultural credibility and legitimacy) and valuation (consecration) from artist to patron. This exchange is, like any exchange of gifts, caught up in a cycle of reciprocity. Gift theorist Komter (2005, 2007) and economist Kolm (2008) have argued that in gift relationships the act of reciprocating is of central importance; it fosters and sustains solidarity and connection. As long as the recipient of a gift has not reciprocated, the giver—in this case: the patron—holds a certain power over the recipient. Balance is restored if and when the recipient—in this case: the artist—takes the step of offering a reciprocal gift in return. If this reciprocal gift is of value to the patron, it will prompt the benefactor to offer new gifts, which will require new reciprocal donations from the artist. This pattern of continual 'back and forth' of giving and reciprocating forms a continuous cycle of interdependency that sustains the relationship and builds trust (Gouldner, 1960, p. 164; Hyde, 1983, p. 37; Kolm, 2008, p. 97).[10]

Based on extensive research into exchange patterns after 1850, van den Braber (2021; in press) has shown that post-Romantic artists tend to offer their patrons non-material reciprocal gifts.[11] These come in the form *cultural capital* and *valuation*; both enable artists to help their benefactors experience as well as signal the importance and legitimacy of their role as patron. Artists work at transferring cultural capital to their patrons by allowing them various types of *access* to their artistic practice, expertise and knowledge (Fig. 3).

With the reciprocal gift of *knowledge* artists offer their patrons the exclusive right to know about their creative choices and plans, have insight in their background story or development, or understand their values, ethos or technique. For the type of invested and involved patron prevalent in post-Romantic times, this reciprocal gift is especially valuable; it allows them privileged involvement in the artist's creative universe.

The same applies to the reciprocal gift of access to the work environment or work process of artists. This gift offers benefactors a sense of *proximity* to the act of creation, and to what Walter Benjamin (2008 [1936], p. 13) has called the aura or 'cultic value' of creation itself. Whether this means visiting a studio, being backstage at shows, or dining with the soprano, it allows benefactors to experience the mysterious

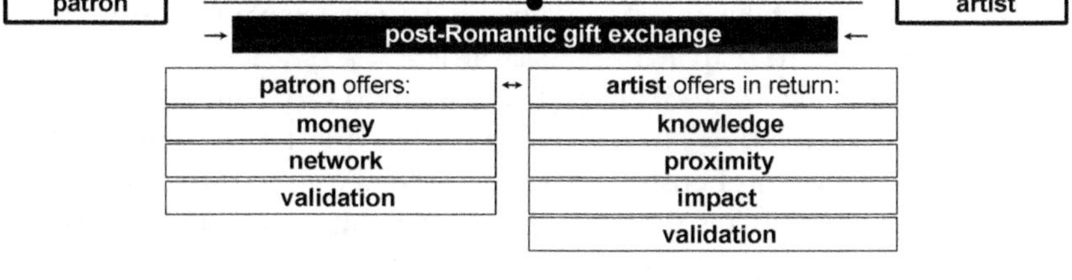

Fig. 3 Partial dynamics of post-romantic gift exchange (*Note* Based on van den Braber [2021, p. 25; 2024, p. 21; in press])

enchantment that lingers around artistic practice and that, as Abbing (2008, p. 288) has argued, is often at the core of post-Romantic patrons' wish to be involved with artists.

The third reciprocal gift is the controversial gift of access to the right to have *impact*: the right to participate in artist's decision-making processes or to exercise a form of controlling ownership over the art work—having a say in the composition of the setlist, in the set-up of the exhibition, or the structure of the sonnet. This can put patrons in the happy position of entering into rewarding forms of co-creation with artists (Hannah, 2015, p. 28), but it can also create tense situations if artists feel that patrons misuse this right to unwelcomely meddle and interfere in their work. We have seen that the issue of autonomy has been pivotal in patronage history: while pre-Romantic patrons could comfortably pull the strings, their post-Romantic counterparts were—and are—expected to absolutely respect the moral and aesthetic vision and autonomy of artists. In case of trespass, the relationship suffers, co-creation breaks down, and the artwork becomes a *contested space*—an unapproachable no-go area for the patron, and a sacred territory that must be defended for the artist (Bourdieu, 1998, p. 238; Hannah, 2015, p. 188).

A last reciprocal gift is the offer of access to important processes of *validation* or meaning-making, by giving patrons a sense of purpose or 'warm glow'. Economist Andreoni (1990) argues that donors gain utility from the act of giving itself, and this assumption is echoed in other research domains: gift theorists Honneth (1995) and Komter (2007) claim that giving enhances the giver's sense of self-respect, psychologists Kahneman and Knetsch (1992) point out the 'contingent value' of giving as "purchase of moral satisfaction", and Smeets et al. (2020, p. 2) argue that the joy of giving has been included in the majority of research in philanthropy studies.

If the transfer of gifts and reciprocal gifts goes well, both parties may—as outlined above—take the step of making their exchange visible to an audience, in order to reap symbolic rewards.

What would Fig. 4 look like if we focused not on post- but on pre-Romantic exchange? The truth is that we don't really know. What is missing is a comprehensive, cross disciplinary literature review that systematically synthesizes insights from existing research on isolated historical cases. A hypothesis would be that before 1850, the ability to offer the reciprocal gift of *impact* would have been a prime asset for artists, and that the gifts of inside *knowledge* and *proximity*—crucially

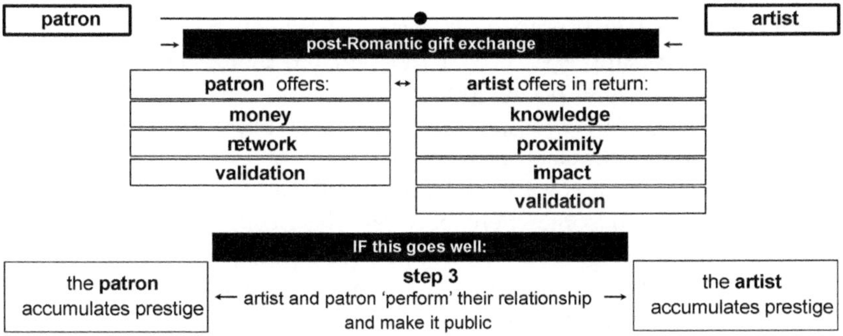

Fig. 4 Full dynamics of post-romantic gift exchange (*Note* Based on van den Braber [2021, p. 35])

important in later centuries to keep the new, 'invested' type of donors on board—would not have been as useful yet. As yet unclear is whether the mutual exchange of the gift of *validation* was as important in pre-Romantic times as it would become later on. What is clear, however, is that the crucial step of 'performing' the relationship to an audience was of prime importance in pre-Romantic times; a firm hypothesis would be that patron and artist aimed for the recognition of a wider, more general public than would be the case later on.

Key Aspect 3: The Issue of Negotiation

At some point in their interaction, patrons and artists enter into negotiations to determine the terms of their exchange. There are many historical examples of both parties entering those negotiations very consciously and deliberately, with full awareness of their aims and expectations; there are also many examples of both sides feeling their way into the exchange and staking out their positions tentatively as they go along. Based on the extensive historical research of van den Braber (2002, 2018, 2021), it seems that after 1850, there have been four clear negotiation strategies open to artists: (a) they can try to control and direct the type of *patron* they (do or do not) engage with; (b) they can control and direct the types of *gifts* that they (do or do not) accept from their patron; (c) they can regulate the types of *reciprocal gifts* that they are (or are not) prepared to offer their benefactors in return or (d) they can try to regulate how patronage relationship is perceived and valuated by (selected) *audiences*.

Regarding the first point (points b, c and d have been discussed above), Zolberg (1982) highlights the prime importance of selecting the right kind of benefactor from 'the pool of possibilities' (2) open to artists. She introduces a useful grid to classify post-Romantic patron types, placing them somewhere between the positions of *status seekers* and *status retainers* on the x-axis, and between *conventional* to *innovative* in artistic taste on the y-axis (16). What all patrons have in common, she argues, is a clear interest in art, a certain availability of means, an evident need for status, and a social environment (big or small) valuing their patronage activities (2). Knowing this, artists hoping to engage with them can leverage each of these attributes and needs to put themselves in the spotlight and solidify their negotiating position.

Yet selecting the right kind of benefactor can be hard. Reflecting on contemporary societal discourse on what it takes to identify a 'good' or legitimate patron, Brewer (2018) argues that

> Historically patronage has been the object of two symbiotically related discourses (…) Since classical antiquity critics, artists and patrons themselves have shaped two exemplary patrons: one with good taste, discernment and discretion, who has nurtured genius and protected skill (…), the other a tasteless, ignorant, interfering and controlling figure (…) whose intervention produces mediocre, compromised or bad work from an alienated client.

The 'bad' or unworthy patron is usually perceived of as all too meddlesome or all too philistine, and the 'good' or exemplary patron as an understanding admirer who is happy to remain in the background. Brewer points out that these double perceptions of the good and bad patron, 'at once enabling and controlling, liberating and inhibiting, facilitating and restricting' have a very long history. Yet it is misleading, he argues, to see them as mutually exclusive. With these archetypes, it is not a question of either—or, but of and—and: they coexist in a symbiotic relationship. Together, they form a powerful cultural framework that shapes conceptions of patronage exchange, both historically and today. These conceptions are constructed first, Brewer argues, through negotiations between artists and patrons themselves, then by the audiences evaluating their exchange, and finally by any academic attempting analysis.

Gift theorist Komter (2005, 2007) proposes a very different take on the issue of negotiation. She organizes the potential positions of donors and recipients into four so-called 'giving modes' (Komter, 2007). She argues that there are four ways in which donors and recipients relate to gifts: through the principle of *community*, *authority*, *equality* or *market* (Komter, 2007, p. 50). For each mode, she presents a set of motives why people—in certain communities, environments or worlds—would or wouldn't engage in either offering or accepting gifts. She also explores their scope for negotiation, and the role that reciprocity and interdependence play in their position-takings. Komter argues that the exchange of gifts can be intended as an expression of love, friendship, respect or the need to care for others (*community*), as an expression of *quid pro quo* or balance (*equality*) or instrumentality (*market*), but also thrives in a less noble context and then may be intended to flatter, manipulate, direct or dominate the other (*authority*) (2007, p. 94).

To researchers analysing the room for negotiation available to artists and patrons, this potentially manipulative or dominating aspect of gift relationships is of extra interest. Recent research shows that for contemporary Dutch artists the fear of having to negotiate with overly meddlesome or intrusive patrons is one of the main reasons for avoiding one-on-one relationships with private benefactors (van den Braber et al., 2025, pp. 26–27). Yet interestingly, Komter explains that that even manipulative gifts can help negotiations between donors and recipients: to the outside world, both parties can use the (controversial) exchange of this type of gifts as valid symbol of the bond that already exists between them, or that they are trying to establish. In this way, each type of gift—even the coercive gift—contributes to their beneficial interdependence.

Key Aspect 4: The Issue of Gift Versus Transaction

It is noteworthy that Komter classifies the instrumental or *market* gift mode (in which the exchange of gifts is intended to deliver more, in the long run, than either party has put in) as a bona fide gift domain. In the context of the arts, we would perhaps be more inclined to view this type of exchange as not philanthropic at all, but as an investment (on the part of the patron) or a market transaction (on the part of the artist). In creative production, entrepreneurial practices and patronage practices have important aspects in common: they are both shaped by artistic as well as economic logics, and they both derive from and build upon the arts sector's timeless and fundamental need for both material and immaterial reward and validation (van den Braber, 2024, p. 2). We have seen that after 1850, patronage as a funding model became largely peripheral, complementing the market model that was becoming more dominant. From then on, if artists wished to combine both models, they had to position themselves as savvy entrepreneurs *and* as worthy recipients of support at the same time. This navigation between market economy and gift economy took (and still takes) some deft manoeuvring. It needs mastering the art of (boldly) selling, but also of (humbly) requesting; of knowing how to persuade potential patrons to not just buy and pay, but to donate or bestow as well.

One of the key debates in patronage research as well as gift theory is whether gifts can function in a context of market exchange. Pierre Bourdieu (1997, p. 231) has pointed out the "dual truth" of the gift: it is imagined as unrequited but functions in a context of exchange. Yet reciprocation seems to invalidate gifts as 'selfless' acts, thereby complicating the notion of disinterestedness (Green, 2019, p. 43). Vecco (2019, p. 87) emphasizes that the shift to market exchange and entrepreneurship after 1850 does not necessarily mean that artists became primarily interested in money and financial success; as 'artpreneurs' they still tried to maximize cultural rather than economic values and were driven by a strong non-monetary internal motivation. This strengthened their position in their interactions with their patrons: a shared belief in the cultural value of their work increased the legitimacy of their requests for support. Abbing (2008, p. 39) claims that 'anti-market values (…) are an important factor in the gift sphere'. However, Velthuis (2019, p. 73) emphasizes that these new, market-oriented attitudes do require specific ways of working and behaving: they call for forms of calculated behaviour and a more formalized, rational relationship with their audiences. In order to successfully ask for help, artists must make sure that audiences—despite the fact that they already have bought a ticket, a cd or a book—still feel 'a sense of guilt, of moral guilt, which prompts [them] to add a gift' (80).

This prompting to feel moral guilt can be awkward for both parties. Individual artists tend to feel some unease at the thought of commodifying the loyalty of their fans and supporters (Baym, 2018, p. 9). Velthuis (2019, p. 78) adds that this sense of moral discomfort stems from a powerful underlying sentiment: the uneasiness felt by both audience and artist in the commercial marketing and selling of objects or experiences they perceive to hold primarily symbolic value, such as music, literature or art. He argues that the marketing and selling of this type of goods can evoke a sense of moral resistance in potential buyers and artists alike. Interestingly, Velthuis suggests that for both parties, entering into gift relationships can help reduce that resistance. To make this happen, artists need to load their gift relationships with 'connotations of friendship based on feelings of gratitude, care, attention or perhaps even love' (83), take care to avoid any suggestion of instrumentality, and conceal all 'commercial connotations of self-interest and calculating behaviour'. Emotional warmth in gift relationships is partly strategy *and* partly sincere. Gifts are about 'the transfer of scarce, valuable resources from one person to another, where the value of those resources is not [and should not be] measured exactly' (77). This aspect of immeasurability is helpful for fostering a viable culture of asking (van den Braber, 2024, p. 7), for it allows artists to help their prospective patrons to put their entrepreneurial price tags in the right perspective. In fact, Velthuis (78) claims, the more they succeed in making their relationships with their potential backers look less like a market relationship, the more successful their gift relationships will become. Gift relationships thrive on indeterminacy, on the grace of what he calls "the ambiguity of the gift" (81): it is advisable, for both parties, not to measure the value of gifts too explicitly.

5 Concluding Remarks

Researchers of contemporary funding models do not often consider the historical roots of those models in their analysis. This is unfortunate, because the way artists deal with and position themselves in those models is often embedded in powerful social, cultural and individual discourses and contexts that have a history that continues to shape their attitudes and behaviour to this day. Current practices of one-on-one patronage interaction are in many ways defined by interaction patterns, values and expectations that go back to influential nineteenth-century notions of how true artists and valid patrons should behave, both towards each other and towards their audiences. Several major historical continuities have been discussed in this chapter, for instance those around the continuing gap between the actual *practice* of patronage, and the way artists and patrons choose to *represent* that practice—both through the works that emerge from their relationship, and in the way they signal that relationship (and their own role in it) to the outside world. Other noteworthy continuities include the continuing importance—for artists, patrons and any researcher analysing their interaction—to recognize and deal with the ambiguity and indeterminacy of the material and symbolic returns of patronage relationships; the enduring benefit for patrons and artist of signalling cultural legitimacy and disinterestedness instead of calculation, and the continuing importance of aiming at long-term exchange and reciprocity instead of at ad hoc profit.

Notes

1. Interestingly, Bonifacio et al. (2023) suggest that individual artists in their crowd patronage efforts, too, tend to gear more and more towards long-term career support rather than short-term projects.
2. Mexican–American artist Ken Taylor entered into a long-term support relationship with American patron-collector Stefan Simchowitz around 2021 (Ruiz, 2021; Westall, 2021).
3. Dutch theatre director Eric Whien received a personal gift of 50.000 euro from theatre aficionado and long-time fan Marcelle Kuipers in 2024. Kuipers insisted that Whien use the money to "just be bored, without worry" and create some free space between performances (Janssens, 2024).
4. UK patrons Sam and Rosie Berwick supported three low income London writers in 2024 with generous early career bursaries (Berwick, 2024); they will continue their support to authors over the next three years (Brown, 2024).
5. In 2022, French film maker Marie Voignier co-created her film "I Like Politics Too" with her private benefactors Soar Gueron and Fanny Spano as part of a larger initiative called 'The New Patrons' (http://www.nouveauxcommanditaires.eu/en/44/protocol).
6. New York band LCD Soundsystem were supported substantially and extensively by their wealthy supporter Tyler Brodie around 2000 (Goodman, 2011), and from 2014 onwards—up to this day—Dutch real estate investor Jan 't Hoen has been donating a six figure sum to rock band The Wild Romance, claiming a permanent role as the band's drummer as a return gift (https://www.imdb.com/title/tt12006864/; van den Braber & Hueting, 2018).
7. In the first decades of the twentieth century patrons sometimes acted collectively rather than on their own, establishing small, informal giving circles to collectively offer support to individual artists. Around 1921, author-patron Ezra Pound brought together

a group of patrons to support poet T. S. Eliot (Materer, 1991), and in 1933 a group of admirers of avantgarde theatre visionary Gordon Craig organized the international *Cercle des Admirateurs et Amis de Edward Gordon Craig* (van den Braber, 2018).

8. KIRAC/Keeping it real art critics addressed Simchowitz' tactics in a critical documentary (KIRAC 2017).
9. Another example: the lavish donations of the controversial Sackler family to a number of UK museums led critics to doubt the balance of the exchange and the legitimacy of the status the Sacklers derived from their patronage. In 2022, artist Nan Goldin released the documentary *All the beauty and the bloodshed* about the Sackler family's position (https://www.imdb.com/title/tt21374850/).
10. There are many examples of long-term post-Romantic relationships involving numerous cycles of reciprocal giving: Irish author James Joyce engaged with his patron Harriet Shaw Weaver between 1917 and 1942 (Crozier 2022, pp. 48–49; Lidderdale & Nicholson, 1971), American patron Elize Hall supported conductor Georges Longy between 1898 and 1922 (Bertels, 2024), and German patron Max Linde supported painter Edvard Munch between 1902 and 1914 (Meyer, 1999).
11. Additionally, they may also offer small material tokens of limited economic value, such as a single copy of their new books, cd's or exhibition catalogues (Dalla Chiesa, 2021, p. 88; van den Braber et al., 2025, p. 25), or offer one-of-a-kind gifts of a certain collectors' value, such as first editions, handwritten manuscripts, musical scores or preliminary sketches (Rainey, 1998, 69).

References

Abbing, H. (2008). *Why Are Artists Poor?: The Exceptional Economy of the Arts.* Amsterdam University Press.

Andreoni, J. (1990). Impure Altruism and Donations to Public Goods: A Theory of Warm-Glow Giving. *The Economic Journal, 100*(401), 464.

Balfe, J. (Ed.) (1993), *Paying the Piper. Causes and Consequences of Art Patronage.* University of Illinois Press.

Baumol, H., & Baumol, W. (2002). Maledizione! Or the Perilous Prospects of Beethoven's Patrons. *Journal of Cultural Economics, 26*(3), 167–184.

Baym, N. (2018). *Playing to the Crowd: Musicians, Audiences, and the Intimate Work of Connection*. New York University Press.

Becker, H. S. (1982). *Art Worlds*. University of California Press.

Bekkers, R., & Wiepking, P. (2011). A Literature Review of Empirical Studies of Philanthropy: Eight Mechanisms That Drive Charitable Giving. *Nonprofit and Voluntary Sector Quarterly, 40*(5), 924–973.

Benjamin, W. (2008, originally 1936). *The Work of Art in the Age of Mechanical Reproduction*. Penguin.

Bertels, K. (2024), Paying and Playing? Elise Hall and Patronage in the Early Twentieth Century. In Bertels, K. & Honnold, A. (Eds.), *The Legacy of Elise Hall. Contemporary Perspectives on Gender and the Saxophone*. Leuven University Press.

Berwick, S. (2024, March 7). *By Supporting Writers and Artists, We Hope to Ensure a Rich and Diverse Cultural Heritage for Future Generations*. The Beacon Collaborative. https://www.beaconcollaborative.org.uk/we-support-writers-and-artists-to-ensure-a-rich-cultural-heritage-for-future-generations

Bilders, G. (2008). *Johannes Kneppelhout (1814–1885) en Gerard Bilders (1838–1865), brieven en dagboek*. Waanders.

Bonifacio, R., Hair, L., & Wohn, D. Y. (2023). Beyond Fans: The Relational Labor and Communication Practices of Creators on Patreon. *New Media & Society, 25*(10), 2684–2703.

Bourdieu, P. (1986). The Forms of Capital. In J. Richardson (Ed.), *Handbook of Theory and Research for the Sociology of Education* (pp. 241–258). Greenwood.

Bourdieu, P. (1997). Marginalia—Some Additional Notes on the Gift. In A. D. Schrift (Ed.), *The Logic of the Gift: Towards an Ethic of Generosity*. Routledge.

Bourdieu, P. (1998). Is a Disinterested Gift Possible? In P. Bourdieu (Ed.), *Practical Reason. On the Theory of Action* (pp. 75–91). Stanford University Press.

Brewer, J. (2018, December 14). Patronage: Beyond the Panegyric and the Jeremiad. Brewer's Blog. https://brewersblog.org/

Brown, L. (2024, September 11). London Writers Awards to Return in 2025 Thanks to £50k Donation. *The Bookseller*. https://www.thebookseller.com/news/london-writers-awards-to-return-in-2025-thanks-to-50k-donation

Chimènes, M. (2004). *Mécènes et musiciens. Du salon au concert à Paris sous la IIIe republique*. Fayard.

Crozier, W. R. (2022). Motivations for Patronage: Early Modernist Literature as a Case Study. *European Journal of Language and Culture Studies, 1*(6), 41–51.

Dalla Chiesa, C. (2021). *Crowdfunding Culture Bridging Arts and Commerce* [Dissertation]. Erasmus University Rotterdam.

de Grefte, E. (2024, December 9). Jan 't Hoen kocht de Wild Romance [Jan 't Hoen Has Bought the Wild Romance']. *De Volkskrant*. https://www.volkskrant.nl/cs-b459c3a5/

Epstein, L. K. (2022). *The Creative Labor of Music Patronage in Interwar France*. Boydell & Brewer.

Gaehtgens, T. W., & Schieder, M. (1998). *Mäzenatisch Handeln. Studien zur Kultur des Bürgersinns in der Gesellschaft*. Fannei und Walz.

Geerdink, N. (2020). Economic Advancement and Reputation Strategies: Seventeenth-Century Dutch Women Writing for Profit. *Renaissance Studies, 34*(3), 345–527.

Gold, B. K. (Ed.). (1982). *Literary and Artistic Patronage in Ancient Rome*. University of North Carolina Press.

Goodman, L. (2011). *Meet Me in the Bathroom. Rebirth and Rock and Roll in New York City, 2001–2011*. HarperCollins.

Gouldner, A. W. (1960). The Norm of Reciprocity: A Preliminary Statement. *American Sociological Review, 25*(2), 161–178.

Green, E. H. (2019). *Dedicating Music, 1785–1850*. University of Rochester Press.

Hannah, M.N. (2015). *Networks of Modernism: Toward a Theory of Cultural Production* [Dissertation]. University of Oregon. https://hdl.handle.net/1794/19663

Honneth, A. (1995, originally 1992). *The Struggle for Recognition: The Moral Grammar of Social Conflicts*. Polity Press.

Hyde, L. (2007, originally 1983). *The Gift: Creativity and the Artist in the Modern World*. Vintage.

Janssens, S. (2024, February 7). Theatermaker Erik Whien ontvangt Stichting Melanie stipendium van 50.000 euro. *De volkskrant*. https://www.volkskrant.nl/cs-bb73b696/

Kahneman, D., & Knetsch, J. L. (1992). Valuing Public Goods: The Purchase of Moral Satisfaction. *Journal of Environmental Economics and Management, 22*(1), 57–70.

Kempers, B. (1992). *Painting, Power and Patronage. The Rise of the Professional Artist in Renaissance Italy*. Allen Lane/Penguin.

KIRAC/Keeping it real art critics. (2017, July 2). *The Art of Stefan Simchowitz* [Video]. YouTube. https://www.youtube.com/watch?v=dK5zh8ZTKO0.

Kocka, J., & Frey, M. (Eds.). (1998). *Bürgerkultur und Mäzenatentum im 19. Jahrhundert*. Fannei und Walz.

Kolm, S. (2008). *Reciprocity. An Economics of Social Relations*. Cambridge University Press.

Komter, A. (2005). *Social Solidarity and the Gift*. Oxford University Press.

Komter, A. (2007). Gifts and Social Relations. The Mechanisms of Reciprocity. *International Sociology, 22*(1), 93–107.

Lidderdale, J., & Nicholson, M. (1971). *Dear Miss Weaver: Harriet Shaw Weaver 1876–1961.* Viking.

Liebregts, M. (2023). *Behind the Red and the Green: Unraveling the history of the Loeb Classical Library (1911–1939)* [Dissertation]. Radboud University Nijmegen. https://hdl.handle.net/2066/297296

Materer, T. (Ed.). (1991). *The Selected Letters of Ezra Pound to John Quinn: 1915–1924.* Duke University Press.

Meyer, C. (1999). Max Linde, MD, a Luebeck Ophthalmologist and Patron of Edvard Munch. *Survey of Ophthalmology, 43*(6), 525–534.

Nelson, J., & Zeckhauser, R. (2008). *The Patron's Payoff: Conspicuous Commissions in Italian Renaissance Art*. Princeton University Press.

Nelson, J., & Zeckhauser, R. (2024). *Risks in Renaissance art: Production, Purchase, and Reception.* Cambridge University Press.

Rainey, L. (1998). *Institutions of Modernism: Literary Elites and Public Culture.* Yale University Press.

Reist, I. (Ed.). (2022). *When Michelangelo Was Modern: Collecting, Patronage and the Art Market in Italy, 1450–1650.* Brill.

Ruiz, C. (2021, March 5). Poacher Turned Gamekeeper? Art World 'Disruptor' Stefan Simchowitz Opens Los Angeles gallery. *The Art Newspaper*. https://www.theartnewspaper.com/2021/03/05/poacher-turned-gamekeeper-art-world-disruptor-stefan-simchowitz-opens-los-angeles-gallery

Smeets, P., Whillans, A., Bekkers, R., & Norton, M.I. (2020). Time Use and Happiness of Millionaires: Evidence From the Netherlands. *Social Psychological and Personality Science 11*(3) 295–307. https://doi.org/10.1177/1948550619854751

Smith, H. (2012). *'Grossly Material Things' Women and Book Production in Early Modern England.* Oxford University Press. https://doi.org/10.1093/acprof:oso/9780199651580.001.0001

Swords, J. (2017). Crowd-Patronage—Intermediaries, Geographies and Relationships in Patronage Networks. *Poetics, 64*, 63–73.

Tingle, L. (2020). Literary Patronage. In *Chaucer's Queens. Royal Women, Intercession, and Patronage in England, 1328–1394* (pp. 173–199). Palgrave Macmillan.

Tyler, E. M. (2017). *England in Europe: English Royal Women and Literary Patronage, c.1000–c.1150.* University of Toronto Press.

van den Braber, H. M. (2002). *Geven om te krijgen. Literair mecenaat in Nederland tussen 1900 en 1940 [To give and to get. Literary patronage in The Netherlands between 1900 and 1940].* Vantilt.

van den Braber, H. M. (2017a). Reciprocal Interactions and Complex Negotiations: Three Nineteenth-Century Models of Patronage. *European Journal of English Studies, 21*(1), 43–60. https://doi.org/10.1080/13825577.2016.1274544

van den Braber, H. M. (2017b). My Intention Is Just to Entertain You a Little...: The Patronage Relationship Between Edward Gordon Craig and Marguerite Caetani. In M. Tortora (Ed.), *Il Novecento di Marguerite Caetani* (pp. 133–144). Storia e Letteratura.

van den Braber, H. M. (2021). *From Maker to Patron (and back): On Gift Exchange in the Arts* [Inaugural Lecture]. Utrecht University. https://www.uu.nl/sites/default/files/2020-01-19_Oratie-Helleke-van-den-Braber-ENGELSTALIG.pdf

van den Braber, H. M. (in press). Patron Saint or Patron Satan? Perceptions of Autonomy in Modern Patronage Interaction. In A. Schramme et al. (Eds.), *Does Autonomy Exist*? Routledge.

van den Braber, H. M. (2017). Reciprocal interactions and complex negotiations: three nineteenth-century models of patronage. *European Journal of English Studies 21*(1) 43–60. https://doi.org/10.1080/13825577.2016.1274544

van den Braber, H. M., & Hueting, R. J. G. (2018, March 22). Welke ruimte willen we rijke rockliefhebbers geven? [What Leeway Will We Allow Rich Rock Lovers?]. *De Volkskrant*. https://www.volkskrant.nl/cs-ba5e4d22/

van den Braber, H. M., et al. (2024). The Anxiety of Asking: Entrepreneurial and Patronage Practices in the Creative Sector. In A. Schramme (Ed.), *Cultural Philanthropy and Entrepreneurship* (pp. 13–27). Routledge.

van den Braber, H. M., Hueting, R. J. G., & van Korven, I. (2025). *Een vinger of een hele hand? Hoe makers zoeken naar balans in hun relatie met particuliere gevers*. [Onderzoeksrapport Leve het Geven 2]. Platform ACCT/Voordekunst. https://www.voordekunst.nl/uploads/medialib/Rapportage_2_Leve_het_geven_-_Drempels.pdf

Vecco, M. (2019). The "Artpreneur". Between traditional and cultural entrepreneurship. A historical perspective. In: W. Byrnes & A. Brkić (Eds), *The Routledge Companion to Arts Management*. Routledge.

Velthuis, O. (2019). Geven om geld. Waarom de marktsamenleving giftrelaties nodig heeft [Giving for Money. Why the Market Society Needs Gift Relationships]. *Sociologie, 15*(1), 69–85. https://doi.org/10.5117/SOC2019.1.004.VELT

Westall, M. (2021, May 3). Ken Taylor "If a Flag Can Reveal the Wind, I Like to Think a Painting Can Reveal the Soul." *FAD Magazine*. https://fadmagazine.com/2021/05/03/ken-taylor-if-a-flag-can-reveal-the-wind-i-like-to-think-a-painting-can-reveal-the-soul/

Wexler, J. P. (1997). *Who Paid for Modernism? Art, Money, and the Fiction of Conrad, Joyce, and Lawrence*. University of Arkansas Press.

Zolberg, V. (1982). *New Art, New Patrons: Coincidence or Causality in the Twentieth Century Avant Garde*. Purdue University.

Open Access This chapter is licensed under the terms of the Creative Commons Attribution 4.0 International License (http://creativecommons.org/licenses/by/4.0/), which permits use, sharing, adaptation, distribution and reproduction in any medium or format, as long as you give appropriate credit to the original author(s) and the source, provide a link to the Creative Commons license and indicate if changes were made.

The images or other third party material in this chapter are included in the chapter's Creative Commons license, unless indicated otherwise in a credit line to the material. If material is not included in the chapter's Creative Commons license and your intended use is not permitted by statutory regulation or exceeds the permitted use, you will need to obtain permission directly from the copyright holder.

CHAPTER 6

Copyright's Contribution to Rewarding Creators and the Digitalisation Paradox

Christian Handke

1 Introduction

Copyright automatically applies to a vast array of creative expressions. The copyright system[1] influences, who enjoys access to copyrighted works, who gets to copy and disseminate, and who gets to generate derivative works. Copyright also affects, whose creative efforts get acknowledged, how works and licenses to use them are traded, and what share of the revenues flow back to creators. The copyright system thus also plays a pivotal role in the process of digitalisation throughout the copyright industries.

Digital information and communication technology (ICT) facilitates reproduction, dissemination, product searches, and modification of copyrighted works. Technically, digital representations of the bulk of extant works are at the fingertips of anyone who has access to the Internet. The potential for exploiting works and generating value is enormous. However, from an economic perspective, rational copyright policy ought

C. Handke (✉)
Erasmus University Rotterdam, Rotterdam, The Netherlands
e-mail: handke@eshcc.eur.nl

© The Author(s) 2026

C. Dalla Chiesa and A. Rykkja (eds.), *Cultural Funding and Financing*, Cultural Economics & the Creative Economy,
https://doi.org/10.1007/978-3-031-96696-5_6

to strike an adequate balance between various interests. This chapter takes stock of divergent interests and options on how to reconcile them, with specific emphasis on creators. It also discusses the interface between the copyright system and recent technological developments, from the emergence of online platforms to blockchain, crowdfunding, and generative artificial intelligence (AI).

The chapter develops two main, somewhat contradictory themes. First, with the diffusion of digital ICT and platform services, the boundaries between producers and users have become more blurred. Successful creators often benefit from value co-creation with amateurs and active users. To cultivate such symbiotic interactions, creators may often benefit from ceding de facto control and putting less emphasis on copyright enforcement and immediate financial rewards. Second, digitalisation is associated with the emergence of highly integrated online platforms, who enjoy considerable market power and exert centralised control over much of the copyright industries. In this context, more robust defences of creators' interests are required. It seems that creators and their representatives must master the art of becoming more flexible in some of their interactions and tougher in others. Arguably, that is a central conundrum in reforming current copyright systems.

2 Basic Economics

Generating valuable copyright works requires scarce resources. [2] Creators face considerable entrepreneurial risk: they have to amortise the fixed and partially sunk costs of creation with market revenues, which only transpire after the full costs of creation have been incurred and the work is released to market. What is more, demand for copyright works is notoriously difficult to predict (Baumol, 1986; Caves, 2000). An important issue for creators and their partners in the copyright industries is thus risk management.

The legal institution of copyright law sets out to address a different challenge. Effective copyright protection reduces market failure due to the attributes of creative works as quasi-public goods (Arrow, 1970; Novos & Waldman, 1984). Important aspects of copyrighted works are that they tend to be non-rival in consumption: the use by other parties hardly compromises the availability of the same work to an agent. Works are also non-excludable, meaning that it is relatively costly to enforce exclusive, quasi-property rights. Thus, works can give rise to substantial positive externalities, where some of their benefits accrue to parties, who do not pay creators and other investors. Without effective copyright protection, the expectation is that the supply of new works would fall below the socially adequate level.

An effective copyright system establishes exclusive rights to make use of works or to license others to do so. Rightsholders thus enjoy a monopoly.[3] Without license/express consent by the rightsholder, no other party is allowed to supply (reproduce and disseminate) the same work without running the risk of litigation. Copyright puts rightsholders in a position to charge prices higher than the miniscule marginal costs of providing another party with access (miniscule at least where digital representations of works are concerned). Creators then have a greater chance of recovering the costs of creation (Towse et al., 2008; Watt, 2000).

As any economist will immediately add, monopolies are associated with another type of market failure due to market power: prices in excess of marginal costs leave users worse off and exclude those potential users, who have a willingness to pay greater than marginal costs but lower than the monopoly price.

However, it is misleading to address this as a straightforward trade-off between creator and user interests. On the one hand, while copyright protection can foster creators' revenues it can also increase their costs (Landes & Posner, 1989). Virtually all creators draw on ideas encapsulated in other peoples' copyright works. With broad and effective copyright protection, current creators either must work around other rightsholders' intellectual property, arrange for a license, or risk litigation. This ambiguous effect of copyright for current creators is a central concern in this chapter.

On the other hand, users are not necessarily better off without copyright protection, either. Users may be better off in the short run, when they enjoy unrestricted access to extant work, but in the long run, users may be worse off should the supply of new valuable works dry up (Handke, 2018). The optimal solution hinges on the discounted current value of any additional works that will come about in the future due to copyright protection. That is one difficult concept to measure.

Overall, the copyright system can be justified as a means to foster the allocation of scarce resources for creativity. In contrast to public provision or direct subsidies, copyright does not replace market mechanisms. It rather seeks to enable markets by establishing exclusive and thus tradable rights (Towse, 1997). In the following, we build on these foundations and complement them with other relevant aspects of generic economics, such as transaction costs, and some specific subjects in cultural economics (the economics of arts and culture), such as intrinsic motivation to create or socially interdependent demand formation.

3 Stakeholders and Industrial Organisation Issues

Copyright industries exhibit considerable complexity (Handke, 2024). For instance, creators often supply several complementary products. They supply various product variants, say different literary texts or different musical compositions. Creators regularly also supply—or license others to supply—various types of goods, for instance original works of authorship, performances, or merchandise. The value chain of copyright industries also exhibits a division of labour, where various functions are conducted within separate organisations. Furthermore, the contracts, which arrange for the cooperation along the value chain and transfer copyrights, contain many scalable elements. This does not only regard prices and modes of payment (e.g.: lump sum advances or revenue sharing), but also the duration of contracts, exclusivity arrangements and territorial scope, termination and resell rights, non-disclosure agreements, and so on. Contract partners of creators also commonly provide in-kind support, such as promotion services to maximise demand for works, in return for some transfer of copyright. The value of these complementary services often exceeds the monetary payments to creators stipulated in a contract.

Overall, there is great scope for diverse experimentation and variety in creators' and other stakeholders' strategies to maximise aggregate rewards from cooperation as well as constant squabbles about the division of rewards among various stakeholders (Vogel, 2020). The copyright system plays a pivotal role.

Market Power, Moral Rights, Inalienability, and Regulations Regarding Fair Remuneration

Creators are at the heart of copyright policy.[4] However, the division of labour in copyright industries is such that specific functions (creation, reproduction, promotion, distribution, and retail) are regularly conducted by separate organisations. Exploitation (copy)rights are tradable assets, and permanent sales or temporary licenses are the goods that generate the bulk of the income of many creators. A consequence of trading is that rightsholders are often not creators themselves, but intermediary firms such as publishers, who acquired rights from the original creators.

Intermediary firms tend to be much more integrated than creators (Caves, 2000). Creators often operate in small, temporary teams, and have limited capacity to engage with several creative projects without compromising quality. Intermediaries often specialise on functions with considerable economies of scale and scope, so that they can efficiently engage with larger volumes of works at the same time. An extreme example are online retailing platforms such as Spotify for recorded music, as well as Netflix or YouTube for audiovisual entertainment. This division of labour can be rationalised as a response to different minimum efficient scales for various functions in the copyright industries, fostering productive efficiency. There is also much concern with the exploitation of market power and asymmetrical information favouring highly integrated intermediaries, when they directly trade with individual creators.

The apparent need to protect creators in this context has justified why in many countries, copyright law regularly defines some 'moral rights' regarding the attribution of authors and performers and modification rights as inalienable (Landes & Posner, 1989). That means creators cannot (be made to) cede them to other parties against payment. Many national copyright systems even stipulate 'fair remuneration' of creators, who are the original rightsholders, as an inalienable right. From an economic perspective, such inalienable rights are an ambiguous means to benefit creators.

Regarding moral rights, attribution ensures creators are easily recognizable. However, at times creators may rather avoid attribution when 'their' works are used in disagreeable contexts (say a contentious political rally), or when others alter and distort aspects of their works (say in user-generated content). Modification rights, or rather the right to veto alterations of a finished copyright work, protect creators from haphazard changes to works they are associated with. Attribution rights and exclusive modification rights can help creators develop and sustain a positive reputation over time and foster demand across all products they supply.

However, contract partners' willingness to pay will be reduced if creators retain some decision rights. As Caves (2000) discussed, inalienable rights may even be associated with hold-up problems, where creators can act opportunistically and insist on contract revisions in their favour (higher payments or other perks) for not invoking their de facto veto, after a contract partner has invested money or other resources herself. Such problems may be particularly virulent for complex copyright works, such as feature films or technically sophisticated video games, where dozens or hundreds of creators contribute. 'Total buy-outs' that transfer all relevant rights from a creator to another party are thus often permitted after all.[5] Furthermore, the potential for lucrative repeat transactions with the same partners and the need to develop a positive image within the industry can also reduce creators' incentives to (ab)use the power that moral rights provisions in copyright law endow them with.

Fair remuneration arrangements can take different shapes. In some territories, unions or collective copyright management organizations (CMOs) set minimum prices. However, many creators are intrinsically motivated or enjoy non-pecuniary rewards such as peer recognition (Caves, 2000; Frey & Jegen, 2001; Throsby, 2001; Towse, 1997). The plethora of so-called user-generated content online, which often entails little prospects of any immediate pecuniary rewards, provides some illustration. Furthermore, creators may expect to gain in protracted or indirect ways, by gradually building up a reputation if they capture some level of initial attention, or by supplying complementary goods and services, such as consultancy or tuition after they demonstrated their creative skills.[6] Minimum prices seek to protect professional creators from heedless price competition and exploitation by powerful negotiation partners.[7] They can also exclude some intrinsically motivated creators or newcomers.[8]

Uncertainty, Transaction Costs, and CMOs

Besides demand uncertainty, another issue to do with incomplete information and complexity is transaction costs. Creators regularly supply various product variants and related goods and services. End-users have taste for variety, that is they appreciate access to several copyright works over relatively short periods of time. In addition, marginal costs of providing another user with access are regularly low, and so are retail prices for non-exclusive access due to the presence of many different works that are often close substitutes for one another. Therefore, in reasonably efficient markets for copyright works, many mutually beneficial transactions will take place per market participant over time. However, a limiting factor are transaction costs, the costs of conducting mutually beneficial exchanges.

Let's distinguish three types of transaction costs in markets for copyright works (cf. Williamson, 1979).[9] First, there are search costs to identify attractive goods and services and their suppliers. Regarding the demand side, creative works have experience good attributes, meaning that users cannot fully foresee the relative utility they will enjoy from any specific work before fully engaging with it. Users make irreversible decisions on what specific works to consider, purchase, and engage with under incomplete information. To ensure that they end up with reasonably adequate choices, users typically complement experimental, utility-revealing consumption with limited product searches.[10] Users regularly consider signals of quality not only from—inevitably biased—advertising and promotion by suppliers themselves, but also from professional critics and awards, or from other users through word-of mouth from acquaintances, from end-user reviews online, or simply from indicators of use such as sales ranks, for instance. Thus, demand develops in a socially interdependent processes, which can give rise to herd behaviour. Socially interdependent demand formation may explain two reliable observations: first, high concentration of attention and demand on a small minority of works and creators, which are hard to explain with any apparent differences in quality (so-called superstar effects); second, relatively frequent, pronounced and largely unpredictable changes in demand, also often referred to as fads and fashions (cf. Handke & Dalla Chiesa, 2022). Much of the copyright industries' organisation can be explained with users seeking to acquire and process adequate pre-purchase information, and suppliers seeking to disseminate quality signals regarding the works they supply.

Second, there are bargaining and contracting costs to establish mutually acceptable transaction terms. Neither side in a transaction has an incentive to reveal its full willingness to pay or accept upfront. In addition, contracts between creators and their contract partners have many dimensions, which jointly determine the expected value for each side in a transaction. In this respect, money clearly isn't the only concern. Bargaining can be a costly and protracted process.

Third, there are monitoring and enforcement costs. Caves (2000) discusses rife asymmetric information problems in creative industries. Compared to creators, highly integrated intermediaries have more direct and earlier access to information on many deals and revenue streams, which they can use to their own advantage. Not all creators studied accounting and finance, as Mick Jagger of the Rolling Stones did at

London School of Economics.[11] On the other hand, creative processes and works can hardly be evaluated against some objectively measurable minimum standards. Only the creator will know whether she is doing the best she can to meet the expectations of contract partners. Thus, at least regarding intermediaries, who provide upfront finance or in-kind support to creators, Caves (2000) speaks of 'symmetric ignorance', even though each party of course tends to enjoy information advantages regarding different relevant aspects regarding the cooperation between creators and their business partners.

A particularly vexing issue in the copyright industries has to do with the non-excludability of works. For rightsholders, it may not be sufficient to monitor only the extent to which known contract partners adhere to agreements. Ideally, they would also monitor potential unauthorised users and—if necessary—enforce legal conduct and copyright compliance. That goes well beyond the means of virtually any individual creator.

Overall, transaction costs inhibit trading. Compared to an imaginary frictionless market, with transaction costs fewer mutually beneficial interactions take place[12] and there is lower diversity of supply, suppliers, demand and users.

In principle, there are three main methods to reduce average transaction costs in complex markets. The first is integration of suppliers of transaction services, which are essentially information goods. As such, they regularly have high fixed costs and low, non-increasing marginal costs, which entails economies of scale and scope—a larger supplier will have lower, quality-adjusted average costs. The second is setting standard terms, reducing the average bargaining costs per transaction. At the same time, standards can hardly provide a close match to the interests of all creators and all couplings between creators and specific intermediaries or users. What is more, standards are associated with centralised control, and whoever gets to determine standards enjoys market power. The third method to reduce average transaction costs is bundling, reducing the number of transactions across a population of agents, who conduct more than one transaction per accounting period. An obvious adverse effect of bundling are delays in revenue streams to creators. Furthermore, the central bundling agent may inadvertently or deliberately distort the proportion of revenues that creators receive.

Indeed, we see very high levels of integration among suppliers of transaction services throughout copyright industries. So-called CMOs are a case in point, such as Gema in Germany or ASCAP in the USA

(Handke, 2014). Such organisations started springing up over a century ago across the highly developed economies. They jointly administer some rights to the repertoire of many rightsholders, who otherwise compete with each other. CMOs are often not-for-profit organisations controlled by rightsholders—hence the term 'collective'. CMOs entertain databases of works and rightsholders, offer copyright licenses under standardised and transparent terms for huge repertoires of works, monitor usage of specific works, collect royalty payments from license takers, and distribute revenues among rightsholders roughly proportional to usage data after covering their operating costs. This is an extreme case of standardisation and bundling: within the realm of CMOs, license takers and rightsholders each have one direct transaction partner only, the CMO.[13]

Some CMOs also collectively bargain on behalf of the participating rightsholders with outside intermediaries (some intermediaries, such as publishers or record companies are also CMO members) and users. They thus reduce price competition between rightsholders, who instead focus more on (monopolistic) competition based on the differentiated attributes of the products they supply. This may look awkward from an economic perspective but recall that the very point of the copyright system is already to give creators a respite from heedless price competition. The question is whether CMOs push that protection too far, and whether public regulation and arbitration processes are sufficient to come to standard terms that strike a reasonable balance with the interests of license takers, so that the entire copyright industries can thrive.

Interestingly, CMOs are a type of two-sided platform, which is a business model that has received a lot of attention of late. On the one hand, CMOs are not conventional traders, who would purchase copyrights from creators or other rightsholders (as for instance publishers do) and sell or rent rights or related products to other parties. CMOs do not commit to any upfront or guaranteed later payments to rightsholders and do not acquire copyrights outright. Instead, they offer transaction services and take a cut from the revenues that come about with their help. On the other, CMOs exploit indirect network effects: the value of their services for license takers increases in the number of participating rightsholders and vice versa. In this fundamental sense, CMOs have operated in a similar manner as online platforms such as Amazon, Spotify, Netflix or Ticketmaster, who will be discussed below.

4 Current Developments and Challenges

Digitalisation has broad and profound effects on the CCI, and the copyright system is a major influence on this development. In this section, we discuss basic themes in this interaction between the copyright system and specific aspects of recent technological change in the copyright industries from the perspective of creators.[14]

Unauthorised Use and Costly Countermeasures

A first major impact of ICT diffusion among private households has been a swift increase in unauthorised use of copyright works.[15] For now, the emergence of online platforms for disseminating creative works seems to have reduced the prevalence of and concerns with unauthorized copying and dissemination for private consumption purposes, and the 'rogue' platforms that deliberately facilitate such processes. Despite the availability of the 'piracy' option in most affluent societies, private users have flocked to such authorised sites, where they often pay subscription fees but also with their 'eyeballs', when they are exposed to advertising, by deliberately providing commentary, or by less deliberately allowing for the collection and exploitation of personal data. Making these authorised services more attractive than piracy seems like an elegant solution. Nonetheless, the prices and other conditions that creators and rightsholders can bargain for with online platforms (and by extension end-users) may be quite low because of the 'outside option' of piracy. We further discuss commercial online platforms below.

Copyright Limitations, the Public Domain, and User-Generated Content

Any copyright system entails limitations to copyrights, such as the limited duration of exclusive rights and some minimum threshold of originality. As mentioned above, one point of copyright limitations is to thin out the thicket of copyrights and licensing processes that current creators have to overcome. The associated trade-offs have become more complex because the diffusion of ICT facilitates the creation of derivative works and related goods and services, thus altering the opportunity costs of copyright protection.

In addition, virtually all copyright systems feature further 'exceptions and limitations' to copyright (in EU legal jargon), also known as 'fair use' regulations (USA) or 'fair dealing' regulations (in the UK and most Commonwealth countries). For instance, this often allows for unauthorised drawing on protected works for commentary and satire, for research and education, reproduction for sustained private use by people who have rightful access, or modification to enable engagement of people with sensory impairments. In a welfare economic perspective, that is justified where unauthorised use generates greater benefits than harm.[16]

In this respect, a shift in perspective may be required to capture an essential aspect of digitalisation: much more complex and multifarious interactions between all types of agents than in conventional markets. For instance, end-users are often not mere consumers, whose main contribution is to pay suppliers and individually enjoy the goods and services they purchase. Instead, in contemporary digital environments, many end-users take further actions that generate value for other market participants. Cultivating such networks of dispersed value generation has become a key area of development in copyright industries.

One aspect of 'dispersed value generation' is demand formation for specific creative works in socially interdependent processes, where users emanate signals of quality through usage counts, sales charts, word-of-mouth, user reviews, and playlists. Another aspect is the supply of derivative works, which are often complements (rather than substitutes) for professionally supplied works. Regarding the latter phenomenon, modification rights are of central import, not just rights to copy and disseminate.

These types of prosumption or produsage processes (Bruns, 2013) give new urgency to long-standing debates regarding copyright. For creators, a central question is to what extent they seek to operate as owners and suppliers of specific works, or rather as moderators of more complex social processes, in which creators deliberately cede some control in order to activate other agents and cultivate joint value generation. For copyright policy, the central question is how to allow for diverse experimentation in this respect.

A particular concern is how to strike a reasonable compromise between 'market logics' of property and commerce while sustaining non-pecuniary incentives. The specialised economic literature on arts and culture documents that creators regularly receive relatively low average pecuniary rewards. One common explanation are non-pecuniary rewards (such as peer recognition) or proper intrinsic motivation to create (where creative work is more enjoyable than other types of activities, which generate value for others). According to this literature, the incentives provided by pecuniary rewards and intrinsic motivation do not necessarily add up in a straightforward manner, however. Pecuniary rewards may crowd out intrinsic motivation, where payments are associated with restrictions on creative processes. The effectiveness of pecuniary rewards may also be sensitive to perceived arbitrariness or inequity. For instance, when some market participants are perceived as making considerable profits, intrinsic motivation by other market participants may decrease.

For instance, an important recent development is so-called 'user-generated content' online. With the diffusion of digital ICT, the costs of generating novel creative works of high technical quality have fallen. Furthermore, any online media content is technically available to Internet users at miniscule marginal costs. These developments have seen a plethora of creative works made available by agents, who do not rely on corresponding revenues for their means of subsistence. Cultural economists have long discussed non-pecuniary incentives or proper intrinsic motivation for creative labour (Throsby, 2001; Towse, 1997). User-generated content provides an illustration, even though it is hard to disentangle, to what extent any indirect appropriability or the hope for long-term payoffs play a role as well. It is far from clear, how to best cultivate user-generated content without compromising incentives for creators seeking to make a living.

Platforms

A major development throughout the copyright sector is the emergence of online platforms that facilitate the dissemination of all kinds of copyright works, such as YouTube, Spotify, Netflix, Amazon and so on. Platforms fulfil two criteria, as discussed for CMOs in Sect. 3.2.[17] First, they provide transaction services. In contrast to intermediary traders, platforms do not purchase and own the underlying goods. Since platforms make no *ex-ante* payments to 'upstream' suppliers, they avoid much of the entrepreneurial risk. They do not have to worry about which specific copyright works sell, but only about the aggregate volume of transactions conducted. Second, platforms do not just exploit economies of scale and scope in transaction services. They also exploit indirect network effects, where the value of participating in a platform for suppliers increases in the number of participating buyers, and vice versa. On this basis, platforms can grow very quickly and serve large parts of society.

An obvious concern with online platforms is centralised control. On the one hand, it is a contentious issue among micro-economists, to what extent online platforms operate in contestable markets (Decker, 2023; Rochet & Tirole, 2003; Rysman, 2009). There is widespread concern that some come to wield extensive market power, charge prices well above marginal costs and even leverage their privileged access to market data and asymmetrical information advantages for horizontal and vertical integration. In this context, creators must fear that their bargaining position with the most successful commercial platforms will be weak, perhaps weaker than it has been with more traditional intermediaries, such as publishers. On the other hand, platforms may exert considerable control over the types of works and content, which become widely available and popular. Copyright works can have considerable social and cultural value. Platforms already routinely bar some content and creators that are deemed inappropriate, sometimes in excess of boundaries set by law. Platforms also enjoy some control over recommendation systems and can de-monetise or de-amplify content.

It is important to note that commercial platforms' success can be explained in a similar way as the more long-standing operation of CMOs in large parts of the copyright industries. Both types of organisations exploit economies of scale and scope as well as indirect network effects, they set standards, and bundle transactions. They fulfil very similar functions—running directories of works and use, collecting revenues from users of copyright works or advertisers, reporting to rightsholders and paying them. However, commercial online platforms have several advantages over CMOs. First, commercial platforms can leverage prospective future profits and raise considerable capital to invest in technological innovation, whereas CMOs are not-for-profit organisations obliged to pay out any profits to rightsholders. Second, commercial platforms can also develop multi-sided business models, including advertisers and services based on user and market data. Third, commercial online platforms are often multi-national corporations, which so far are even more integrated than CMOs, who are often still focused on a single country.[18]

It thus seems probable that some CMOs will be replaced by commercial online platforms.[19] However, at the same time, the very strength of commercial online platforms increases the need for CMOs, who operate independently of commercial platforms, in two important respects. First, to verify that commercial online platforms adequately assess the royalty payments they owe rightsholders. Second, to bargain on behalf of fragmented rightsholders for sustainable prices and terms.

Big Data

A major trend in copyright industries is easily overlooked: any engagement with copyright works online generates plentiful digital data that is relatively cheap to assemble and jointly analyse. This is a specific aspect of platforms, who routinely collect data on a great number of buyers and sellers making use of their services. This constitutes 'big data', which may be even bigger when platforms co-operate with each other by exchanging data.

One obvious use of this data is for market research, allowing for better matching between supply and demand. Commercially minded creators as well as creators, who care about the apparent appeal of their works, will find this data motivating and helpful.

Another use of this data is to develop sophisticated, personalised recommendation systems. This is an important complementary service to creative works, as without them end-users find it hard to identify the most promising product variants among literally thousands of works available (Fleder & Hosanagar, 2009). Nonetheless, the data and technical procedures by which recommendations are generated private property and not transparent. There is ample scope for asymmetric information problems and centralised control, which will worry economists and well as many creators.

All of these 'big data' processes are an aspect of multi-sided platform business models. Digital platforms can supply targeted advertising services. They can also supply data and data-driven consultancy services to their extant users as well as to additional customers (another side in multi-sided operations, besides suppliers of content, users of content, and advertisers). Big data applications also extend the network logic that the overall value of using a platform increases in the number of other users.

At the current state of technology and regulation, online platforms have privileged access to data. On the one hand, this incentivises platform service suppliers to invest in developing new goods and services. On the other hand, it raises concerns for market power, centralised control, asymmetric information problems, and privacy of Internet users.

In this context, a specific concern is also moral hazard for platforms to develop pricing strategies across their multiple 'sides' that discriminate against creators. One of the few definite insights from the microeconomic literature on multi-sided platforms is that rational platforms usually can and must develop pricing strategies that combine minimal prices for some participants and high, profit-generating prices for other types of participants. One consideration is to charge high prices for participants, who usually participate in multiple competing platforms (multi-home), and low prices among single-homing types of participants. However, for creators, a more straightforward issue arises. When a platform sells subscriptions or advertising, they have to share revenues with rightsholders. For revenues from exploiting data in other ways, platforms are under no such obligations. Platforms thus have incentives to maximise revenues from the exploitation of data at the expense of revenue streams they must share. For creators, a central issue is whether they can ensure that they participate in all major revenue streams that come about due to their contributions.

Generative Artificial Intelligence (Gen-AI)

One of the most exciting issues over recent years have been advances in generative artificial intelligence (AI) services available to the wider public.[20] In a nutshell, the technology is based on learning algorithms, which analyse large volumes of input works—texts, code, sound, as well as still and moving images—from the Internet or databases and identify patterns. Users can enter texts, so-called prompts, and the service generates novel texts (e.g.: ChatGPT), music and sound (e.g.: Soundraw), or still and moving images (e.g.: Dall-E).

The value proposition of AI is that it lowers to the costs of generating personalised media content. Whether AI output constitutes 'copyright works' in the legal sense—and whether the rights ought to be given to authors of prompts, the suppliers of the AI infrastructure, or the rightsholders of input works—remains a contentious issue. For now, copyright is largely ineffective in this area.

In any case, creators may become more productive, where AI lowers their need to acquire, sustain, and implement technical skills, and facilitates creators to conduct rapid prototyping and 'dream up' new types of works that are technically sophisticated and interactive. On the other hand, AI puts into question to what extent the CCI will remain labour-intensive, as AI output displaces demand for some human-generated works. Some of this displacement may be mitigated if professional creators develop new complementary services, for instance helping with AI training or advising other (end-)users on how to use AI. What is more, professional creators may cultivate human labour as a 'unique selling point', which requires reliable certification of AI-generated and human-generated content, however.

At the same time AI entails a fundamental challenge to the copyright system and the interests of creators. Unauthorised copying is problematic already, infringing on reproduction and dissemination rights, but at least it leaves some scope for indirect appropriability—creators can benefit from peer recognition and increased demand for related, more excludable goods and services they supply. That works as a mitigating factor because works are still attributed to creators, even if there are reproduced and disseminated without their consent. What is more, some enforcement of modification rights has been apparent, for instance on social media, at least where derivative works became very popular and generated income. With AI, modification of input works is the very point. What is more, attribution of creators of input works hardly happens at all. In this sense, generative AI is an even more comprehensive challenge to effective copyright protection and associated creator interests than unauthorised copying has been.

Suppliers of generative AI services claim that technical restrictions make attribution virtually impossible. Allegedly, the learning neural networks cannot be 'reverse engineered' to reliably identify and attribute input works. To what extent this is valid is beyond the scope of this chapter, and for most stakeholders and regulators, AI is very much a 'black box'. There may also be too many input works used for more general training or even associated processing of some specific prompts to make attribution meaningful. Furthermore, it may be challenging to establish the relative contribution of various input works, the AI infrastructure, and the 'prompt design' by an AI user to start calculating, who should be entitled to IP rights and any royalty payments. However, from an economic perspective it needs to be clear that suppliers of AI services have little incentives to invest in effective attribution. Attribution could make them liable to pay copyright royalties and/or enable creators to withhold or withdraw copyright works from the databases used to train AI.

For creators, this raises several concerns. First, AI output may displace demand for works generated by humans. This would undermine pecuniary incentives for creators and their business partners. Creators may also be cut off from indirect appropriability and non-pecuniary rewards and receive less reliable signals, to what extent they generate value for others. There may even be some crowding out of intrinsic and altruistic incentives to create where creators feel their own works are used to replace them, while other stakeholders (AI suppliers) receive huge investments and market revenues.

Blockchain Technology, Smart Contracting, and Non-Fungible Tokens

As discussed above, transaction costs and non-transparency are fundamental problems in much of the contemporary copyright industries. A couple of years ago, there was great hope that blockchain technology would help resolve such matters (e.g.: Potts & Rennie, 2019). In a nutshell, blockchain technology is a decentralised mode of storing and transferring data that no single party controls and that is allegedly impossible to crack and manipulate in illegitimate ways. The blockchain system permanently records extensive meta-data, which is technically available to all participants.

There are obvious applications of blockchain technology to inhibit copyright infringement. What is more blockchain technology has been used for so-called 'smart contracting', to stipulate and effectively enforce very detailed and specific terms of use for creative works. So far, an important limiting factor has been high energy consumption of blockchain applications. In contrast to cryptocurrencies, digital rights management and smart contracting in copyright industries has remained even more limited.[21]

5 Conclusions

This chapter surveys main elements of current copyright systems and how they relate to creator interests in the context of various aspects of digitalisation. Arguably, there are two overarching challenges, which amount to a paradoxical situation for most creators.

On the one hand, there are many opportunities for creators to benefit from joint value generation with other parties. Money isn't everything in the copyright industries on two separate levels. First, intrinsic motivation and use value far in excess of market value characterise the copyright industries. Second, complex co-ordination arrangements between creators and other parties are also typical, where much of the value exchanged is not denominated in money (but in social esteem donations, or in-kind support). The costs of creation and of dissemination works online have allowed much more intrinsically motivated supply by amateurs and lowered barriers to entry for ambitious newcomers. What is more, active users of digital ICT and copyright works often provide signals of quality and complementary services, which can decisively influence the success of specific works and creators. Creators often try and develop symbiotic cooperation and become deliberate moderators of complex social processes—co-creation and valorisation—rather than acting as lone geniuses, who express their own ideas and then jealously guard the exclusive rights to the fruits of their labour. The copyright system is ambiguous in this respect. It retains some privileges for creators and allows them to appropriate some of the value that comes about. It is also associated with transaction costs and often with considerable legal uncertainty that inhibits diverse experimentation and new developments. Arguably, standardised processes for licensing and compensation of creators are required to keep the bargaining, monitoring, and enforcement costs manageable, and thus to allow for new modes of joint value generation.

On the other hand, creators are in a weak position as increasingly rely on highly integrated commercial online platforms to reach out to users. To be sure, these platforms offer productively efficient processes, as they exploit economies of scale and scope as well as network effects, and they managed to raise the means to finance innovation. However, commercial online platforms also appear to enjoy considerable market power and asymmetrical information advantages—probably more so than major publishers, record labels, film studios, and wholesalers have in the past. This begets the question, whether creators are in any position to benefit from the exclusive copyrights they enjoy. After all, they may be forced to accept conditions that allow platforms to capture much of the profits generated in the market for creative works. Thus, whereas value co-creation may thrive on flexibility and some generosity by creators, a more robust defence of creators' rights seems required to cope with online platforms.

Arguably, it far exceeds the capacity of individual creators to cope with either of these two challenges by themselves. A tried-and-tested method for standardisation and for strengthening the position of creators by collective bargaining is joint copyrights management by CMOs. Whether extant CMOs and their statutory regulators can be trusted to rise to that challenge is yet another question. A fundamental problem is that technological change requires swift responses and great investments, and CMOs neither have comparable means nor incentives to commercial firms when it comes to investing in new technology. Nonetheless, CMOs are regularly collectives of creators (and other rightsholders), so that it largely depends on creators whether and how quickly CMOs contribute to safeguarding sustainable and efficient processes in the copyright industries.

Notes

1. This chapter refers to 'copyright system' as authors' rights for creators of a first fixation of an original work, to related rights of performers, as well as to institutions and organisations set up by governments or private stakeholders to monitor use, enforce copyright compliance, and to efficiently trade works or copyright licenses.
2. This includes adequate technical artefacts, the time required to acquire relevant skills, and the time and effort to implement these resources to create specific works (cf.: Handke, 2018; Johnson, 1985; Landes & Posner, 1989; Novos & Waldman, 1984; Towse et al., 2008).
3. This monopoly state is temporary due to the limited duration of copyrights. More precisely, rightsholders operate under conditions of monopolistic competition due to the presence of other creators supplying close substitutes.
4. Copyright is sometimes also referred to as 'authors' rights'.
5. Another solution are work-for-hire contracts, where creators work under conditions similar to conventional employees, and the employer becomes the only or main original rightsholder.
6. On 'indirect appropriability', see Liebowitz (1985).
7. Minimum prices are only effective if they exceed the market clearing price. Stakeholders may try and circumvent them, say by complementing formally contracted activities with unpaid work or 'gifts'.
8. Furthermore, in the European Union, the latest copyright directives stipulate additional inalienable rights for original creators

(Directive (EU) 2019/790). Creators are to receive a fair share of unforeseen, high revenues from sales or licensing of their works. Creators must also be able to reclaim any copyrights they have sold, in case the buyer makes insufficient efforts to market these works.

9. Williamson (1979) distinguishes four types of transaction costs: search costs, contracting costs, monitoring costs, and enforcement costs. For conciseness, we merge the latter two categories.
10. According to economic rational choice theory, agents conduct product searches up to the point where the marginal expected additional utility from improving choices is equal to marginal search costs.
11. Caves (2003) suggests revenue sharing rather than profit sharing, so that at least, there will be no strategic massaging of data regarding costs incurred by the various parties involved.
12. An exception could be a narrow, short-run discussion, counting instances of unauthorised use.
13. To be sure, CMOs usually set a range of standards, where for instance license prices vary across categories of license takers, or the calculation of rightsholders' distribution entitlements depend not only on usage metrics but vary also on the types of works concerned.
14. For reasons of space, we do not discuss crowdfunding in this chapter. For a detailed discussion, also regarding the interface with copyright, see Handke and Dalla Chiesa (2022).
15. There is little space in this format to rehash the issue of unauthorised copying online. For a concise and reasonably current introduction by the author of this very chapter, see Handke (2020).
16. More technically speaking, these measures would then fulfill the Kaldor-Hicks compensation criterion (Kaldor, 1939). A corrective to make copyright exceptions and limitations more consistent with rightsholder interests are copying levies. Overall, this kind of welfare economic reasoning is roughly consistent with the three-step test in international copyright law (the Berne Convention; Geiger et al., 2013), which allows for national copyright law to feature copyright exceptions and limitations if these are (1) limited to well-defined, "special cases", (2) do not to conflict "with normal exploitation of the work", and (3) do not "prejudice legitimate interests" of the rightsholders. Of course, the adjectives "special",

"normal", and "legitimate" are hardly self-explanatory nor do they reflect the more precise trade-offs that a welfare economic analysis emphasises. There is much scope for empirical work to help prepare updates of copyright limitations and exceptions.

17. For a popular concept in contemporary economics, the definition of platforms in two- or multisided markets is somewhat contentious.
18. Finally, at least where movies and tv series are concerned, firms who operate commercial platforms such as Netflix or Amazon, have also started directly investing in their 'own' content (that is vertical integration), deviating from a pure platform model. Due to platform's large market shares and privileged access to data, this raises concerns for competition policy. In any case, such hybrid models, where platforms directly and selectively invest in content, also put the trustworthiness of platforms for other content suppliers into question.
19. In this context, note that the US American collecting society Broadcast Music Inc. (BMI) has been acquired by the investment firm New Mountain Capital (BMI, 2024).
20. A review of academic literature is published in a series of reports by the U.S. Copyright Office (2025).
21. Another application of blockchain technology are non-fungible tokens (NFTs). In contrast to digital rights management and smart contracting, NFTs are not about transaction processes. NFTs simply constitute a derivative, excludable good that creators can supply—similar to limited-edition merchandise, but allegedly impossible to reproduce and forge for technical reasons and regardless of any copyright law. NFTs do not entail any exclusive rights regarding the actual creative work. Their appreciation may tell creators a lot about how much some potential customers value the feeling they relate to creative works in a special way, over and beyond their use-value from enjoying access to the work. NFTs can also be understood as a means for creators to cultivate revenues that do not depend on effective copyright protection, similar to some types of crowdfunding.

References

Arrow, K. (1970). Political and Economic Evaluation of Social Effects and Externalities. In J. Margolis (Ed.), *The Analysis of Public Output* (pp. 1–30). National Bureau of Economic Research.

Baumol, W. J. (1986). Unnatural Value: Or Art Investment as Floating Crap Game. *The American Economic Review, 76*(2), 10–14.

BMI. (2024). *New Mountain Capital Announces the Closing of Its Majority Growth Investment in BMI*. Online: https://www.bmi.com/news/entry/new-mountain-capital-announces-the-closing-of-its-majority-growth-investment-in-bmi

Bruns, A. (2013). From Prosumption to Produsage. In R. Towse & C. Handke (Eds.), *Handbook on the Digital Creative Economy* (pp. 67–78). Edward Elgar Publishing.

Caves, R. E. (2000). Creative Industries: Contracts Between Art and Commerce. *Harvard University*.

Caves, R. E. (2003). Contracts Between Art and Commerce. *Journal of Economic Perspectives, 17*(2), 73–83.

Decker, C. (2023). *Modern Economic Regulation: An Introduction to Theory and Practice*. Cambridge University Press.

Fleder, D., & Hosanagar, K. (2009). Blockbuster Culture's Next Rise or Fall: The Impact of Recommender Systems on Sales Diversity. *Management Science, 55*(5), 697–712.

Frey, B. S., & Jegen, R. (2001). Motivation Crowding Theory. *Journal of Economic Surveys, 15*(5), 589–611.

Geiger, C., Gervais, D., & Senftleben, M. (2013). The Three-Step Test Revisited: How to Use the Test's Flexibility in National Copyright Law. *American University International Law Review, 29*, 581–626.

Handke, C. (2014). Collective Administration. In R. Watt (Ed.), *Handbook on the Economics of Copyright* (pp. 179–204). Edward Elgar Publishing.

Handke, C. (2018). Intellectual Property in Creative Industries: The Economic Perspective. In C. Waelde & A. Brown (Eds.), *Research Handbook on Intellectual Property and Creative Industries* (pp. 57–76). Edward Elgar Publishing.

Handke, C. (2020). Music Industry. In R. Towse & T. Navarrete (Eds.), *Handbook of Cultural Economics* (3rd ed., pp. 358–370). Edward Elgar Publishing.

Handke, C. (2024). God Is in the Detail: Intellectual Property in Light of Cultural Economics. In W. G. Park (Ed.), *Handbook of Innovation and Intellectual Property Rights* (pp. 191–205). Edward Elgar Publishing.

Handke, C., & Dalla Chiesa, C. (2022). The Art of Crowdfunding Arts and Innovation: The Cultural Economic Perspective. *Journal of Cultural Economics, 46*(2), 249–284.

Johnson, W. R. (1985). The Economics of Copying. *Journal of Political Economy, 93*(1), 158–174.

Kaldor, N. (1939). Welfare Propositions of Economics and Interpersonal Comparisons of Utility. *The Economic Journal, 49*(195), 549–552.

Landes, W. M., & Posner, R. A. (1989). An Economic Analysis of Copyright Law. *The Journal of Legal Studies, 18*(2), 325–363.

Liebowitz, S. J. (1985). Copying and Indirect Appropriability: Photocopying of Journals. *Journal of Political Economy, 93*(5), 945–957.

Novos, I. E., & Waldman, M. (1984). The Effects of Increased Copyright Protection: An Analytic Approach. *Journal of Political Economy, 92*(2), 236–246.

Potts, J., & Rennie, E. (2019). Web3 and the Creative Industries: How Blockchains Are Reshaping Business Models. In S. Cunningham & T. Flew (Eds.), *A Research Agenda for Creative Industries* (pp. 93–111). Edward Elgar Publishing.

Rochet, J. C., & Tirole, J. (2003). Platform Competition in Two-Sided Markets. *Journal of the European Economic Association, 1*(4), 990–1029.

Rysman, M. (2009). The Economics of Two-Sided Markets. *Journal of Economic Perspectives, 23*(3), 125–143.

Throsby, D. (2001). *Economics and Culture.* Cambridge University Press.

Towse, R. (1997). Copyright as an Economic Incentive. In H. MacQueen & B. G. Main (Eds.), *Innovation, Incentive and Reward* (pp. 32–45). Edinburgh University Press.

Towse, R., Handke, C., & Stepan, P. (2008). The Economics of Copyright Law: A Stocktake of the Literature. *Review of Economic Research. on Copyright Issues, 5*(1), 1–22.

U.S. Copyright Office. (2025). *Copyright and Artificial Intelligence.* Online: https://www.copyright.gov/ai/

Vogel, H. L. (2020). *Entertainment Industry Economics: A Guide for Financial Analysis* (10th ed.). Cambridge University Press.

Watt, R. (2000). *Copyright and Economic Theory: Friends or Foes?* Edward Elgar Publishing.

Williamson, O. E. (1979). Transaction-Cost Economics: The Governance of Contractual Relations. *The Journal of Law and Economics, 22*(2), 233–261.

Open Access This chapter is licensed under the terms of the Creative Commons Attribution 4.0 International License (http://creativecommons.org/licenses/by/4.0/), which permits use, sharing, adaptation, distribution and reproduction in any medium or format, as long as you give appropriate credit to the original author(s) and the source, provide a link to the Creative Commons license and indicate if changes were made.

The images or other third party material in this chapter are included in the chapter's Creative Commons license, unless indicated otherwise in a credit line to the material. If material is not included in the chapter's Creative Commons license and your intended use is not permitted by statutory regulation or exceeds the permitted use, you will need to obtain permission directly from the copyright holder.

PART II

Extended (Digital-Based) Funding and Financing Models

CHAPTER 7

Trends in Crowdfunding for Arts and Culture

Douglas Noonan

1 Introduction

Crowdfunding in the arts and culture has an interesting history that includes strong trends, profound impacts, and complexities. Its future promises to be even more interesting—both for how its impact and role evolves and for what that tells us about the relationships between the public, resources, and arts and culture. But before we can get to the future, I will offer some perspectives on the development of crowdfunding in arts and culture over the past few decades. Where it has come, and the lessons we have learned thus far, can help inform where we think it might go next.

This review of crowdfunding in the arts and culture narrows its gaze in two important respects. First, it focuses exclusively on reward-based crowdfunding. This is because the reward-based form of crowdfunding dominates the arts and culture activity using crowdfunding tools (and also the published research about it). Second, I will draw on experiences

D. Noonan (✉)
Indiana University Indianapolis, Indianapolis, IN, USA
e-mail: noonand@iu.edu

© The Author(s) 2026

C. Dalla Chiesa and A. Rykkja (eds.), *Cultural Funding and Financing*, Cultural Economics & the Creative Economy,
https://doi.org/10.1007/978-3-031-96696-5_7

at Kickstarter and the US experience for the most part. Kickstarter was an early leader and dominant platform for reward-based crowdfunding in the US and globally. Its mission centres on "creativity", and its projects lean heavily towards arts and culture. Of course, there are other platforms like Indiegogo and Goteo. But this review returns again and again to Kickstarter because of its long-running and dominant position in the market. Examining Kickstarter, whose activity is increasingly overseas, can help us draw some interesting lessons by contrast with crowdfunding experiences elsewhere in the world (Lazzaro & Noonan, 2021).

2 Nature of Crowdfunding in Arts and Culture

A basic conceptualization of (reward-based) crowdfunding sees it from two vantages: what it is and what it is not. It is the financing of ventures or projects directly from the public with an emphasis on individual funders (in addition to, potentially, more institutional funders). It harkens to a musician passing the hat around the room for voluntary donations or a street performer asking for their "tip jar" to be filled. In its contemporary form, crowdfunding typically refers to fundraising via online platforms that feature many projects and allow for backers to contribute via digital transactions. Importantly, crowdfunding is typically not contractual and involves no equity stake or ownership by backers. Rather, backers pledge to support a project in the hopes that the creator will perform as intended and (possibly) deliver rewards to backers as promised. Without a warranty or contractual recourse for nonperformance, however, this sort of crowdfunding is more like a "donation that might get rewarded" than it is "pre-sales" or early-stage financing. Some crowdfunding models try to regularize contributions from backers, such as annual or monthly subscription via Patreon or Substack, with special perks for paying subscribers.

Seen in this way, crowdfunding functions to bring creators and their audience/backers into more direct contact (moderated only by an online platform) rather than having the relationship moderated financially by gatekeepers like distributors, publishers, venues, etc. who collect fees from the audience and then, in a separate contractual relationship, pay the creators. Crowdfunding lets the audience, users, or patrons fund creators (more) directly.

In theory, crowdfunding refers to a variety of arrangements and practices that ultimately involve appeals to a broad public for financial support for some specified "project". As Handke and Dalla Chiesa (2022) usefully note, the practice—and variety of practices—of crowdfunding can be seen through an economic lens as responses to several fundamental challenges in markets for creative and cultural products. Crowdfunding platforms facilitate learning about highly uncertain demand and about supply when creators' quality can be hard to discern. They also enable producers to cover fixed costs, especially important for products with low marginal costs (Lazzaro & Noonan, 2021), through price discrimination. Importantly for the public goods aspects of much of arts and culture, crowdfunding seeks to offer assurance contracts to address free-riding problems (Cason et al., 2021).

The economics of crowdfunding would do well to start with markets for or associated with crowdfunding. The online platforms themselves serve as a sort of marketplace, bringing together the creators (supply) and backers (demand) for transactions. Even though no final product is being delivered or guaranteed in these transactions, the elements of a marketplace are present. Competing creators offer to supply various goods, and many backers voluntarily choose which projects to back, if any, and how much to purchase. Creators can act as price-setters in deciding the rewards they would offer at different prices, but they are constrained by competition in the form of alternative crowdfunding projects or alternative investments or purchases outside of crowdfunding. There can be high levels of transparency in these marketplaces as well. This is important in reducing problems of information asymmetry and allowing for enforcement of norms and good practices via reputational mechanisms. In principle, these crowdfunding platforms have many features that we might expect to see in functioning markets.

In practice, however, crowdfunding platforms too rarely achieve operating conditions that one would associate with robust marketplaces. The elements are there in principle, but in practice the scale or "thickness" of the marketplaces is often lacking. This may change over time if these platforms become more popular for creators and (especially) backers. Typically, creators seeking more financing might turn to crowdfunding platforms to raise additional funds for their project. Out of shrewdness or desperation, their appearance in that marketplace is more idiosyncratic than integral to their normal revenue-generating efforts, and they typically do not sustain themselves in that marketplace. They seek to sell their project, and they happen to use the platform to raise funds in this case. Once the campaign ends, they return to business as usual. And, more importantly, many of the backers for that project find themselves in that marketplace just for that project—arriving at the platform due to the networking and marketing of the creator rather than because they regularly shop for that kind of venture in that (or any other) marketplace. While at any given moment the crowdfunding platform might have thousands of creators and backers, this does not mean those backers are actively *shopping* among the creators or that creators *compete* with one another. Instead, many (especially in the arts) creators post their campaign to the platform, advertise and bring their own networks to the platform to handle the transactions, and their campaign exists largely or entirely in isolation from anything else on the platform. When I hear that my favourite author is crowdfunding their next book, I go to the platform and back it—but I do not generally (or ever) go to the platform when shopping for books. For many or most campaigns, the platform is just an effective tool to collect contributions rather than a marketplace with competition among suppliers. Lowering transaction costs is important to understanding crowdfunding (Lazzaro & Noonan, 2021), but it is not the same as a full-blown public marketplace for entrepreneurial ideas that reaches masses of would-be funders, catalyses competition and innovation among creators, and renders conventional institutions obsolete. The markets are often "thin", campaigns can essentially operate monopolistically, and they are often limited to the demand that they bring to the platform themselves.

There are some exceptions where crowdfunding platforms function more like marketplaces with active communities of users. In these pockets on the platforms, significant numbers of creators and backers follow the crowdfunding in their area of interest, returning again and again. A prominent example of this sort of density or "thickness" are tabletop games on Kickstarter. The gaming community—professionals and amateurs, hobbyists, and even more casual enthusiasts—have flocked to Kickstarter and established it as the go-to place for new game development in the industry worldwide (Butticè & Noonan, 2020; Dalla Chiesa & Rykkja, 2024; Silva, 2020; Wachs & Vedres, 2021). This rapidly growing niche industry (including board games, dice and card games, various accessories and related content) found a critical mass early on Kickstarter and flourished, becoming a primary home for market R&D. The artistic and creative content of these projects prominently feature artistic and design elements, craftmanship in physical components, and storytelling and writing. It serves as a pre-sale platform in large part, but highly successful campaigns—many of which fill the ranks of the biggest campaigns in Kickstarter history—often become acquired by larger, established companies or launch startup companies.

The importance of context and industry highlights the varied roles served by crowdfunding platforms (Dalla Chiesa, 2021; Rykkja, 2023). In terms of production processes, *what* gets funded can vary tremendously—from development to distribution and beyond. In this sense, crowdfunding interacts with (and substitutes or complements) different markets based on context and category. Crowdfunding does not occur in a vacuum and generally never includes all facets of production. Projects in some categories tend to use crowdfunding for only distribution, others for procurement, while others for multiple aspects. Hence, the entrepreneurial nature of creators on these platforms varies, from rather narrowly entrepreneurial cultural campaigns to more comprehensively entrepreneurial tech startups. Where crowdfunding platform markets are thickest, we might expect not merely more creators and backers but also campaigns encompassing more aspects of the production process (e.g. development, production, distribution) than in thinner corners of crowdfunding marketplaces that target more narrowly, say, studio time to record or exhibitions to advertise.

Even when crowdfunding platforms play a limited "marketplace" role this does not mean, however, that markets do not matter for crowdfunding. Quite the opposite. Here, we need to look at ancillary markets, which might be upstream, downstream, or even midstream to a crowdfunding campaign. It is through these other markets that we see crucial elements of the crowdfunding world. Upstream of a crowdfunding campaign, creators engage with other important markets such as their labour markets and markets for other sources of revenue. Crowdfunding often contributes to the "gig economy" with creators engaging in crowdfunding as a "side hustle" or a "moonlighting" activity. Other times, creators pursue crowdfunding with or through their employer. Creators' crowdfunding decisions generally depend on opportunities and constraints in their labour markets, whether it is part of, a complement to, or a substitute for their employment. In addition, upstream crowdfunding decisions depend on the availability of other (non-crowdfunding) resources to support the project. Markets for venture capital, retail sales, charitable donations, or other revenue may factor prominently in which projects use crowdfunding and which do not. Much of the hype behind crowdfunding, at least initially and superficially, has centred on the potential for crowdfunding to fill in gaps where conventional financing would not cover or where local markets were too small to make projects viable. Crowdfunding can allow creators to sidestep gatekeepers in conventional markets.

Downstream from the campaign are other, potentially critical markets. Downstream markets include post-campaign retail sales markets (Aygoren & Koch, 2021), markets for more investment, and markets for charitable donations. Seen as market R&D with valuable signals of market demand, crowdfunding campaigns have improved creators' abilities to attract venture capital and other forms of financing (Kaminksi et al., 2018). More generally, campaign performance can affect creators' reputations (Buttice et al., 2017). In turn, reputational impacts can influence creators' longer-term career prospects and subsequent endeavours. Arguably, these post-campaign markets are much more important to understanding crowdfunding (decisions to launch a campaign, impacts of the campaign) than the campaign itself.

Outside of the campaign itself, other markets can also play a role in crowdfunding *during* the campaign. These "midstream" markets include the market for platforms themselves, as creators can choose among alternative websites (e.g. Indiegogo, Kickstarter, GoFundMe) to host their campaign. Platforms vary of course in their terms, visibility, and features, and more platforms have entered the market. Rykkja et al. (2020) highlight the close connection between project characteristics (e.g. production complexity, language) and platform choice. Related markets for consultancies and other enterprises to support creators also play roles of varying importance. Thus, understanding the markets for crowdfunding must go beyond simply the marketplace *on* the platforms themselves. The markets *outside* of the campaign can be far, far more important to understanding the drivers and impacts of crowdfunding.

The low barriers to entry on crowdfunding platforms have spawned great variety. And the inherently public nature of campaigns provides a wealth of data from which to learn. But the high visibility of crowdfunding campaigns themselves—where other markets and context are harder to observe—influences the literature. Much scholarship and discussion around crowdfunding focuses on determinants of campaign success (i.e. meeting goals) and reflects readily available indicators of campaigns. Less abundant are richer measures of creators' context, such as where their campaign fits in a broader production cycle (e.g. creating prototypes, manufacture, distribution) or fundraising strategy (e.g. VC, grants, pre-sales). Different creators come to platforms with different needs, underlining the blurry distinctions and complex heterogeneity in crowdfunding (Dalla Chiesa, 2021; Rykkja, 2023). The music creator may seek funding for studio time, while an author offers pre-sales and a designer pursues capital to finance product development, manufacture, and distribution. The convenience of pooling large datasets of crowdfunding data alone (funding, backers, counts of words and images, thematic categories) only takes us so far. Yet crowdfunding for a video game, a smartwatch or a painting exhibition serves very different entrepreneurial functions. Conducting market R&D, financing a startup, building reputation, covering fixed costs of production, expanding a donor base, and so many more functions can be found across (and even within) campaigns. Advancing our understanding of "success" in crowdfunding will require a better understanding of what is being funded or how that fits in a broader context.

3 Trends in Crowdfunding

To appreciate trends in arts and culture crowdfunding, I use Kickstarter data to ground the discussion in empirical evidence. Kickstarter is used because of its historical—and current—dominant position in the reward-based crowdfunding space and its overt specialization in "fostering creativity". In Kickstarter's own words, "Our mission is to help bring creative projects to life" (Kickstarter, 2025). Since its inception in 2009, over 23 million backers have pledged real dollars—exceeding $8 billion in funding. Some 15 years later, Kickstarter reports 259,179 projects being successfully funded on its platform. At the time of writing, almost 3000 unique projects are currently live on Kickstarter. Nearly 8 million individuals have backed multiple projects on the platform. Among the successful campaigns—those that raise pledges over a pre-specified goal within a limited window (usually 30 days)—almost two-thirds of them raised less than $10,000, whereas 826 projects have raised over $1 million. Kickstarter has become a household name in reward-based crowdfunding in the US. It has attracted much of the crowdfunding market, and a good deal of press coverage, over the past 15 years. It has also helped launch some very famous products (e.g. Pebble Smartwatch, Oculus Rift VR goggles, Peloton exercise bikes), which went on to spur significant commercial development. Among its biggest campaigns, however, are projects steeped in creative content like novels (Brandon Sanderson's latest project is the current leader in largest Kickstarter projects at $41 million), animated series (e.g. Legend of Vox Machina), and games (e.g. Frosthaven). The large pool of projects at Kickstarter is sufficient to include many exceptional, big-name projects alongside hundreds of thousands of small-scale campaigns for very niche audiences. Over time, Kickstarter's dominant position might be eroding as new platforms enter the market. Some of these platforms offer different models, different terms, or have different specializations. Today, a multitude of smaller crowdfunding platforms exist and proliferate across niches (e.g. DonorsChoose for education, Seed&Spark for movies). While Kickstarter's market share may be slowly fading, it appears more a trend away from concentration rather than the rise of a new, dominant alternative.

Kickstarter welcomes a wide range of projects and does not restrict project content to certain goods or services or particular themes. Campaign creators self-select into Kickstarter's category classification scheme (art, theatre, technology, etc.), but this is a matter of self-identification and not something based on clear objective standards. Many projects straddle between these categorical classifications (Soublière et al., 2024). In the earlier days of Kickstarter, Ethan Mollick (2016) tried to classify Kickstarter campaigns as more "product" or "art" oriented. But even today, that kind of distinction is problematic to apply. Quite simply, the creativity found on Kickstarter spans the categories, and campaigns' "artistic" or "cultural" content can be important irrespective of their category. Of course, categories like "Art" and "Dance" will fit nicely in the "arts and culture" classification, but one can find considerable arts and cultural content within projects across the platform including categories like Games or Crafts that do not align with traditional fine arts. The blurred lines between categories and the pervasiveness of arts and cultural aspects of projects are such that Kickstarter does not use Mollick's product/art distinction and remains agnostic about which categories contain greater creativity or intensity of arts and culture.

Furthermore, the categories themselves (and the many subcategories within each category) have evolved over time as campaign content on the platform has evolved. Using the 15 top-level categories of today, this sort of evolution can be seen in an examination of the scraped data from Kickstarter. Table 1 shows the average success rate, and the share of overall Kickstarter funds raised within each category. The variation across project categories stands out in Table 1. Some categories boast high success rates (e.g. comics, theatre) as others exhibit low success rates (e.g. journalism, technology). The high and low success rates do not obviously track closely with categories that might be most readily associated with retail products or commercial opportunities, or even with those categories with more activity (more competition or more popularity). Crowdfunding activity on Kickstarter spans a wide range of categories and eschews a simple pattern.

To see the trends in crowdfunding activity on Kickstarter—arguably indicative of trends in the larger crowdfunding arena—the next set of tables reports key indicators by year. Table 2 shows mean and median values for pledges, goals, backers, and more for each year from 2009 to 2021 (a partial year). A first lesson from the tables is the rapid rise in the size of the platform from 2009 to 2015, and then a sort of plateauing after 2016. Even as the annual number of projects has stopped growing, the size of the projects (in dollars pledged and in the number of backers) has continued to grow over time. The average pledge size in more recent years is considerably less than in previous years. This suggests a sort of evolution or maturation of the most common Kickstarter projects: they are fewer, bigger, and appealing to a much larger base of backers than the initial wave of campaigns. Similar trends can be seen between all projects and only successful ones. Success rates hover around 50% in recent years,

Table 1 Distribution of Kickstarter activity by project category

Category	*Success rate*	*Share of total pledges*
Art	55%	2.4%
Comics	72	2.6
Crafts	31	0.4
Dance	63	0.3
Design	58	20.5
Fashion	42	3.5
Film & Video	53	7.4
Food	42	3.1
Games	55	26.8
Journalism	23	0.3
Music	56	3.5
Photography	48	1.0
Publishing	43	3.4
Technology	29	17.8
Theatre	81	1.0
Total	50%	100%

down from the higher rates in the early days of Kickstarter but well above the low point (2016) as Kickstarter transitioned into its more current form.

Another lesson that emerges from Table 2 holds that the distribution of crowdfunding activity is highly skewed: a handful of *very* large projects makes mean values of pledges, backers, etc. much greater than medians. Considering only the successful campaigns can amplify this skewness by removing all those projects that raise close to $0. This skewness reflects distributions throughout the broader arts and culture sector, long known for its tendencies towards Superstar economies (Chen & Noonan, 2023). Superstars or not, the reality that a great deal of activity or traffic on crowdfunding platforms accrues to a minority of elite projects is a defining characteristic that can affect how platforms operate and how creators or backers behave as well.

Modern crowdfunding often boasts a sort of geographic inclusivity or egalitarian nature owing to its predominantly online nature. Several crowdfunding studies (e.g. Breznitz & Noonan, 2020; Lazzaro & Noonan, 2021; Mendes-Da-Silva et al., 2016; Noonan et al., 2021; Yu & Fleming, 2022; Yu et al., 2017) have investigated the geography of crowdfunding in greater detail than permitted here. A few key observations merit reinforcement. First, despite the online nature of the crowdfunding platform (allowing platforms to reach distant participants at low cost) and the digital nature of many projects (allowing global product distribution at low-cost), crowdfunding tends to have very strong local effects. Friends and family, professional networks, and key assets (e.g. venues, subjects) tend to cluster locally. And so, support follows locally. Second, crowdfunding has supported some geographic disconnection by allowing for more fundraising success in new places. Traditional venture-capital hubs do not dominate the crowdfunding geography. Third, crowdfunding still thrives in big markets, perhaps disproportionately so. Bigger markets contain more backers *and* attract (or supply) more creators. If anything, geographic concentration appears to be strengthened by crowdfunding (much like IT advances seem to not have reversed trends towards urbanization). That crowdfunding enables creators to launch campaigns from *anywhere* in the world does not mean that creators will launch from *everywhere*.

An important trend in the geography of crowdfunding involves its globalization. Its diffusion took some time and was hardly uniform. Again, market size figures into this story in a model where larger crowds

Table 2 Trends in Kickstarter activity

	2009	*2010*	*2011*	*2012*	*2013*	*2014*	*2015*	*2016*	*2017*	*2018*	*2019*	*2020*	*2021*
All projects													
success %	66%	69%	71%	65%	68%	52%	40%	36%	43%	46%	50%	53%	50%
Mean total pledge ($)	3163	4281	5834	12,837	18,441	13,751	13,703	12,560	14,167	14,290	16,427	21,277	24,494
Median total pledge ($)	1436	2090	2200	2384	3226	1456	620	598	876	1035	1197	1517	2086
Mean goal ($)	4995	10,745	7848	13,992	20,137	33,657	59,046	54,060	42,352	28,611	25,943	34,916	25,145
Median goal ($)	2500	3000	3500	4950	5000	5000	5636	7000	5600	5000	5000	4568	4168
Mean backers (#)	36	45	60	123	169	111	106	141	148	160	185	241	265
Median backers (#)	14	21	24	25	33	14	7	11	16	20	24	30	39
Mean pledge($)/goal($)	13	5	2	2	3	3	5	6	3	5	9	6	5
Median pledge($)/goal($)	1	1	1	1	1	1	0	0	0	0	1	1	1
Mean pledge/backer ($)	255	296	269	290	357	365	339	78	83	73	66	68	74
Median pledge/backer ($)	62	70	68	64	68	63	64	47	49	42	38	39	44
Total # projects	874	8050	20,210	34,675	36,980	60,077	77,935	45,817	44,374	41,645	39,104	35,339	15,889
Successful projects only													
Mean total pledge ($)	4553	5932	7965	19,098	26,139	25,256	31,459	32,172	31,284	29,689	31,734	38,989	40,834

(continued)

Table 2 (continued)

	2009	*2010*	*2011*	*2012*	*2013*	*2014*	*2015*	*2016*	*2017*	*2018*	*2019*	*2020*	*2021*
Median total pledge ($)	2828	3248	3610	4941	6082	6303	6111	6216	5923	5630	5245	5615	5854
Mean goal ($)	3707	4422	5551	9472	12,680	11,365	11,753	11,033	9690	8547	7948	7255	7170
Median goal ($)	2363	3000	3000	3750	5000	5000	4606	4408	4000	3500	3000	2508	2417
Mean backers (#)	50	60	80	178	233	195	232	359	323	331	356	440	456
Median backers (#)	29	36	39	49	59	52	50	88	86	84	86	102	110
Mean pledge($)/goal($)	20	7	2	3	5	6	13	14	7	10	18	10	9
Median pledge($)/goal($)	1	1	1	1	1	1	1	1	1	1	1	2	2
Mean pledge/backer ($)	318	367	332	385	468	568	522	98	96	91	84	80	79
Median pledge/backer ($)	77	83	79	79	86	99	101	64	61	57	53	49	51
Total # projects	580	5592	14,276	22,493	25,194	31,145	30,889	16,405	18,876	18,990	19,413	18,727	7936

mean larger benefits from crowdfunding (Lazzaro & Noonan, 2021). Types and qualities of projects may also evolve as crowdfunding diffuses (Barbi & Bigelli, 2017). As startup platforms emerged, competed, and survived in different markets around the world, studies of crowdfunding across international markets remain very limited. Little is known about how creators and backers navigate crowdfunding in the presence of both domestic platforms and global platforms (See Rykkja et al. (2020) for rare insights into the complexities of creators' platform choice in a global setting. Project scale and marketability internationally, especially with language differences, should play a role).

Nonetheless, crowdfunding has become increasingly a global business for platforms such as Kickstarter. Table 3 shows the steady downward trend in the share of projects that originate in the US. The increasing globalization of Kickstarter can be seen in numbers of projects or in funds raised. Whether this platform is reaching a steady-state of roughly half its projects being overseas remains to be seen, of course. (In addition, these data do not reveal the location of the backers—only the projects.) Nonetheless, the strong growth in use of the Kickstarter platform by overseas creators stands out as an important trend in crowdfunding in the US.

Table 3 Trends in domestic projects on Kickstarter[1]

	% of all projects in US		*% of successful projects in US*	
	by count	*by pledged ($)*	*by count*	*by pledged ($)*
2009	100%	100%	100%	100%
2010	100%	100%	100%	100%
2011	100%	100%	100%	100%
2012	99%	99%	99%	99%
2013	88%	89%	90%	90%
2014	78%	80%	85%	85%
2015	72%	75%	83%	84%
2016	68%	69%	77%	78%
2017	63%	64%	74%	75%
2018	60%	62%	69%	69%
2019	59%	60%	70%	71%
2020	55%	57%	67%	68%
2021	54%	57%	61%	60%
Total	72%	76%	82%	84%

Returning to the different categories of projects on Kickstarter allows us to examine whether these trends in project sizes, successes, and globalization differ across major themes. The representation of more traditional arts on Kickstarter appears to be largely constant over time. Categories of Arts, Crafts, Dance, and Theatre accounted for 25% of successful projects prior to 2012 and for 19% of successful projects in 2021. These projects' share declined in the early years of that decade, but these traditional art categories have largely held their own over time. Conversely, categories that might be associated with more commercial ventures—Film & Video, Music, Photography, Publishing—exhibited a steep decline in popularity on Kickstarter during this timeframe. Originally accounting for over half of all successful Kickstarter projects, these categories account for under a quarter of successful projects since 2020. Yet this classification fails to capture the driving forces behind these shifts. Since 2020, Dance and Theatre projects have nearly disappeared from the platform. The decline in more commercial categories has been especially steep for music and video (12.1%, down from 46.7%), but publishing projects account for 10% of all successful projects post-2019. The Mollick distinction between *product* categories (Design, Food, Technology, Games, Fashion) and *art* categories (Comics, Publishing, Journalism, Music, Art, Photography, Crafts, Dance, Theatre, Film & Video) also fails to capture the underlying dynamic at Kickstarter, especially in recent years. Mollick's *art* projects originally accounted for 89% of successful projects prior to 2012, but account for less than 52% after 2019. Again, this largely reflects the drop-off in a few formerly popular *art* categories (music and video) and the fading of smaller *art* categories (dance and theatre) while other *art* categories (art, comics, crafts, and publishing) have grown in relative popularity in recent years. The rise in *product* projects, on the other hand, reflects the rise in popularity of *product* categories Fashion and Technology and most especially those in Design and Games (See Figures 2 and 3 in the Appendix to visualize these trends.)

Table 4 illustrates these stark changes in the composition of Kickstarter projects from its early days to its more current incarnation. The table shows the dramatic increase in the prevalence of Games and, to a lesser extent, Design and Technology. It also shows the dramatic decline in the prevalence of Film & Video, Music, and Theatre. Table 4 also shows the difference in the relative sizes of projects in these categories. Larger projects can be found in Design, Games, and Technology. Conversely, projects in Art, Comics, Fashion, Music, and Publishing tend to be much smaller. In terms of popularity—as measured by the numbers of backers summed across the projects in each category—the Games and Design categories again stand out as attracting the lion's share of backers. Interestingly, several categories (Art, Crafts, Fashion, Film & Video, Journalism, Music, Photography, Theatre) attract a share of backers than is less than half of their share of overall projects. Among successful campaigns, these projects tend to attract small numbers of backers. This was not the case for Film & Video and Music projects in Kickstarter's early years, suggesting that a new equilibrium for those sorts of projects as involving smaller projects with smaller crowds.

Another way to appreciate the "size" crowdfunding markets for different categories is to look at the average sizes of projects in terms of funds raised, numbers of backers making pledges, and pledges per backer. Table 5 shows the distributions of these indicators across different categories in the early years of Kickstarter versus more recent years. All averages are median values here to mitigate the influence of outlier campaigns. Median pledges and backers have both grown substantially in the past decade, although the slower growth in pledges means that

Table 4 Share of Kickstarter by category over time

	2009–2011			*2020–2021*		
Category	*% of successful projects*	*% of funds raised*	*% of backers*	*% of successful projects*	*% of funds raised*	*% of backers*
Art	10.5%	6.7%	7.2%	15.7%	3.1%	4.5%
Comics	3.5	2.6	3.1	9.4	3.5	6.0
Crafts	0.7	0.3	0.3	1.7	0.2	0.3
Dance	3.6	1.7	1.4	0.2	0.0	0.0
Design	2.4	10.3	11.0	10.3	22.1	18.2
Fashion	2.0	1.7	1.2	6.0	2.2	2.3
Film & Video	25.0	31.8	27.5	5.9	3.1	2.7
Food	3.2	3.9	3.0	2.4	2.0	1.5
Games	2.3	4.3	5.9	25.0	41.9	49.4
Journalism	1.4	1.0	0.9	0.4	0.2	0.2
Music	21.7	15.9	20.5	6.2	1.6	1.9
Photography	5.1	3.3	2.7	1.5	0.5	0.5
Publishing	6.1	4.7	6.0	9.7	3.9	4.6
Technology	1.9	6.4	4.4	5.1	15.5	7.8
Theatre	10.4	5.6	4.8	0.6	0.1	0.1

projects' average pledge sizes have declined. Against those overall trends, median funds raised declined for Art, Fashion, and Film & Video campaigns even as they tend to attract more backers. Every category's median backers grew. Campaigns in the categories in ascendency (Comics, Design, Games, and Technology) have exhibited more success in reaching crowds on Kickstarter. Each of those ascendent categories currently ranks in the top four in median backers-per-project, suggesting relatively "thick" markets. Yet only Technology projects tend to attract high average pledge values. These categories' robust performances in recent years appear to be owed to the larger crowds they attract rather than premium products or high-value contributions.

These descriptive statistics make plain some of the many ways in which the crowdfunding markets on Kickstarter have evolved. Campaigns are bigger in terms of total funds raised and numbers of backers attracted, but some of this is driven by "superstar" campaigns. Median pledges per backer have fallen and median total pledges have stagnated, leaving the growth in average projects to be driven by greater numbers of backers. Notable is the rapid growth, modest decline, and general plateauing of the

Table 5 Median pledges and backers for successful Kickstarter projects

	2009–2011			*2020–2021*		
Median: Category	*Pledges ($)*	*Backers*	*Pledges ($)/ backer*	*Pledges ($)*	*Backers*	*Pledges ($)/backer*
Art	2648	31	72	2135	55	38
Comics	2860	29	87	4515	133	35
Crafts	1541	19	72	1958	40	44
Dance	2685	17	119	5481	62	77
Design	8370	68	82	15,462	149	80
Fashion	3641	17	146	3501	71	45
Film & Video	5083	44	91	4227	49	79
Food	5514	43	123	11,475	116	83
Games	6713	79	64	9329	225	43
Journalism	3065	25	118	5189	87	64
Music	3313	47	63	4973	71	63
Photography	3052	20	114	5488	75	65
Publishing	3005	41	60	5110	89	50
Technology	7125	48	135	22,001	183	114
Theatre	2586	22	90	2826	41	63

platform's fundraising over its 15-year history. The other major maturation has occurred in the composition of marketplace in terms of the types of campaigns being launched. Over time, some categories have grown tremendously in popularity while others have faded. Those growing and shrinking do not neatly correspond to prior classifications of arts- and product-oriented projects.

The evolution of Kickstarter might be seen in two distinct periods: before and after 2016. Until 2016, the platform's total funds raised per year grew rapidly, but growth stagnated after that. The year 2016 also brought a low point in the success rates and a major drop-off in the number of new campaigns launched. Lower success rates reflect more than just the average quality of campaigns. More campaign launches with a finite pool of supporters—competition—can lower success rates just as poorly implemented campaigns, declining demand, or other factors can (See Wessel et al. (2017) for discussion of changes in competition, and policy, at Kickstarter around this time. Changes in eligibility for campaigns can affect the equilibrium pool and performance of campaigns). The recovery of success rates (to roughly 50%) in recent years may be consistent with an equilibrium of greater competition for scarce funds from the crowd and better campaigns (if not better products, ideas, or content). Creators who return to Kickstarter for multiple campaigns tend to learn from their past experiences and quality improves (Butticè & Noonan, 2020). The share of projects being brought by repeat-creators has been growing steadily over time. In 2021, 49% of projects were launched by repeat-creators, up from 31% in 2016. Furthermore, some of the more intensive or successful categories on Kickstarter have the highest rates of repeat-creators (e.g. 53% for Games, 53% for Comics, 33% for Design, 33% for Art), while other categories in decline tend to have higher first-time creator rates (e.g. 86% for Film & Video, 84% for Music, 84% for Theatre). The prevalence of repeat-creators on Kickstarter may speak to the formation of a more robust marketplace, where entrepreneurs bring ideas and products to market to compete with other sellers, just as much as it might signal improving quality.

4 Superstars and Concentration

The dynamics of crowdfunding and repeat-creators raise other concerns. Creators might return to the platform because they found great success or promise on their previous attempt, which suggests that repeat-creators are associated with the superstar phenomenon. Superstars may crowd-out other new entrants by outcompeting them or attracting most of the available resources. Alternatively, crowdfunding can lead to greater downstream success *outside of* the platform. This suggests that repeat-creators are merely associated with a lack of off-platform fundraising options. Chen and Noonan (2023) examine the trends in these superstars absorbing more and more of the available resources. They show how highly concentrated the distribution of pledges are across successful projects, and how that concentration increased over time. In the first few years of Kickstarter, the Gini coefficient—an indicator from 0–1 measuring concentration of funds—was a 0.7. Although 0.7 indicates a high degree of inequality, the Gini coefficient grew to 0.90 in more recent years. Put another way, the top 1% of all Kickstarter campaigns from 2009–2011 raised 19% of the funds. That figure reached 36% for 2017–2018, and then 42% for 2020–2021. The superstar campaigns' domination and inequality in the distribution of funds raised on Kickstarter has grown alongside the growth in average project size.

The tendency of fundraising to concentrate in a few superstar campaigns is widespread but not uniform. Although inequality in funding across projects has plateaued somewhat in the recent era, substantial variation in this concentration exists across project categories. Figure 1 shows this variation with Gini coefficients, with highly concentrated categories (e.g. Journalism, Technology) standing apart from less concentrated categories (e.g. Dance, Music, Theatre). The more dominant categories today are the ones with the highest concentration, perhaps reflecting more commercial activity and more professional or high-quality campaigns being launched there. Figure 1 also shows how the Gini coefficients for each category have all increased from the early years to the later years. Some categories' growth was much larger (e.g. Fashion, Food) than others' (e.g. Music, Technology). Overall, there appears to be some convergence across categories. Though categories' Gini coefficients appear positively correlated with their share of overall Kickstarter activity, a category's concentration of funding is unrelated to the share of its creators that are first-time creators. Superstars may be accruing ever-larger shares of funding, but they do not seem to be deterring new entrants. They could, however, signify more established organizations or firms entering in lieu of individual freelancers or independent creatives. Future research into the evolving nature of the creators entering different crowdfunding spaces is needed.

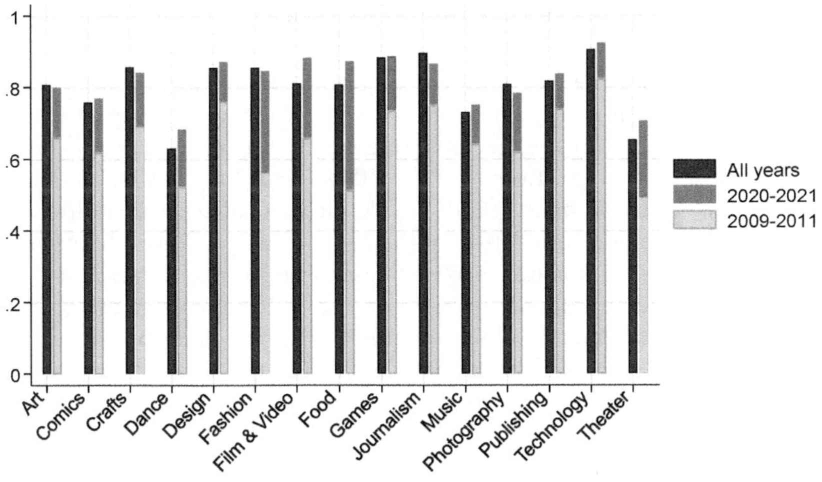

Fig. 1 Gini coefficients by category

5 Impacts

The past 15 years of Kickstarter has provided a long time-series of data through which to observe its evolution and maturation. This also afforded scholars time to research its impacts on society. Although studies of behaviour on crowdfunding platforms—who creates and backs, which campaigns succeed, etc.—were legion and quick to publish, research on its implications for society is rarer and slower to arrive. The literature has identified impacts in various dimensions, including quality of work and downstream commercialization, subsequent financing, and macroeconomic impacts (e.g. Murray & Fisher, 2023; Stanko & Henard, 2017). Crowdfunding creators build social capital on the platform and learn how to harness the input—the co-design feature—provided by backers (Butticè & Noonan, 2020). Experienced crowdfunders can harness the power of the crowds to improve their (Tabletop Games) product quality when it eventually arrives at the retail stage. Research also suggests that hundreds of (non-hobby) video game campaigns on Kickstarter make it to market (Weber et al., 2023) and, in turn, earn millions of dollars in revenue on average (Aygoren & Koch, 2021). Although only a small fraction of movie campaigns gets released theatrically, crowdfunding nonetheless kickstarts millions of dollars annually in box office (Roma et al., 2023).

Arguably more relevant than retail impacts, the effects of crowdfunding on subsequent funding stand out. Successful crowdfunding has been shown to attract more angel investments (Yu et al., 2017) and other professional financing (Roma et al., 2017; Tasneem, 2020). Kaminski et al. (2018), for instance, find "a 1% increase in total crowdfunding investments effects a cumulative 4% increase in total VC investments at lag (month) 4 and a cumulative 10% increase at lag 6, respectively" (p. 12). Though this literature tends to focus on the Technology category, where professional financing is more common, the broader, post-campaign economic impacts of Kickstarter activity extend well beyond Technology. Successful campaigns drive substantial increases in new startups (Yu et al., 2017) and employment (Lambert et al., 2024). Just as the initial wave of findings regarding Kickstarter is illuminating, these impacts are sure to evolve as crowdfunding practices change over time. A key message throughout this literature on impacts holds that crowdfunding activity itself may be just the tip of the iceberg of its societal and economic impact.

6 Where to Next?

Crowdfunding has much to offer its participants as well as its observers. Participants and researchers alike can learn from crowdfunding campaigns. One of the first and most prominent lessons I learned from studying Kickstarter experiences was the prominence of *learning* as a key benefit. Creators and backers learned whether that was their primary goal or not. Campaigns provide "market R&D", the kind of insights evidenced by real-world financial payments that outcompete focus groups run in shopping malls. Further, financial supporters and professional networks learned about creators via strong reputational effects. The arguably paltry sums at stake in crowdfunding—seen in the aggregate against other revenue sources in arts and culture—were never the best indicator of crowdfunding's value. Rather, information gained serves as the better currency. Creators' early-stage information gathering process propels their later-stage developments and career advancements.

We have much more to learn from crowdfunding campaigns. Clearly, the Kickstarter platform has evolved greatly since its rise to prominence, both in the types of projects launched there and in the ways creators and backers operate. Such is the next big lesson: Kickstarter of 2021 is far more specialized and more mature than it was in 2011. How crowdfunding participants learned about and from the platform remains an important subject for future inquiry. This learning is especially important in light of evolution and dynamics within and among crowdfunding platforms.

Even as crowdfunding in arts and culture matures, more research is needed to better understand how crowdfunding fits into the broader ecosystem of funding, career development, networking, and innovation in arts and culture. The dynamics and trends in crowdfunding as a marketplace suggests a need for great attention to creators developing their networks, before and after campaigns, and how it factors into crowdfunding decisions and impacts. As researchers continue to study the post-campaign effects of crowdfunding, more research on public goods aspects of arts and culture merit more attention. Matched crowdfunding, civic crowdfunding, and other ways to couple crowdfunding mechanisms with government funds or public policy remain largely experimental, at least in the US, with more learning to be done.

Furthermore, there is still much to learn from developments on platforms like Kickstarter, especially along the lines of crowdfunding's role in fostering creativity and innovation, altering "gatekeeper" functions and forces, and enabling projects that might not otherwise have launched. Within the crowdfunding arena, complex economic and sociological dynamics warrant more scrutiny. How do creators learn from one another, adapt to competition, fill niches, build on prior successes and the crowd's wisdom? How do thicker markets form and sustain themselves? How do platforms support creativity, and what forms does that creativity take? What affects the overall inflow of resources or funding—in addition to the inflow of idea and innovations—to the platforms? Future research would do well to explore these sorts of questions.

In their overview of crowdfunding in arts and culture, Handke and Dalla Chiesa conclude: "Arguably, the main boon of crowdfunding for cultural economics is not so much that it makes markets … much more efficient and fosters growth. Instead, crowdfunding enables sophisticated empirical research on central topics of cultural economics" (p. 249). I might quibble, rather than argue, with this bold claim. Indeed, both facets of their conclusion hold great truth. Crowdfunding has not obviously transformed cultural and creative industries (CCI), and it has enabled a bounty of fascinating research (e.g. Greenberg & Mollick, 2017; Mollick & Nanda, 2016). Yet the learning that crowdfunding has enabled is not just for empirical researchers and academics. It is for producers, consumers, and financiers in the field. A primary benefit of crowdfunding thus far has been *informational*. Campaigns provide market R&D about novel products and build reputations for creators. This learning can have profound "downstream" benefits. Certainly, crowdfunding pledges account for a "tiny fraction" (p. 276) of CCI revenues, but this may not be the best metric for appreciating its impact on the sector.

Crowdfunding has been shown to facilitate major post-campaign financing, revenues, innovations, startups, employment, and more. The best promise of crowdfunding might be in enabling new projects to be realized, which should lead us to measure projects' downstream fundraising, retail revenues, and public goods values created—not just the revenues raised on the platform. For example, the Kickstarter campaign for *The Legend of Vox Machina*—an animated show based on the Critical Role web series of voice actors playing Dungeons and Dragons—demonstrates this. The *Legend of Vox Machina* campaign raised over $11 million in 2019, overwhelming their initial goal of $750,000, and leading the creators to expand their project from a 22-minute special to a 10-episode series (Spangler, 2021). A few months later, Amazon Studios purchased the streaming rights and expanded it to an ongoing series (season 3 just dropped in 2024) on Amazon Prime video. Its strong performance on the streamer underscores just how far the value of crowdfunding goes beyond the pledges received. Crowdfunding can bring creative projects to life, and those lives after the campaign can be legendary.

Appendix

See Figs. 2 and 3.

Notes

1. Data derived from Web Robots (2025), through 16 August 2021. These are webscraped data, cleaned by the author.

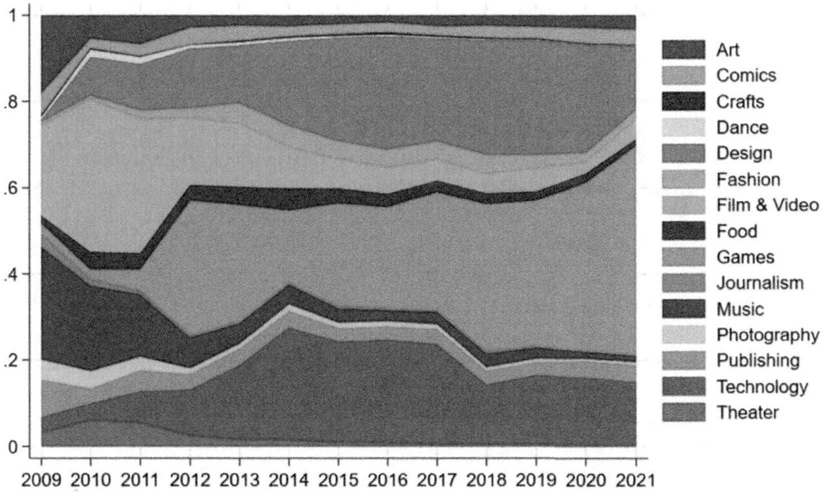

Fig. 2 Share of funds raised over time, by category

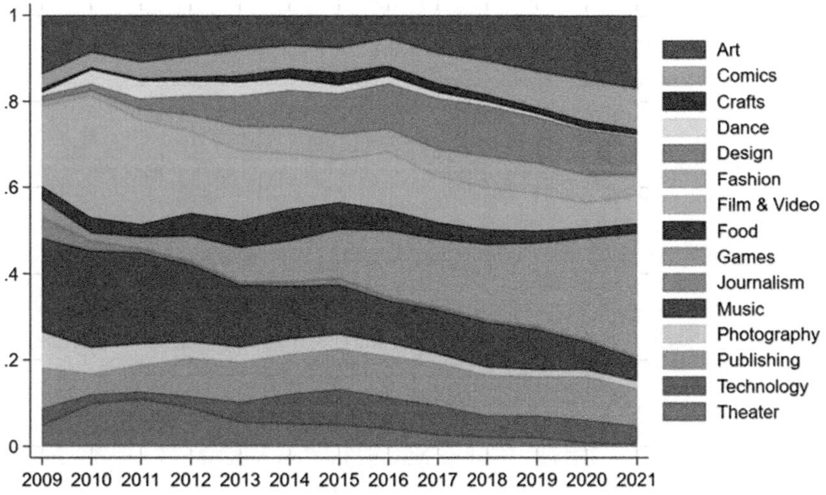

Fig. 3 Share of successful projects over time, by category

References

Aygoren, O., & Koch, S. (2021). Community Support or Funding Amount: Actual Contribution of Reward-based Crowdfunding to Market Success of Video Game Projects on Kickstarter. *Sustainability, 13*(16), 9195.

Barbi, M., & Bigelli, M. (2017). Crowdfunding Practices in and Outside the US. *Research in International Business and Finance, 42*, 208–223.

Breznitz, S. M., & Noonan, D. S. (2020). Crowdfunding in a Not-So-Flat World. *Journal of Economic Geography, 20*(4), 1069–1092.

Buttice, V., Colombo, M. G., & Wright, M. (2017). Serial Crowdfunding, Social Capital, and Project Success. *Entrepreneurship Theory and Practice, 41*(2), 183–207.

Butticè, V., & Noonan, D. (2020). Active Backers, Product Commercialisation and Product Quality after a Crowdfunding Campaign: A Comparison Between First-time and Repeated Entrepreneurs. *International Small Business Journal, 38*(2), 111–134.

Cason, T. N., Tabarrok, A., & Zubrickas, R. (2021). Early Refund Bonuses Increase Successful Crowdfunding. *Games and Economic Behaviour, 129*, 78–95.

Chen, W., & Noonan, D. (2023). Sharing the Stage: Exploring Inequities in Resources for the Arts Across Funding Institutions. *American Behavioural Scientist*, 00027642231179923.

Dalla Chiesa, C. (2021). *Crowdfunding Culture: Bridging Art and Commerce* (Doctoral Dissertation PhD). Erasmus University of Rotterdam.

Dalla Chiesa, C., & Rykkja, A. (2024). Bridging the Urban-Digital Divide: Crowdfunding as an Online Middleground Space. *City, Culture and Society, 37*, Article 100580.

Greenberg, J., & Mollick, E. (2017). Activist Choice Homophily and the Crowdfunding of Female Founders. *Administrative Science Quarterly, 62*(2), 341–374.

Handke, C., & Dalla Chiesa, C. (2022). The Art of Crowdfunding Arts and Innovation: The Cultural Economic Perspective. *Journal of Cultural Economics, 46*(2), 249–284.

Kaminski, J., Hopp, C., & Lukas, C. (2018). Who Benefits From the Wisdom of the Crowd in Crowdfunding? Assessing the Benefits of User-Generated and Mass Personal Electronic Word of Mouth in Computer-Mediated Financing. *Journal of Business Economics, 88*, 1133–1162.

Kickstarter. (2025, March 29). About. https://www.kickstarter.com/about

Lambert, T., Ralcheva, A., & Roosenboom, P. (2024). Crowdfunding Entrepreneurship: Evidence from US Counties. Available at SSRN 4244733.

Lazzaro, E., & Noonan, D. (2021). A Comparative Analysis of US and EU Regulatory Frameworks of Crowdfunding for the Cultural and Creative Industries. *International Journal of Cultural Policy, 27*(5), 590–606.

Mendes-Da-Silva, W., Rossoni, L., Conte, B. S., Gattaz, C. C., & Francisco, E. R. (2016). The Impacts of Fundraising Periods and Geographic Distance on Financing Music Production via Crowdfunding in Brazil. *Journal of Cultural Economics, 40*, 75–99.

Mollick, E. R. (2016). Containing Multitudes: The Many Impacts of Kickstarter Funding. Available at SSRN 2808000.

Mollick, E., & Nanda, R. (2016). Wisdom or Madness? Comparing Crowds with Expert Evaluation in Funding the Arts. *Management Science, 62*(6), 1533–1553.

Murray, A., & Fisher, G. (2023). When More is Less: Explaining the Curse of Too Much Capital for Early-Stage Ventures. *Organization Science, 34*(1), 246–282.

Noonan, D. S., Breznitz, S. M., & Maqbool, S. (2021). Looking for a Change in Scene: Analyzing the Mobility of Crowdfunding Entrepreneurs. *Small Business Economics, 57*(2), 685–703.

Roma, P., Petruzzelli, A. M., & Perrone, G. (2017). From the Crowd to the Market: The Role of Reward-based Crowdfunding Performance in Attracting Professional Investors. *Research Policy, 46*(9), 1606–1628.

Roma, P., Natalicchio, A., Panniello, U., Vasi, M., & Messeni Petruzzelli, A. (2023). Crowdfunding Performance, Market Performance, and the Moderating Roles of Product Innovativeness and Experts' Judgment: Evidence From the Movie Industry. *Journal of Product Innovation Management, 40*(3), 297–339.

Rykkja, A. (2023). *Take a Chance on Me: Cultural Crowdfunding as a Necessary, Complementary, or Substitutive Business Model in the Nordic Countries and in Spain*. Inland University of Applied Sciences.

Rykkja, A., Munim, Z. H., & Bonet, L. (2020). Varieties of Cultural Crowdfunding. *Baltic Journal of Management, 15*, 261–280.

Silva, C. (2020, July 5). A Look Into the Wild Economy of Tabletop Board Game Funding. *National Public Radio*. https://www.npr.org/2020/07/05/887283058/a-look-into-the-wild-economy-of-tabletop-board-game-funding

Soublière, J. F., Lo, J. Y., & Rhee, E. Y. (2024). Coherence Within and Across Categories: The Dynamic Viability of Product Categories on Kickstarter. *Academy of Management Journal, 67*(1), 61–91.

Spangler, T. (2021, October 14). Inside Critical Role's Growing D&D Fantasy Empire and the Making of 'The Legend of Vox Machina' for Amazon. *Variety*. https://variety.com/2021/digital/features/critical-role-amazon-legend-of-vox-machina-1235088274/

Stanko, M. A., & Henard, D. H. (2017). Toward a Better Understanding of Crowdfunding, Openness and the Consequences for Innovation. *Research Policy, 46*(4), 784–798.

Tasneem, T. (2020). *Venture Capital Funding After Crowdfunding Success: A Study of Successful Kickstarter Campaigns* (Doctoral dissertation, Concordia University).
Wachs, J., & Vedres, B. (2021). Does Crowdfunding Really Foster Innovation? Evidence From the Board Game Industry. *Technological Forecasting and Social Change, 168*, Article 120747.
Weber, C. E., Steigenberger, N., & Wilhelm, H. (2023). After Successful Fundraising: How Overfunding and Category Spanning Affect the Release and Audience-Perceived Quality of Crowdfunded Products. *Small Business Economics, 61*(3), 1009–1026.
Webrobots. (2025, February 20). Kickstarter Datasets. https://webrobots.io/kickstarter-datasets/
Wessel, M., Thies, F., & Benlian, A. (2017). Opening the Floodgates: The Implications of Increasing Platform Openness in Crowdfunding. *Journal of Information Technology, 32*, 344–360.
Yu, S., Johnson, S., Lai, C., Cricelli, A., & Fleming, L. (2017). Crowdfunding and Regional Entrepreneurial Investment: An Application of the CrowdBerkeley Database. *Research Policy, 46*(10), 1723–1737.
Yu, S., & Fleming, L. (2022). Regional Crowdfunding and High-Tech Entrepreneurship. *Research Policy, 51*(9), Article 104348.

Open Access This chapter is licensed under the terms of the Creative Commons Attribution 4.0 International License (http://creativecommons.org/licenses/by/4.0/), which permits use, sharing, adaptation, distribution and reproduction in any medium or format, as long as you give appropriate credit to the original author(s) and the source, provide a link to the Creative Commons license and indicate if changes were made.

The images or other third party material in this chapter are included in the chapter's Creative Commons license, unless indicated otherwise in a credit line to the material. If material is not included in the chapter's Creative Commons license and your intended use is not permitted by statutory regulation or exceeds the permitted use, you will need to obtain permission directly from the copyright holder.

CHAPTER 8

Matched-Money in the Arts and Culture: Conceptualising Online and Offline Matchfunding Models

Carolina Dalla Chiesa, Ellen Loots, and Yosha Wijngaarden

1 Introduction

Cultural organisations and individual creators have historically relied on various funding mechanisms to make their cultural projects viable, e.g. in-kind contributions (labour, materials, advice) and money (investments, funds, grants, subsidies, donations), thus "mixing" different forms and sources of support (Loots et al., 2025). This chapter focuses on a specific type of funding arrangement, where different partners or donors match

C. Dalla Chiesa (✉) · E. Loots · Y. Wijngaarden
Erasmus University Rotterdam, Rotterdam, Netherlands
e-mail: c.dallachiesa@eshcc.eur.nl

E. Loots
e-mail: loots@eshcc.eur.nl

Y. Wijngaarden
e-mail: wijngaarden@eshcc.eur.nl

© The Author(s) 2026
C. Dalla Chiesa and A. Rykkja (eds.), *Cultural Funding and Financing*, Cultural Economics & the Creative Economy,
https://doi.org/10.1007/978-3-031-96696-5_8

each other's contributions. More recently, this arrangement has been popularised in the form of so-called *matchfunding*,[1] a co-funding taking place online with the crowd's individual donations matched with public or private institutions.

Studies of *matching grants*, *matchfunding, or matched funds* precede digitalisation (see Eckel & Grossman, 2006; Diamond & Hausman, 1994; Karlan & List, 2007; Meier, 2007; Rushton, 2008). While terms are used interchangeably, most mechanisms reveal forms of "co-financing" theorised by Schuster (1989). Key findings show that individuals tend to give more under matched grant programs than via tax rebates (Bekkers, 2015; Eckel & Grossman, 2006) and that matched donations increase the likelihood of follow-up donations (Karlan & List, 2007). Pre-digitalisation evidence also confirms positive outcomes from matched funds, as they induce higher average donations (Meier, 2007) and, furthermore, tend to reduce inefficiencies in the public sector (Gong & Grundy, 2010).

With digitalization, matchfunding became relatively more complex and accessible. New intermediaries offer novel ways to connect cultural projects to donors, for example, by using crowdfunding technology. Crowdfunding's capacity to reveal demand and facilitate quality screening serves the purposes of matchfunding rather well. Nevertheless, while artists, creators, and CCS organisations vastly use multiple funding sources, scholarship on novel matchfunding options is scarce. A few recent empirical studies show the potential of matched funds to leverage additional funds from the crowd or individual donors (Baeck et al., 2017; Dalla Chiesa et al., 2025; Fang et al., 2021), often using EU-based case studies (Dalla Chiesa & Alexopoulou, 2022; Loots et al., 2023; Morell et al., 2020; Rykkja & Bonet, 2023). Generally, it has been shown that matchfunding can contribute to the success of fundraising campaigns (Davies, 2015; De Voldere & Zeqo, 2017; Van Montfort et al., 2020), but the differences between the digital and non-digital mechanisms remain unclear.

Existing research on arts funding typically focuses on understanding common funding gaps and organisational portfolios (Ashton, 2022), motivations of funders (D'Andrea, 2017), and the various mechanisms through which funding is acquired or allocated (Loots, 2015). New funding formats (e.g. Loots et al., 2022), such as NFTs, crowdfunding, online busking, and online investment options, also play a role. Yet, there is a lack of understanding of how online matchfunding translates into benefits for funders, fund-seekers, and governments seeking cost-sharing strategies in the CCS. To address this gap, this chapter first provides a framework that compares online and offline matchfunding from a signalling or informational perspective (Spence, 1981). Secondly, it discusses the main challenges and benefits of online matchfunding for the arts and culture. As such, our research questions are: (1) What is the matchfunding phenomenon, and what are its different formats? (2) How do online and offline matchfunding differ? (3) What potential benefits and challenges do new matchfunding formats reveal for the cultural sectors?

Our chapter contributes to scholarly debates in arts funding by providing a framework to compare the various matchfunding formats. We further elect the online matchfunding option as a powerful tool to harness broader audiences while also benefiting from institutional support from public or private entities. In line with previous research (Handke & Dalla Chiesa, 2021), we argue that online intermediaries can reduce the costs associated with quality screening and signalling for institutional funders, as well as allowing creatives to reveal demand online before incurring substantive costs of creation. More broadly, the online matchfunding mechanism can be seen as a partial *Rawlsian* (Rawls, 1971) solution to arts funding by governments, as it maintains some neutrality in public authorities' decision-making. As such, it sustains a modern liberal view of arts funding (Rushton, 2000), with some limitations, as public authorities can still direct cultural outcomes to the extent that the crowd is validated.

This ties in well with current debates, testified by for example the Dutch Council for Culture, which states it is promising "to coordinate public and private funding better so that public money can work more as a lever for private money; think of matching, impulses for crowdfunding or forms that make cultural organisations more likely to be eligible for bank financing" (Raad voor Cultuur, 2024, p. 133 [translated from Dutch by authors]). In what follows, the chapter first discusses definitions related to matchfunding, followed by a description of the online-based format operated through crowdfunding platforms. We then describe the traditional (offline) matchfunding model to compare both options. Each model further reflects the challenges and benefits for creators and funders. We then conclude by elaborating hypothetically on the limitations of channelling public funding through the online matchfunding model, as we examine the consequences of relying on the "crowd's" judgment to decide on additional institutional funding.

Defining Matchfunding

Matchfunding is part of a broader discussion about the desirability and capacity to diversify funding sources (Frumkin & Keating, 2011; Koumou, 2020) and strike an efficient balance between public and private funding (Anheier, 2005; Morris, 2000). While matchfunding implies the combination of monetary support from different sources (Schuster, 1989), a financing mix can be understood as a broader phenomenon characterised by pooling monetary and non-monetary support (e.g. in-kind donations, patronage, and volunteers' time) next to revenues from selling cultural and ancillary products and services (e.g. ticket sales, art commissioning, hospitality services, museum shop sales, etc.) (Hughes & Luksetich, 2004). As such, matchfunding is a more specific phenomenon, part of a mixed economy, in which funders and/or the market intentionally pool monetary resources simultaneously, differing in their co-financing strategy.

According to McClelland (2024), a large body of evidence suggests that *matching funds/grants* are a better incentive than tax rebate systems (see, for example, Beckers, 2015; Davis, 2006; Davis et al., 2005; Eckel & Grossman, 2006; Hungerman & Ottoni-Wilhelm, 2021). Some authors (Karlan & List, 2007) find that charities can increase the revenue per solicitation and the response rate of donors by simply announcing that a match offer is available. The reasons for this effect are unclear (McClelland, 2024). Still, the relative indifference to *price* in matching donations, as found in empirical evidence (Karlan & List, 2007), suggests that moral satisfaction or a *warm glow* is part of donors' reasoning (Andreoni, 1990).

When initiated by a major public or private funder, matchfunding can be translated into a cost-sharing strategy that (a) invites other institutional partners to fund or that (b) imposes budget requirements on fundees to tap into other sources to raise additional funds. In the case of the former (a), major institutional funders can arrange agreements with other funders to fund. This can occur in various ways, including pooling funds a priori. In the case of the latter (b), typically, institutional funders require fundees to tap into private capital or "the market" (revenue streams such as sales, merchandising, tickets and others) to collect financial resources. Such matching requirements can occur at three stages of a funding cycle: in the program announcements where they constitute an eligibility criterion a priori, at the proposal review processes a posteriori where an evaluation criterion is used to accept or reject matching funds, or in the pre-award budget negotiations where cost-sharing requirements can be made explicitly, at the case level (Feller, 2000).

More recently, the term *matchfunding* gained prominence with its incorporation into digital platform technologies, in part due to its connection to and derivative of *crowdfunding* (Dalla Chiesa & Alexopoulou, 2022; Loots et al., 2023; Morell et al., 2020; Passeri, 2020). The novel matchfunding strategy is argued to "offer communities an alternative means of financing social projects that are normally funded by the government" (Van Montfort et al., 2020: 2), as well as a conveyor of a collaborative funding mechanism with unique civic potential (Morell et al., 2020). We discuss the online model in the following section.

Matchfunding can be understood as a funding model requiring recipients to raise a predetermined amount of financial support from sources other than their earned income, then subsequently matched by an institutional funder. Based on this broader view, we define matchfunding as *the intentional process of providing funding by funders to fundees, in a manner that encourages or enforces additional funders to contribute to the targeted goal, either prearranged or not by the initial funder/or mediated by the efforts of the fundee.* Some matchfunding happens through online platforms, while others take place offline. In the following sections, we discuss both formats, starting with the most recent of them.

2 Matchfunding Facilitated by Online Platforms: The *New* Model

Key Characteristics

In recent years, online platforms have started to facilitate a specific type of matchfunding with the intermediation of crowdfunding platforms.[2] Crowdfunding is an online-based system operated by two-sided markets offering an open call for projects of various purposes. Typically, a crowdfunding platform is an infrastructure allowing creators to raise funds from dispersed donors, consumers, or investors who commit to funding a project if the fundraising campaign reaches its target goal (Handke & Dalla Chiesa, 2021). When "matchfunding" integrates crowdfunding, institutional donors, public or private, match the *crowd* (dispersed individual donors or consumers). Some examples include the platform *Voordekunst* and *Voor Je Buurt* in the Netherlands, *Goteo* in Spain, *Benfeitoria* and *Juntos Pela Saude* in Brazil, *CrowdCulture* in

Sweden, *Growfunding* in Belgium, and *CharityDigital* in the UK. In all these cases, the online platform acts as a "two-sided market" (Rochet & Tirole, 2003) matching the crowd with institutional donors (e.g. governments, municipalities, foundations, international or national parties, and, in some cases, private companies). To cover the fixed costs of operating the online intermediation, the platform typically charges a fixed fee on the full amount raised, deducted before the platform transfers the funds to the cultural project.

The matchmaking procedures can happen in either of three mechanisms: (a) In-First, when the matchfunder contributes to the project before the crowd's donations; (b) Top-Up, when the matchfunding contributes to the project after the crowd's donations; (c) Bridge, when the matchfunder contributes after an initial amount has been collected through crowd donations, yet far from reaching the target goal. Baeck et al. (2017) thoroughly describe these mechanisms in a seminal work supported by NESTA[3] (UK). A fourth alternative is the *real-time* model (Baeck et al., 2017) when matching happens automatically. In this case, the contributions from funders are automatically matched (usually doubled, i.e. as Goteo does, as described by Senabre and Morell, 2018). The real-time mechanism, although more complex and expensive for the platform (cf. Baeck et al., 2017), is important because the signals will be immediate to any new funder/backer and thereby causing herding behaviour—a typical success factor in crowdfunding studies (Shneor & Vik, 2020).

Although many models apply, typically, the online-based matchfunding operates, through *challenge grants* (Schuster, 1989)—i.e. if you manage to reach amount x in new sources of funding, we will match this by a bonus consisting of percentage x of the money you got at first—or *reverse matching grants*—i.e. if you fundraise x, we will more or less automatically support you with y funds). These mechanisms, discussed in a seminal paper by Schuster (1989), thus resemble mostly the *first-in* and *top-up* options, widely used as they provide either a clear confirmation of the crowd's preferences or institutional preferences.

The Benefits of Online Matchfunding Operated Through Crowdfunding Mechanisms

This model conveys key benefits: (a) fewer costs of communication and standardisation of information for all parties; (b) an established quality criteria by which the platform runs its operation to ensure high success rates; (c) reduced information asymmetry between parties involved as there is no communication happening outside of the platform (cf. Dalla Chiesa & Alexopoulou, 2022; Loots et al., 2023).

For campaigners, the online platform can provide access to a diverse pool of institutional funders before the campaign starts or after the campaign is published online, if a prearranged matchfunding is not in place. The platform typically collects information about the partners' preferences (e.g. theatre, visual arts, music) or thematic preferences (e.g. diversity-related projects, environmentalism, democracy, etc.) to match institutional preferences with existing or incoming crowdfunding campaigns. Furthermore, the involvement of institutional funders in crowdfunding campaigns is likely to partially resolve the assurance problem in crowdfunding (cf. Handke & Dalla Chiesa, 2021; Hudik & Chovankuliak, 2018) by conferring a credibility signal (Steigenberger, 2017) based on which campaigners can collect more crowd-based donations. The confirmation of assurance can also work the other way round, whereby campaigners can collect the matchfunding contribution by offering institutional donors an assurance of the crowd's appreciation. In this case, the assurance mechanism works for two different types of donors (individuals and institutions) rather than among individuals only.

For civil society in general, this model puts the public authority's decision-making in check, as a project will only meet the target goal with enough contributions from the fans, consumers, or patrons who scrutinise projects submitted online. It also puts the interests of these *crowds* in check if the public funds arrive only after demand is revealed. Public grants thus follow through if cultural projects align with the thematic interests of policymakers, either before or after the crowd's donation. Specifically in the domain of civic crowdfunding, which "offers communities an alternative means of financing social projects that are normally funded by the government", matchfunding is already applied by governments that act as co-financiers in the arts (Van Montfort et al., 2020: 2).

From an informational viewpoint, crowdfunding technology can reduce search and negotiation costs for funders, too. As the mechanism of funding is outsourced, communication problems and transactions are dealt with outside of the public authority's jurisdiction. Quality screening is also shared with other parties (initially, the platform; then, the public). Lastly, it also provides the expert opinion of cultural policymakers with legitimation by the public, which aligns with a more liberal approach to arts funding.

Figure 8.1 below depicts a stylised three-step process for match-funding, where the platform conducts an initial search and negotiation with potential matchfunders to determine funding capacity. In the second step, individual projects submitted on the platform are scrutinised by both the crowd and the institutional funder (top-up or first-in), who decides whether to match the crowd's donation. When all parties contribute to the campaign and reach the target goal, the campaign receives the amount raised minus the platform fee.

Furthermore, we assume that the online crowdfunding system benefits when reputable institutions contribute to the campaign, thus conferring an *external* credibility signal (Mavlanova et al., 2016) to the crowd-funding project. This can generate more individual donations or higher average donation values (Baeck et al., 2017; Dalla Chiesa et al., 2025; Meier, 2007). Due to the high asymmetry of information in cultural markets (cf. Caves, 2000), we assume that individual donors are unlikely to donate without first screening online campaigns (Kang et al., 2016).

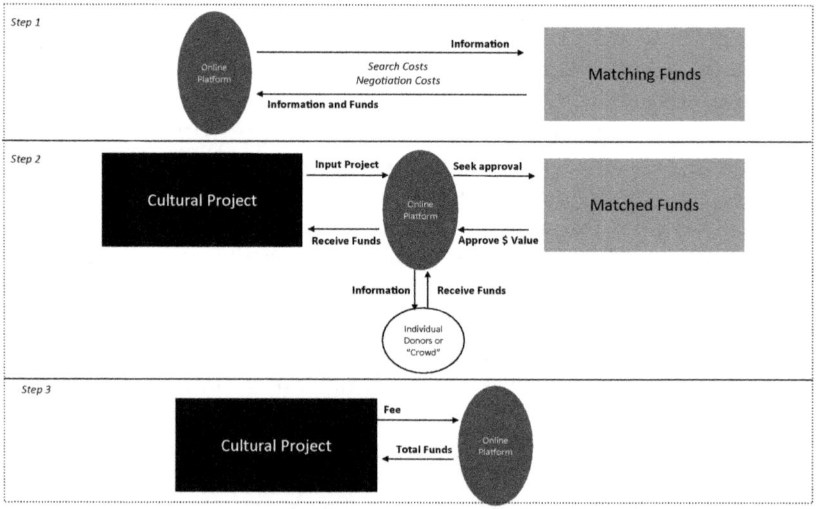

Fig. 1 Matchfunding with private platform intermediation (*Source* Authors' own elaboration)

This may indicate that institutional funders improve campaign success and effectively serve as a credibility signal for uncertain private donors seeking status signals (Feder, 2017). As such, matchfunding, in theory, provides a powerful premise for crowding in private support. Evidence suggests that, in some cases, public investment crowds out private contributions (Payne, 2009). The crowd-out hypothesis is highly contested due to its endogeneity and omitted variables (Wit & Bekkers, 2017) or incomplete crowd-out (Andreoni, 1993). Furthermore, Andreoni and Payne (2003) theorise that the crowding-out hypothesis emerged not from private investment disincentives but rather from the cultural project's reduced fundraising efforts after acquiring a public grant.

3 Matchfunding with Public Grants[4]: The *Traditional* Model

Key Characteristics

As discussed in Section 1, matchfunding can be defined as the intentional process of providing funding in a manner that triggers other funders or the fundee to contribute to a cost-sharing strategy. These have happened pre-digitalisation, also in various forms. Because the emergence of matching grants is motivated by the efficiency argument of public funding, we discuss the offline model primarily organised by public authorities in this section. We understand that private actors (corporate sponsorship, patrons and investors) can always decrease their contribution to the arts due to a different moral justification of arts support, while civil society, especially arts interest groups, expect otherwise from public authorities.

Schuster (1989) identifies three key manifestations of matching grants involving public partners.[5] First, (1) *Co-funding* relies on the principle that governments co-fund part of the costs of artistic or cultural projects. Other funding sources are expected to contribute to the project's execution. Second, matchfunding via (2) *Challenge Grants* rests on the principle that a funder (typically the government) challenges an artist or organisation to secure private funding (tax rebates typically incentivise private contributors) or market contributions, with a promise to reward the successful completion of a challenge at a given ratio if successful (for example, 1:3 or 1:4 in public grants[6]). Third, (3) *Reverse matching grants* rely on the principle that the government will match any other private contribution, more or less automatically, based on defined eligibility criteria. *Reverse* is thus a descriptor for reversing the logic of governance in that the public, not appointed civil servants, members of arts councils, or politicians, decides on allocating public resources.

Schuster (1989) explains that challenge grants should be preferred over the other two formats when policymakers want to *proactively* support artistic projects that cannot rely on private arts funding or typical market exchange. Conversely, reverse matching is preferred if policymakers wish to take a *reactive* approach, taking its cues from what is already funded through the existing private arts funding marketplace. According to Schuster, most governments prefer co-funding since these two grants are the extremes on a continuum.

We can also extend the analysis of these three mechanisms to private institutions that wholly or partially sponsor particular cultural projects using matchfunding principles. While in principle, the reasons for funding may differ, mechanisms can be quite similar. In a private matchfunding scheme, the typical corporate arts-sponsorship logic applies (see Kirchberg, 2003). We will zoom into two actors triggering such match funding below: first, initiated by cultural organisations themselves; second, triggered by public authorities. A third option follows, which we call a *hypothetical* mechanism resembling a public crowdfunding fully operated by the public authorities' administrative powers.

Option 1: Cultural Organisations Matching Funds Offline

Matchfunding can be triggered by any cultural project/organisation seeking funds to match a first donor's contributions (e.g. a public or private institution) (Fig. 8.2), or revenues originating in its internal operations (e.g. revenues from ticket sales, etc.) (Fig. 8.3). When seeking *external* support, we assume that the costs of securing the matchfunding are greater for the cultural organisation than for the partner institution(s). The initiator first incurs search costs while searching for potential matchfunders, then negotiation costs when securing a deal regarding the value of matched support, and finally reports the results to the matchfunder, who screens the quality according to its compliance procedures. These are time-costly activities for organisations, which most likely benefit from existing contacts with potential donors and in-house fundraisers.

As such, most transaction costs (i.e., information, negotiation, bargaining, and search costs) involved in this relationship are upheld

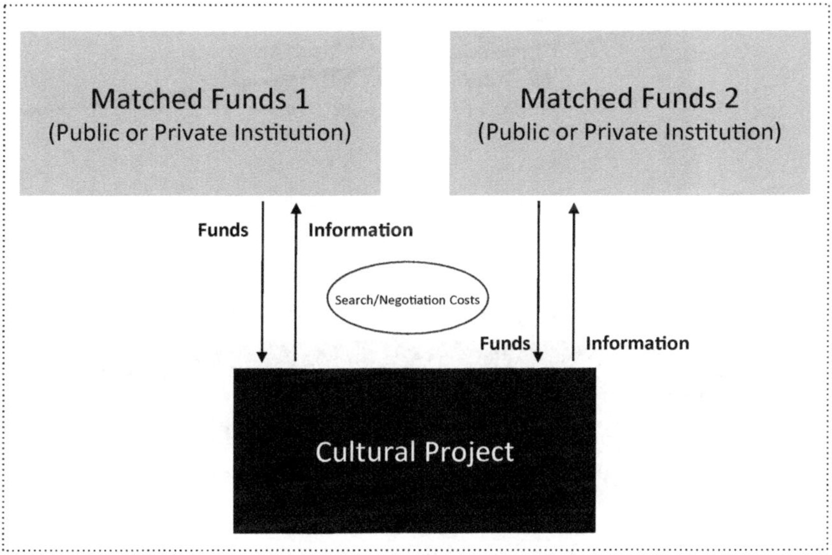

Fig. 2 Matchfunding with external funds only (*Source* Authors' own elaboration)

by the organising party, which seeks an institutional funder willing to contribute, offers a project, and negotiates a deal. While cultural projects benefit from pooling funds from a matchfunding entity, the private matching entity likely benefits from tax-deductible or tax-credit mechanisms (when applicable), as well as from the non-monetary values associated with sponsoring culture and the arts. Thus, the external funder's role is to acquire information and provide funds, but not to actively engage in the project's decision-making processes, which differs from investment-based models where the expectation of monetary returns applies. This mechanism resembles a typical corporate sponsorship engaging in co-financing (Schuster, 1989). We thus suppose that private foundations, corporations, and nonprofits can actively match existing revenues from cultural projects, with or without the involvement of public agents, and with or without the presence of internal revenues to match external funds.

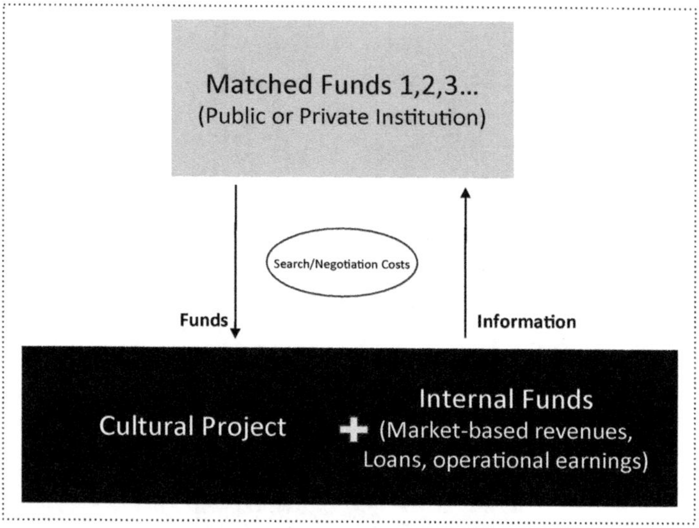

Fig. 3 Matchfunding with internal funds included (*Source* Authors' own elaboration)

Option 2: Governments Triggering Matching Funds Offline

When the matchfunding mechanism is primarily organised by a public authority, it primarily incentivises donations from other parties, non-governmental or corporate. For example, in Canada, the Canadian Cultural Investment Fund (CCIF) encourages private sector investment, partnership, and sound business practices to help arts organisations be better rooted and recognised in their communities. In this model, eligible applicants can receive funds from the public authority aimed at matching the funds raised from private donations, up to a maximum of one dollar of public money for each private dollar raised (Government of Canada, 2025).[7] Project creators still bear the search and negotiation costs delineated in the previous section. Still, they are facilitated by a centralised system that pursues a cost-sharing strategy and welcomes matchfunding from other (private) parties that commit to financial support. For public authorities, this has benefits such as (a) cultural organisations acquire public grants after private agents approve of the cultural project's qualities; (b) reduced costs of screening quality; (c) decentralisation of public grants and spreading costs of cultural production.

Option 3: The Public Authorities' Online Matchfunding Model

We discuss a potential last (hypothetical) model in which public authorities trigger matchfunding through an online information aggregator, similar to online crowdfunding platforms. Figure 8.4 depicts a hypothetical public agent acting as an intermediary that sets a matchfunding mechanism by gathering information from cultural projects and potential funders. The public authority thus acts as a matchmaker of private funds, the crowd and artistic projects. Instead of letting the private market decide on the matchfunding mechanisms and paying the costs of a private matchmaker, the public authority acts proactively as a mediator, funder, and screener of the private funds, thus providing the matchmaking mechanism as a *public good*. This model is thus similar to a crowdfunding mechanism. The main difference lies in the possibility of acquiring matching funds without paying for the intermediary's fees.

This model is hypothetical, as we lack information on any existing governmental platform acting as an all-centralised matchmaking of various funding types. This model facilitates the work of cultural organisations in that part of the search costs can be reduced by a public authority

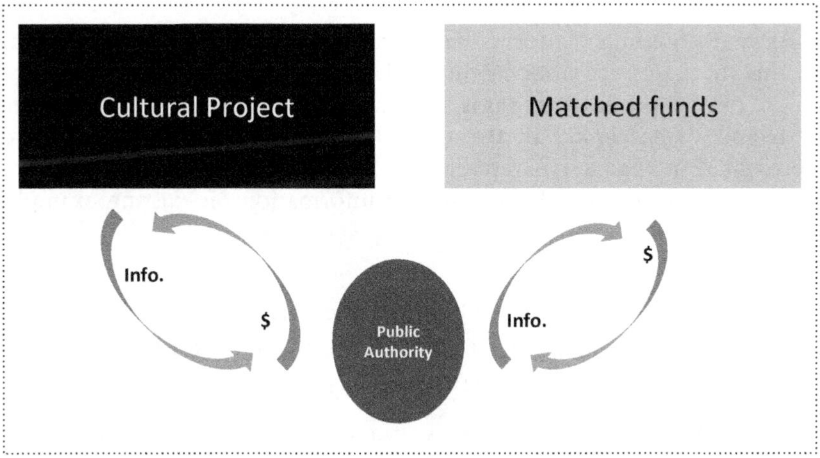

Fig. 4 Matchfunding centralised by public authorities (*Source* Authors' own elaboration)

responsible for compiling information on the various (often private) partners willing to fund the arts. The public authority assesses matchfunding partners by reacting to private requests, or actively searching for suitable institutions.

The downside of this model is the cost of *making* the system instead of *buying* it. If private partners offer a similar service for a fee and demand is price-inelastic, we can suppose that there is no need for public authorities to incorporate the costs of matchmaking and offer it as a public good. As such, it is unlikely that public authorities will take on the burden of search and negotiation costs between matchmakers and cultural projects, as the latter are more numerous than the former and will likely dispute funding opportunities. Because the CCS are expected to oversupply art due to infinite variety and intrinsic motivation (Caves, 2000), we suppose this is less likely to happen. More projects are willing to take public grants than public grants are available, thus there are fewer incentives for governments to integrate an online matchfunding fully as a public good, as this may represent significant costs for public authorities. Another limitation of this model is the over-centralisation rationale, which competes with the liberal foundations of crowdfunding. Technically, if private suppliers provide matchmaking functions for a limited fee, the greater efficiency of centralisation is disputable.

As crowdfunding platforms have already incurred the costs of setting up this mechanism, public agents will likely outsource this service to a private or non-profit entity (as is the case with *Voordekunst* in the Netherlands and *Crowdfunder* in the UK). In this case, the public authority represented in Fig. 8.4 is replaced by a private matchfunding platform. To the best of our knowledge, we lack information on existing examples of option 3.

4 Discussion: Assessing Matchfunding as a Primary Source of Public Support for the Arts

We have highlighted the benefits and challenges of different matchfunding formats, showing how online intermediaries enhance credibility, screening, and communication. In the following, we discuss the potential consequences should online matchfunding fully integrate how public money for the arts is distributed.

The Crowd's Ruling

Many scholars have theorised how the emergence of cultural policy stems from a market failure of the arts (Fullerton, 1991; Potts & Cunningham, 2008): (a) artists are more numerous than the available public funds or consumers' willingness-to-pay for the wide variety of available art (Caves, 2000); (b) consumers cannot fully access information on the variety and quantity of art supplied; (c) technological progress seems to impact the arts differently, or relatively more slowly in sectors like the performing arts (Baumol & Bowen, 1966); (d) artist frequently aspire to provide art as a public good, or with public good attributes uncaptured by market value (Frey, 2000). As some art forms are provided based on their meritorious value (Srakar & Čopic, 2012), crowd validation is less important. For all other goods where demand revealing is welcome, the crowdfunding mechanism offers a vote via monetary means with obvious fiscal, moral and economic implications for the public economy.

Second, the pure crowd's ruling of public funding implies a redefinition of cultural policy and a paradigm shift in terms of allocating public funds for the arts. Mangset (2020) discusses whether the contemporary approaches to cultural policymaking—like crowdsourcing—would imply the end of cultural policy as we know it. Ultimately, less centralisation of decision-making coupled with the *desacralisation* of the arts suggests that new decision-makers have a stake in how the arts are distributed. While this approach relatively democratises art by providing easy access to funds to unknown artists, it also incorporates market logics at the centre of arts funding. Artists would first compete for consumers, then for public grants depending on the matchfunding system in place (top-up or first-in, as described above). If so, arts-making would resemble a *competitive model* (Potts & Cunningham, 2008) similar to any open market mechanism, with potential dire consequences for artists whose public appeal is minor, hence returning to the merit-good argument for public funding without demand-revealing tools.

The non-prescriptive nature of the crowd-driven crowdfunding selection model compared with how public funders select projects and artistic works (i.e. through formal application and instrumental criteria dictated by experts, cf. Rykkja & Bonet, 2023) is a more liberal mechanism aligned with a *Rawlsian* (Rawls, 1971) view that public authorities are not meant to interfere in defining what the good culture is for society. Rushton

(2000) debates such issues, demonstrating competing versions of liberalism (by Richard Dworkin) within the framework of arts funding, where a positive outcome of public funding for the arts is an intended aim for innovation in structured funding systems. The channelling of public money through matchfunding mechanisms is a way to partially influence decision-making on the needed sources of innovation for the future good, and at the same time, a partial appreciation of expert opinions (i.e. cultural policymakers) on what good art is.

The problems it entails are far beyond the scope of this essay, yet it unveils important trade-offs between centralisation and decentralisation of cultural policy, fiscal consequences and an ethical assessment on how much centralisation/decentralisation is necessary to ensure diversity. Yet, it is unlikely that matchfunding operated through crowdfunding precludes policy goals. It is also unlikely that all decision-making regarding funding provisioning polarises the crowd's ruling and policymaking on different sides of the spectrum. However, just like Mollick and Nanda's (2016) study on amateurs versus expert funding decision-making, new studies can assess the differences between the crowd's opinions (amateur, consumers, audiences) and the expert opinion to evaluate if differences also apply in matchfunding more accurately.

Equity and Access

Though many public funding schemes are organised nationally, the prevalence of the CCS clustering in urban areas has led to an overrepresentation of funding for urban dwellers. In contrast, makers in more peripheral settings often struggle more to find financing for their projects. Similarly, funding organisations have usually favoured nationally dominant groups, leaving ethnic organisations underfunded (Feder & Katz-Gerro, 2015). Funding organisations also tend to support established organisations that have successfully leveraged funding in the past (Peters & Roose, 2022). If such makers or organisations without easy access to existing arts funding are to harness individual donors in a matched crowdfunding campaign, online matching through crowdfunding may be able to increase equity in arts funding. However, evidence from debt-based crowdfunding suggests that donors are more likely to contribute to projects in their current location (Li et al., 2024). Considering that most consumers of cultural products are more likely to be higher educated, white, upper-middle-class, and live in urban areas (Brook et al., 2020), this might further exacerbate unequal access to funding. To provide most public grants via crowdfunding, we should first ensure that a significant—and more diverse—portion of the population actively participates in direct (online) crowd-voting.

Other issues to revisit are failures to address the tricky legal and fiscal debate on whether crowdfunding income constitutes gifts or sales of production (Lazzaro & Noonan, 2020). We do not cover the legal and fiscal implications of this debate, but they relate to equity and access through assessing how taxed income reaches arts projects and how it would, hypothetically, arrive through matchfunding. It is important to consider that we want to avoid, in plain English, the poor paying for the rich once again through novel digital ways. This would simply reinforce existing disparities without welfare improvement.

"Make or Buy" Decision

The more public authorities use crowdfunding platforms to supply public money, the more cultural projects will integrate crowdfunding mechanisms. In short, the public authority's decision to provide matchfunding through crowdfunding is like a make-or-buy decision where *make* is the typical grant-giving mechanism without online intermediaries, and *buy* is the grant-giving with a private online intermediary. There are consequences to using an all-encompassing crowdfunding option (buy) to supply public grants versus using centralised grant procedures (make).

In the current grant-giving system, artists compete for scarce funds while having to adapt their artistic narratives each time (Peters & Roose, 2020). The time spent on each application form is supposedly significant and could potentially displace valuable art creation time. The buy option would partially decentralise fund-seekers' approval while centralising the application mechanisms through a single platform. Suppose public grants for the arts were supplied via the online matchfunding mechanism. In that case, artists will vary the application narrative regarding their potential consumer base to seek the crowd's validation, rather than crafting narratives tailored for public authorities each time. In either case, artists already craft narratives to different funding agents (individuals or institutions; public or private).

In essence, not all art engages donors/consumers at this very moment, or will prove valuable in the future (e.g. avant-garde art forms). Requesting funds through a standardised private (buy) crowdfunding platform can be overly restrictive to art innovation with less commercial appeal, but it is beneficial for liberal principles. Future choice-experimental research methods can investigate the willingness of creators and funders to match funds through such mechanisms compared to disengaging from any online participatory mechanisms.

Furthermore, the barriers to implementation of matchfunding through crowdfunding include technological and administrative challenges, its perception as a marginal funding mechanism, and regulatory barriers (Lazzaro & Noonan, 2020), impeding a complete picture of its welfare consequences.

5 Conclusion

The present chapter explored the matchfunding phenomenon, distinguishing between different matchfunding formats and arrangements, primarily between online and offline options. Matchfunding, as a cost-sharing strategy, can be defined as the intentional process of providing funding by funders to fundees, in a manner that encourages or enforces additional funders to contribute to the targeted goal, either prearranged by the initial funder and/or mediated by the efforts of the fundee. We specifically identified a new online matchfunding model and a traditional matched grants mechanism, which differ in how the matchmaking function occurs: with or without intermediation.

Examining the potential of matchfunding as a cost-sharing strategy, we argue that institutions are key to the future of the cultural sector. At a minimum, institutions can play an essential role by conveying credibility signals to cultural project owners seeking to develop a financing mix. More groundbreaking formats are those in which institutional funders take leading roles, by prearranging matchfunding modalities, foreseeing benefits for matchfunders, and closing the budget gaps of cultural projects. As such, we argue that public and private, matching institutional and individual partners, can stimulate a burgeoning funding landscape for the cultural sector with money and credibility.

On the other hand, more matchfunding may threaten the role, status and access to funding of civil servants, Art Councils, established artists, and institutions because they become sidelined. From a theoretical perspective, this may not be an issue, but it could explain why, at least in the European context, matchfunding has not become more prevalent. Schuster (1989) discusses the difficulties in making these institutional changes as a way to explain why most governments prefer co-funding, so as to at least allow decision-making powers by at least two parties and share the costs of cultural incentives.

While the present chapter conceptualises matchfunding, empirical studies can illuminate the efficiency and workable elements of the various identified formats. For example, the hypothesised signalling and minimised transaction costs could be tested on sufficiently large samples, and online and offline formats can be compared. Future studies could also demonstrate how matchfunding formats relate to other forms of public–private partnerships, mainly when conceived as cost-saving strategies in the arts, distinguishing between sectors and contexts.

Lastly, a limitation of our study is that we purposely excluded investment-based options because we found less evidence of investment funds in the arts engaging in typical matchfunding, hence our narrower focus in this chapter. We are also limited in our discussion of the moral and fiscal outcomes of centralising and decentralising funding mechanisms, a discussion that match/crowdfunding brings to the fore. We suggest further research on matchfunding options with equity and repayable grants to compare the effectiveness of matching with and without financial returns for funders, as well as a debate on the fiscal and moral implications of fully adopting such a system to distribute public money. Recent studies in the field of public health have questioned the effectiveness of novel blended mechanisms proposed in the public sector for its tendency to favour middlemen in both private and public sectors (cf. Stein & McNeil, 2025). This could also be explored in the cultural sectors where actors increasingly incorporate varied funding options for the CCS while tapping into the potential of public–private funding mix.

Competing Interests This chapter results from a joint research project supported by Platform ACCT, Cultuur + Ondernemen, Voordekunst, the Dutch Research Council (NWO/KIEM). The authors also thank the support of interns from the Erasmus School of Culture and Communication during the development of this research project.

Notes

1. We are aware of the various ways in which the term matchfunding has been used (e.g., matched funding, match funding, match-funding, matched-funding, matching funds). In this chapter, we use

the combined version "matchfunding" to highlight its connection to another term: "crowdfunding." Similar to how the separate words "crowd" and "funding" come together to form a new concept, we treat "matchfunding" as a term that describes a novel phenomenon. Since the integration of matchfunding into crowdfunding platforms is a relatively recent development, we use "matchfunding" throughout our analysis to specifically refer to match funds within crowdfunding contexts.

2. Crowdfunding platforms are not the only way in which online matchfunding can happen. In theory, any institution, public or private, can provide an online intermediary matchmaker for matchfunding. Examples other than the crowdfunding mechanisms are, however, scarce.
3. National Endowment for Science, Technology and the Arts.
4. *Grants* are typically the types of funds provided for a specific purpose awarded on the basis of merit, need, or quality following a "call for proposals" (European Union, 2025). *Subsidies* follow a similar logic but often emerge as a financial support to reduce the cost of a product or service or aiming at impacting prices or output levels (European Union, 2025). According to the World Bank (2014), subsidies, grants, and other social benefits include all unrequited, nonrepayable transfers on current account to private and public enterprises".
5. Schuster (1989) discusses matching grants in the context of arts organisations. We extend his understanding also to individual artists who can constitute a *firm* from an economic standpoint.
6. For example, the Norwegian Ministry of Culture ran a challenge grant scheme between 2014–2022 whereby any artist or organisation that raised NOK 100,000 (about EUR 8,000) in private funding through private philanthropy or donations would receive an additional grant of 25% (capped at some extent) of the value of the private funding (see Rykkja & Bonet, 2025). Also, the Dutch government experimented with a matching scheme for major cultural organisations; an income standard was introduced in 2013 to foster the cultural entrepreneurship of those organisations, but soon abolished (Loots, 2015).
7. Since its inception in 2001, the Endowment Incentives component has provided a total of $367 million in matching grants, leveraging private sector donations of $516 million, for a total of $883

million invested in 107 public charitable foundations and benefitting the long-term financial health of 307 professional arts organisations across Canada (Government of Canada, 2025).

References

Andreoni, J. (1990). Impure Altruism and Donations to Public Goods: A Theory of Warm-Glow Giving. *The Economic Journal, 100*(401), 464–477.

Andreoni, J. (1993). An Experimental Test of the Public-Goods Crowding-Out Hypothesis. *American Economic Review, 83*, 1317–1327.

Andreoni, J., & Payne, A. A. (2003). Do government grants to private charities crowd out giving or fund-raising? *American Economic Review, 93*(3), 792–812.

Anheier, H. K. (2005). *A dictionary of civil society, philanthropy and the third sector* (1st ed.). Routledge. https://doi.org/10.4324/9780203403372

Ashton, D. (2022). Funding arts and culture: Everyday experiences and organisational portfolio precarity. *European Journal of Cultural Studies, 26*(3), 388–407.

Baeck, P., Bone, J., & Mitchell, S. (2017). *Matching the Crowd: Combining Crowdfunding and Institutional Funding to Get Great Ideas off the Ground.* NESTA.

Baumol, W. J., & Bowen, W. G. (1966). *Performing Arts—The Economic Dilemma.* Twentieth Century Fund.

Bekkers, R. (2015). When and Why Matches Are More Effective Subsidies than Rebates. In *Replication in Experimental Economics* (Vol. 18, pp. 183–211). Emerald Group Publishing Limited.

Brook, O., O'Brien, D., & Taylor, M. (2020). *Culture is Bad for You.* Manchester University Press.

Canada (2025). Canada Cultural Investment Fund. Government of Canada. https://www.canada.ca/en/canadian-heritage/services/funding/cultural-investment-fund.html

Caves, R. E. (2000). *Creative Industries: Contracts Between Art and Commerce.* Harvard University Press.

Dalla Chiesa, C., & Alexopoulou, A. (2022). Matchfunding Goes Digital: The Benefits of Matching Policymaking with the Crowd's Wisdom. European Journal of Cultural Management and Policy, 12.

Dalla Chiesa, C., & Handke, C. (2020). Crowdfunding. In R. Towse & T. Navarette (Eds.), *A Handbook of Cultural Economics*(3rd ed., pp. 158–167). Edward Elgar.

Dalla Chiesa, C., Loots, E., Brandelli Bucco, G., & Wijngaarden, Y. (2025). Matchfunding momentum: The effect of institutional funding on the success of crowdfunded cultural and creative projects. *Journal of Alternative Finance, 2*(3), 274–301.

Davis, D. D. (2006). Rebate Subsidies, Matching Subsidies and Isolation Effects. *Judgment and Decision Making., 1*(1), 13–22.

Davis, D. D., Millner, E. L., & Reilly, R. J. (2005). Subsidy Schemes and Charitable Contributions: A Closer Look. *Experimental Economics, 8*, 85–106.

Davies, R. (2015). Three provocations for civic crowdfunding. *Information, Communication & Society, 18*(3), 342–355.

De Voldere, I., & K. Zeqo, K. (2017). *Crowdfunding: Reshaping the crowd's engagement in culture*. European Commission, Directorate-General for Education, Youth, Sport and Culture.

Diamond, P. A., & Hausman, J. A. (1994). Contingent Valuation: Is Some Number Better than no Number? *Journal of Economic Perspectives, 8*(4), 45–64.

Eckel, C. C., & Grossman, P. J. (2006). Subsidizing Charitable Giving with Rebates or Matching: Further Laboratory Evidence. *Southern Economic Journal, 72*(4), 794–807.

European Union. (2025). Glossary: Subsidies. In: *Statistics Explained*. https://ec.europa.eu/eurostat/statistics-explained/index.php?title=Glossary:Subsidies

Fang, Z., Tan, X. J., Xiao, S., & Tan, Y. (2021). More than Double Your Impact: An empirical study of match offers on charitable crowdfunding platforms. *Kelley School of Business Research Paper*, (2021–36).

Feder, T. (2017). *Intentions and Consequences of Arts Funding: Arts Policy and Arts Consumptio*n (Doctoral dissertation, University of Haifa (Israel).

Feder, T., & Katz-Gerro, T. (2015). The Cultural Hierarchy in Funding: Government Funding of the Performing arts Based on Ethnic and Geographic Distinctions. *Poetics, 49*, 76–95.

Feller, I. (2000). Social Contracts and the Impact of Matching Fund Requirements on American Research Universities. *Educational Evaluation and Policy Analysis, 22*(1), 91–98.

Frey, B. (2000). *Arts & Economics: Analysis & Cultural Policy*. Springer.

Frumkin, P., & Keating, E. K. (2011). Diversification reconsidered: The risks and rewards of revenue concentration. *Journal of Social Entrepreneurship, 2*(2), 151–164. https://doi.org/10.1080/19420676.2011.614630

Fullerton, D. (1991). On Justifications for Public Support of the arts. *Journal of Cultural Economics., 15*(2), 67–82.

Handke, C., & Dalla Chiesa, C. (2021). The art of crowdfunding arts and innovation: The cultural economic perspective. *Journal of Cultural Economics*.

Hungerman, D. M., & Ottoni-Wilhelm, M. (2021). Impure Impact Giving: Theory and Evidence. *Journal of Political Economy, 129*(5), 1553–1614.

Hudik, M., & Chovankuliak, R. (2018). Private Provision of Public Goods via Crowdfunding. *Journal of Institutional Economics, 14*(1), 23–44.

Hughes, P., & Luksetich, W. (2004). Nonprofit arts Organizations: Do Funding Sources Influence Spending Patterns? *Nonprofit and Voluntary Sector Quarterly, 33*(2), 203–220.

Kang, M., Gao, Y., Wang, T., & Zheng, H. (2016). Understanding the determinants of funders' investment intentions on crowdfunding platforms: A trust-based perspective. *Industrial Management & Data Systems, 116*(8), 1800–1819.

Karlan, D., & List, J. A. (2007). Does Price Matter in Charitable Giving? Evidence from a Large-Scale Natural Field Experiment. *The American Economic Review, 97*(5), 1774–1793.

Kirchberg, V. (2003). Corporate Arts Sponsorship, Chapters. In Ruth Towse (ed.), A *Handbook of Cultural Economics,* chapter 16, Edward Elgar Publishing.

Koumou, G. B. (2020). Diversification and Portfolio Theory: A Review. *Financial Markets and Portfolio Management, 34*, 267–312.

Lazzaro, E., & Noonan, D. (2020). A comparative analysis of US and EU regulatory frameworks of crowdfunding for the cultural and creative industries. *International Journal of Cultural Policy, 27*(5), 590–606.

Li, J., Zhou, Y., Hu, J., & Guo, F. (2024). Local Bias Versus Home Bias: Evidence from Debt-Based Crowdfunding. *Applied Economics, 56*(23), 2705–2719.

Loots, E. (2015). The Income Standard for the Performing and Visual Arts in the Netherlands: A Simple Indicator of Financial Performance or a Transition to Another Mode of Supporting Non-profit Organizations? *Zeitschrift Für Kulturmanagement, 1*(1), 53–74.

Loots, E., Betzler, D., Bille, T., Borowiecki, K. J., & Lee, B. (2022). New Forms of Finance and Funding in the Cultural and Creative Industries. Introduction to the Special Issue. *Journal of Cultural Economics, 46*(2), 205–230.

Loots, E., Piecyk, K., & Wijngaarden, Y. (2023). At the Juncture of Funding, Policy, and Technology: How Promising is Match-Funding of Arts and Culture through Crowdfunding Platforms? *International Journal of Cultural Policy, 30*(1), 118–134.

Mangset, P. (2020). The End of Cultural Policy? *International Journal of Cultural Policy, 26*(3), 398–411.

Mavlanova, T., Benbunan-Fich, R., & Lang, G. (2016). The Role of External and Internal Signals in E-commerce. *Decision Support Systems, 87*, 59–68.

McClelland, R. (2024). Encouraging Charitable Giving: Matching Grants Versus Rebates. *Tax Policy Center.* https://taxpolicycenter.org/sites/default/files/publication/165827/encouraging-charitable-giving-matching-grants-versus-rebates.pdf

Meier, S. (2007). Do Subsidies Increase Charitable Giving in the Long Run? Matching Donations in a Field Experiment. *Journal of the European Economic Association, 5*(6), 1203–1222.

Mollick, E., & Nanda, R. (2016). Wisdom or madness? Comparing crowds with expert evaluation in funding the arts. *Management Science, 62*(6), 1533–1553.

Morell, F. M., Hidalgo, E. S., & Rodríguez, E. (2020). Goteo.org civic crowdfunding and match-funding data connecting Sustainable Development Goals. *Scientific Data, 7*(1), 132.

Passeri, F. (2020). Lessons Learned from Civic Crowdfunding and Match-Funding Schemes in Europe. In *Crowdasset: Crowdfunding for Policymakers* (pp. 211–255).

Payne A. A. (2009). Does Government Funding Change Behavior? An Empirical Analysis of Crowd Out. In Eds. Jeffrey R. Brown & James M. Poterba (Eds.), *Tax Policy and The Economy,* (Vol. 23, pp. 159–84).

Peters, J., & Roose, H. (2020). From Starving Artist to Entrepreneur. Justificatory Pluralism in Visual Artists' Grant Proposals. *The British Journal of Sociology, 71*(5), 952–969.

Peters, J., & Roose, H. (2022). The Matthew Effect in Art Funding. How Reputation Affects an Artist's Chances of Receiving Government Support. *Poetics, 92*, 101578.

Potts, J., & Cunningham, S. (2008). Four Models of the Creative Industries. *Revue D'economie Politique, 120*, 163–180.

Raad voor Cultuur. (2024). *Toegang tot Cultuur. Op weg naar een nieuw bestel in 2029.* Raad voor Cultuur.

Rawls, J. (1971). *A theory of justice.* Harvard University Press.

Rochet, J.-C., & Tirole, J. (2003). Platform competition in two-sided markets. *Journal of the European Economic Association, 1*(4), 990–1029.

Rushton, M. (2000). Public funding of controversial art. *Journal of Cultural Economics 24*, 267–282.

Rushton, M. (2008). Who Pays? Who Benefits? Who Decides? *Journal of Cultural Economics, 32*(4), 293–300.

Rykkja, A., & Bonet, L. (2023). Governments Matching of Cultural Crowdfunding: An Exploratory Comparative Analysis of the Spanish and Swedish Case. *Debats Revista de cultura, poder i societat, 137*(1).

Rykkja, A., & Bonet, L. (2025). From Intent to Inaction: Factors Conditioning Cultural Institutions From Embracing Crowdfunding as a Fundraising Tool. *Journal of Alternative Finance, 2*(1), 3–23.

Schuster, J. M. D. (1989). Government Leverage of Private Support: Matching Grants and the Problem with New Money. In M. J. Wyszomirski & P. Clubb (Eds.), *The Cost of Culture: Patterns and Prospects of Private Arts Patronage*. ACA Books.

Senabre, E. & Morell, M. (2018). Match-funding as a formula for crowdfunding: A case study on the Goteo.org platform. In *OpenSym '18: Proceedings of the 14th International Symposium on Open Collaboration* (pp. 1–5).

Shneor, R., & Vik, A. A. (2020). Crowdfunding success: A systematic literature review 2010–2017. *Baltic Journal of Management, 15*(2).

Spence, M. (1981). Signaling, Screening, and Information. In *Studies in Labor Markets* (pp. 319–358). *University of Chicago Press.*

Srakar, A., & Čopic, V. (2012). Private Investments, Public Values: A Value-Based Approach to Argumenting for Public Support to the Arts. *Cultural Trends, 21*(3), 227–237.

Steigenberger, N. (2017). Why supporters contribute to reward-based crowdfunding. *International Journal of Entrepreneurial Behaviour & Research, 23*, 336–353.

Stein, F., & McNeill, D. (2025). Blended Finance to the Rescue? Subsidies, Vaccine Bonds and Matching Funds in Global Health. *Global Public Health, 20*(1), 2468338.

Van Montfort, K., Siebers, V., & De Graaf, F. J. (2020). Civic Crowdfunding in Local Governments: Variables for Success in the Netherlands? *Journal of Risk and Financial Management, 14*(1), 8.

de Wit, A., & Bekkers, R. (2017). Government Support and Charitable Donations: A Meta-Analysis of the Crowding-out Hypothesis. *Journal of Public Administration Research and Theory, 27*(2), 301–319.

World Bank. (2014). *Data Bank.* https://databank.worldbank.org/home

Open Access This chapter is licensed under the terms of the Creative Commons Attribution 4.0 International License (http://creativecommons.org/licenses/by/4.0/), which permits use, sharing, adaptation, distribution and reproduction in any medium or format, as long as you give appropriate credit to the original author(s) and the source, provide a link to the Creative Commons license and indicate if changes were made.

The images or other third party material in this chapter are included in the chapter's Creative Commons license, unless indicated otherwise in a credit line to the material. If material is not included in the chapter's Creative Commons license and your intended use is not permitted by statutory regulation or exceeds the permitted use, you will need to obtain permission directly from the copyright holder.

CHAPTER 9

"I Would Do Anything for Funds, but I Won't Do That": On Artists' Reluctance to Adopt Investment Crowdfunding and Possible Ways to Overcome It

Rotem Shneor

1 Introduction

Crowdfunding is a fundraising mechanism in which small amounts are collected from many contributors over the Internet and often without the involvement of traditional financial intermediaries (Mollick, 2014). It manifests in a variety of fundraising models distinguished by the types of benefits being offered to prospective backers, which range from non-investment (such as reward/prepurchase, donation, and patronage/subscription) to investment offers (such as equity, lending, profit- and revenue-sharing) (Shneor, 2020). Its digital embeddedness, democratic nature, and relatively low entry requirements offer new opportunities for effective project fundraising on a more levelled playing field. All of which

R. Shneor (✉)
School of Business and Law, University of Agder, Kristiansand, Norway
e-mail: rotem.shneor@uia.no

© The Author(s) 2026

C. Dalla Chiesa and A. Rykkja (eds.), *Cultural Funding and Financing*, Cultural Economics & the Creative Economy,
https://doi.org/10.1007/978-3-031-96696-5_9

leads some to find evidence that crowdfunding helps underserved and underfunded groups gain improved access to finance (Dolson & Jagtiani, 2024; Jagtiani & Lemieux, 2018; Mollick & Robb, 2016; Serwaah, 2022; Stevenson et al., 2019).

Growth in global crowdfunding volumes is primarily driven by increasing participation in investment schemes, which represented 93% of volumes in 2020 in comparison to non-investment schemes, which captured only 7% of volumes during the same year (Ziegler et al., 2021). At the same time, when comparing models, project fundraising campaigns utilising investment models raise significantly larger sums than those raised via non-investment models (Shneor, 2020). In contrast to these trends, research into the use of crowdfunding in the cultural sector finds a strong preference for non-investment crowdfunding models, while only a small minority of creators attempt to use investment crowdfunding models (De Voldere & Zeqo, 2017; Loots et al., 2022).

Such a choice seems surprising, especially when considering that artists exhibit higher degrees of risk tolerance and openness to new experiences when compared to other workers (Arenius et al., 2021). It is also somewhat counterintuitive because crowdfunding serves as a mechanism to reduce income uncertainty by ensuring coverage of necessary upfront project costs (Handke & Dalla Chiesa, 2022), often with no preset requirements (Tosatto et al., 2019), as well as that a fairer and/or larger share of generated income is left with the creator (Thorley, 2012), thanks to reduction in number of intermediaries between artist and end consumers (Tosatto et al., 2019). Furthermore, this choice is at odds with the reality in which artists suffer from chronically limited funding thanks to trends of public funds' shrinkage, stagnation, or growth that fail to catch up with the growing demand (Boeuf et al., 2014; Bonet & Sastre, 2016; Inkei, 2019; Papadimitriou, 2017) as propelled by constant increase in the number of new income-seeking artists entering the market annually (Abbing, 2002).

Accordingly, in the current chapter, an attempt is made at understanding this choice, while suggesting the Fear-Prejudice-Ignorance framework (hereafter referred to as the "FPI" framework), which outlines the mental barriers triggering artists' aversion to using investment fundraising models. Such an approach builds on psychological theory (e.g. Conroy, 2004; Elliot & Church, 1997; Gray, 1987), which is then anchored in the realities of artists' attitudes and preferences with respect to their economy and fundraising options (e.g. Abbing, 2002; Feder &

Woronkowicz, 2022; Haynes & Marshall, 2018; Rykkja et al., 2024). Accordingly, each of the FPI framework's mental barriers is defined, and its origins and implications are outlined. Furthermore, each barrier's relationship with the others is considered and explained. Later, several methods for potentially addressing these mental barriers are suggested, including education (Shneor & Flåten, 2020; Wenzlaff & Spaeth, 2023), match-funding schemes (Dalla Chiesa & Alexopoulou, 2022; Rykkja & Bonet, 2023), and strategic integration of value chains (Foà, 2019; Quero et al., 2017).

As such, the current chapter presents a conceptual discussion and development that builds on a blend of findings from earlier research, as well as reflections on the author's own multiple-year engagement in research and educational experiences covering crowdfunding in support of workers in the cultural sector broadly, and artists specifically. Moreover, since research on artists' perspectives on crowdfunding choices remains in short supply (Rykkja et al., 2020, 2024), some arguments need to be made while drawing on insights from broader literature.

The remainder of the chapter first presents each of the core conditions of the FPI framework and suggests its links to artists' aversion of investment crowdfunding models. Next, inter-relations between these conditions and their effects are also discussed. The chapter then discusses approaches to help address these adverse conditions. Finally, the chapter concludes by highlighting some of its contributions, limitations, and implications.

2 Conceptual Development

Research into adoption decisions concerning new technologies, services, and products usually builds on well-established general theories such as the Theory of Planned Behaviour (TPB) (Ajzen, 1991), and versions of the Technology Acceptance Model (TAM) (Venkatesh & Davis, 2000). The TPB stresses the importance of favourable attitudes, sense of perceived behavioural control, and subjective norms as critical in volitional decision-making such as technological adoption. TAM, on the other hand, focuses more on user perspectives, highlighting the importance of perceived usefulness and ease-of-use of the technology considered. Unsurprisingly, conceptual parallels have been drawn between the two theories, mostly linking notions of perceived usefulness to favourable attitudes, and perceived ease-of-use with perceived self-efficacy and behavioural control.

In the context of artist adoption of crowdfunding in general, two studies in Norway have provided interesting insights. First, artists with crowdfunding experience exhibited significantly higher levels of favourable attitudes towards using crowdfunding, perceived behavioural control (i.e. having an independent choice in use of crowdfunding), reported self-efficacy (i.e. having skills needed to use crowdfunding), and subjective norms (i.e. encouragement from close social circle to use crowdfunding), when compared to artists without crowdfunding experience (Rykkja et al., 2024). Second, while favourable attitudes towards crowdfunding and levels of subjective norms were significantly and positively associated with crowdfunding use intentions, levels of behavioural control and self-efficacy were not (Shneor et al., 2024).

While informative and helpful, some decisions can be better understood with further specification of contextual conditions shaping individuals' mindsets and dispositions, which in turn form their attitudes and perceptions towards technological adoption decisions. Accordingly, the current chapter suggests several mental barriers arising from the unique circumstances and realities of artistic work within the cultural and creative sectors. These circumstances influence attitudes and perceptions underlying the development of attitudes and intentions toward using investment crowdfunding for financing artistic and creative work. More specifically, fear of failure, prejudice towards commercial activities, ignorance of both crowdfunding and investment framing of work, as well as their interactions, are all suggested to discourage the use of investment crowdfunding by artists.

Fear

Fear is an emotional reaction to any threat or stimulus that other members of a species will work to terminate, escape from, or avoid (Gray, 1987). The idea that fear plays a role within creative work processes is well in tune with the assumption that creative work is an emotionally laden process, as it involves giving feelings a symbolic form that is then manifested in creative outputs (Averill, 2004). Furthermore, artists pay emotional costs when engaging in emotional expression in their creative work (Hamilton, 1997). Hence, creating art may feel dangerous and revealing for artists, leading many to find it difficult to draw a fine line between themselves and their creations (Bayles & Orland, 1993).

Accordingly, one of the most relevant forms of fear in an artist's professional experience may be the fear of failure. Broadly, the fear of failure captures how strongly individuals believe or anticipate that certain aversive consequences will occur should they experience failing (Conroy, 2001), causing them to feel anxiety in evaluative situations (Conroy, 2004). In this context, the main aversive consequences most dreaded include: the experience of shame and embarrassment, devaluing one's self-estimate, having an uncertain future, loss of interest from important others, and upsetting important others (Conroy et al., 2002).

In a similar fashion, fears concerning disclosure, visible failure, and projecting desperation have been found to hamper crowdfunding adoption in general (Gleasure, 2015), and investing forms of crowdfunding, such as equity crowdfunding more specifically (Estrin et al., 2018). In the cultural and creative industries, research showed that fear of failure, and concerns with reputational damage that may follow it, served as important disincentives for artists to engage in repeated crowdfunding campaigns (Dalla Chiesa, 2022), and so did the intensity of the emotional labour and disclosure requirements that come with crowdfunding practice (Davidson & Poor, 2015).

Overall, typical reactions to the sense of fear manifest in three forms (Gray, 1987): approaching the threat aggressively (fight), avoiding the situation (flight), or becoming paralyzed (freeze). Accordingly, in the case of fear of failure from using investment crowdfunding, these reactions may translate into either engaging in delegitimization of the use of investment crowdfunding (fight), avoiding the use of it (flight), or dropping out of the process after initiating a campaign (freeze).

Prejudice

Financial and economic considerations are often frowned upon in artistic circles. According to Abbing (2002), the economy is denied in the arts, and money is viewed as a necessary evil, despite the arts operating in both market and gift spheres (including public grants). While the latter is viewed as of higher status and attractiveness thanks to its recognition of artistic and aesthetic value, the former is tolerated as a necessity where some sacred art is traded in veiled transactions. Commercial activity represents a reluctant acceptance that survival is not just a matter of natural talent, as monetary and aesthetic value may coincide, donors and grant providers are not always selfless and unlimited, and art is not always open and independent. And while it may sometimes pay off commercially to pose as non-commercial in the arts, caring less about money than in other professions leads to overcrowding, increasingly lower income, and relative poverty in the sector. This situation is closely anchored in the paradox of creative production, where economic logics tend to crowd out artistic logics, and thus endanger the resources vital to creative production (Eikhof & Haunschild, 2007).

While donation crowdfunding activities may be framed as the financing of public goods, in promoting culture and arts for their own sake, and hence may be more easily accepted among artistic circles, the primacy of financial considerations in investment crowdfunding may taint its legitimacy among more idealistic artists. The sacrifices artists are willing to make while discounting the importance of monetary benefits in favour of artistic value creation (Abbing, 2002) clash directly with investors' primary interest in attractive material returns (Shneor, 2020). Furthermore, the notions of creative freedoms in artistic work and artists' control over IPR linked to creative outputs clash directly with the influence that comes with shared ownership in equity investments. Finally, the notions of time-flexible muse-inspired creative work clash directly with rigid repayment schedules outlined in loan agreements. Such clashes in fundamental views lead to further strengthening of commercial scepticism and economic denial.

Ignorance

Generally, cultural actors that have good business competencies are associated with more successful fundraising (Betzler, 2015). However, artists often report feeling less skilled at business functions such as marketing and sales (Leyshon et al., 2016), as well as disinterest in developing commercial skills (Lee et al., 2018).

Recognizing that most artists will end up as either partly or fully self-employed due to limited availability of full-time positions in existing cultural organizations, brought forth various offerings of entrepreneurial training as part of art education programs in higher education institutions (Bridgstock, 2012; Thom, 2017). However, such offerings often fail to strike an effective balance because they are either offered by business school professionals lacking deep understanding of cultural sector particularities or delivered by art faculty members that lack knowledge and skills relevant to market-oriented entrepreneurship (Bridgstock, 2012;

Thom, 2017). One of the results is the emergence of artists as reluctant entrepreneurs who engage in entrepreneurial activities but object to the label because it implies a for-profit orientation while denying business and commercial aspects of their work (Haynes & Marshall, 2018).

More specific to crowdfunding, a large-scale European study has shown that artists had limited awareness and understanding of crowdfunding, as well as limited entrepreneurial competence necessary for successful crowdfunding practice (De Voldere & Zeqo, 2017). Even when using crowdfunding, artists seem to lack the expertise to persuade people to participate and/or the will to accommodate fans' needs in their creative work (Thorley, 2012), as may be expected in commercial marketing logic aimed at satisfying demand.

The case of investment crowdfunding presents an even greater knowledge gap, as it goes well-beyond fundamental understanding of promotional marketing and project budgeting. It requires a shift from a project to a business mindset in which opportunities are framed as investments where financial returns are expected. As such, this requires deeper understanding of financial planning, resource management, and how to estimate financial valuations and expected return on investment. While artists are gradually opening to the need to improve their understanding of, and preparations for, entrepreneurial realities (Albinsson, 2018), the notion of needing to have a financial focus and develop related expertise may seem a stretch too far for most. In investment fundraising, artists are fully pushed towards the entrepreneur side of the artist-entrepreneur phenomenon. This position is often rejected by most artists as part of their inherent willingness to trade financial gains for self-fulfilment and artistic value creation, deemed as normatively superior in their professional circles (Abbing, 2002).

Interactions Between Fear, Prejudice, and Ignorance

Thus far, the FPI framework building blocks have been presented separately, however, it is also important to acknowledge the interactions between them and their resulting effects. First, the *interaction between fear and prejudice* may be closely aligned with fear of peer reactions in terms of exclusion and/or rejection. Here, the adoption of investment crowdfunding may be viewed by peers (and fans) as an act of "selling out" for financial gain (Klein et al., 2017). Purist peers' rejection may emerge from viewing the use of investment crowdfunding by an insider as philosophical treachery, tilting the balance towards commercial value at the expense of artistic value. Alternatively, pragmatist peers' rejection may emerge from growing anxiety about a possible resulting reduction in resource availability from traditional providers (such as public funding), as well as growing pressures on them to use it for funding their own projects.

Second, an *interaction between fear and ignorance* can be anchored in notions of fear of the unknown. According to psychological theory, fear of the unknown emerges when individuals perceive the absence of information at any level of consciousness, leading to automatic appraisal of the unknown as something to be averted (Carleton, 2016). As presented earlier, the research found that artists had limited awareness and understanding of crowdfunding broadly (De Voldere & Zeqo, 2017), and, therefore, may represent an unknown that can trigger anxiety that results in aversion.

Finally, evidence for an interaction between ignorance and prejudice can be traced to research showing that ignorance enhances negative effects of prejudice. At the core of this lies the fear of change because it threatens existing structures in one's life through revisiting views on how the world is (Bugental & Bugental, 1984). When the core assumptions by which we live are challenged, some choose to resist change in both active and quiescent manners (Thomas, 2015). In arts, artists not only express limited interest in developing commercial skills but even develop an anti-entrepreneurial mindset (Lee et al., 2018) which can easily result in aversion towards investment crowdfunding. However, at the same time, ignorance reduction through the crowdfunding experience and the learning from it enhance both the extent to which artists sense social support to engage in crowdfunding (and hence the legitimacy of such engagement), as well as the intentions to do so (Rykkja et al., 2024; Shneor et al., 2024).

In summary, Fig. 1 graphically represents the FPI framework, its core concepts, their interactions, and their overall impact on aversive attitudes. Aversive attitudes imply unfavourable views of the use of crowdfunding, which results from assessing it as more damaging than beneficial. In the next section, several mechanisms for a better-informed consideration of investment crowdfunding are suggested while highlighting how they address each of the mental barriers that need to be crossed.

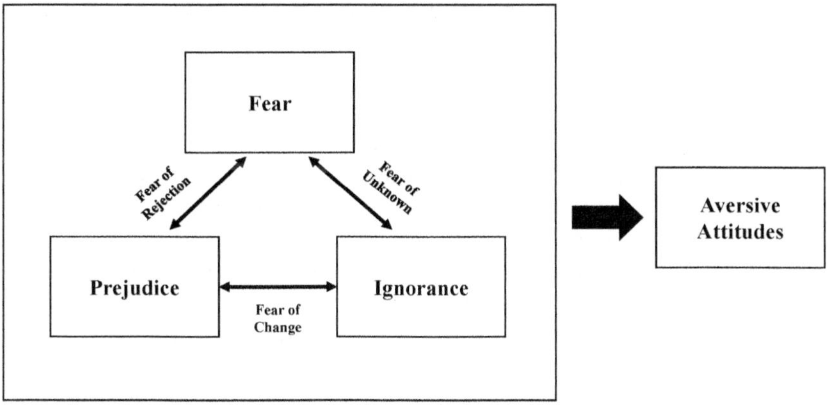

Fig. 1 The Fear-Prejudice-Ignorance (FPI) framework

3 Potential Mitigators of the FPI Mental Barriers

Several actions may be taken to help tackle the impact of excessive fear, prejudice, and ignorance. In the current section, the effects of education, match-funding schemes, and functional integration will be discussed as such potential mitigators.

Education

Education may help lift the veil of ignorance currently deterring more careful consideration of investment crowdfunding. Through the critical transfer of knowledge concerning the opportunities, challenges, and best practices in investment crowdfunding, artists can make better judgements about its relevance to supporting their own work. Here, it is important to stress that crowdfunding education should not serve as an act of (less critical) advocacy but rather one of critical information sharing that reviews successes and failures, rewards and costs, possibilities, and their boundaries.

As a starting point, one may consider some of the programs already developed and used in various higher education institutions (see: Shneor & Flåten, 2020; Wenzlaff & Spaeth, 2023). Such programs are built on modules that can be adjusted to the realities of the cultural and creative sectors while building on relevant examples from these settings and anchored in concrete projects art students (or people they work with) are engaged in anyway. Such real-time case-driven experiential learning may enable taking relevant lessons from the theoretical to the concrete and practical. Moreover, dual supervision by art and business faculty in such processes may help negotiate different interests and value-creation objectives in a pragmatic manner, while better understanding trade-offs and the conscious choices between them.

Accordingly, one may adopt modules fundamental to understanding crowdfunding practice. These include modules focused on the different types of fundraising models, different stakeholders, and the benefits they seek, campaign design elements, project planning and budgeting, digital and social media marketing, as well as regulatory and ethical considerations. To these, one may add modules dedicated to the particularities of crowdfunding public goods, art marketing, art financing, cultural and artistic value chains, and fandom build-up and management, which are critical for crowdfunding artists' campaigns. In addition, units dedicated to strategies for framing projects as investment objects, introduction to basic methods of project valuation and estimation of returns, as well as key aspects of corporate governance and owners' rights will all demystify the investment leg of investment crowdfunding.

Overall, such an approach will go beyond lifting the veil of ignorance. It will also reduce fears of failure thanks to acquiring relevant skills and strengthening perceptions of self-efficacy. It will reduce fear of the unknown by making it known and explicit. It will reduce fear of change by creating safe opportunities to experience change through controlled and bounded simulations. And it will reduce fear of rejection through signalling legitimacy by the very incorporation of investment crowdfunding into the formal curriculum and the use of real examples from peers in the educational materials. The latter is also likely to at least moderate prevailing prejudices against commercial activities thanks to the provision of real-life example cases, learning through experiences, and the realization that sometimes the artistic and commercial are not necessarily opposing ends but can also be parallel objectives that can be achieved simultaneously through careful strategy, planning, and framing.

Match-Funding Schemes

Match-funding in crowdfunding involves a third party contributing a part of the requested sum—at the beginning, midway, or the end of the crowdfunding campaign (Dalla Chiesa & Alexopoulou, 2022; Loots et al., 2024; Rykkja & Bonet, 2023). It is viewed as an extension of the funding toolbox at the disposal of organizations for the provision of public goods under the wider roof of civic crowdfunding (Davies, 2015). As such, it contributes both towards a public budget by increasing resource availability to already funded public services, as well as outside a public budget by providing resources to unfunded or underfunded public services (Wenzlaff, 2020). Regardless, at its core, match-funding implies that resources from government and quasi-public institutions are matched under various schemes with funds that are raised from the crowd and other private contributors (Loots et al., 2024).

According to Dalla Chiesa and Alexopoulou (2022), match-funding schemes represent a set of incentives for all stakeholders involved in the funding of cultural and creative work. Artists enjoy an opportunity to tap into a wider resource base, as well as enhanced legitimacy through endorsement from both public institutions and the wider crowd. Public institutions can reduce resource demands associated with project screening through partial outsourcing to the public in the form of hybrid democracy. Crowdfunding platforms enjoy enhanced legitimacy and credibility of their services through the engagement of public institutions and the growing volumes of funds being raised. And backers enjoy both greater opportunities to influence decisions, as well as enhance the likelihood of success for the projects of their choice.

While match-funding schemes in crowdfunding represent interesting opportunities, they are not free of controversy (Dalla Chiesa & Alexopoulou, 2022; Davies, 2015; Loots et al., 2024). On the one hand, they present a potential to increase the overall resource base, allocate public funds in a more democratic way, and increase citizen engagement, sense of ownership, and accountability. However, on the other hand, match-funding raises concerns with issues of responsibility, quality assurance, increasing indirect tax burdens, fit with public policy priorities, and the capacities of public administration to accommodate necessary flexibilities and technology adjustments. Such tensions may be addressed through the selective use of match-funding schemes when considering specific types of projects, specific types of fundraiser groups, within specific time frames, within specific geographies, and as parts of specific programs and policy initiatives. This is to say, match-funding should not be viewed as a dramatic replacement to existing sources but rather a supplement to existing schemes, programs, and tools that can be used selectively based on needs and priorities.

Accordingly, match-funding schemes for supporting cultural and creative projects represent an opportunity to both boost resource allocations to a sector struggling to catch up with demand, and hence provide needed funds to currently unfunded and underfunded cultural and creative work. Such mechanisms are already in use and include schemes often devised as collaborations between relevant authorities and dedicated crowdfunding platforms. Examples here include schemes involving platforms like Goteo in collaboration with regional government in Spain, CrowdCulture in collaboration with local government in Sweden, Voordekunst in cooperation with local government in the Netherlands, and Crowdfunder in collaboration with the national agency of Creative Scotland in the UK (Dalla Chiesa & Alexopoulou, 2022; Loots et al., 2024; Rykkja & Bonet, 2023). Alternatively, public organizations may also consider operating their own platforms. However, in such cases, they need to balance related costs (human and financial resource allocations) and benefits (greater curation control and quality assurance) when making such choices.

Thus far, most experimentations with match-funding have focused on non-investment crowdfunding models. Considering match-funding in investment models may create additional challenges in terms of the legitimacy and capacity of public organizations to share ownership or serve as credit providers. However, these have already been implemented in other sectors, such as entrepreneurial financing (Cumming, 2007; Wonglimpiyarat, 2016), regional development (Passeri, 2019), as well as financing of education, energy, and infrastructure projects (Pasicko & Petrovic, 2019) and hence could be extended to the cultural and creative sector as well. The easiest case here may be matched financing of credit offered under better conditions than that available from commercial entities, either by charging lower interest or foregoing interest altogether, all while crowd investors still receive interest and enjoy the public body serving as loan guarantors. Such offers may make lending more bearable for artists and cultural organizations. In the case of equity, public organizations may hold commitments to sell out ownership taken within a set number of years and hence turning them into temporary passive owners that help bridge funding needs without developing commercial interest. In public authorities, where investment of public funds is allowed and exercised, such investments can be allocated into existing relevant public investment funds as part of the diversification of related portfolios.

Assuming the suggestions outlined above can be used to alleviate related challenges, incorporating match-funding into investment crowdfunding initiatives can help mitigate the barriers presented under the FPI framework. Specifically, the involvement of public and semi-public organizations in the process will enhance legitimacy that can moderate existing prejudices while also alleviating fears of rejection and change. Furthermore, the availability of such schemes will incentivize artists (and other creative workers) to learn about the workings of investment crowdfunding while lowering fears of the unknown and reducing related ignorance. To further enhance this effect, public organizations can also create their own dedicated training programs for artists aimed at preparing them for a successful campaign that can both qualify for and enjoy matched funding upon successful fundraising.

Functional Integration

Functional integration is concerned with leveraging the opportunities provided by the platform economy in creating a one-stop shop where multiple artist needs can be met. Such a solution is well in tune with reintermediation by online market makers, where the core value offering is embedded in helping users become less overwhelmed by information overload through trust facilitation and superior information collection, processing, filtration, and evaluation services (Chircu & Kauffman, 1999). Furthermore, not only is information better organized and made available, but it also may incorporate value creation through the benefits of complementary offerings, novelty, efficiency, and personalization (Amit & Zott, 2017).

Here, one can envision digital market aggregators that offer crowdfunding as part of a series of services required by artists, which may include promotional support, fandom management, financial planning and budgeting, agent recruiting and contracting, material sourcing, distribution services, booking gigs or gallery placement, IPR protection, legal advice, etc. Such service integrators can offer a common interface for exchanges and recruitment of multiple sub-suppliers or offer service packages involving multiple components. For example, a relevant package may include crowdfunding campaign management services that will include public relations and promotional services, creation of marketing materials, legal advice, and financial planning consultancy.

Some examples of such integration trends are already available on a much smaller scale than the one suggested above in certain segments of the cultural and creative sector. For example, websites such as Qrates and Corite offer musicians combined services that include crowdfunding, album production, and distribution; other websites such as Unbound and Inshares offer authors services that include crowdfunding, editorial support, book production, and distribution. Similarly, Seed&Spark offers film producers services that include both crowdfunding and distribution.

While these examples represent steps in the direction of functional integration, they still incorporate a limited set of offerings vis-à-vis the needs of artists. The more ambitious range of service offerings suggested above renders such services uneconomical and too expensive for small-scale non-investment fundraising efforts (raising a few hundred or thousands of euros). However, they may make greater economic sense when raising large sums (raising hundreds of thousands to millions of euros) using investment crowdfunding. Thus far, it seems no entity has taken up this challenge, and hence, the idea remains somewhat theoretical.

Nevertheless, if such service integrators emerge in the future, they may also help address the mental barriers currently holding artists away from using investment crowdfunding. First, by concentrating services on one solution provider, processes may seem less overwhelming to prospective artists. The use of professional sub-suppliers and advisors for all related aspects of commercial thinking and execution of projects may partially relieve artists from tasks they dread and make change more palpable. Moreover, unlike earlier mechanisms that aim to educate or incentivize the education of artists, the current solution alleviates ignorance through the engagement of and reliance on professional support. While, in principle, the execution of commercial tasks can be outsourced to external actors, they will engage the artist in critical decision-making, implying an indirect learning process will still take place and contribute to reducing ignorance in related matters. Furthermore, the outsourcing of business dealings to professionals may allow the artist to more easily maintain their artistic credentials by focusing on artistic and creative work, and hence also reduce fear of rejection from peers based on sectoral prejudices.

4 Setting the FPI Framework in Context

While the FPI Framework concerns the individual level of decision-making, it is important to acknowledge that such decisions are made in specific contexts and that contextual conditions may moderate the relative salience and impact of the various barriers underlying the FPI. Here, one may consider the contexts of national cultural policy, as well as specific sub-sectors of the cultural and creative industries.

Cultural Policy Context

Cultural policy is broadly defined as "governmental strategies and activities that promote the production, dissemination, marketing, and consumption of the arts" (Mulcahy, 2006, p. 320). Cultural policy is deeply interwoven in the political discourses of different societies. It is motivated by a varied set of objectives, the configuration of which is defined by the political, social, and economic orientations and capacities of each nation. According to Mulcahy (2006), the main dilemmas underlying cultural policy formulation and execution revolve around tensions between elitism (provision to access to high art previously reserved for higher class citizens only) and populism (allowing citizens of all classes to engage in art on own terms); and between utilitarian views of art (as directly and indirectly benefiting economic well-being of citizens) and intrinsic value view of art (as an essential element allowing fulfilment of citizens lives in its own right).

In recent years, these tensions have been placed under growing social, political, and technological pressures towards ever-greater public participation in cultural policy initiatives and activities (Bonet & Négrier, 2018). Crowdfunding is just one manifestation of such enabling technologies that incorporate greater degrees of public participation. In this respect, environments guided by ideologies of cultural democracy may be more attuned to the opportunities afforded by investment crowdfunding to support a wider plurality of creative expressions (including costly productions, novice artists, etc.). At the same time, those more attuned to cultural democratization may hold more conflicting views, as crowdfunding both provides greater access to artistic expressions, but at the same time, does not necessarily guarantee their aesthetic qualities and values. Moreover, while utilitarian approaches may herald investment crowdfunding for encouraging creators to think of their creations as something to be consumed and invested in, purists of the intrinsic value of arts may view non-donation forms of crowdfunding as mechanisms that erode and corrupt such values and artistic freedom. Accordingly, one may assume that barriers to investment crowdfunding adoption may be lower in environments where cultural policy is focused on cultural democracy and utilitarian values.

Beyond the objectives and delivery modes of cultural policy, nations also vary in terms of the extent to which the cultural and creative sectors have access to and are dependent on public funding. Here, while some environments tend to depend more on commercial and non-profit private patronage, others depend on public funding and grant schemes (Mulcahy, 2006). For example, in Europe, during 2022, public cultural funding (including recreation and religion) ranges from relatively low levels of 0.4% of GDP in Ireland and 0.6% in Bulgaria to relatively higher levels of over 3.1% of GDP in Iceland and 2.7% in Hungary (EuroStat, 2024). Nevertheless, the general trend in most Western countries is one of public funds' shrinkage, stagnation, or growth failing to catch up with the growing demand (Boeuf et al., 2014; Bonet & Sastre, 2016; Inkei, 2019; Papadimitriou, 2017) due to constant increase in the number of new income-seeking artists entering the market annually (Abbing, 2002). Hence, while cultural funding represents a small portion of national budgets overall, some environments are more challenging than others and may require artist-entrepreneurs to seek funding from alternative channels more vigorously, either through crowdfunding broadly or investment crowdfunding specifically.

Varieties of Cultural and Creative Work

Thus far, we have treated cultural and creative work without acknowledging the particularities of certain creative works versus others. A popular conceptualization distinguishing between different cultural creations was suggested by Throsby (2008), capturing how the content being produced is aligned along a continuum from a core of cultural value and layered circles of creative work with growing commercial value attached to it.

While non-investment forms of crowdfunding may be relevant for all cultural and artistic expressions either through consumption-oriented reward crowdfunding or public-good-oriented donation crowdfunding, investment forms of crowdfunding represent a unique challenge in the cultural and creative sector. While investment crowdfunding may come in non-profit forms, such as buying equity in community shares (i.e. cooperatives) or offering loans in prosocial lending (i.e. zero or very low interest-bearing loans), most investment activities are strongly profit-oriented (Shneor, 2020). As such, profit orientation by definition implies an expectation of commercial value creation, pushing the sectoral relevance of investment crowdfunding towards outer layers of Throsby's (2008) concentric model.

In this respect, one may expect a weakening of the FPI barriers' impact the further one's creative work is from the core of pure cultural or artistic value or a strengthening of their impact the closer one's creative work is to the core. To clarify, investment crowdfunding is relevant for all types of creative expressions, but the process becomes more demanding and selective when involving creative expressions at the core, requiring creative works not only to be of exquisite cultural value but also a commercial one. The question of whether to use it or not for such purposes becomes one of ideology and necessity.

5 Conclusion

Investment crowdfunding represents an untapped opportunity for artists' fundraising involving larger amounts and, hence, greater rewards for the promotional efforts involved. The current chapter suggests a framework outlining the key mental barriers leading to artists' reluctance to use investment crowdfunding in their fundraising. Specifically, the framework highlights the roles played by fear of failure (and potential reputational damage), prejudice against commercial activities in the arts (and the supremacy of artistic value), and relative ignorance of both crowdfunding as a fundraising tool and how to frame creative work as an investment opportunity. Furthermore, interactions between these barriers further enhance the aversion of investment crowdfunding through the power of the fear of rejection (interaction of fear and prejudice), fear of the unknown (interaction of fear and ignorance), and fear of change (interaction of ignorance and prejudice). Finally, opportunities that may help mitigate these concerns are outlined, including education, match-funding schemes, and functional integration around crowdfunding platforms.

While helpful and well-anchored in both research and reality, the framework is primarily suggested as a conceptual starting point for better understanding artists' aversion to investment crowdfunding. As such, it may be further expanded to include additional influential factors, which may include contextual settings such as cultural policy regimes and regulatory maturity of investment crowdfunding, to name a few. Other elements may include inherent characteristics of the creative outputs being funded, especially when comparing those that may be more easily replicated and scaled versus non-replicable and scalable projects. Moreover, even if one remains within the individual unit of analysis and his/her psychological domain, personality dimensions, such as extraversion, introversion, neuroticism, and agreeableness, may all play moderating roles in the extent to which FPI elements exert their influence. Indeed, earlier work suggests that crowdfunding more broadly may better fit artists with extroverted rather than introverted personalities (Davidson & Poor, 2015). Accordingly, future research may seek to empirically validate the assertions underlying the FPI framework in different contexts, as well as consider its potential extension in line with the suggestions above.

Finally, while uncovered in the context of cultural and creative work, the FPI may be relevant for understanding aversive attitudes in other sectors at the fringes and beyond the cultural and creative industry. One such sector may warrant special attention in future research involving academic research itself. Academic research can also be viewed as the result of the "love labour" of professional researchers working in a sector heavily dependent on public funding, as well as on peer approval and acceptance. Researchers see fundraising as a hassle, taking resources and time away from their main professional objective of working on research. Here as well, researchers may find themselves pushed towards more or less "reluctant entrepreneurship" when engaged in various consultancy projects. Moreover, similar policy debates also involve clashes of values between independent quality research versus popular research, between making high-quality research widely accessible versus allowing for a wider plurality of research practices, and between utilitarian approaches to research of what is needed versus researching what is interesting. Here, while initial studies in the context of academic research have uncovered the importance of fear of failure and rejection by peers (i.e. Lenart-Gansiniec & Chen, 2023), most other elements of the FPI remain unexplored.

Competing Interests The writing of this chapter was supported by a grant from the Research Council of Norway [301291].

References

Abbing, H. (2002). *Why Are Artists Poor? The Exceptional Economy of the Arts.* Amsterdam University Press.

Ajzen, I. (1991). The Theory of Planned Behavior. *Organizational Behavior and Human Decision Process, 50*(2), 179–211.

Albinsson, S. (2018). Musicians as Entrepreneurs or Entrepreneurs as Musicians? *Creativity and Innovation Management, 27*(3), 348–357.

Amit, R., & Zott, C. (2017). Value Drivers of e-Commerce Business Models. In *Creating Value: Winners in the New Business Environment* (pp. 13–43).

Arenius, P., Chuah, S.-H., Coate, B., & Hoffmann, R. (2021). The Economic Psychology of Creating and Venturing: A Comparative Behavioural Portrait of Artists and Entrepreneurs. *Small Business Economics, 57*(2), 721–737.

Averill, J. R. (2004). Emotions as Mediators and as Products of Creative Activity. In J. C. Kaufman & J. Baer (Eds.), *Creativity Across Domains: Faces of the Muse* (1st ed., pp. 225–243). Psychology Press.

Bayles, D., & Orland, T. (1993). *Art & Fear: Observations On the Perils (and Rewards) of Artmaking.* Image Continuum Press.

Betzler, D. (2015). Factors of Board Governance and Fundraising Success. *Journal of Cultural Economy, 8*(2), 144–165.

Boeuf, B., Darveau, J., & Legoux, R. (2014). Financing Creativity: Crowd-funding as a New Approach for Theatre Projects. *International Journal of Arts Management, 16*(3), 33–48.

Bonet, L., & Négrier, E. (2018). The Participative Turn in Cultural Policy: Paradigms, Models, Contexts. *Poetics, 66*, 64–73.

Bonet, L., & Sastre, E. (2016). Le financement participatif, une alternative à la politique culturelle ? [Crowdfunding, an alternative to cultural policy?]. *Nectart, 2*(1), 121–129.

Bridgstock, R. (2012). Not a Dirty Word: Arts Entrepreneurship and Higher Education. *Arts and Humanities in Higher Education, 12*(2–3), 122–137.

Bugental, J. F., & Bugental, E. K. (1984). A Fate Worse than Death: The Fear of Changing. *Psychotherapy: Theory, Research, Practice, Training, 21*(4), 543–549.

Carleton, R. N. (2016). Fear of the Unknown: One Fear to Rule them All? *Journal of Anxiety Disorders, 41*, 5–21.

Chircu, A. M., & Kauffman, R. J. (1999). Strategies for Internet Middlemen in the Intermediation/Disintermediation/Reintermediation Cycle. *Electronic Markets, 9*(1–2), 109–117.

Conroy, D. E. (2001). Progress in the Development of a Multidimensional Measure of Fear of failure: The Performance Failure Appraisal Inventory (pfai). *Anxiety, Stress, & Coping, 14*(4), 431–452.

Conroy, D. E. (2004). The Unique Psychological Meanings of Multidimensional Fears of Failing. *Journal of Sport and Exercise Psychology, 26*(3), 484–491.

Conroy, D. E., Willow, J. P., & Metzler, J. N. (2002). Multidimensional Fear of Failure Measurement: The Performance Failure Appraisal Inventory. *Journal of Applied Sport Psychology, 14*(2), 76–90.

Cumming, D. (2007). Government Policy Towards Entrepreneurial Finance: Innovation Investment Funds. *Journal of Business Venturing, 22*(2), 193–235.

Dalla Chiesa, C. (2022). The Artists' Critique on Crowdfunding and Online Gift-Giving. *The Journal of Arts Management, Law, and Society, 52*(1), 20–36.

Dalla Chiesa, C., & Alexopoulou, A. (2022). Matchfunding Goes Digital: The Benefits of Matching Policymaking with the Crowd's Wisdom. *European Journal of Cultural Management and Policy, 12.*

Davidson, R., & Poor, N. (2015). The Barriers Facing Artists' Use of Crowdfunding Platforms: Personality, Emotional Labor, and Going to the Well One too Many Times. *New Media & Society, 17*(2), 289–307.

Davies, R. (2015). Three Provocations for Civic Crowdfunding. *Information, Communication & Society, 18*(3), 342–355.

De Voldere, I., & Zeqo, K. (2017). *Crowdfunding: Reshaping the Crowd's Engagement in Culture* (E. Commission, Ed.). European Commission https://op.europa.eu/en/publication-detail/-/publication/7e10916d-677c-11e7-b2f2-01aa75ed71a1/language-en

Dolson, E., & Jagtiani, J. (2024). Which Lenders are More Likely to Reach Out to Underserved Consumers: Banks Versus Fintechs Versus Other Nonbanks? *Journal of Alternative Finance, 1*(1), 35–66.

Eikhof, D. R., & Haunschild, A. (2007). For Art's Sake! Artistic and Economic Logics in Creative Production. *Journal of Organizational Behavior, 28*(5), 523–538.

Elliot, A. J., & Church, M. A. (1997). A Hierarchical Model of Approach and Avoidance Achievement Motivation. *Journal of Personality and Social Psychology, 72*(1), 218–232.

Estrin, S., Gozman, D., & Khavul, S. (2018). The Evolution and Adoption of Equity Crowdfunding: Entrepreneur and Investor Entry into a New Market. *Small Business Economics, 51*(2), 425–439.

EuroStat. (2024). *General Government Expenditure by Function (COFOG)* https://ec.europa.eu/eurostat/databrowser/view/gov_10a_exp__custom_14958257/default/table?lang=en

Feder, T., & Woronkowicz, J. (2022). Reluctantly Independent: Motivations for Self-Employed Artistic Work. *Journal of Cultural Economics, 47*, 589–607.

Foà, C. (2019). Crowdfunding Cultural Projects and Networking the Value Creation: Experience Economy between Global Platforms and Local Communities. *Arts and the Market, 9*(2), 235–254.

Gleasure, R. (2015). Resistance to Crowdfunding Among Entrepreneurs: An Impression Management Perspective. *The Journal of Strategic Information Systems, 24*(4), 219–233.

Gray, J. A. (1987). *The Psychology of Fear and Stress* (2nd ed.). Cambridge University Press.

Hamilton, L. H. (1997). The Emotional Costs of Performing: Interventions for the Young Artist. *Medical Problems of Performing Artists, 12*(3), 67–71.

Handbook of Research on Crowdfunding. In H. Landström, A. Parhankangas, & C. Mason (Eds.), *Handbook of Research on Crowdfunding*. Edward Elgar Publishing.

Handke, C., & Dalla Chiesa, C. (2022). The Art of Crowdfunding Arts and Innovation: The Cultural Economic Perspective. *Journal of Cultural Economics*.

Haynes, J., & Marshall, L. (2018). Reluctant Entrepreneurs: Musicians and Entrepreneurship in the 'New' Music Industry. *The British Journal of Sociology, 69*(2), 459–482.

Inkei, P. (2019). *Public Funding of Culture in Europe, 2004–2017* (T. B. O. R. O. o. C. i. E.-C. Europe, Ed.). The Budapest Observatory: Regional Observatory on Culture in East-Central Europe. http://www.budobs.org/files/Public%20cultural%20funding%202004-2017.pdf

Jagtiani, J., & Lemieux, C. (2018). Do Fintech Lenders Penetrate Areas that are Underserved by Traditional Banks? *Journal of Economics and Business, 100*, 43–54.

Klein, B., Meier, L. M., & Powers, D. (2017). Selling Out: Musicians, Autonomy, and Compromise in the Digital Age. *Popular Music and Society, 40*(2), 222–238.

Lee, B., Fraser, I., & Fillis, I. (2018). Creative Futures for New Contemporary Artists: Opportunities and Barriers [Article]. *International Journal of Arts Management, 20*(2), 9–19.

Lenart-Gansiniec, R., & Chen, J. (2023). When will Scientists say yes? Antecedents, Consequences and Limitations of Crowdfunding in Research. *Studies in Higher Education, 48*(8), 1159–1171.

Leyshon, A., Thrift, N., Crewe, L., French, S., & Webb, P. (2016). Leveraging Affect: Mobilizing Enthusiasm and the Co-Production of the Musical Economy. In B. J. Hracs, M. Seman, & T. E. Virani (Eds.), *The Production and Consumption of Music in the Digital Age* (pp. 248–262). Routledge.

Loots, E., Betzler, D., Bille, T., Borowiecki, K. J., & Lee, B. (2022). New Forms of Finance and Funding in the Cultural and Creative Industries. Introduction to the Special Issue. *Journal of Cultural Economics, 46*(2), 205–230.

Loots, E., Piecyk, K., & Wijngaarden, Y. (2024). At the Juncture of Funding, Policy, and Technology: How Promising is Match-Funding of Arts and Culture Through Crowdfunding Platforms? *International Journal of Cultural Policy, 30*(1), 118–134.

Mollick, E. (2014). The Dynamics of Crowdfunding: An Exploratory Study. *Journal of Business Venturing, 29*(1), 1–16.

Mollick, E., & Robb, A. (2016). Democratizing Innovation and Capital Access: The Role of Crowdfunding. *California Management Review, 58*(2), 72–87.

Mulcahy, K. V. (2006). Cultural Policy: Definitions and Theoretical Approaches. *The Journal of Arts Management, Law, and Society, 35*(4), 319–330.

Papadimitriou, L. (2017). Transitions in the Periphery: Funding Film Production in Greece Since the Financial Crisis. *International Journal on Media Management, 19*(2), 164–181.

Pasicko, R., & Petrovic, M. (2019). Crowdfunding for Civic and Development Projects. In O. Gajda, D. Marom, & T. Wright (Eds.), *CrowdAsset* (pp. 437–443). World Scientific.

Passeri, F. (2019). Lessons Learned from Civic Crowdfunding and Match-Funding Schemes in Europe. In O. Gajda, D. Marom, & T. Wright (Eds.), *CrowdAsset* (pp. 211–255). World Scientific.

Quero, M. J., Ventura, R., & Kelleher, C. (2017). Value-in-Context in Crowdfunding Ecosystems: How Context Frames Value Co-Creation. *Service Business, 11*(2), 405–425.

Rykkja, A., & Bonet, L. A. (2023). Adjudicació de fons de contrapartida al micromecenatge cultural per part dels governs: Una anàlisi comparativa exploratòria dels casos espanyol i suec [Government Matching of Cultural Crowdfunding: An Exploratory Comparative Analysis of the Spanish and Swedish Cases]. *Debats, 137*(1), 117–141.

Rykkja, A., Maehle, N., Munim, Z. H., & Shneor, R. (2020). Crowdfunding in the Cultural Industries. In R. Shneor, L. Zhao, & B.-T. Flåten (Eds.), *Advance in Crowdfunding: Research and Practice* (pp. 423–440). Palgrave MacMillan.

Rykkja, A., Shneor, R., Maehle, N., & Munim, Z. H. (2024). Cultural Crowdfunding: Does Experience Matter? *Beta, 37*(1), 1–18.

Serwaah, P. (2022). Crowdfunding, Gender and the Promise of Financial Democracy: A Systematic Review. *International Journal of Gender and Entrepreneurship, 14*(2), 263–283.

Shneor, R. (2020). Crowdfunding Models, Strategies, and Choices Between Them. In R. Shneor, L. Zhao, & B.-T. Flåten (Eds.), *Advances in Crowdfunding: Research and Practice* (pp. 21–42). Palgrave MacMillan.

Shneor, R., & Flåten, B.-T. (2020). Crowdfunding Education: Objectives, Content, Pedagogy, and Assessment. In R. Shneor, L. Zhao, & B.-T. Flåten (Eds.), *Advances in Crowdfunding: Research and Practice* (pp. 475–497). Palgrave MacMillan.

Shneor, R., Maehle, N., Munim, Z. H., & Rykkja, A. (2024). What Drives Crowdfunding Intentions of Artist-Entrepreneurs?—Evidence from Norway. *The International Journal of Entrepreneurship and Innovation* (in Press). https://doi.org/10.1177/14657503241282939

Stevenson, R. M., Kuratko, D. F., & Eutsler, J. (2019). Unleashing Main Street Entrepreneurship: Crowdfunding, Venture Capital, and the Democratization of New Venture Investments. *Small Business Economics, 52*(2), 375–393.

Thom, M. (2017). The Rough Journey into Arts Entrepreneurship. *Education + Training, 59*(7/8), 720–739.

Thomas, R. (2015). Resisting Change and Changing Resistance. In N. Beech & C. Gilmore (Eds.), *Organising Music* (pp. 61–71). Cambridge University Press.

Thorley, M. (2012). An Audience in the Studio–The Effect of the Artistshare Fan-Funding Platform on Creation, Performance, Recording and Production. *Journal on the Art of Record Production* (7), 1–29. https://www.arpjournal.com/asarpwp/an-audience-in-the-studio-%E2%80%93-the-effect-of-the-artistshare-fan-funding-platform-on-creation-performance-recording-and-production/

Throsby, D. (2008). The Concentric Circles Model of the Cultural Industries. *Cultural Trends, 17*(3), 147–164. https://doi.org/10.1080/09548960802361951

Tosatto, J., Cox, J., & Nguyen, T. (2019). An Overview of Crowdfunding in the Creative and Cultural Industries

Venkatesh, V., & Davis, F. D. (2000). A Theoretical Extension of the Technology Acceptance Model: Four Longitudinal Field Studies. *Management Science, 46*(2), 186–204.

Wenzlaff, K. (2020). Civic Crowdfunding: Four Perspectives on the Definition of Civic Crowdfunding. In R. Shneor, L. Zhao, & B.-T. Flåten (Eds.), *Advances in Crowdfunding: Research and Practice* (pp. 441–472). Palgrave MacMillan.

Wenzlaff, K., & Spaeth, S. (2023). Experiences in Educating Students and Professionals About Crowdfunding. In R. Lenart-Gansiniec, K. Wenzlaff, & S. Späth (Eds.), *Crowdfunding in Higher Education Institutions: Theory and Best Practices* (pp. 71–102). Springer International Publishing.

Wonglimpiyarat, J. (2016). Government Policies Towards Israel's High-Tech Powerhouse. *Technovation, 52–53*, 18–27.

Ziegler, T., Shneor, R., Wenzlaff, K., Suresh, K., Paes, F. F. d. C., Mammadova, L., Wanga, C., Kekre, N., Mutinda, S., Wang, B. and Closs, C.L.,. (2021). The 2nd Global Alternative Finance Market Benchmarking Report. In T. Ziegler, R. Shneor, & K. Wenzlaff (Eds.), *Cambridge Centre for Alternative Finance*. https://www.jbs.cam.ac.uk/faculty-research/centres/alternative-finance/publications/the-2nd-global-alternative-finance-market-benchmarking-report

Open Access This chapter is licensed under the terms of the Creative Commons Attribution 4.0 International License (http://creativecommons.org/licenses/by/4.0/), which permits use, sharing, adaptation, distribution and reproduction in any medium or format, as long as you give appropriate credit to the original author(s) and the source, provide a link to the Creative Commons license and indicate if changes were made.

The images or other third party material in this chapter are included in the chapter's Creative Commons license, unless indicated otherwise in a credit line to the material. If material is not included in the chapter's Creative Commons license and your intended use is not permitted by statutory regulation or exceeds the permitted use, you will need to obtain permission directly from the copyright holder.

CHAPTER 10

The Rise of Online Crowd-Patronage: Models, Challenges, and Providing Security to the Creative Worker

Wojciech Hardy

1 Contextualizing Online Patronage

Online crowd-patronage is a new form of financing that offers exciting opportunities for creative workers. In the most popular model of this form, creators establish online profiles presenting their work, while patrons can support the creators with monthly payments of self-declared amounts. These exchanges are facilitated by platforms, which also handle subscriptions, payment processing and offer additional services like interaction spaces or tiered content (i.e. available only to those who pay specific amounts) or—in some cases—a way of distributing the product directly within the platform. The platforms, in exchange, take a percentage from all transactions or include ads.

Existing forms of such platforms can be broadly categorized into two types. The first variety is online patronage, proposed by platforms such

W. Hardy (✉)
University of Warsaw, Warsaw, Poland
e-mail: wojciechhardy@uw.edu.pl

© The Author(s) 2026

C. Dalla Chiesa and A. Rykkja (eds.), *Cultural Funding and Financing*, Cultural Economics & the Creative Economy,
https://doi.org/10.1007/978-3-031-96696-5_10

as Patreon, built around communication—often on top of other distribution channels—and relying on subscription-based support or spontaneous tips. Such platforms allow for the promotion of various types of creative work. The second kind is content-specific platforms, often combining specific types of creative work directly with monetization within a single ecosystem.

For creators, the key distinguishing elements of online crowd patronage as a whole are its flexibility, the direct reach to niches and—typically—the recurring payments fostering stable income. While different alternative models have historically offered some elements of these features, their focus was typically centred on individual projects instead of continuous creative activity or lacked the infrastructure for its scaling beyond "superstars". Moreover, more traditional models of funding were historically more "elitist" in character—targeting wealthy sponsors whose support for the art was not purely altruistic.

Indeed, patronage isn't a new concept. For much of the world's history, a few artists benefited from wealthy sponsors or patrons. These people, typically representatives of the upper classes, would provide support (sometimes over long periods of time) in exchange for some form of exclusive access to the artists' works and performances, which resulted in increased prestige and social standing. Later on, particularly during the renaissance, this relationship evolved as artists became more likely to produce works on commissions from networks of patrons (religious orders, authorities, merchant families, guilds, etc.).[1] Swords (2017) also names corporate and government patronage, as well as once-popular subscription lists, precursors to the crowd-patronage discussed in this chapter.

The early patronage systems gradually disappeared across different art sectors, especially with the development of the public funding of arts, including museums and theatres. Moreover, the 20th introduced new distribution channels that allowed creative workers to reach broader audiences and monetize their work (e.g. radio, TV and recorded media). The rapid spread of the internet created even more opportunities in this vein but it also lowered many of the barriers to creative work. The easier access to production tools, distribution, and promotional channels contributed to an inflow of new creative workers often with niche audiences that were previously overlooked by the major mainstream studios and production companies.

The internet enabled the return of patronage, only this time with a focus on a "crowd" of enthusiastic supporters instead of one wealthy sponsor. The changes reached further, as online patronage relies less on exclusivity (though it is not devoid of it) and is more likely to reach a specific niche for whom a particular creator is exceptionally appealing. In contrast to the early days of patronage, this means that creators can find their niches and superfans, even those small and scattered. These audiences, in contrast to typical funders or funding schemes, are offered the ability to become patrons at the level they choose. Even small contributions from a crowd of patrons can amount to a meaningful income. As such, becoming patrons of art and creativity has become easier and less dependent on one's status.

This inclusivity (anyone can create, and anyone can be a patron) stands in stark contrast to the early patronage focused on exclusivity (a select few could afford sponsoring a select group of artists and receive exclusive access for doing so). Now, not only superstars benefit but also smaller artists. With the growing number of artists (as enabled by digitization), this feature highlights the importance of the platform infrastructure in allowing matching between creators and even distant supporters.

Crowd patronage connects creators and their audiences beyond just the superstars. This is similar to online crowdfunding. However, the latter replicates the common issues faced by creative workers—namely, that they often lack financial stability with income dependent on project-oriented work. Crowdfunding supports short and long-term projects but ends when the product is delivered. Moreover, payouts aren't guaranteed if projects do not reach funding goals. This lack of stability contributes to the precarious nature of creative labour.

The patronage platforms instead provide the opportunity for smaller but stable support with no definitive commitments. Swords (2017) identifies three key differences from crowdfunding: first, the continuous small-scale support instead of one-time large payments; second, the fact that the money is transferred unconditionally and not tied to specific goals or total amounts pledged; and third, that it is (usually) not tied to specific deliverables, implying continuous support and nurture rather than a buyer-seller relationship. While specifics vary, steady support remains crucial. Indeed, supporters' beliefs in creators can provide stable, if partial, income.

This chapter follows with a description of the key online patronage models and the most popular platforms that represent them. I offer a brief explanation of the motivation between different platforms and their models, describe their popularity, as well as key distinguishing features. I then provide a more academic discussion on how these platforms fit within the context of the CCIs, creative labour and cultural consumption, relying on existing research and reports. Finally, I provide a selection of potential avenues to explore in future research, highlighting the importance of potential data sources that could be used to understand these markets better.

2 Key Online Patronage Platforms and Their Models

Online platforms offer several models of support for the creative and cultural workers that tap directly into crowds of fans. These fans, in turn, can become patrons by providing monetary support to their favourite creators, effectively providing a revenue stream that is not tied to specific projects. The Table 1 summarizes the different models, with the following subsections discussing the most popular examples.

Patreon

Likely the most well-known format of online patronage is represented by the platform Patreon—the largest of its type. While not the only platform, many mimic its model, often focusing on specific regions or sectors. Patreon allows creators to build an online space on the platform for sharing updates or asking for funds. The other side of the platform—the patrons—can support creators with changeable monthly pledges. The platform offers a flexible set of tools, which can be further used for a customized approach from the creators. They can, for example, use the platform either to capture an additional source of income or as a vehicle to directly interact with their closest supporters. Creators can provide exclusive content, early access, or special offers based on support levels.[2]

Patreon was created in 2013 as a joint effort by Sam Yam and Jack Conte—a musician disenchanted by the revenue prospects from streaming platforms such as YouTube (Skid, 2022), at a time when online piracy challenged creative sectors and ad revenues proved unstable. In 1.5 years, the company boasted more than 125,000 patrons (Constine, 2017). By 2017, this number had grown to a million, and the number of

Table 1 Main types of patronage-based online platforms

Category of online patronage	*Prominent examples*	*Primary categories of work*	*Primary support*	*Distribution options*
Subscription-based patronage	Patreon, Patronite (local)	Any—e.g. adult and non-adult: podcasts, games, video, animation, cosplay, 3D printing, drawing and painting, dance and theatre and more.	Perpetual	Limited (embedding)
Online tipping	Buymeacoffee, Busking Project	Any; sometimes platform-specific - (e.g. for street performers). Other examples include podcasts, videos, news, and activism.	Ad hoc	None
Fan-powered distribution platforms	Twitch	Live-streaming (e.g. gaming)	Perpetual/ad hoc	Within the platform
Fan-powered distribution platforms (adult)	OnlyFans	Adult live-streaming	Perpetual/ad hoc	Within the platform
Fan-based royalty systems	Soundcloud	Music	Consumption-based	Within the platform

active creators reached 50,000. Graphtreon, a platform aggregating high-frequency statistics on the Patreon platform and its creators, reported that the site had approximately 100,000 paid creators at the start of 2020, a number that grew to 250,000 by May 2024. This figure is coupled with more than 15 million paid memberships (i.e. paid member subscriptions to creators) and an estimated 24 million USD in monthly payouts to the creators (Graphtreon, 2024).

Patreon offers full flexibility on the created content (barring illegal activities). As of May 2024, the platform had the most creators in the Video category, followed by Drawing & Painting and Games.[3] However, the Podcasts replace Drawing & Painting in the top three in terms of numbers of paid memberships and monthly payouts to creators, highlighting different supply and demand dynamics across the categories.

Importantly, Patreon doesn't force its creators into single categories. A creator can represent several different types of work, combining, e.g. performing music, recording videos, doing podcasts and writing blog posts. In this regard, crowd-patronage often focuses on supporting a creative person in general rather than focusing on a single aspect of their creation.

Another distinction between creators comes from adult content, which constitutes a significant part of some content categories (despite the platform's algorithm omitting it from its Featured sections). Adult games constitute a smaller share among game creators but take the majority of paid memberships and monthly payouts. The adult category is similarly important for the Drawing & Painting, Comics and Animation categories. The popularity of adult content highlights both the creators' needs for reliable monetization channels and the consumers' readiness to pay for it when provided with a safe transaction service. A different, adult-themed, patronage-based service—OnlyFans—is described later in this subsection.

Buymeacoffee, Ko-Fi, and the Busking Project

While both Buymeacoffee and Ko-fi bear many resemblances to Patreon, they target different creators and donators, which pervades both their design and user base. Instead of promoting continuous support of creators through monthly subscriptions (which are actually also possible on the platforms), the platforms encourage the supporters to buy a „coffee" for the creators. This boils down to contributing one-time payments to the amount of approximately $5 (although creators can pick something else than a "coffee" and customize the price as well).

Because of this, these platforms attract different creators and donations than Patreon. At the time of this writing, Buymeacoffee reports more than 1 million creators (although it does not report on how many of them are active and actually receive "coffees"). A quick look at the featured creators shows that the subscription option is (by far) not the default, with many creators focusing only on single tips, with some combining two options (and the number of tipping supporters outnumbering that of the subscribers).

The Busking Project is a specific subtype of tip-based platform that provides an online support channel for street performers. Though smaller in scope, it provides an extension of the monetization opportunities by introducing a secondary online patronage channel. As many buskers cannot directly move their creative acts online, the platform allows them to still tap into the advantages of online support. Buskers receive space for self-promotion and can receive tips from their fans. The platform also provides the option of hiring the performers (e.g. for parties), should they choose to enable it.

Twitch

Twitch remains the most popular platform for live streaming. Creators can run their own channels, most of which focus on gaming-related content. However, Twitch also remains a popular outlet for eSports transmissions, with some users signing deals for official retransmissions of tournaments. Twitch offers several monetization options, including subscriptions, tips, ads included in the live stream or promoting products on Amazon.[4]

Despite the potential for subscription-based support, Twitch differs from Patreon in several important dimensions. First, it only allows for a specific kind of content in the form of live streaming. Second, Twitch acts as both the monetization and distribution channel for its creators. Third, the live-streaming scene is known for a fiercer competition between the platforms, with numerous notorious cases of exclusivity deals made with prominent high-profile streamers. In this sense, the platforms play a larger role than just providing the tools for their users and instead also enter strategic partnerships with their members. Finally, Twitch does not allow for streaming of content that is not suitable for work.

OnlyFans

OnlyFans is a 2016-started platform connecting creators and their fans, allowing for monetization through subscriptions, tips and pay-per-view. It is currently dominated by and mainly associated with being a platform for online sex workers, with most of its content labelled as not safe for work. Still, the platform doesn't exclude other forms of content and is also home to other categories. By May 2023, the platform boasted 3 million registered creators and 220 million registered users (Mann, 2023)[5]. Also, as in the case of Patreon, the success of OnlyFans led to the launch of several other platforms with similar models (e.g. Fansly). Due to the high focus on adult content, the platforms have often been the subject of controversies and legal trouble. A notable difference from Patreon lies in that OnlyFans acts as both the monetization and distribution platform for its creators. It is the creators who choose what is shared at different subscription tiers, and the content itself is hosted on the platform.

Soundcloud

In 2021, the music streaming platform Soundcloud introduced what it called "fan-powered royalties." While more focused on independent musicians from the start,[6] the new royalty system differentiated Soundcloud from other streaming services even further by putting a stronger focus on direct relationships between artists and their audiences.

All the major streaming services (e.g. Spotify, Deezer, Apple Music, etc.) operate through a pro-rata royalty system. In this system, paid subscriptions are aggregated into a large pool. This pool is then distributed across artists based on the shares of streams of their songs.[7] The approach has been criticized for its preferential treatment of star artists. Indeed, niche artists might have their devoted fan bases whose paid subscriptions nevertheless primarily go to the currently trending pop stars. The distribution of streaming revenues has been the subject of several recent studies and reports (e.g. Jensen, 2024).

Soundcloud's alternative approach fits in this chapter because it turns the focus to direct fan support. While it is expressed through streams—rather than direct payments—it still represents a form of support that can be leveraged through monetization of a creator's user base. In other words, in an industry dominated by *pro rata* approach, Soundcloud's case offers a direct way of supporting artists. Another service—Bandcamp—remains another example of a music service fostering direct relationships where users purchase music or merchandize from specific artists—rather than paying money into a pool that is afterwards redistributed.

3 What We Know from Research and Statistics

Some of the dynamics behind online patronage have been outlined in prior academic research and reports. On the one hand, to truly understand the role of online patronage, it is key to understand the labour market situation of creative workers. This has been studied by multiple authors and also through larger reports. On the other hand, online patronage can be conducted through many different platforms, but only some of them have been studied so far. Even among those, questions remain to be addressed, as the market continues to evolve. Below, I provide an overview of the current knowledge on these topics.

The Need for Sustainable Support

Creative workers tend to work under precarious conditions. Across the EU27 in 2018, 44% of the cultural and creative labour force was self-employed (a share higher than in other sectors). Moreover, creative workers are more likely to work on part-time, non-permanent contracts or need to combine creative work with other jobs (Woronkowicz & Noonan, 2019; Snijders et al., 2020). Due to these non-typical work arrangements and non-stable project-based work, creative workers are often not eligible for social protection schemes (OECD, 2022) and find it hard to sustain themselves purely from creative work (Snijders et al., 2020). Bridgstock (2005) described the artists' labour market situation as a prominent example of the new protean careers that require transferable skills, taking on multiple occupation roles, combining different income sources and contract-based work for clients rather than a singular employer. Throsby and Zednik (2011) also showed that artists tend to need to combine different jobs, even if the additional ones also rely on creativity.

These precarious conditions also mean that creative workers are particularly exposed to negative shocks. The COVID-19 pandemic disrupted all venue-based and performative cultural activities—from museums and concerts to theatres and cinemas (OECD, 2020). Unsurprisingly, this resulted in a drop-in work hours for creative workers, which often resulted in workforce shrinkage—particularly among those on freelance and temporary contracts (OECD, 2022). The street performers were also hit by the onset of COVID-19, as much of their life (including payments) moved online (Elkins & Fry, 2022b). Comunian and England (2020) argue that COVID-19 exposed the stern conditions of cultural and creative work rather than acting as a crisis by itself. Some subsectors—like gaming—seem to have benefitted instead, despite production delays (OECD, 2022) but are currently (in 2024) facing unprecedented massive layoffs in turn.

Statistics from a variety of patronage-based platforms show the potential of such platforms in boosting resilience to negative shocks. A large part of the recent growth in Patreon took place directly as the pandemic started, with many creators seemingly entering with their pre-existing audiences (see, e.g. Church, 2020). Similarly, many buskers registered to The Busking Project with the onset of the pandemic, and increased donations followed (Elkins & Fry, 2022a); the number of Twitch concurrent streamers and viewers doubled between 2019 and 2020;[8] OnlyFans noted a 75% spike in user registrations between March and April of 2020.

The constant struggle of creative workers for sustainable and stable income has been glaring, and the pandemic fleshed it out even further. Traditional crowdfunding offers an alternative source for the realization of projects. However, it is online patronage that addresses the other key worry of artists' situation, as it provides a steady and stable source of income.

Online Patronage Dynamics

Regner (2021) provides a comprehensive exploration of the role Patreon can play for creators. Analysing the platform creators and their audiences, Regner found that it follows typical superstar distributions. Specifically, between May 2013 and October 2015, only the top 1% of profiles earned at least $2500 monthly, which amounted to around 250 creators. The vast majority of active profiles received no income, with only 5% making more than $750. In February 2025, as inferred from the Graphtreon stats, the top 50 creators received nearly 12% of all monthly incomes (out of almost 300,000 creators with at least one patron).

While these statistics might seem stark, they do not stand out much from typical long tail dynamics in creative industries. For example, in 2022, it's been reported that only around 20% of artists on Spotify had a monthly audience of at least 50 people (Ingham, 2022). A 2023 engagement report from Netflix shows that about 100 titles (or show seasons) make up for around 20% of all hours viewed in the streaming services and near to. 700 titles/seasons are responsible for 50% of all hours (while around 18,000 titles/seasons comprised 99% of viewership; Netflix, 2023). Thus, the number of creators on Patreon should not surprise, although the distribution also shows that the income obtained through crowd-patronage is rarely large enough to singlehandedly sustain a living.

Still, even a partially stable income could reduce the employment insecurity associated with artistic work. Moreover, typical crowdfunding often adopts an all-or-nothing mechanism (i.e. a creator might launch a project but fail to gather enough support and ultimately not get any money despite initial work). Subscription-based crowd-patronage (as well as other fan-based support systems outlined before), on the other hand, often builds on mutual trust (i.e. that the creator will eventually deliver with proper support) or simply functions as an expression of ongoing support to the creators' activities—regardless of whether they are largely project-based (e.g. game creation) or continuous (e.g. weekly newsletters and blog posting). The patrons might still express their displeasure by cancelling their subscriptions, but the effect is distinct from an all-or-nothing outcome.

Creators engaging in monetization through online patronage via Patreon vary not only in terms of audience size but also in terms of its diversity (creators came from more than 90 countries in 2016—Swords [2017]—and from more than 113 countries by 2022—Patreon, 2022), and dynamics such as loyalty or giving feedback and verbal support. El Sanyoura and Anderson (2022) analysed data from Patreon to find several such differences. The most profitable creators attract larger audiences who are less likely to contribute to other creators. This finding casts new light on the large inflow of audiences in the advent of COVID-19—it is likely that the sudden rise in users focused on specific creators (especially newly registered ones) did not spillover to existing creators. The authors also show that "specializing" patrons (i.e. ones focused on particular types of creators) tend to provide larger support but are also more likely to leave the platform altogether.

In principle, it is possible for the patrons to become large donors or sponsors, covering the bulk of the contributions for a specific creator. Such situations would make them more similar to traditional historic patronage from wealthy sponsors or institutions. For the latter case, an additional transaction could include a form of advertising for the sponsor. Still, with the online nature of the platforms, the relationship no longer tends to be exclusive. It is also difficult to identify whether such cases are common across the platforms, as the levels of individual donations are typically hidden. Still, as the payment scheme is largely on a pay-what-you-want basis, one can expect a certain level of self-induced price discrimination and—hence—differences between contribution levels.

Regner (2021) notes important advantages of the patronage channel: transparency and direct support from the actual audience. On the one hand, this means that creators receive direct information on their fees and number of contributors. On the other, they receive a direct communication channel with their most devoted supporters. Maintaining this relationship is important, similar to what has been found about communication activities on other crowdfunding platforms. Analysing the relationship between the creators and supporters, Hair (2021) found that it often takes the form of a close social relationship—at least as evidenced by the wording used by the creators who reference their patrons as, for example, friends and offer direct looks into their private lives. Simultaneously, they avoid making explicit references to the economic nature of the relationship. More quantitatively, Regner (2021) found that the amount of outreach (e.g. posts, images, videos) from creators positively relates to their success on the platform. Still, while Patreon offers some outreach options, most creators combine Patreon with other channels for distribution and potential monetization. According to the same analysis, approximately 75% of the Patreon creators linked other social media profiles on their Patreon pages.

This multi-homing and diversification of channels extends beyond just communication. Regner (2021) highlights that such efforts allow to combine revenue streams, e.g. from advertising in some services, with subscriptions in online patronage—as is typical in the media industry in general (see also Peukert, 2019 for a discussion on the role of online advertising in the supply of culture). In a 2019 study of music creators on Patreon, Dalla Chiesa and Hardy (2019) found that the majority of creators used social media platforms (Facebook, Twitter and, to a lesser extent, Instagram), with more than 80% of those with more than 10 patrons also having YouTube channels (often launched prior to entering Patreon). With smaller shares, the creators also used a variety of other channels, such as Spotify, Twitch, Soundcloud or Bandcamp.

From the point of view of the platform itself, the degree of such interpenetration with other services constitutes both an opportunity and a risk and requires strategic decisions. Swords (2020) describes how Patreon approaches this at several levels, e.g. finance, regulation or network management. Reliance on third-party payment processing requires careful considerations preventing sudden loss of revenue streams (as was the case for a different patronage platform - Subbable). Limiting content hosting—allowing some embedding features and relying on hosting through other platforms—in turn, eases up moderation measures that the platform has to apply to comply with regulations. The previously mentioned integration with social media channels has to be considered in terms of how much Patreon is willing to "outsource" community management and engagement services. Swords (2020) argues that this web of connections also shapes the involved cultural work and the way it is accessed, discovered, and appreciated.

4 Studying Online Patronage

While crowdfunding has received some attention from scholarly research, its fan-focused, patronage subtype seems to be understudied. However, while some features are shared between the traditional crowdfunding and crowd-patronage platforms, there are enough differences to warrant separate inquiries or—instead—to offer different opportunities for research. Below, I summarize the most important differences between the different channels, highlighting the uncharted territories as well as opportunities for further research.

Labour Market of Creative Workers

As previously noted, the labour market of creative workers is characterized by high job precarity. Subscription-based models and monetary support from a devoted fan base may seem like a promising solution to at least some of these problems. However, crowd patronage is still utilized by only a fraction of creative workers. It is also unclear how it affects its users and their work, whether it protects them from shocks such as pandemics or war, and what are the best strategies for incorporating it in a career. A labour economics perspective could contribute some of the necessary answers to these questions, including:

1. What prevents creative workers from utilizing crowd-patronage platforms? What are the barriers to entry? Are crowd-patronage platforms a viable channel for all creative workers?

Studies such as Regner (2021) try to distinguish between creators with patrons and those without any by incorporating a selection equation in his analysis. Still, the study considers only those already registered on the platform, while a broader pool of artists would have to be surveyed from other sources. Understanding how universal the crowd-patronage platforms can be in their support could help develop pathways for successful implementation of such channels, including, e.g. training in community management or maintaining an online presence.

2. Is online patronage a viable option at all career stages? Does it pay off for new artists? Does it work as an alternative to traditional channels for established artists?

To achieve a successful position at online patronage platforms one needs to build an audience willing to contribute monetarily. However, it is unclear whether these channels should be used simultaneously or after building a portfolio and gaining at least some recognition. Experiences from the COVID-19 pandemic show that established artists can join patronage platforms if need-be and to carry over their audiences. This suggests that, at least for some, traditional channels are preferable unless they are disrupted. However, it is unclear what are the exact dynamics for other creators, as well as how their success depends on the starting point.

3. Does crowd-patronage increase perceived job security? Does it affect the time distribution between other jobs and creative activities? Does it affect productivity and quality of the creative work?

By offering a stable source of income which is not strictly tied to any one project, crowd-patronage could alleviate some of the pressures of having to manage multiple jobs. For creative workers, this could mean more time for creative work, a clearer focus on creative work, fewer feelings of job insecurity, etc., which could potentially translate into higher productivity, higher quality of work or higher job quality and satisfaction. Scholars could analyse how productivity and quality of work depend on the level of support and the start of patronage profiles for artists with established audiences. Another venue would be to compare the labour market conditions of artists leveraging patronage channels with those who don't.

4. Does crowd patronage increase resilience to shocks? Are artists with established crowd support less vulnerable to negative economic trends or potentially disrupting shocks?

Patronage platforms and researchers reported an inflow of creators with the onset of the COVID-19 pandemic. This outcome shows that many creators sought alternative support schemes during this turbulent time. It could also mean that other individuals (including workers of different professions) found themselves with more time resources as restrictions and lockdowns forced people to stay home. These new arrivals often brought their own audiences with them. What remains less clear is how the pandemic affected those who already had established patronage channels as opposed to those who had not. Scholars could investigate whether patronage shielded such creators from the adverse effects of the pandemic, supporting their continued work—as opposed to creators without such pre-established channels. Similar questions could be asked in less disruptive contexts, such as poorer economic market conditions, unemployment, wars, etc.

5. What is the optimal monetization strategy for different types of creative workers? How do we successfully combine crowd-patronage with various distribution and outreach channels? What is the optimal moment for launching additional optimization channels (e.g. after establishing an audience or before)?

Prior findings for music creators show that they often build their presence across several platforms, including social media and distribution. This means multi-homing in terms of community outreach, distribution modes and monetization channels. Yet, it is difficult to map how this differs between sectors, what is the optimal portfolio of platforms and functions, and what is the proper order of them. Scholars could conduct a network analysis of these relationships while also incorporating information on the launch dates of the connected channels.

Community Management

Community relationships, management, and outreach remain key ingredients of a successful crowd-patronage campaign. Multiple studies have highlighted these factors in relation to traditional crowdfunding, and existing studies of Patreon show that outreach activities are associated with higher and more pledges. Yet, such models differ significantly from project-based crowdfunding, as communities need to be maintained continuously. Platforms such as Patreon offer an interesting opportunity for study, as they host creators through long periods of time and include data on the community size and their level of support. They also allow us to measure the level and content of outreach activities, although they simultaneously need to strategically manage integrations with other social media channels. Scholars could seek answers for questions such as:

1. What are the standard retention rate and attrition rate of supporters in crowd-patronage? What factors influence churn and retention?

With no particular end period for crowd-patronage, creators should focus not only on acquiring pledges but also on maintaining their existing communities and minimizing their attrition. An open question remains on how to best approach this, but scholars could analyse this by looking at the creator and patron dynamics in such platforms, as well as by operationalizing the ongoing activities of the creators.

2. What is the role of feedback from the community? Does providing feedback options (e.g. surveys) affect community loyalty? Does the feedback affect the productivity or quality of work? What's the impact on the creative process?

Patronage platforms often offer dedicated tools for collecting contributor feedback. These range from comments under posts to surveys targeted at assessing the preferences of the supporters. However, it is so far unclear how these relate to the actual engagement of the supporters, how it affects the creative process, and whether it translates to further community building. Scholars could study these relationships by analysing the text content of posts in crowd-patronage platforms and comparing it to the observed patterns of support and outputs.

3. What is the role of exclusivity tiers, and how does it translate into pledges and supporter numbers? How does it fit with the typical motives of supporters?

Much has been said about the difference between the modern crowd-patronage and the early patronage. Historically, patrons were often wealthy individuals who sought exclusive access to an artist or their work. With online platforms, the creators often choose to make their work public to everyone. They do, however, sometimes additionally include exclusive tiers with earlier access or access to exclusive content and feedback opportunities. Moreover, in the early days, patronage was typically restricted only to the upper classes, who could boast contributing to the development of arts. Online patronage, instead, is inclusive in that anyone can become a contributor—even at small level—and can thus join a group of art supporters. It is unclear how these factors contribute to retention churn and how they fit in with the typical motivations for supporting artists. Are the modern-day patrons acting altruistically? Do they receive a form of a warm glow? Are they pledges related to a sense of belonging to an exclusive community, thus increasing their loyalty? Does access to exclusive content drive pledges or their amount? These questions could be addressed through a survey or ethnographic studies of patrons.

4. 4. What is the community's reaction to official partnerships between the platforms and creators?

Some of the platforms with patronage features offer specific perks or partnerships to their creators. These range from additional exposure through appearance in a Featured section to official partnerships associated with additional monetization options and payments. These partnerships might affect both the number of contributors and audience sizes, as well as their willingness to pay and contribute to the creators' success.

5. What is the importance of communication channel multi-homing, such as established networks in social media platforms?

Patronage platforms need to decide on how much communication they manage directly on the platform and how much exposure they want to provide to third-party channels such as social media platforms. This can take the form of simple integrations, such as displaying links to specific platforms in dedicated fields. Similarly, creators need to decide whether to limit their outreach to specific platforms or whether to multi-home and engage audiences across different channels. These decisions might shape the creator's popularity and contributions, but also the cultural work itself.

Navigating Controversies and Legal Issues

Legal and political scholars could turn their attention to the controversies surrounding patronage platforms. The platforms in question typically claim they stay clear of illegal content, extremism or hate speech. However, moderation is often lacking. Bogle (2021) maps funding channels for right-wing extremism, noting a prominent role of patronage (whether subscription- or tip-based) platforms. Twitch has often been updating its guidelines on types of the allowed content, either prohibiting adult streams or requiring their proper labelling. Another issue came with streaming video games with explicit imagery—whether in terms of sexual or violent content. Twitch creators have been notably pushing the boundaries of what's allowed, prompting Twitch to make ad hoc decisions on drawing the line between adult and non-adult content.[9] Adult content on Patreon has been the subject of controversies as some creators produced illegal content in various formats while attracting monetary contributions through the platform. Whether through the lenses of political science, policy or law research, these topics have received little to no scrutiny.

Other Topics and Data Access

Finally, patronage platforms can be used to extend research previously conducted for traditional crowdfunding platforms or in the context of industrial organization in general. These topics might include the issues of, e.g. inequality, gender gaps, effects of the pandemic, role of adult content, multidisciplinary or specialized creators, leaders and followers, etc. Many of these platforms offer a potent ground for such research, by publicizing much of the underlying data related to the creators, their supporters and the occurring transactions.

As many of these platforms are not owned by large corporations, they are often less restrictive in terms of what data is available. Graphtreon is a platform, which collects and shares frequently updated information on all Patreon creators with at least one contributor. These data are available at creator-level, with historical information, with browsable content categories and can be either scraped or purchased from the platform. For live-streaming services like Twitch, similar data aggregators exist in the form of, e.g. Sullygnome or Streamscharts—offering historical data at a channel level, including information on time streamed, audience size and the type of content streamed. These data are often further disaggregated by language, nationality, etc. Numerous creators in such profiles offer links to other platforms, including social media, and sometimes provide contact information. These, in turn, could be used for ethnographic or survey studies.

5 Summary

Crowd-patronage is a non-standard type of crowdfunding that moves away from project-related work and instead focuses on continuous subscription-based support or spontaneous support expressions in the form of monetary tips. Due to its continuous nature, it presents different dynamics to other funding models and offers advantages to creative workers who suffer from high job precarity and unstable income. One of the most promising features of crowd-patronage is its inclusivity, allowing both smaller artists and less wealthy consumers to connect, conduct meaningful transactions and develop reciprocal support networks. Due to their promising offer, platforms like Patreon have been consistently growing, providing monetization options to creators from all over the world (Patreon, 2022; Swords, 2017), despite the simultaneous appearance of country-specific Patreon-inspired services (e.g. the Polish Patronite platform).

While most creators do not earn enough through patronage to abandon other income sources, the platform growth during the onset of the pandemic showed that crowd-patronage can act as a viable alternative even for established artists with existing audiences. This sudden migration to online patronage also highlighted the role of such platforms in increasing resilience to sudden crises, even if it has not previously been the primary channel for monetization for many of the migrating creators.

Yet, despite the observable promise of such platforms, many of their underlying dynamics remain under-researched. With existing data access and publicly visible expressions of communication (e.g. posts, comments, polls, etc.), engagement (views, likes, etc.), or support (contributors and contributions), crowd-patronage represents a promising area for new scholar interest, as well as an interesting field in general.

Notes

1. For a broader description with sources, of the changes in patronage over the centuries, see Swords (2017).

2. Similarly, to typical crowdfunding, these options essentially allow the creators to introduce second degree price discrimination, as patrons increase their support dependent on preferences and budgets.
3. Not counting a joint "Other" category.
4. Twitch is currently owned by Amazon, which allows streamers to earn commissions when their linking leads to a purchase.
5. It is unclear how many of these were actually active when the statistic was provided.
6. Soundcloud had a tumultuous relationship with major labels, having problems in establishing and maintaining licensing deals (source).
7. This is, of course, a simplification as numerous stakeholders take their cuts along the way (e.g. the service itself, the labels, etc.). However, this does not affect the proportionality issues discussed in the paragraph.
8. Concurrent means same time. The actual numbers of unique active streamers and viewers within a month time are much higher (e.g. app. 8 million active streamers at the beginning of 2024).
9. Notable examples include a trend of streaming from inflatable pools or hot tubs, or yoga videos with ASMR sound setup (see Chalk, 2021; Diaz, 2021).

References

Andres, R., Rossi, M., & Tremblay, M. (2023). *YouTube 'Adpocalypse': The Youtubers' Journey From Ad-Based to Patron-Based Revenues* (ZEW Discussion Paper 23–059). ZEW - Leibniz Centre for European Economic Research. https://econpapers.repec.org/paper/zbwzewdip/283579.htm

Bogle, A. (2021). *Policy Brief: Buying and Selling Extremism: New Funding Opportunities in the Right-Wing Extremist Online Ecosystem.*

Bonifacio, R., Hair, L., & Wohn, D. Y. (2023). Beyond Fans: The Relational Labor and Communication Practices of Creators on Patreon. *New Media & Society, 25*(10), 2684–2703.

Bridgstock, R. (2005). Australian Artists, Starving and Well-Nourished: What Can We Learn from the Prototypical Protean Career? *Australian Journal of Career Development, 14*(3), 40–47.

Chalk, A. (2021, December 31). Twitch 2021: A Year in Controversies. *PC Gamer*. https://www.pcgamer.com/twitch-2021-a-year-in-controversies/

Church, M. (2020). COVID-19 and the Creative Economy: Takeaways From Patreon's Data Science Team. *Patreon*. https://news.patreon.com/articles/covid-19-and-the-creative-economy-takeaways-from-patreon-s-data-science-team. Accessed November 2024.

Comunian, R., & England, L. (2020). Creative and Cultural Work Without Filters: COVID-19 and Exposed Precarity in the Creative Economy. *Cultural Trends, 29*(2), 112–128.

Constine, J. (2017). Patreon Doubles in a Year to 1M Paying Patrons and 50K Creators. *TechCrunch*. https://techcrunch.com/2017/05/18/patreon-pushes-as-youtube-stutters/ Accessed November 2024.

Dalla Chiesa, C., & Hardy, W. (2019). *Presented at 17th Interdisciplinary European Conference on Entrepreneurship Research (IECER), "Entrepreneurship for a Better World"*. Utrecht, The Netherlands.

Diaz, A. (2021, June 21). Twitch Bans Popular Streamers Amouranth and Indiefoxx After Yoga ASMR Streams. *Polygon*. https://www.polygon.com/22543478/twitch-amouranth-indiefoxx-yoga-asmr-stream-hot-tub-meta-ban

Elkins, M., & Fry, T. R. L. (2022a). Beyond the Realm of Cash: Street Performers and Payments in the Online World. *Journal of Cultural Economics, 46*(2), 231–248.

Elkins, M., & Fry, T. R. L. (2022b). Street Performers and Donations in an Online Environment in the Wake of COVID-19. *City, Culture and Society, 28*, Article 100438.

Graphtreon. (2024). *Patreon Stats*. https://graphtreon.com/patreon-stats. Accessed November 2024.

Hair, L. (2021). Friends, Not ATMs: Parasocial Relational Work and the Construction of Intimacy by Artists on Patreon. *Sociological Spectrum, 41*(2), 196–212.

Hair, L., Bonifacio, R., & Wohn, D. Y. (2022). Multi-platform Practices Among Digital Patronage Creators. *Convergence, 28*(5), 1438–1456.

Ingham, T. (2022). Nearly 80% of Artists on Spotify Have Fewer Than 50 Monthly Listeners. *MusicBusiness Worldwide*. https://www.musicbusinessworldwide.com/over-75-of-artists-on-spotify-have-fewer-than-50-monthly-listeners/. Accessed February 2025.

Jensen, F. J. (2024). Rethinking Royalties: Alternative Payment Systems on Music Streaming Platforms. *Journal of Cultural Economics*. https://doi.org/10.1007/s10824-024-09507-z

Lankoski, P., Apperley, T., & Harviainen, J. T. (2023). Platform-produced Heteronormativity: A Content Analysis of Adult Videogames on Patreon. *Games and Culture, 18*(1), 102–123.

Mann, J. (2023). OnlyFans Now Has More Than 3 Million Content Creators and Is a 'Global Business', Says the CEO. Business Insider.https://www.businessinsider.com/onlyfans-has-more-than-3-million-creators-global-business-2023-5?international=true&r=US&IR=T. Accessed November 2024.

Mixon, F. G., Jr., Asarta, C. J., & Caudill, S. B. (2017). Patreonomics: Public Goods Pedagogy for Economics Principles. *International Review of Economics Education, 25*, 1–7.

Netflix. (2023). *What We Watched: A Netflix Engagement Report*. https://about.netflix.com/en/news/what-we-watched-a-netflix-engagement-report. Accessed February 2025.

OECD. (2020). *Culture Shock: COVID-19 and the Cultural and Creative Sectors.*

OECD. (2022). *The Culture Fix: Creative People, Places and Industries*. Organisation for Economic Co-operation and Development. https://www.oecd-ilibrary.org/urban-rural-and-regional-development/the-culture-fix_991bb520-en

Patreon. (2022). The First-Ever Patreon Creator Census. https://news.patreon.com/articles/the-first-ever-patreon-creator-census. Accessed February 2025.

Peukert, C. (2019). The Next Wave of Digital Technological Change and the Cultural Industries. *Journal of Cultural Economics, 43*(2), 189–210.

Regner, T. (2021). Crowdfunding a Monthly Income: An Analysis of the Membership Platform Patreon. *Journal of Cultural Economics, 45*(1), 133–142.

Sanyoura, L. E., & Anderson, A. (2022). Quantifying the Creator Economy: A Large-Scale Analysis of Patreon. *Proceedings of the International AAAI Conference on Web and Social Media, 16*, 829–840.

Skid, N. (2022). How a Mental Breakdown Launched This $4 Billion Start-Up: 'I Sat There in a Puddle of Bottled Water, Crying Like a Baby'. *CNBC*. https://www.cnbc.com/2022/03/31/how-jack-conte-sam-yam-built-a-4-billion-start-up-called-patreon.html. Accessed November 2024.

Snijders, J., Clarke, M., van der Graaf, A., De Stefano, V., Kimenai, F., & Tajtakova, M. (2020). The Status and Working Conditions of Artists and Cultural and Creative Professionals: Report of the OMC (Open Method of Coordination) Group of EU Member States' Experts: Final Report. Publications Office of the European Union. https://doi.org/10.2766/46315

Swords, J. (2017). Crowd-Patronage—Intermediaries, Geographies and Relationships in Patronage Networks. *Poetics, 64*, 63–73.

Swords, J. (2020). Interpenetration and Intermediation of Crowd-Patronage Platforms. *Information, Communication & Society, 23*(4), 523–538.

Throsby, D., & Zednik, A. (2011). Multiple Job-Holding and Artistic Careers: Some Empirical Evidence. *Cultural Trends, 20*(1), 9–24.

Woronkowicz, J., & Noonan, D. S. (2019). Who Goes Freelance? The Determinants of Self-Employment for Artists. *Entrepreneurship Theory and Practice, 43*(4), 651–672.

Open Access This chapter is licensed under the terms of the Creative Commons Attribution 4.0 International License (http://creativecommons.org/licenses/by/4.0/), which permits use, sharing, adaptation, distribution and reproduction in any medium or format, as long as you give appropriate credit to the original author(s) and the source, provide a link to the Creative Commons license and indicate if changes were made.

The images or other third party material in this chapter are included in the chapter's Creative Commons license, unless indicated otherwise in a credit line to the material. If material is not included in the chapter's Creative Commons license and your intended use is not permitted by statutory regulation or exceeds the permitted use, you will need to obtain permission directly from the copyright holder.

CHAPTER 11

Beyond Likes: Social Media Remuneration and Financing of Digital Cultural Production

Sophia Gaenssle

1 Introduction: Social Media and Cultural Production

Digitalisation and the development of social media introduced new avenues to distribute art and personal creations. While the early years of social media started with amateur content and simple videos or images, the field has drastically professionalised within the last two decades (Döring, 2014; Gaenssle & Budzinski, 2021). Typically, social media platforms focus on different types of content (inter alia, text *X/Twitter*, images and short videos *Instagram*, short videos *TikTok*, videos *YouTube*). However, there are trends to diversify, such as *YouTube* and *Instagram* offering short videos. As such, those platforms give content creators new opportunities to publish their own creations and ideas. Among these creations are contents of conventional nature, such as music or audio-visual art. But also new forms of entertainment came to life, e.g., vlogs

S. Gaenssle (✉)
Economic Theory Group, Ilmenau University of Technology, Ilmenau, Germany
e-mail: sophia.gaenssle@outlook.com

© The Author(s) 2026

C. Dalla Chiesa and A. Rykkja (eds.), *Cultural Funding and Financing*, Cultural Economics & the Creative Economy,
https://doi.org/10.1007/978-3-031-96696-5_11

(video blogs) and gaming (such as "Let's Plays"). Moreover, people found new ways to express themselves and their creativity in publishing their DIY ("Do-It-Yourself") projects, special crafts, tutorials, or life hacks. Traditional artists could join the digital market to find new career and marketing options. Social media fuelled the reach and enabled the publication of those contents at very low costs (Waldfogel, 2018). Digitalisation reduced the cost of (i) content production, with digital cameras and smartphones recording high quality and (ii) content publication, with broadband internet, social media, and international sides, enabling an international reach of digital goods. Hence, digital developments lower specific technological barriers to enter the creative industries (Gaenssle, 2024). However, consumer attention became even more scarce,[1] since information "consumes the attention of its recipients" (Simon, 1971, p. 40) and the quantity of information and content increased rapidly in the digital age. Content creators need to build an audience and maintain it in the long run to succeed (Budzinski & Gaenssle, 2020). In the digital realm which is influenced and controlled by the power of algorithmic selection (Budzinski et al., 2022), content creators compete for consumer attention to generate income. Their increasingly professional businesses became a vital part of the creative economy (Kolo, 2024; Shapiro, 2018). See Sect. 2 on the remuneration mechanisms and how they may exacerbate inequalities among creators, especially regarding platform favouritism, algorithmic biases, and disparities in access to resources.

This chapter is going to shed light on digital artists and creators to reflect on their production as well as their digital avenues of income. The main questions are: *How do social media mechanisms of remuneration work?* Or putting it even easier: *(1) How do social media creators monetise their content and works of art?* to draw conclusions and answer the second question: *(2) What does this mean for financing and funding cultural production, in particular core arts?* The chapter is structured as follows. Section 2 provides an introduction to social media creators and their work. Section 3 contains detailed information on remuneration in the field (question 1) and Sect. 4 summarises and concludes on a meta level (question 2).

2 Social Media Creators and Contents

Social media creators (SMC) are providers of self-produced content on pages like YouTube, TikTok, Instagram, Twitch, etc. Many of them are active on multiple platforms. They build their own audiences and regularly produce content. While there are many non-commercial providers (private accounts for friends and family), this chapter focuses on commercial SMC, who received monetary rewards for their publications. Very popular creators are called influencers or social media stars, who can be defined as people who dominate the activities in which they engage (Jung & Nüesch, 2019; Rosen, 1981), in this case, their social media activities and uploads dominate their field and reach a huge target group. They earn top incomes and represent a novel superstar type of the digital era (Budzinski & Gaenssle, 2020; Gaenssle & Budzinski, 2021). Their fame is native to social media (Marwick, 2016), while the lines between stars of traditional and new media become more and more blurry (Gaenssle & Budzinski, 2024). As mentioned above, attention in online markets is scarce and the competition for target groups and consumer engagement is high. While social media decreases the barriers to publish creative content, the success (measured mostly in popularity and quantity of people reached) remains hierarchical (Gaenssle & Budzinski, 2021).

There are various factors that influence the popularity of uploads. The following list is not intended to be comprehensive; however, it includes the main factors influencing the popularity of an SMC's activity. Firstly, the creator is in the control of:

i. Quality and type of the content: The medium (e.g., video, text form, pictures, audio); the cost and level of inputs (e.g., professional shooting of pictures, etc.); market segment (i.e., target group and market size)?
ii. Quantity of publications: At which frequency is content uploaded? A higher frequency might correlate with lesser quality, or pressure to reduce costs.
iii. Engagement and community building: Interaction with followers, e.g., responding to comments, DMs, and engaging in discussions. But also, collaborations and cross-promotion (i.e., partnering with other influencers or brands).

iv. Market optimisation: SEO and hashtags, thumbnails and titles, selection of platforms, i.e., where to publish. Publication strategies might include multiple platforms and multiple use of contents, slightly varying between outlets.

Secondly, the factors beyond the sphere of the artist's influence are:

v. Technical and legal requirements: Some creators might face technical barriers. For instance, a poet needs to create pictures or provide videos of her poems on *Instagram*, due to the nature of the (picture sharing) platform. Moreover, there might be terms of condition that limit the creative output. Nude content, for instance, is not permitted on many social media sites. A photographer expressing herself and her art with nude content might be banned and uploads blocked by the platform.
vi. Market and audience dynamics: Demographic shifts and changes in audience preferences, economic conditions, market saturation (increased creators in the same niche), cultural and societal trends, e.g., political events or social movements shaping content reception.
vii. Platform and algorithmic influences: Platform operators use algorithms (so-called recommender systems) to order and select content according to (1) consumer preferences, (2) their characteristics, and (3) additional factors that are typically not revealed in full detail. Content visibility depends on algorithm chances, virality pushes, shifts, ranks, etc. according to the algorithmic rules.

Especially, (vii.) algorithmic search and recommendation services play a vital role in many digital markets like e-commerce, but also in social media (Budzinski et al., 2022). Social media recommender systems are pivotal in shaping online visibility, influencing which content is prominently displayed and which remains unseen (Leerssen, 2020). Platforms might prioritise highly engaging content, disproportionately benefiting already popular creators while making it harder for emerging talent to gain visibility. Algorithmic biases may further marginalise certain groups by favouring specific aesthetics, languages, or content types that align with commercial interests. An example found by Richard et al. (2020) was *Instagram* favouring nude contents, pushing pictures showing more naked skin. Additionally, financial and technological barriers—such as access to high-quality production equipment, professional networking opportunities, or advertising budgets—can deepen the gap between well-resourced creators and those with limited means, ultimately shaping which accounts can sustain the creative social media career.

Regarding the contents, there are limitations to the type of creative contents publishable due to the digital nature of social media. Only reproducible cultural goods that can be captured in bits, i.e., information goods (Shapiro & Varian, 1999), can be published. These are, for example, sound recordings, films, or e-books. Non-reproducible artistic and cultural products such as performances, paintings, or sculptures (Towse, 2020) cannot be made available online in their original form. However, artists found creative ways to market and promote their work on social media (Salo et al., 2013). Both avenues, for digital as well as non-digital goods will be analysed within the next section to shed light on different options depending on the creative products. While it may appear that core arts are not inherently suited to leveraging social media channels for commercial purposes, there exist viable strategies for their integration. The following section will examine these approaches and provide critical insights into their potential applications.

3 Social Media Remuneration

Depending on the social media platform, there are different avenues to generate revenue as a content producer. The remuneration depends on the page's features and rules. Gaenssle (2024) differentiates between platform internal and external revenues; this approach is extended and enhanced in the following section: (i) platform internal payments, i.e. those revenues that are distributed via the social media platform itself (see Sect. 3.1, types 1–4), and (ii) platform external payments, i.e., revenues that are collected through social media activity but not directly paid via the platform but through external parties (advertisers and companies) (see Sect. 3.2, types 5–7).

Figure 1 illustrates an exemplified social media ecosystem and possible revenue sources for SMC. The social media platform as well as the SMC serve two or more market sides and act as an intermediary. Therefore, both parties are displayed as a *platform* in the economic sense.[2] The types of payment are visualised in (i) platform internal payments (types 1–4) coming from the social media platform and (ii) platform external payments (types 5–7) from external parties. There are two types of advertisers. Firstly, advertisers placing ads directly on the social media page and, secondly, advertisers collaborating with commercial SMC. The different types of payments are discussed in detail in the following sections. Notably, platforms and SMC can mix and combine different types; for analytical reasons, there are explained individually.

Platform Internal Payments

Ad Revenue Sharing (Type 1)

Some social media platforms offer the possibility of sharing ad revenues. These are generated from ad displayed on and around the SMC's content. Content providers agree to ads before, during and/or after their content and get paid per view. In Fig. 1, the advertisers are directly connected to the social media platform on the right side of the figure. Consumers pay with their attention to advertisement, advertisers pay to place their ads, and the platform and content providers share the revenues. The more ads are consumed, the higher the revenues for SMC. *YouTube* and *TikTok*, for instance, offer creators a share of ad revenue. There could also be integrated ads or banners in video content, where creators receive a percentage per view or click. This payment type is especially suitable for audio and audio-visual artists with digital content.

Subscription Models and Memberships (Type 2)

There is also the option of subscription models, either in (i) à la carte (pay what you consume) or (ii) all you can eat (flat rate) variation (Gaenssle, 2024). On pages like *Patreon* or *OnlyFans*, you can support specific content providers of your choice. By paying a membership, you receive access to the content and support, e.g. your favourite artist. *YouTube's* "Join" feature lets creators offer exclusive perks to paying subscribers, from early access to behind-the-scenes content. These are paywall systems to make contents excludable.[3] It is also possible that platforms like *Telegram*, *Facebook* or *Twitch* offer users access to special events, emojis, or exclusive content. Thus, mixing revenue forms of ad financed and subscription models. Comparably to payment type 1, type 2 is also suitable for audio and audio-visual art, i.e. the digital good itself is being sold.

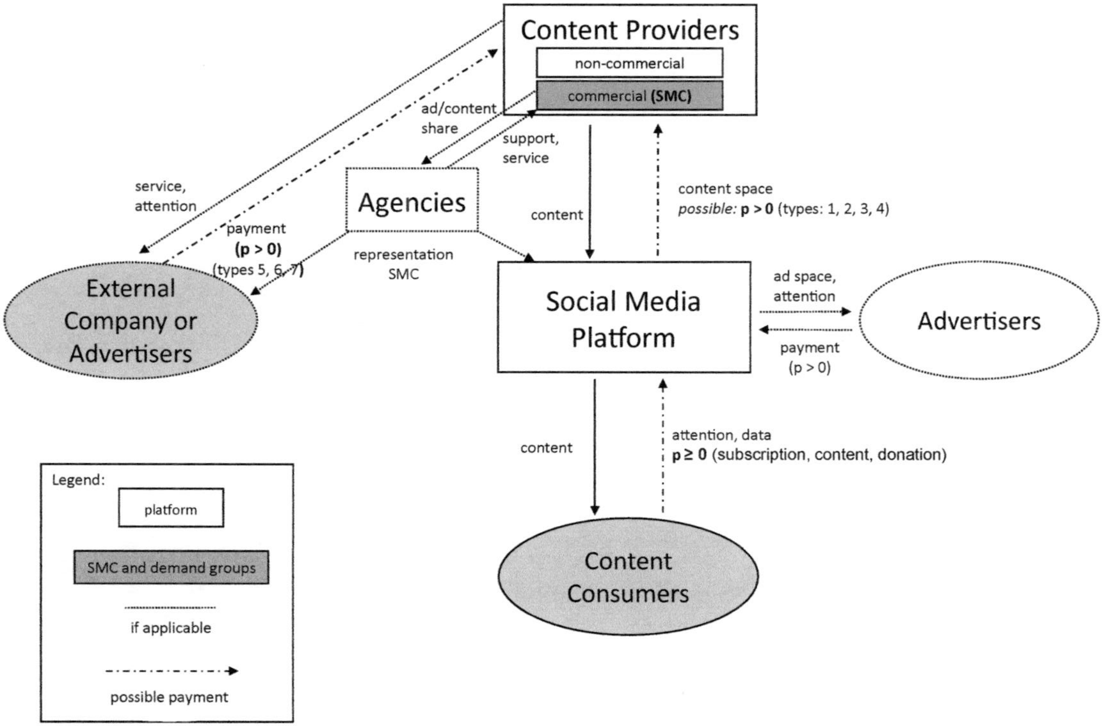

Fig. 1 SMC—Ecosystem and payment types (enhanced from Gaenssle and Budzinski [2024])

Creator Funds and Bonuses (Type 3)
Some platforms offer bonuses or rewards for content performance or metrics. *TikTok* or *Snapchat* tried different models to reward content creators for high numbers of views and engagement. Introducing short videos, so-called Reels (on *Instagram*) and Shorts (on *YouTube*), these platforms also tested performance-based bonuses for short-form video creators, incentivising consistent, engaging content. As of now, payment type 3 seems to favour fast-paced, highly engaging content with high entertainment value.

Tips, Donations, and Gifting (Type 4)
It is possible to send money directly to a content provider via the platform, i.e. tip them. This is very common in live streams on *Twitch*, for example (Partin, 2020). These would be direct donations from fans within a stream that are coordinated via the platform. In Fig. 1, consumers would pay money to their favoured SMC via the social media page (in a vertical line). There are also some gifting features, inter alia, on *TikTok*, *Twitch*, and *YouTube*, that allow viewers to purchase digital gifts and send them the SMC's way, so they can cash them in. This payment type is mainly found in live events or formats where consumers directly interact with SMC. Therefore, it is most suitable for audio-visual goods with direct communication.

Platform External Payments

Merchandise Sales (Type 5)
Some artists use social media to market their work of art and creations. With growing reach and popularity, these pages are powerful tools to promote products, brands, or companies. There is platform-integrated merchandise option, enabling sales of works and content through the platform like *Teespring* on *YouTube* or *Taobao* on *WeChat* in China (Zhou, 2022). Admittedly, these shops fall between the separation of external versus internal payments. Since the revenues are generated within the shop system where consumers are referred to, I place them with external payments.

Moreover, artists can promote their own shops or external sites, e.g. on *Shopify* or *Etsy*, linking these to their social media accounts. By posting pictures of sculptures or paintings, artists can introduce themselves to consumers and generate a bigger audience. Social media can be a channel to publish behind the scenes information, for instance on performances, or background information on ideas and creations. Payment type 5 can therefore be a powerful (marketing) tool for non-digital goods. In Fig. 1, there are own companies or shops on the left-hand side to sell (external) work.

Sponsorships and Brand Partnerships (Type 6)
Another important source of income on social media is sponsored content or brand collaborations (Ibáñez-Sánchez et al., 2022). In Fig. 1, external companies or advertisers are placed on the left side. These are typically not owned by the SMC themselves (in contrast to type 5). Brands pay creators to promote specific products or services in their posts. These might be single posts, or longer campaigns and cooperations. This ad-financed, or sponsored content, is prevalent on *Instagram* but can also be found on most other social media platforms. These cooperations can start very small with single product samples but have the potential to generate millions of USD for single posts, if the influencer is very popular (Gaenssle, 2024). Social media influencers can take different roles in advertising collaborations (Rundin & Colliander, 2021) and act as opinion leaders, fuelling online word-of-mouth (Kozinets et al., 2010). Artists might choose to work with a suitable brand that is in line with their creative identity. However, as most ad cooperations, this payment type has a strong commercial nature.

Commission and Affiliate Marketing (Type 7)
SMC can generate a commission for sales through custom links or promo codes (Dajah, 2020). So-called affiliate links (for instance, *Amazon*) can be shared on social media, accessed by consumers, and SMC receive a share for click-throughs or purchases. Promotion codes also fit within this category; influencers have an individual voucher code (e.g. their name and percent discount) that can be used for discounts at checkouts while shopping online. The SMC gets a commission for each of these affiliated sales. This is very popular on *Instagram*, *TikTok*, and *YouTube*. Typically, this payment category has strong commercial and marketing connotation in line with the "influencer" character of social media (Gräve, 2017). Artist might use links or gift codes to promote performances, sell tickets to events, or similar.

Co-Creator Features, Revenue Split, and Crowdfunding (Special Type)
There are more options to raise awareness and money on social media for art projects and creative production. These are listed here to complete the overview. However, they are not considered as main sources of payment for social media in the narrow sense (and not part of Fig. 1).

Naturally, creatives want to collaborate and co-create. SMC cooperate, co-produce content, and might want to split revenues. In many cases, visiting other social media hosts can create buzz and boost attention for both accounts (Kozinets et al., 2010). Being part of a multi-channel network on YouTube, for example, is an option for cross-promotion and increasing attention across fan bases (Zabel et al., 2017). Split revenue models and labels are being discussed and might offer new ways to co-produce online.

Lastly, bigger art projects can be funded via *Kickstarter* or *GoFundMe* for creative ventures. Social media is a potent marketing tool to introduce and promote projects that go beyond the everyday content. However, in this case, social media merely serves the purpose of a medium to increase awareness for external funding.

4 Conclusion: Social Media—One of Many Avenues

Social media platforms can offer new avenues to finance art and creative ventures. To sum up the findings and answer the question *"(1) How do social media creators monetise their content and works of art?"*: There are different options to earn monetary rewards (i) directly via the platform and (ii) indirectly through external payments.

(i) Direct payments, though embedded advertising, subscription models, etc. (see 3.1) are specifically suitable for primary digital goods (the main good is an information good), such as music and audio-visual entertainment. Creators can monetise their content via ad shares or claim rewards through copyright ownership on the platform.
(ii) Indirect payment options, offer diverse avenues. On the one hand, merchandise sales and shops directly connected to the social media pages might be specifically interesting for creators of non-tangible

art. They have the possibility to promote and sell their products via social media pages. On the other hand, commissions, affiliate links, and promo codes have a highly commercial "influencing" character that are especially suitable for marketing avenues.

Notably, a combination of payment methods is possible for SMC to generate income via social media. For instance, a visual artist paints a new piece, records the process, and posts the video online (on *YouTube*, *TikTok*, *Twitch*, and *Instagram*). She receives ad shares per view of the video, while she embeds a link to her shop (e.g., on *Etsy* or *Artsy*) or studio (physical or selling NFTs). Moreover, she might have a *Patreon* page with a subscription fee for true fans, where she publishes behind-the-scenes information or further, more exquisite, art. In this example, the artist collects ad shares, subscription fees, and possibly sells her physical art.

As such SMC have the option to monetise their content through ad revenue, brand sponsorships, memberships, crowd-patronage (e.g., Patreon), direct sales (e.g., merch, NFTs), and platform-based tipping (e.g., YouTube Super Chats, TikTok gifts). *(2) What does this mean for financing and funding cultural production, in particular core arts?* This shifts cultural production, especially core arts, toward market-driven models, relying more on engagement metrics and commercial partnerships rather than traditional funding sources like grants or public subsidies, potentially privileging entertainment-oriented content over experimental or non-commercial artistic expressions. However, social media not only shifts financing models but also fosters innovation in cultural production. New formats—such as short-form artistic storytelling, immersive digital experiences, audience-driven narratives—have emerged. These developments allow creators to experience beyond traditional artistic boundaries and institutional gatekeepers, offering fresh avenues of creative expression and sustainable artistic careers. SMC can create and upload content in line with their recent personal development and ideas, without producers or gatekeepers adjusting their content to a target group or forcing them to fit in. The means of publication are direct, if wanted, "raw"; leaving the consumers to judge whether they like it or not. This enables unfiltered possibilities for self-expression without, e.g. the media altering the artistic appearance. However, it might also put artists in the crosshairs of the public's harsh online judgement. These innovations still operate within platform-driven economic constraints, influencing which artistic practices can thrive. Overall, social media gives some new options and avenues to generate income from arts in the digital age. Eventually, it serves as one of many avenues to finance art and creative production today.

Regarding future studies and areas of research key questions remain: How do algorithmic selections (including self-learning AI systems) affect social media popularity and monetary success in the long term? How do algorithmic changes impact creators' financial stability? Another avenue for investigation is the role of decentralised digital economies, such as blockchain-based monetisation (e.g., NFTs, DAOs). Finally, comparative studies between digital and traditional funding models could provide deeper insights into whether social media is truly democratising artistic careers or reinforcing new forms of gatekeeping. Addressing these gaps will be essential for understanding how social media shapes not only the financial, but also the cultural and artistic landscape in the long run.

Notes

1. For an overview on attention economics, see (Taylor, 2014).
2. For more details on platform theory, see (Anderson & Gabszewicz, 2006; Evans, 2013; Rochet & Tirole, 2003) and social media influencers acting as a platform (Gaenssle et al., forthcoming).
3. As discussed in Sect. 2, the online contents are information goods, which makes them non-rival (see detailed explanation of non-rivalry and non-excludability introduced by Musgrave (1969) in the economic sense. However, by establishing a pay wall, it is possible to ensure copyrights and excludability.

References

Anderson, S. P., & Gabszewicz, J. J. (2006). The Media and Advertising: A Tale of Two-Sided Markets. In V. A. Ginsburgh & D. Throsby (Eds.), *Handbook of the Economics of Art and Culture* (pp. 567–614). Elsevier.

Budzinski, O., & Gaenssle, S. (2020). The Economics of Social Media (Super-)Stars: An Empirical Investigation of Stardom and Success on YouTube. *Journal of Media Economics, 31*(3–4), 75–95.

Budzinski, O., Gaenssle, S., & Lindstädt-Dreusicke, N. (2022). Data (R)Evolution—The Economics of Algorithmic Search and Recommender

Services. In S. Baumann (Ed.), *Handbook of Digital Business Ecosystems* (pp. 349–366). Elgar.

Dajah, Dr. S. (2020). Marketing Through Social Media Influencers. *International Journal of Business and Social Science, 11*(9). https://www.researchgate.net/publication/347385520_Marketing_through_Social_Media_Influencers

Döring, N. (2014). Professionalisierung und Kommerzialisierung auf YouTube. *Merz Medien + Erziehung, 58*(4), 24–31.

Evans, D. S. (2013). Attention Rivalry Among Online Platforms. *Journal of Competition Law and Economics, 9*(2), 313–357.

Gaenssle, S. (2024). Income Distribution and Nudity on Social Media: Attention Economics of Instagram Stars. *Kyklos, 77*(1), 184–212.

Gaenssle, S., & Budzinski, O. (2021). Stars in Social Media: New Light Through Old Windows? *Journal of Media Business Studies, 18*(2), 79–105.

Gaenssle, S., & Budzinski, O. (2024). The Economics of Influencers and Social Media Stardom. In U. Rohn, T. Raats, & M. B. Rimscha (Eds.), *De Gruyter Handbook of Media Economics* (1st ed.). De Gruyter.

Gaenssle, S., Lindstädt-Dreusicke, N., & Budzinski, O. (forthcoming). *Understanding Consumer Preferences in the Digital Landscape—Empirical Evidence from Instagram* (Ilmenau Economics Discussion Papers, pp. 1–20).

Gräve, J.-F. (2017). Exploring the Perception of Influencers Vs. Traditional Celebrities. In Association for Computing Machinery (Ed.), *Proceedings of the 8th International Conference on Social Media & Society—#SMSociety17* (pp. 1–5). ACM Press.

Ibáñez-Sánchez, S., Flavián, M., Casaló, L. V., & Belanche, D. (2022). Influencers and Brands Successful Collaborations: A Mutual Reinforcement to Promote Products and Services on Social Media. *Journal of Marketing Communications, 28*(5), 469–486.

Jung, C., & Nüesch, S. (2019). The More Others Care, the More You Share?—Social Contagion as a Stardom Trigger of Social Media Superstars. *Applied Economics, 51*(9), 881–888.

Kolo, C. (2024). Social media influencers as content creators in the creative economy. *Journal of Creative Industries and Cultural Studies, 11,* 52–82.

Kozinets, R. V., De Valck, K., Wojnicki, A. C., & Wilner, S. J. S. (2010). Networked Narratives: Understanding Word-of-Mouth Marketing in Online Communities. *Journal of Marketing, 74*(2), 71–89.

Leerssen, P. J. (2020). The Soap Box as a Black Box Regulating: Transparency in Social Media Recommender Systems. *European Journal of Law and Technology, 11*(2), 1–34.

Marwick, A. E. (2016). You May Know Me from YouTube: (Micro-)Celebrity in Social Media. In P. D. Marshall & S. Redmond (Eds.), *A companion to celebrity* (pp. 333–350). Wiley Blackwell.

Musgrave, R. (1969). Provision for Social Goods. In J. Margolis & H. Guitton (Eds.), *Public Economics: An Analysis of Public Production and Consumption and Their Relations to the Private Sectors*. Proceedings of a Conference held by the International Economic Association (pp. 124–144). Macmillan.

Partin, W. C. (2020). Bit by (Twitch) Bit: "Platform Capture" and the Evolution of Digital Platforms. *Social Media + Society*, *6*(3), 2056305120933981.

Richard, É., Duportail, J., Kayser-Bril, N., & Schacht, K. (2020). *Undress or Fail: Instagram's Algorithm Strong-Arms Users into Showing Skin*. https://algorithmwatch.org/en/instagram-algorithm-nudity/

Rochet, J.-C., & Tirole, J. (2003). Platform Competition in Two-Sided Markets. *Journal of the European Economic Association*, *1*(4), 990–1029.

Rosen, S. (1981). The Economics of Superstars. *The American Economic Review*, *71*(5), 845–858.

Rundin, K., & Colliander, J. (2021). Multifaceted Influencers: Toward a New Typology for Influencer Roles in Advertising. *Journal of Advertising*, *50*(5), 548–564.

Salo, J., Lankinen, M., & Mäntymäki, M. (2013). The Use of Social Media for Artist Marketing: Music Industry Perspectives and Consumer Motivations. *International Journal on Media Management*, *15*(1), 23–41.

Shapiro, C., & Varian, H. R. (1999). *Information Rules: A Strategic Guide to the Network Economy*. Harvard Business School Press.

Shapiro, R. (2018). *Unlocking the Gates: America's New Creative Economy* (Americans for the Arts, p. 99). http://www.recreatecoalition.org

Simon, H. A. (1971). Designing Organizations for an Information Rich World. In M. Greenberger (Ed.), *Computers, Communications, and the Public Interest* (pp. 37–72). Johns Hopkins Press.

Taylor, G. (2014). Scarcity of Attention for a Medium of Abundance. In M. Graham & W. H. Dutton (Eds.), *Society and the Internet: How Networks of Information and Communication are Changing Our Lives* (pp. 257–271). Oxford University Press.

Towse, R. (2020). Creative Industries. In R. Towse & T. Navarrete Hernández (Eds.), *Handbook of Cultural Economics*. Edward Elgar Publishing.

Waldfogel, J. (2018). *Digital Renaissance: What Data And Economics Tell Us About the Future of Popular Culture*. Princeton University Press.

Zabel, C., Seemann, C., & Pagel, S. (2017). Youtube-Creators in Deutschland – Motive, Produktionsroutinen und Finanzierung von deutschen Online-Video-Produzenten. In W. Seufert (Ed.), *Media Economics revisited: (Wie) Verändert das Internet die Ökonomie der Medien?* (pp. 125–145). Nomos.

Zhou, W. (2022). The Social Shopping Movement in China: From TaoBao to WeChat. In A. Hanlon, T. L. Tuten, & EBSCOhost (Eds.), *The Sage Handbook of Social Media Marketing*. Sage.

Open Access This chapter is licensed under the terms of the Creative Commons Attribution 4.0 International License (http://creativecommons.org/licenses/by/4.0/), which permits use, sharing, adaptation, distribution and reproduction in any medium or format, as long as you give appropriate credit to the original author(s) and the source, provide a link to the Creative Commons license and indicate if changes were made.

The images or other third party material in this chapter are included in the chapter's Creative Commons license, unless indicated otherwise in a credit line to the material. If material is not included in the chapter's Creative Commons license and your intended use is not permitted by statutory regulation or exceeds the permitted use, you will need to obtain permission directly from the copyright holder.

CHAPTER 12

Making Money from Streaming: Benefits and Barriers in the Music Industry

Sigbjørn Hjelmbrekke

1 Streaming Services

Once upon a time, people purchased copies of recordings and owned those copies indefinitely. They could replay the recordings freely for their own personal usage. They paid for such products only once, and rights holders and middlemen got paid once. This model existed through different technologies, such as phonograph cylinders, vinyl records, magnetic tapes, compact discs, and paid downloads, including ringtones for mobile phones. Although many might have purchased the same recording in multiple formats, the simple story is that rights holders mostly got their revenues relatively quickly, as the majority of sales took place in the months following a release.

Over the past 20 years, people have shifted from buying recorded music to subscribing to paid access that requires recurring monthly payments. Music streaming services had a slow start from around the turn of the century and finally gained substantial traction from 2007 to 2008.[1]

S. Hjelmbrekke (✉)
University of South-Eastern Norway, Bø, Norway
e-mail: sigbjorn.hjelmbrekke@usn.no

© The Author(s) 2026
C. Dalla Chiesa and A. Rykkja (eds.), *Cultural Funding and Financing*, Cultural Economics & the Creative Economy,
https://doi.org/10.1007/978-3-031-96696-5_12

Some preconditions needed to be in place for this to work well. On the technical side, capacity of internet transmission was the most important bottleneck. But these services also required entirely new licensing agreements, something that was difficult to obtain (Silver, 2013).

Money is collected and distributed in a very different way on digital streaming services compared with non-digital music sales. In the case of subscription services, consumers pay a fixed monthly fee independent of how much the consumers listen to music, and independent of how many different recordings are listened to. Rights holders are paid a small compensation for each replay. In the case of ad-supported services, consumers do not pay money, but "pay" in the form of watching or listening to ads. Ad-supported services are aimed at consumers with a low willingness to pay. They also allow consumers to experience a streaming service before they are potentially converted into a paying subscriber.

The transition to music streaming is essentially one from purchasing copies of recordings owned indefinitely, to a system of renting access to music for a limited period. This fundamental change is discussed in detail in Hjelmbrekke (2021). Streaming services shook up established models for the distribution of music as well as how revenues are shared among stakeholders. All such changes have winners and losers, and there will always be those who are unhappy with the new order.

In this chapter, we look at the characteristics of streaming as a financing model for the music industry. Among other methods of financing artistic and cultural products, such as government grants, patronage from individuals, corporate sponsorships, live performance revenues, crowdfunding or royalties distributed through collecting societies, streaming revenues are arguably among those that are most akin to direct market compensation. However, as streaming revenue rests heavily on copyright protection, the royalties can be considered a publicly enabled entitlement.

Distribution through streaming was pioneered in the music sector, later followed by other reproducible cultural goods. Particularly audiobooks and films have followed suit. Although the technologies have much in common with music streaming, the differences in terms of stakeholders, cost of production, exclusivity deals, and complementary goods are vastly different. Discussing streaming as one phenomenon, across all types of cultural goods, mostly does not seem very useful. However, some parallels remain.

This chapter will discuss the financing of music through market revenues, by looking at the specific case of music streaming services, and the different revenue sharing models employed for such services. Some key differences to other cultural industries will be mentioned towards the end of the chapter to discuss potential research avenues.

2 Who Gets the Money?—What We Know

Many artists and songwriters have claimed that the compensation they get per replay is far too low. Although the numbers are low, they might be the same as when people bought CDs. Sinnreich (2016) claims: "To put it simply, if one fan were to buy Swift's CD and listen to it 100 times and another were to stream the same album 100 times on Spotify, she'd net more revenue from the second fan than from the first".

A recent change in revenue distribution is the relative lag in revenues introduced by the payment-per-play model (Hjelmbrekke, 2021). Catalogue recordings (more than 18 months old) might now make up more than 70% of streams (Hesmondhalgh et al., 2021; Ingham, 2022; Luminate, 2025; Pedersen, 2018). Before streaming, record companies got most of the sales related to a recording within a shorter period after release. Listeners could continue to listen to works, without rights holders getting paid again. With the introduction of the payment-per-play model of streaming services, revenues only accrue upon replay in the decades to come. Thus, there is a lag in revenues associated with new recordings (Page, 2017), while old recordings have become a much more important source of revenue to the record companies.

Discussing how little streaming services pay artists is misleading, as streaming services do not pay artists at all. They pay publishers and record companies. These in turn pass some of the money on to creators. Recordings usually come into existence as a collaboration between songwriters, artists, and a record company. All parts of this effort need financing. How much record companies pass on to creators depends on costs and contracts set with the intermediary firms.

According to Hesmondhalgh et al. (2021), artists have been offered similar terms for streaming revenues as for physical sales, with recoupable advances, although with some adjustments. A 25% royalty rate is regarded as average in the case of exclusive contracts, somewhat higher than the 15–20% that might have been more common for physical records. An alternative is for artists to keep control of recording rights and instead partner with a digital distribution company, like DistroKid or TuneCore. There are several different options in this case, and distributors may take anything from 10 to 40% commission dependent on service level, but the artist cannot expect any advance, and must carry the full expenses (Hesmondhalgh et al., 2021, p. 66). Creators that self-release and own all rights can earn significant sums even from limited amounts of streaming.

Hesmondhalgh et al. (2021) estimate what they believe are average revenue sharing in Britain in 2021. It seems artists receive a similar share of recording rights irrespective of format. Publishing rights holders gain substantially from streaming, at the expense of recording rights owners. Record companies receive a smaller share, but their costs have also been reduced over time. This sounds all good for artists and songwriters, but one must keep in mind that these revenues are distributed to many more creators than before. Both due to access to a huge pool of catalogue material, and due to increasing amounts of new music being released. Thus, while creator revenues go up, revenues per creator do not (Hesmondhalgh et al., 2021, Chapter3).

Discussions on the economic situation of musicians/creators/artists are complicated because there is no unified definition of who are members of these groups, and thus no unified measure of how many musicians exist. Nevertheless, there appears to be an increasing number of musicians, at least in some countries. This is especially true for musicians with music present on digital streaming services (Hesmondhalgh et al., 2021). Average earnings of musicians depend on the definitions of musicians in each specific study. It also depends on which types of revenues are included.

At least in some countries, there are debates on which type of licensing rules streaming should be subject to. If regulation was more like that for broadcasting, then session musicians would have a slice of royalties, not only an upfront payment for the job. This would also give artists a larger percentage of royalties, and it will provide an ongoing source of income even from unrecouped recordings. However, record industry representatives claim that such a model would greatly benefit service providers at the expense of both record companies and artists (Hesmondhalgh et al., 2021, Chapter 3).

Evaluating the effect of streaming on artist revenues is further complicated by the long-existing practice of advance payments from record companies, and the recoupment of both advance and expenses from the artist's share of royalties. If the artist never recoups, and there is no more royalty after the initial advance, then the lag in revenues has arguably not harmed artists. However, for those that eventually recoups, this will take longer. The lag in revenues to record companies presumably also make them less inclined to pay large advances to artists. This might especially be true for small, independent record companies with modest catalogues and modest opportunity to take risk. Furthermore, the prevalence of using digital distribution platforms implies that a smaller fraction of recordings will be subject to recoupment contracts. Crowdfunding can, in some cases, diminish the dependence on a record company advance.

The monetisation of catalogue content associated with streaming services might benefit heritage acts. However, if those artists have not recouped expenses according to contract, or if their contracts are badly suited for digital revenues, this redistribution of income is not to the benefit of any artists, only the record companies with the largest catalogues.

Financing Model: "Pro Rata" or "User-Centric"

In markets for most other goods, the money a person spends is distributed to the sellers and producers of the goods the person buys. This is different for music in the time of streaming. The model of royalty distribution employed by most music streaming services is what has been termed the *pro rata model*.[2] Streaming services collect revenues in one big pool. Rights holders then get paid proportional to their share of the total number of streams, and the total amount of consumer expenditure.[3]

An alternative model of royalty distribution that has gained quite a few proponents is called the *user-centric model*.[4] The idea behind this is that the fee a consumer pays is distributed among the rights holders of the music this particular consumer listens to in a given month. Assuming a listener pays €10 for the subscription and the streaming service takes a 30% cut. If the subscriber only listens to one song once and nothing else during that month, then the rights holders will get $\approx$ €7 for that single replay. The terms *pro rata* and *user-centric* were first applied by the music research project *Clouds and Concerts*, which also was the first to empirically compare the distributional aspects of the two models (Maasø, 2014).

Figure 1 shows the two distribution models with some simplifications. Under the current pro rata model, a rights-holder's payout is calculated per territory and tier. Each stream within this segment triggers a payout.

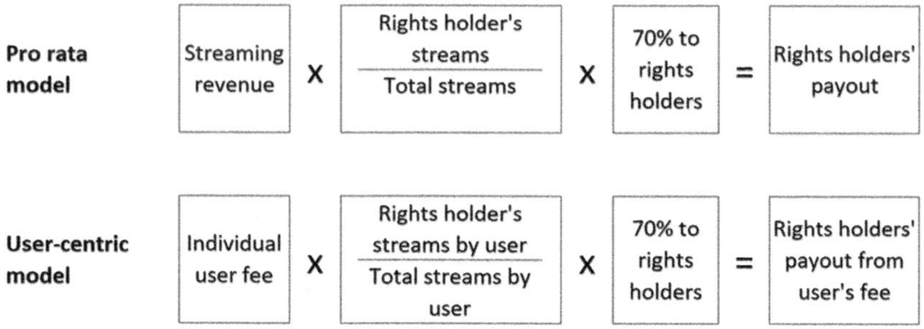

Fig. 1 Pro rata model and user-centric model compared

A listener who listens to a lot of music has a large say in where the royalties go, while one who does not listen a lot has little effect. Under the user-centric model, a rights-holder's payout is calculated based on each subscriber's use. Thus, each subscriber has the same influence on royalty distribution, irrespective of how much they listen. A key implication of the models is that music that is listened to by sporadic consumers will gain from the user-centric model, while music that is listened to by frequent consumers will gain from the pro rata model.

While the pro rata model dominates among music streaming services, Soundcloud's "fan-powered royalties' model" is based on a user-centric model (Soundcloud, Not dated). Deezer has also adopted a mixed model where the model is pro rata for subscribers that stream less than 1000 streams in a given month, while it is user-centric for subscribers that stream more.

Pro Rata or User-Centric—Who Gains?

Many stakeholders have voiced their opinions on the pros and cons of the models. Academic papers are mostly more balanced, although Dimont (2017) call it a "disastrous flaw" that revenues are collected by subscription and paid out per stream. The service has an incentive in increasing the number of subscribers, while individual artists are more concerned with increasing the number of streams. I agree that a pro rata royalty model might be said to be a better fit along with a per-play payment system. It is not immediately apparent that the user-centric model has a natural relation to fixed subscription payments, however.

Several contributions have modelled the consequences of a transition from a pro rata to a user-centric model. The pioneering investigations were made by analysing Norwegian and Danish data from 2012 and 2013, provided by the streaming service Wimp (Danielsen & Maasø, 2016; Maasø, 2014; Pedersen, 2014, 2018, 2020). I will also mention a paper by Muikku (2017). More recently, there are two important contributions. The first is by Meyn et al. (2023) and is based on German survey data. Moreau et al. (2023) is based on streaming data supplied by the French market leader Deezer.[5] I will cite findings from these papers in the sections below.

Superstars and the Long Tail

Many appear to believe that the existing pro-rata model inherently favours superstars. We argue that it only favours superstars to the extent that their songs are listened to more times per listener than other songs are.

Maasø (2014) as well as Danielsen and Maasø (2016) claim that it is the user-centric model that works to the benefit of the most-streamed artists, and especially the most popular local acts.[6] Two out of three local artists would benefit more from user-centric settlement. In a related paper, Pedersen (2014) analyses Wimp data for the Danish market. He finds that the most popular artists tend to have the least active listeners. Those who listen a lot tend to listen to artists outside the superstars. Thus, the top 50 artists will on average earn more under user-centric settlement. Pedersen (2020) expands on the same study and finds that among all the 5000 artists included in the study, more than 70% will lose out from a transition. Pedersen also finds that user-centric favours local artists, and indeed that many of the top artists are local favourites rather than global superstars.

Muikku (2017) presents an analysis of a sample of streams from Spotify in Finland. Contrary to Pedersen (2014) and Maasø (2014), Muikku finds that the pro-rata model favours the top tier artists while the user-centric model favours the tail of the popularity distribution. Pedersen (2020) raises concerns about the sampling procedure. It is not clear if any superstars are included in the sample, and thus if results apply to them. A different sample might have given different results. Furthermore, Muikku's division into artist popularity tiers challenges direct comparison with the other contributions. Moreau et al. (2023, Fig. 1) report findings that are more in line with the Finnish findings than with the Scandinavian: The top 10 artists, as well as those ranked eleven to hundred, profit most from the pro rata model. Less popular artists would thus gain from the user-centric model.

Evidence from the studies cited above thus give an ambiguous picture. If we lean more on the most recent study, evidence so far appears to indicate that the user-centric model will give less to global superstars, but possibly more to local stars.

Old vs New

When judging the fairness and efficiency of revenue distributions, it is important to also keep in mind the distribution between new recordings on the one hand and catalogue content on the other. The tail of the distribution consists largely of catalogue content (Pedersen, 2018).

Hesmondhalgh et al. (2021, p. 150) report that 60% of streaming in the UK in 2019 was of tracks more than 2 years old. Analysing Danish streaming of Sony Music's artists Pedersen (2018) finds that among artists streamed at least 1000 times in 2016, catalogue (more than 18 months since release) makes up half of all streams. This is down from between 60 and 70% in the years prior. Ingham (2022) reports that catalogue made up 72.4% of music consumption in the US during the first 6 months of 2022. Pedersen (2018) finds that new releases (less than 18 months old) dominate only one section of the popularity distribution: the top 1%. For the category 1–10% on the popularity rank, catalogue (more than 18 months old) music makes up approximately two-thirds of the streams, and this domination of catalogue is steadily stronger towards the tail of the distribution. If young people listen more to music than older people, then a shift to a user-centric model implies that each replay by an older person will on average pay better than one from a young person. As older people presumably are more inclined to listen to old music, a user-centric model can be suspected to be intrinsically in favour of old music (Hesmondhalgh et al., 2021, p. 101). Moreau et al. (2023) investigate this. They divide recordings in three categories: Frontline, which is less than 18 months old, a category of recent back catalogue, less than ten years old, and a category of old catalogue, more than 10 years. They find that the user-centric model will take away 10% of revenues from frontline music, while old catalogue will gain 21%. Recent catalogue does not see much change. Music from the US has a particularly strong position in the back catalogue. Lumeau et al. (2024) finds that US music dominates the back catalogue substantially more for streaming services than what is the case for downloaded music. It is therefore likely that distributing revenues from the head to the tail of the distribution would imply distributing revenues from active young artists to older stars that may no longer be active.

Genre

Based on German data, Meyn et al. (2023) find that for most genres, the most important determinant for whether artists gain or lose from a user-centric settlement is how much their listeners stream the music. The exception is metal, which gains from a user-centric model because metal songs tend to be long, and fans will therefore hear fewer replays for the same given amount of listening time. Meyn et al. (2023) find that international rock, metal and classical will all gain substantially from a transition to a user-centric royalty distribution system. Rap, Hip-Hop and EDM are the genres that will lose the most. Other genres see more modest changes.

In the French market, Moreau et al. (2023) find that Blues, Classical and Jazz are the genres that will benefit most from a transition to user-centric. The genres that will lose are most likely "urban", R&B/Soul and Electronic Music. The results mostly align well with those from Meyn et al. (2023).

3 Contemporary Challenges in the Streaming Model and Potential Measures

In this section, I will list some much-discussed issues related to streaming services. I will also go through some measures that have been tested or suggested to address the challenges. Jensen (2024) is a plentiful source for several of the suggestions found here.

Streaming Bots

It will typically take 31 seconds to trigger a royalty payment from a streaming service. It is thus theoretically possible to trigger 86,400 such payments in a 31-day month. If royalties per stream are around €0.01, then 1000 replays are enough to trigger royalties higher than a €10 user payment. The existing model thus provides ample scope for fraud.

Streaming bots are becoming a rising problem and, reportedly, major labels hire bots to push their releases up the charts (Boyer, 2020). Third-party intermediaries can also sell spots on playlists they subsequently have bots replaying. These artificial replays boost the streaming numbers of those artists. Artificial replays can also potentially ruin recommendation algorithms, unless the streaming service has the means to weed such replays out of organic listening.

Streaming bots and botted playlists have the potential to break the business model completely. The model may not provide the right incentives to create. The system for remuneration will lose legitimacy, and music listeners may just as well resort to unlicensed alternatives if the money does not reach the artist anyway.

Streaming services have several specific measures to counter bots. They monitor patterns of streaming activity and can clamp down on unwanted users and playlists. Streaming bots are getting increasingly sophisticated, with activity mimicking humans. It is a challenge for streaming services to distinguish between bots and real users, even if they want to. This is an arms race (Lucas, 2024). In 2024, Spotify implemented a principle that says a track must have a minimum number of unique listeners in order to be eligible for royalties (Spotify for artists, 2024). This is a measure to mitigate the problem of tracks having royalties triggered by a few active bots. They also state that they have begun charging labels and distributors when "flagrant artificial streaming" is detected on their content.

Converting to the user-centric model would solve this issue. A more drastic measure would be to leave the flat rate user payment system for a pay-per-replay system. An intermediate alternative of payment tiers, dependent on the amount of listening, would also remedy the problem of streaming bots.

Non-Music, Functional Sound, and Fake Artists

Streaming services have enormous amounts of content available. Not all of it is genuinely creative or innovative content. Some recordings are simply generic recordings of birds, cars, washing machines, etc. Some may find this pleasant to listen to, but there is no reason anyone should be paid royalties for such content. There is also content that is borderline between music and generic noise. These may be cover versions with little creative input, or entirely machine-created music. People listening to such music will usually not be concerned about which artist they listen to but just want a certain mood.

Somewhat related to the issue of functional sound is the issue with fake artists. A relatively unknown Swede has been disclosed as the composer behind more than 650 "artists" on Spotify. He has created more than 2,700 works published on the service. Added together, these 650 "artists" are streamed more than superstars such as Michael Jackson and Metallica. The explanation is his presence on more than a hundred of Spotify's official instrumental playlists (Bryant, 2024). It is not clear whether such fake artists are subject to standard royalty agreements with Spotify. If fake artists have less favourable terms in exchange for heavy promotion through playlists, this may result in lowered costs for Spotify but may also allow higher royalties to other creators.

In 2023, Deezer implemented measures specifically to target this issue. Branded as an "artist-centric" model, the main points of the measures can be summed up as such (Stassen, 2023):

1. Artists who attract over 1,000 listens a month from over 500 unique listeners gets a "double boost".
2. It rewards replays that result from users actively searching for a song, as opposed to being served it by an algorithm.
3. Deezer will replace "non-artist noise content" with its own Deezer-made "content in the functional music space". Deezer will then demonetise "noise" content.

These measures appear to be both specific and effective, at least so far as the service can identify the non-music properly. The second measure above is likely a well-suited tool to reward real artists instead of fake artists. Spotify has also embraced similar measures to Deezer's artist-centric model (Ingham, 2023).

Song Length and Repeatability

The current system of allocating royalties after 30 seconds of replay, means that any length of song longer than this receives no remuneration. An album with 20 short songs will give higher royalties than an album with ten longer songs. These properties of the current settlement model have led to redistribution compared to sales of CDs or album downloads. Metal, jazz and blues have on average longer song lengths than other music genres, while the category hip-hop and rap has shorter songs (Meyn et al., 2023). This means the former are disadvantaged when it comes to royalty allocation, and they would benefit from royalties being calculated per minute instead of per replay. For hip-hop and rap, it is the other way around. Reworking streaming royalties to be calculated per minute has been suggested, and some distributional consequences of this are investigated by Moreau et al. (2023).

The user-centric model can also work to the benefit of creators of long songs. Users who tend to listen to long songs will listen to fewer tracks, at least for a given time spent on music listening. Thus, a user-centric model will increase royalties per play. Meyn et al. (2023) calculate that metal, jazz, and blues have the longest average works, while hip-hop and folk music have the shortest. Moreau et al. (2023) estimate not only the difference between pro-rata and user-centric but also how both of those would differ if royalties were calculated per minute instead of per play. This "temporis" mode would benefit jazz, and negatively impact urban music. It would also harm new music and benefit old music, possibly because new music has adapted to the existing revenue model through shorter songs (Kopf, 2019; Meyn et al., 2023; Moreau et al., 2023).

4 Fairness and Efficiency

Some Considerations of Fairness

Deezer's mixed model, mentioned in Sect. 2.1, might have advantages compared to the pure user-centric model. For instance, if I do not use my streaming service at all for a month, what happens to the money I have paid? If I do not listen a lot, or, very variably from month to month, then the allocation of royalties per stream will be very arbitrary. If you are a "lucky" artist, I will listen to your music in a month that I do not listen a lot to music. If you are less fortunate, I may listen to your music during a month when I also listen to many other artists, resulting in you receiving significantly lower royalties. This is not immediately sensical. By only applying the user-centric model in cases where this limit of a thousand streams is reached, such issues are strongly reduced. Whether thousand is an optimal cut-off is of course open for discussion, but the limit of a thousand streams is in the order of magnitude where the triggered royalties equate the average revenue per user.

Both Deezer and Spotify have recently introduced measures that take revenues out of the long tail and distribute them to those further up. Under the heading "Focusing on artists", Deezer announced that a double boost will be given to all artists who have a minimum of 1,000 streams per month by a minimum of 500 unique listeners. Deezer designates these as "professional artists" (Universal, 2023). Spotify has stopped paying royalties for tracks that have been streamed less than 1000 times during the last twelve months. The reasoning is that such small royalties are often not paid out. When they are, these royalties are often not paid by distributors to artists. This accounts for 0.5% of all royalties (Spotify for artists, 2023).

Discussions around the distribution of revenues sometimes make a distinction between "stars" and everyone else. A "fair" distribution might be assumed to be one where revenues are distributed as evenly as possible among a wide range of artists and creators. Such an assumption is debatable, and I will make three points in that regard. First, is it necessarily better to distribute revenues to as many amateurs as possible, rather than to ensure a decent living for borderline professional artists? Second, it seems often to be assumed that the long tail consists of an endless number of poor artists. That might not be the case, as discussed in Sect. 2.4. The third point I would like to make is that there is a possible fallacy of composition when deducing from concentration in national markets to the remuneration of global superstars. Many artists found in national charts are far from global superstars.

Whether the pro rata model or the user-centric model provides the "fairest" distribution of revenues depends entirely on the criteria one has for fairness. Such criteria must be quite specific in terms of which groups should have more, and which should have less. What is perceived as "fair" is often a question of framing (or on whether something benefits of harms yourself). Rethink Music (2015) asks the overarching question: Are the compensation structures fair? The main part of their answer to this question relates to transparency in who takes which cut of the pie. They voice a concern that the lack of transparency is to the benefit of various middlemen.

Transparency into the distribution of streaming revenues has been a hot topic for many years. The transparency issues have changed. While it is easier for artists to access and understand data on replays of their music, there has been growing emphasis on how recommendation algorithms work, and how music can become part of important playlists. Computer algorithms as well as human curation guide the choices of music consumers (Maasø & Spilker, 2022). A lot of invisible power is exercised, and artists have little influence on, or knowledge of, how their music is recommended or suppressed (Pilati et al., 2025).

The introduction of streaming services brought along a lag in revenues to rights holders. In combination with unfavourable contracts with record companies, this might be the most likely explanation behind why so many creators feel they get too little from streaming services. If rights holders agree to new recordings receiving higher royalties than old ones, this issue could potentially be remedied. It is unlikely, however, that those losing out from such a measure would agree to it. A shorter copyright term might bring along a revenue distribution that better serves the purpose of financing new art.

One possible starting point for discussions of fairness could be that external factors that shift revenue distribution, without there being changes in artist popularity or effort, would be unfair. Such shifts inevitably arise from many technological or political developments. Another notion of fairness may be that fair rules provide efficient outcomes in terms of bringing music from creators to listeners in a sustainable manner. For a general discussion of fairness in remuneration from music, see Hesmondhalgh (2021). For a discussion of fairness specifically connected to the user-centric and pro rata models, see Pedersen (2020).

Efficient Supply of Music

Economists' view on the purpose of copyright protection is conventionally that it should aim to bring the supply of protected works closer to a socially optimal level (Handke, 2010). Public discussion on copyright in general, and revenues from streaming services specifically, often revolves around another justification for copyright, namely the natural rights of artists to benefit from their works. Concerns of a "just" distribution of revenues between stakeholders is much more prominent within this latter approach, but there is no agreement on which criteria should be used to evaluate outcomes. Economists may to some degree weigh in on the relative efficiency of different models based on given criteria, but the criteria themselves will continue to be subject to political and ethical discussions.

Hjelmbrekke (2021) discusses criteria for the evaluation of efficiency and attempts to evaluate the efficiency of streaming compared to traditional sales. A finding is that concentration around one single streaming service is likely to be inefficient, as it will have detrimental effect on consumer surplus, and will also give the service provider great leverage over creators and rights holders.

For consumers, access to a wide variety of music is a great boon. An efficient price model is one that excludes as few listeners as possible, while providing sufficient funding for the creation of new music. It seems likely that an introduction of differentiated subscription tiers based on the number of streams replayed would improve efficiency. Services can thus extract larger share of the willingness to pay, while also accommodating better those with a low willingness to pay. A full out metered pricing, on the other hand, is likely less efficient, as consumers are willing to pay a premium for not being bothered by a ticking meter (Altmann & Chu, 2001).

A mathematical model of consumer valuation is presented by Hjelmbrekke (2021, Chapter 9). Under various assumptions, the distribution of surplus is calculated as a service provider serves consumers' music while maximising rights holder revenues. A result is that suppliers are better off with a subscription service compared to sales, while consumers may be slightly worse off. If this sounds counter-intuitive, it may be because today's existing subscription prices probably do not maximise rights holder revenues, due to competition. In the model, the total social surplus is somewhat higher from subscriptions, due to a smaller "deadweight loss". I.e. it is more efficient in matching consumers' willingness to pay with music on offer. The model also suggests that for a given fundamental valuation of songs and variety, subscriptions will send a somewhat larger share of revenues to artists further down the popularity ranking. Thus, if equity in royalties is an objective, then subscriptions may be more efficient also in that respect.

For a business model and a market structure to be efficient, it must be able to bring goods to the market in the first place. That implies that creators must be able and willing to create. While artists are certainly motivated by factors other than money only, I assume they will at least need some revenue to be able to bring goods to market to their full potential. It seems reasonable that distributing revenues to a substantial number of artists will bring more music to market than if revenues are strongly concentrated among the superstars. Thus, a reasonably equitable distribution of revenues is not only "fair", but also efficient. It is not straightforward to say how equitable it should be, however.

5 Financing Culture Through Streaming—Extending to Other Markets

Music subscriptions serve as a prominent example of how streaming data over the internet has dramatically changed access to cultural goods. Some goods are more affected by digitisation than others, and music has been at the forefront. Reproducibility, the quality that a good can be easily and infinitely copied, is a prerequisite for digital subscriptions. This trait is present for music, film, and audiobooks. Transmitting over the internet does not compromise the quality. For non-reproducible goods, the impact of digitisation mostly limits itself to ticketing and retailing (Handke et al., 2016).

Streaming has a potential as a very important source of revenue for producers of cultural goods. For some, this is straightforward and is already the norm. For others, such as performing arts or visual arts, digital transmission usually results in something quite different from the original experience. That does not rule out a commercial potential.

Video streaming services have become very successful. With media outlets combining linear airing with online replays, and with some content owners such as Disney and HBO having launched subscription services, demarcations between the different stakeholders are much more blurred than what is the case for music streaming. Video streaming services also mostly have separate content, so you must subscribe to one specific service to have access to specific content. Lastly, most people tend to watch video content only once before they move on to new content. This is unlike music, where the same songs are listened to repeatedly. Thus, the challenges laid out in Sect. 3 has little relevance for video streaming.

E-books and audiobooks are often bundled together in one and the same subscription. Such services have been slower to establish in markets than those for music. The reason might be that reading is very heavily skewed: A few people read a lot while most people read few or no books at all. And many of those who read books prefer paper books. A subscription sold to an avid reader may cannibalise many book sales, which are the traditional revenue stream of publishers and authors. This reduces the profitability of offering books through subscriptions. Any subscription is a sort of bundle, and bundling must be profitable for the bundle to be offered in the first place. While either pure or mixed bundling is profitable under fairly general assumptions (Bakos & Brynjolfsson, 1999; McAfee et al., 1989), a subscription service has substantial fixed costs, and likely has some minimum efficient scale.

One way to make bundles profitable is to exclude bestsellers from the bundle. That is commonly the case for e-book subscriptions. They have limited libraries, and often few bestsellers (Hill, 2023). Even if you subscribe to several services, you will not have access to "everything" in the same way as you will with a music subscription. Similarly to video streaming, books are commonly read only once by each reader, so the pattern of reading is not as different from the pattern of buying.

Performing arts are not as easily reproducible, but are also being streamed. Some theatres, like The Royal National Theatre in London, offer a subscription with access to previously recorded theatrical performances. Offering theatrical performances as a digital product requires significant additional effort, but it can be profitable because one can reach a much larger audience. In case of the most renowned institutions, the audience is global, and the digital product is not likely to cannibalise the theatre's own live performances to any significant degree. In the case of theatrical performances, and music concerts, the digital product is not a perfect substitute because it is probably considered an inferior substitute.

Theatres are often much more heavily subsidised by governments than is the case for most music creators and performers. That has raised questions about how government funding should be affected by the presence of the digital product (King, 2018). Some have argued that governments should also subsidise the digital product, as it has potential to bring high-quality cultural experiences to new groups. Others have raised concerns that the digital offering from major national theatres may threaten regional and independent theatres (King, 2018).

Theatres and concerts have often emphasised live transmission rather than recordings and is thus an extension of the venue. Buying a ticket for a single digital performance is not too different from a traditional performance. The digital offering does not alter the distribution of revenues in the same way music streaming services do.

6 Concluding Remarks

Streaming emerged as a functional model for financing music after a period where the music industry struggled with unlicensed copying. Paid subscriptions have more or less replaced sales. On-demand music also competes heavily with radio stations. Existing revenue streams have dried out, and new ones have emerged. Whenever such things happen, there are both challenges and opportunities to explore.

Digitisation has made its impression on most other cultural goods as well, but in different ways. Many cultural goods can be streamed, audio-books: e-books, theatrical performances, and concerts as a way to generate revenues to creators and intermediaries. These goods typically differ from recorded music in various ways, and the transition from record sales to music subscriptions do not really have any close parallels. "Streaming" is not per se a financing model, but a "bundle of models" that allow financing of reproducible goods, each with their own particularities.

Knowledge about the distributional effects from streaming is still lacking. More research on how income streams have changed over timeand how different revenue-sharing models can affect this is much needed. There are many questions where researchers are not yet in a position to offer confident advice to policymakers.

Just as technological change allows for new business models to thrive, it also allows for new policy models to emerge. Cultural policy should aim to shape cultural markets in ways that benefit creators and the audience. As streaming has changed how existing regulations work for financing writers and composers of music, policymakers may want to consider whether licensing regulations as well as intellectual property law should be revised in order to help streaming services be the best tools of financing that they can be.

Notes

1. Music streaming services are commonly called "platforms". I will only call them *services*, however, as such services are not necessarily best understood as multi-sided market platforms (Hjelmbrekke, 2021).
2. The pro rata model is also called the *Big Pool model* or the *service-centric model.*

3. There is not a single sum of money that applies to all streams: This will depend on which market the song is replayed in and on which tier of the service it is replayed through, and it varies from month to month. It also depends on the contract the rights holders have with the service. Spotify supposedly has around 800 different rates for a replay (Herstrand, 2021). So only in a very limited sense is it exactly true that royalty is proportional to the number of streams. Soundcharts Team. (2019) provides a good explanation on how and why rates vary.
4. The user-centric model has also been called the *per-subscriber model* or *subscriber-share model.*
5. Moreau et al. (2024) is the published version of this paper. The emphasis changed somewhat between revisions, and some of the results most relevant to this chapter are unfortunately not included in the final version. I therefore cite a working paper version.
6. Wimp was first launched in Norway in 2010. It was later rebranded as Tidal.

References

Altmann, J., & Chu, K. (2001). How to Charge for Network Services—Flat-Rate or Usage-Based? *Computer Networks, 36*(2001), 519–531.

Bakos, Y., & Brynjolfsson, E. (1999). Bundling Information Goods: Pricing, Profits, and Efficiency. *Management Science*, *45*(12), 1613–1630. https://doi.org/10.1287/mnsc.45.12.1613

Boyer, D. (2020). *How Streaming Bots Are Ruining Careers of Independent Musicians*. Retrieved November 18th from https://www.venturemusic.com/blog/streaming-bots-will-ruin-your-career?curator=MusicREDEF. Accessed 24 April 2025.

Bryant, M. (2024). Swedish Composer Becomes Spotiy's Most-Famous Musician You've Never Heard Of. *The Guardian*. Retrieved November 10th from https://www.theguardian.com/uk-news/2024/mar/19/swedish-composer-johan-rohr-becomes-spotifys-most-famous-musician-youve-never-heard-of?fbclid=IwAR03rByCF5BlKSI2fu-K7GXdSSYDgaymTr7EcnK4n7smiRe-f_2kXXGEkVo. Accessed 10 November 2024.

Danielsen, A., & Maasø, A. (2016). *Main Findings (from the Clouds and Concerts Research Project)*. Department of Musicology, University of Oslo. https://www.hf.uio.no/imv/english/research/projects/cloudsandconcerts/findings/index.html

Dimont, J. (2017). Royalty Inequity: Why Music Streaming Services Should Switch to a Per-Subscriber Model. *Hastings LJ*, *69*, 675.

Handke, C. (2010). *The Economics of Copyright and Digitisation: A Report on the Literature and the Need for Further Research*. S. A. b. f. i. P. policy. https://papers.ssrn.com/sol3/papers.cfm?abstract_id=2707153

Handke, C., Stepan, P., & Towse, R. (2016). Cultural Economics and the Internet. *Handbook on the Economics of the Internet*, 146–162.

Herstrand, A. (2021). *How Much Each Distributor Pays for Spotify and Apple Music*. https://aristake.com/distributor-payment/. Accessed 2 May 2024.

Hesmondhalgh, D. (2021). Is Music Streaming Bad for Musicians? Problems of Evidence and Argument. *New Media & Society, 23*(12), 3593–3615.

Hesmondhalgh, D., Osborne, R., Sun, H., & Barr, K. (2021). *Music Creators' Earnings in the Digital Era*. Intellectual Property Office. https://papers.ssrn.com/sol3/papers.cfm?abstract_id=4089749

Hill, S. (2023). *The Best Ebook Subscription Services for Every Kind of Reader*. https://www.wired.com/gallery/best-ebook-subscription-services/#61e7e3e8f355cd4b798a0006. Accessed 9 November 2024.

Hjelmbrekke, S. (2021). *From Ownership to Access: The Economics of Music Subscription Services*. Erasmus University Rotterdam. http://hdl.handle.net/1765/137027

Ingham, T. (2022). *It's Official: New Music is SHRINKING in Popularity in the United States*. Music Business Worldwide. https://www.musicbusinessworldwide.com/its-official-new-music-is-shrinking-in-popularity-in-the-united-states/. Accessed 4 March 2025.

Ingham, T. (2023). *Spotify Is Embracing Elements of Universal Music Group's 'Artist-Centric' Royalties Model—Following a New Multi-Year Licensing Deal Between UMG and Daniel Ek's Platform*. Music Business Worldwide. https://www.musicbusinessworldwide.com/spotify-is-embracing-elements-of-universal-music-groups-artist-centric-royalties-model-following-a-new-multi-year-licensing-deal-between-umg-and-daniel-eks-platf/ (accessed 13 May 2024)

Jensen, F. J. (2024). Rethinking Royalties: Alternative Payment Systems on Music Streaming Platforms. *Journal of Cultural Economics, 48*(3), 439–462.

King, T. (2018). Streaming from Stage to Screen: Its Place in the Cultural Marketplace and the Implication for UK Arts Policy. *International Journal of Cultural Policy, 24*(2), 220–235.

Kopf, D. (2019). *The economics of streaming is making songs shorter*. Retrieved April 22nd from https://qz.com/1519823/is-spotify-making-songs-shorter (accessed 22 April 2025)

Lucas. (2024). *Understanding Spotify's Streaming Metrics*. https://themarketingheaven.com/can-spotify-detect-fake-streams/. Accessed 9 February 2024.

Lumeau, M., Moreau, F., Haampland, O., Johannessen, R., & Wikström, P. (2024). *A Geographical Bias in a Music Streaming Market*. https://hal.science/hal-04570806/

Luminate. (2025). *2024 Year-End Music Report*. https://luminatedata.com/reports/yearend-music-industry-report-2024/

McAfee, R. P., McMillan, J., & Whinston, M. D. (1989). Multiproduct Monopoly, Commodity Bundling, and Correlation of Values. *The Quarterly Journal of Economics, 104*(2), 371–383.

Meyn, J., Kandziora, M., Albers, S., & Clement, M. (2023). Consequences of Platforms' Remuneration Models for Digital Content: Initial Evidence and a Research Agenda for Streaming Services. *Journal of the Academy of Marketing Science, 51*(1), 114–131.

Moreau, F., Wikstrom, P., Haampland, O., & Johannessen, R. (2023). Implementing a User-Centric Payment System in the Music Streaming Market: A Comparative Static Approach from User Data. SSRN 4432605. https://doi.org/10.2139/ssrn.4432605

Moreau, F., Wikström, P., Haampland, O., & Johannessen, R. (2024). Alternative Payment Models in the Music Streaming Market: A Comparative Approach Based On Stream-Level Data. *Information Economics and Policy, 68*, Article 101103.

Muikku, J. (2017). Pro Rata and User Centric Distribution Models: A Comparative Study. *DIGITAL MEDIA,2*, 14. https://www.fim-musicians.org/wp-content/uploads/prorata-vs-user-centric-models-study-2018.pdf

Maasø, A. (2014). *User-Centric Settlement for Music Streaming*. https://www.hf.uio.no/imk/english/people/aca/arntm/usercentric-cloudsandconcerts-report.pdf

Maasø, A., & Spilker, H. S. (2022). The Streaming Paradox: Untangling the Hybrid Gatekeeping Mechanisms of Music Streaming. *Popular Music and Society, 45*(3), 300–316.

Page, W. (2017). *Does the Music Industry Definition of 'Catalogue' need an Upgrade?* https://www.musicbusinessworldwide.com/music-industrys-definition-catalogue-need-upgrade/. Accessed 16 April 2025.

Pedersen, R. R. (2014). Music Streaming in Denmark: An Analysis of Listening Patterns and the Consequences of A'per User'settlement Model Based on Streaming Data from WiMP. https://forskning.ruc.dk/en/publications/music-streaming-in-denmark-an-analysis-of-listening-patterns-and_

Pedersen, R. R. (2018). Exploring Bounty and Spread: Key Changes in the Danish Music Streaming Economy. *International Journal of Music Business Research,7*(1), 6–25. https://musicbusinessresearch.wordpress.com/wp-content/uploads/2018/04/volume-7-no-1-april-2018-pedersen_final.pdf

Pedersen, R. R. (2020). A Meta Study of User-Centric Distribution for Music Streaming. https://forskning.ruc.dk/en/publications/a-meta-study-of-user-centric-distribution-for-music-streaming

Pilati, F., Antoine, H., & Sacco, P. L. (2025). Mirroring the Inequalities of Mainstream Music Platforms: Popularity, Revenue, and Monetization Strategies on Bandcamp. *International Journal of Cultural Policy, 31*(3), 338–357.

Rethink Music. (2015). *Fair Music: Transparency and Payment Flows in the Music Industry* (Rethink Music, Issue). https://college.berklee.edu/news/fair_music_report

Silver, J. (2013). *Digital Medieval—The First Twenty Years of Music on the Web...and the Next Twenty*. Xstorical Publications Media.

Sinnreich, A. (2016). Slicing the Pie: The Search for an Equitable Recorded Music Economy. In *Business Innovation and Disruption in the Music Industry* (pp. 153–174). Edward Elgar Publishing.

Soundcharts Team. (2019). What Music Streaming Services Pay Per Stream (And Why It Actually Doesn't Matter). *Soundcharts Blog, 26*. https://soundcharts.com/blog/music-streaming-rates-payouts (accessed 24 april 2025)

Soundcloud. (Not dated). *Fan-Powered Royalties* https://help.soundcloud.com/hc/en-us/articles/1260801306810-Fan-powered-Royalties-FAQs. Accessed 3 May 2024.

Spotify for artists. (2023). *Modernizing Our Royalty System to Drive an Additional $1 Billion toward Emerging and Professional Artists*. https://artists.spotify.com/blog/modernizing-our-royalty-system. Accessed 12 May 2024.

Spotify for artists. (2024). *Track Monetization Eligibility*. https://support.spotify.com/us/artists/article/track-monetization-eligibility/. Accessed 13 May 2024.

Stassen, M. (2023). *Popular Artists to Get 'Royalty Boost' on Deezer as Platform Readies 'artist-Centric' Model with Universal Music Group*. Music Business Worldwide. https://www.musicbusinessworldwide.com/popular-artists-to-get-royalty-boost-on-deezer-as-platform-strikes-artist-centric-agreement-with-universal-music-group/. Accessed 24 April 2025.

Universal. (2023). *Universal Music Group and Deezer to Launch the First Comprehensive Artist-Centric Music Streaming Model*. https://www.universalmusic.com/universal-music-group-and-deezer-to-launch-the-first-comprehensive-artist-centric-music-streaming-model/. Accessed 11 May 2024.

Open Access This chapter is licensed under the terms of the Creative Commons Attribution 4.0 International License (http://creativecommons.org/licenses/by/4.0/), which permits use, sharing, adaptation, distribution and reproduction in any medium or format, as long as you give appropriate credit to the original author(s) and the source, provide a link to the Creative Commons license and indicate if changes were made.

The images or other third party material in this chapter are included in the chapter's Creative Commons license, unless indicated otherwise in a credit line to the material. If material is not included in the chapter's Creative Commons license and your intended use is not permitted by statutory regulation or exceeds the permitted use, you will need to obtain permission directly from the copyright holder.

PART III

Case-Studies and Illustrations

CHAPTER 13

Digital Funding and Financing in Museums and Cultural Heritage

Elisabetta Lazzaro

1 Introduction

Museums are characterised by high levels of fixed costs (Frey & Meier, 2006), making them crucially dependent on a steady income, which has been historically ensured by public subsidies and traditional forms of private funding, such as sponsorships, philanthropy and patronage. In addition, North American museums, especially larger ones, have been relying on interest and endowment income (Temin, 1991).

Museums' access to traditional private financing, such as bank lending, depends on their collateral capacity, which is high for flagship museums with important assets, but more problematic for small and private museums (Shaked, 2022). In addition, private loans can represent an important source of funding for public museums, yet with the risk of exposing them to public criticism (Berg & Larsen, 2024). Lately, private wealth has fuelled the phenomenon of private art museums, which are

E. Lazzaro (✉)
Epsom School of Creative Business, Fashion and Enterprise, University for the Creative Arts (UK), Epsom, England
e-mail: elisabetta.lazzaro@uca.ac.uk

© The Author(s) 2026

C. Dalla Chiesa and A. Rykkja (eds.), *Cultural Funding and Financing*, Cultural Economics & the Creative Economy,
https://doi.org/10.1007/978-3-031-96696-5_13

directly established, sustained and controlled by the wealth of their funders, usually business or finance tycoons (Kolbe et al., 2022).

Compared to other cultural and creative sectors, museums have been less inclined to adopt innovative financing modes, such as private venture capital, individual angel investors, and networks (Prokůpek et al., 2023). A relative exception has been represented by the largest museums, which might dispose of a greater capacity to experiment new forms of financing, and dampen the associated possible risks (ICOM, 2021).

More recently, following other cultural and creative sectors, in particular non-profit ones, museums have increasingly embraced an entrepreneurial approach, also in their financing (Lazzaro & Noonan, 2021). To cope with structural market inefficiency marked by suboptimal allocation of resources, uncertain demand, and market failure (Loots et al., 2022), plus their relatively high fixed costs, museums are increasingly inclined to complement a decreasing traditional public support with a combination of funding modalities. Among other possible avenues of museums' financial sustainability, Prokůpek et al. (2023) have pointed to crowdfunding and blockchain technology as novel digital funding tools that may, besides digital content, constitute a new source of income.

Overall, financing avenues in the cultural and creative sectors are oriented towards collaborative funding, which goes beyond the traditional public-private separation in terms of stakes and modes, and allows for privatisation and hybridisation, as suggested by Loots et al. (2022). In such a context, the latest innovation in cultural financing and investment practices looks at an array of technology-driven and collaborative modalities and different sources, including crowdfunding, peer-to-peer lending platforms, pooled investments, such as incubators and accelerator finance, and digital fundraising technologies that facilitate new modes of asset finance and tokenised funding. These modalities can be enabled or supported by a variety of emergent digital technologies, such as online platforms, blockchain, the metaverse, artificial intelligence (AI), recommender systems, mobile applications, and gamification.

In the general domain of digital technologies, museums have noticeably been early adopters. Yet this has been for scientific—rather than financing—purposes, such as preservation, cataloguing and study of collections, followed by education and audience development (Srinivasan et al., 2009). In museums, similarly to other cultural and creative sectors, digital solutions can be applied to develop and differentiate the digital offering and corresponding audiences, through the expansion and differentiation of cultural services and contents (e.g. new modalities to access new digital collections, configurations of new digital experiences, etc.), and hence expand sources of income. This perspective has been a significant concern of marketing and management research, specifically how social media, co-creation, and audience engagement enhance the value of museums and their income, which again have more-or-less impact on museums' fundraising, and hence financing (Najda-Janoszka & Sawczuk, 2023).

When applied to finance, digital solutions are aimed to expand funding sources, and secure additional resources and investments, including fostering the engagement of younger generations of donors and investors (Giachino et al., 2024). The main models of technology-based funding and financing include crowdfunding, blockchain, and licensing (Prokůpek et al., 2023). They can increase museums' efficiency, by reducing transaction costs of funding, as well as information asymmetries. The first instance is typically contributed by crowdfunding (Handke & Dalla Chiesa, 2022), while blockchain can reduce information asymmetries, particularly about provenance and authenticity (Fincham, 2019). If museums own endowment funds, they can recur to digital management platforms, to better track fund performance and compliance with donor restrictions,as exemplified by the Metropolitan Museum of Art in New York or the Museum of Contemporary Art in Los Angeles.[2]

Through an explorative approach, this chapter offers an original mapping of major incumbent digital financing models in the museums and heritage sector, shedding light on which factors lead museums to adopt innovative digital funding and financing models. By leveraging scholarly, industry, and media secondary data, each innovative model is illustrated by means of a real-world case study, namely, a museum, highlighting implied changes in the uptake, the main reasons behind these changes, and the effectiveness and efficiency of these innovative models. Since capacity constraints, as explained above, may favour larger museums in terms of uptake, the examined cases focus on smaller museums, also for the sake of suggesting possible modalities that enable other smaller and less resource-rich museums to take up some of these innovative financial models.

To more neatly account for funders' motivations, the presented models, and corresponding examples, are divided into, respectively, digital funding and digital financing. The former covers digital models of financial support without an expected financial return, thus only expecting cultural and/or social benefits or impacts. The latter encompasses digital models of investment, where, instead, a monetary repayment of funds is expected (Betzler et al., 2021), at or below market values (Medda et al., 2021). For each financial model, the involved digital technologies are briefly introduced.

2 Digital Funding Models

Digital funding mechanisms are mainly operated by individual members of the museums' visitors or other individual stakeholders.[3] While some digital funding mechanisms are virtually available to any museum through outsourced dedicated platforms (e.g., crowdfunding), other mechanisms imply a certain technical, structural and financial capacity, which constitute entry barriers for especially smaller museums, similarly to other innovation adoptions (Camarero et al., 2011). Main digital funding models in museums and heritage include reward- and donation-based crowdfunding, contactless donations, digital payments for ticketing and purchases, and loyalty programs and digital tokens.

Reward- and Donation-Based Crowdfunding

In the cultural and creative sectors, reward- and donation-based crowdfunding are the commonest modes of crowdfunding (e.g. Rykkja et al., 2020). As crowdfunding is typically used to fund projects with even relatively low budgets, crowdfunding is virtually within the reach of cultural organisations of any size and capacity, especially when relying on existing specialised crowdfunding platforms (e.g. Kickstarter, GoFundMe, Indigogo, etc.). On the other hand, many major museums directly organise and manage crowdfunding campaigns on their own web platforms (Izzo, 2017).

As it has been highlighted in related theoretical and empirical literature, raising funds is not the only benefit of crowdfunding, as a whole body of direct and indirect benefits are contributed, including community involvement and interaction and co-creation with backers, fostering entrepreneurship and business skills, and democratisation of funding (Koch & Siering, 2015; Lazzaro & Nordgård, 2025). The additional social benefits of crowdfunding are particularly relevant for museums, as they foster community engagement, and the promotion of their artistic missions (Najda-Janoszka & Sawczuk, 2024).

A successful case of a museum that raised substantial money through crowdfunding, while also fostering community involvement, interaction, co-creation with backers, and improving entrepreneurship skills, is the state museum for Christian art and culture Catharijne Convent in Utrecht, in the Netherlands. In 2021, the museum launched a crowdfunding campaign to restore an eighteenth-century Neapolitan nativity scene on its own crowdfunding platform (https://museumcatharijneconvent.creativefunding.nl). The campaign successfully raised more than €80,000 from 900 backers (Museum Catharijne Convent, 2021).

This campaign not only achieved its financial goal but also engaged the community in a meaningful way. The museum implemented a strategy known as "crowdkeeping", which focuses on nurturing relationships with backers long after the campaign has ended (Carr, 2014). This approach transformed one-time donors into lifelong supporters, enhancing their connection to the museum and encouraging ongoing participation in future initiatives. The campaign emphasised transparency and active participation, allowing backers to feel involved in the restoration process. By utilising social media effectively and maintaining communication with supporters, the museum created a sense of ownership among backers, which contributed to their commitment to the institution. This model exemplifies how crowdfunding can democratize funding for museums while simultaneously building a supportive community around them (Loots et al., 2024).

Noticeably, this case can rely on a favourable environment among cultural institutions and the population, as crowdfunding is quite developed in the Netherlands, in terms of campaigns turnover and money raised, and successful dedicated platforms also at national level, such as Voordekunst (De Voldere & Zeqo, 2017).

Contactless Donations

Contactless donations are a novel fundraising method that allows individuals to contribute to charities and other organisations by simply tapping their contactless-enabled debit or credit cards, or mobile payment applications, on a designated terminal. This approach has gained traction in various sectors, including museums and cultural heritage institutions, as it aligns with an increasing trend towards using cashless transactions. Fostered by the post-COVID era, such digital transactions allow consumers to carry limited or no cash, favouring a better transparency, scalability and accountability in organisations (Ramya et al., 2017).

Contactless donations are flexible, as terminals can be placed in different locations, and convenient, as they are quick and easy to make, encouraging spontaneous giving (Csongrádi et al., 2018). Unlike cash donations, contactless contributions can be tracked and analysed, which allows museums to gather valuable data on donors for future fundraising strategies (Wright & Walmsley, 2022). Contactless donations also reduce possible risks associated with handling cash and fraud. At the same time, the security of contactless donations should be ensured by encrypting personal information about the individual donors (Gebken et al., 2021).

A successful case of a museum adopting contactless donations is the national museum of People's History in Manchester, United Kingdom. Their implementation of a contactless donation terminal at the front desk in 2019 to supplement cash donations has yielded significant results. The free-entrance People's History Museum experienced a rapid return on investment from their contactless donation terminal, recouping the initial costs in just 42 days. This swift financial recovery was complemented by an increase in contributions and visibility for the museum's fundraising efforts. The museum noted that weekends, particularly Fridays through Sundays, were the most lucrative days for donations, with a peak donation time between 1 and 2 pm (Turner, 2022).

Several factors contributed to the observed increase in donations. The contactless terminal was strategically located at the front desk, a high-traffic area where staff could encourage donations and greet visitors warmly. This positioning, accompanied by a modest suggested donation amount of £5, likely enhanced visitor engagement and willingness to donate (Wright & Walmsley, 2022). Thanks to the new technology, the museum gained valuable insights into donor behaviour, allowing them to tailor their fundraising strategies more effectively. For instance, understanding peak donation times enabled them to focus their efforts when visitors were most inclined to give. Finally, contactless payments provided a more convenient option for visitors who may not carry cash, aligning with broader trends towards digital transactions in society (Wilson, 2022).

Digital Payments for Ticketing and Purchases

Digital payments for ticketing and purchases in museums have transformed the visitor experience, operational efficiency, and financial performance (Calderon, 2025). Museums increasingly offer their visitors the possibility to book their tickets in advance, online or over the phone, by paying with their credit cards or via other digital payment methods. The integration of digital payment systems allows museums to implement timed entry booking operations, which help manage visitor flow and comply with capacity constraints and health guidelines. This system enables museums to set predefined capacity limits, ensuring a safe environment for visitors, while maintaining operational efficiency (Digital Culture Network, 2020). The use of online ticketing reduces wait times, enhances visitors' experience and satisfaction, and minimises the risk of overcrowding during peak hours. Online ticketing systems can generate more revenue by allowing advance purchases, reducing the likelihood of sold-out situations. Visitors can buy tickets virtually from anywhere, avoiding long queues at the entrance. Digital payments can also include museum merchandise and other services, including membership programmes, which increase museum's sales and revenues. In addition, digital systems facilitate the collection of visitor data, which can be used for future marketing strategies and improving services. On the other hand, this technology implies some challenges, as initial investments in digital infrastructure can be substantial. Moreover, staff must be trained to manage new systems effectively (Nikolaou, 2024).

A notable case of a museum successfully adopting digital payments for ticketing and purchases is the Royal Albert Memorial Museum & Art Gallery (RAMM) in Exeter, UK. This museum implemented an open-access strategy along with digital payment options, which significantly transformed its operations. Following the adoption of digital payment systems, RAMM observed a notable increase in visitor numbers. The ease of digital transactions encouraged more people to visit and engage with the museum's offerings. The integration of digital payments facilitated a rise in memberships, as visitors found it easier to sign up and pay online. This shift contributed to a more loyal audience base, enhancing community engagement and support for the museum (Farmer & Wallace, 2024).

Digital payment systems streamlined ticketing and purchase processes, reducing wait times and improving overall visitor experience. This efficiency led to better resource allocation within the museum, allowing staff to focus on enhancing visitor engagement rather than managing cash transactions. The combination of increased visitor numbers and memberships resulted in a more stable financial footing for RAMM. The museum reported expectations of greater overall income from diverse revenue streams beyond just ticket sales, thanks to enhanced visibility and engagement with its collections. By embracing digital payments, RAMM not only improved its operational model but also strengthened its role within the community as a modern cultural institution that values accessibility and innovation. This has fostered a sense of belonging among visitors, further solidifying their support for the museum (Li et al., 2024).

Loyalty Programs and Digital Tokens

Digital tokens in loyalty programs represent a transformative approach to customer rewards, leveraging blockchain technology to enhance the way businesses engage with their customers, as well as streamline operations. Digital tokens are cryptographic assets issued by businesses to reward customers for specific actions, such as making purchases or engaging with the brand. Unlike traditional loyalty points, which are often limited in use and can expire, these tokens are securely recorded on a blockchain, providing a more flexible and transparent system for managing rewards. Research in tourism has shown that tokenised rewards increase booking intentions to the hotel and the perceived values of a discount, besides enhancing the attractiveness of reward schemes for customers; although, such benefits hold with luxury hotels only and not for budget ones (Boukis, 2024).

This innovative model can allow museums to create digital tokens that incorporate various benefits, rewards, and membership privileges, making loyalty programs more appealing and efficient. Tokenisation can foster deeper connections between museums and their audiences. By using digital tokens, museums can gamify the experience, offering rewards for activities such as attending events or participating in discussions. For instance, Nimi, a Web3 tech startup, has developed a membership system where attendees earn tokens that can be redeemed for benefits. Nimi collaborated with the Goethe-Institut Lisbon, in Portugal, to create an innovative membership system that rewards participants with tokens for their attendance. This initiative is designed to enhance engagement among younger audiences by incorporating gamification and loyalty models, allowing users to earn various benefits through their participation in events and activities at the institute (Nelson, 2024). Tokenised loyalty programs allow patrons to choose from a wider range of rewards. Instead of fixed rewards, tokenization enables customers to redeem tokens for various experiences or items, enhancing the perceived value of the rewards (Boukis, 2024). Digital tokens simplify the redemption process, allowing for instant and hassle-free access to rewards. This efficiency improves customer satisfaction and encourages more frequent participation in museum activities (Cadence, 2019).

Some museums are exploring decentralised autonomous organisations (DAOs), where token holders can influence decision-making processes regarding exhibitions and programming. This model not only empowers patrons but also creates a sense of ownership among community members (Nelson, 2024). Blockchain technology ensures that all transactions related to loyalty programs are transparent and secure. This builds trust with patrons who can see how their engagement translates into tangible benefits (Wang et al., 2019).

Real-world examples in the museum and heritage sector are still limited. For instance, tokenised loyalty programs were implemented by the Museum of Kansas City Chiefs quarterback Patrick Mahomes in the United States, which showcases sports memorabilia through NFTs (Non-Fungible Tokens) and physical artefacts on its website (https://www.museumofmahomes.com). Tokenised rewards have also been used by a major international museum, in combination with gamification and NFTs. In 2022, the Museum of Fine Arts in Boston has launched a collection of NFTs featuring rarely exhibited Impressionist pastels by artists such as Monet and Degas. This initiative, in collaboration with the French startup LaCollection, aimed to raise funds for the conservation of two Degas paintings: *Edmondo and Therese Morbilli* and Degas's *Father Listening to Lorenzo Pagans Playing the Guitar*. The museum gamified the purchasing experience by offering rewards based on the number of NFTs bought: purchase of two NFTs to receive a third for free; buying three NFTs to access to an NFT of one of the conserved Degas paintings; and a special "Secret Box" containing one of three selected pastels available during the sale (Museum of Fine Arts Boston, 2022).

3 Digital Financing Models

This section covers digital financing models that more explicitly imply a monetary return for investors, and that have also been utilised by in museum and organisations in the cultural heritage sector, although to a limited extent, and with particular features. The considered mechanisms include investment crowdfunding, non-fungible tokens (NFTs) and blockchain.

Investment Crowdfunding

Models of crowdfunding other than reward and donation include lending, equity, and royalty crowdfunding, more generally grouped under investment crowdfunding (see e.g., Belleflamme et al., 2015). Lending crowdfunding, also known as debt-based crowdfunding or peer-to-peer lending, involves raising debt capital by dividing loans among multiple investors. Equity crowdfunding involves selling company shares to raise venture capital online. This model establishes a long-term relationship between companies and investors. In royalty-based crowdfunding, investors receive a predefined percentage of future revenue generated by the project in exchange for their investment, without acquiring ownership rights.

Investment crowdfunding is underutilised in the nonprofit cultural sector (e.g., Handke & Dalla Chiesa, 2022), especially within the heritage sector, where it remains an exception (Jelinčić & Šveb, 2021). This pattern is also reflected by the scarcity of literature dedicated to the topic. Borin and Donato (2023) present a successful, and rare, case of equity crowdfunding by a private heritage site in France, where financial success is accompanied by a more participatory model of cultural management. The study could not, however, access information on potential dividends or the rate of return on investments. Yet it highlights main success factors, which essentially rely on an effective communication not only towards the media but also, more specifically, towards investors, clearly and explicitly informing them about the percentage of offered equity, how the funds were spent, and a diffused involvement of shareholders in the governance of the project, also through a dedicated platform. An additional success factor was the explicit support by the heritage civil society, contrary to the professional financial sector. Noticeably, investors were not professional and were not used to this novel investment mechanism.

From this case, we can possibly argue a similarity with the variety of benefits offered by reward- and donation-based crowdfunding beyond monetary ones. Indeed, investment crowdfunding applied to cultural heritage can develop additional forms of returns other than monetary ones. Remarkably, sense of belonging and supporting a good cause are more important drivers than profitability for equity backers (Marchegiani, 2018).

Non-Fungible Tokens (NFTs) and Blockchain

NFTs are unique digital assets that represent ownership of a specific item, which can be digital (like digital art, music, or videos) or physical (such as real estate, fine art, or luxury fashion). NFTs are used in various sectors, including art, gaming, fashion, and the metaverse. They enable creators to monetise digital content and provide a new form of digital ownership, conferring scarcity value. NFTs are stored on a blockchain, ensuring their uniqueness and authenticity. NFTs are non-fungible, meaning they cannot be exchanged for another identical asset. They are also cryptographically verifiable and easily transferable. Blockchain technology authenticates and validates NFTs, providing a secure and transparent way to prove ownership and provenance. Smart contracts, typically built on platforms like Ethereum, facilitate the creation, purchase, and sale of NFTs. Blockchain is a decentralised, distributed ledger that records transactions across many computers. It ensures transparency, security, and immutability of data. NFTs emerged in 2014 and exploded in 2021 (see, e.g., Wang et al., 2021).

Artworks and other items in museums' collections are assets that are worth a considerable value and can be digitally exploited through NFTs, to generate additional financial streams paid by cryptocurrencies, At the same time, they can attract novel segments of tech-loving audiences. NFTs offer an efficient way to raise funds without deaccessioning physical artworks. NFTs allow museums to maintain their collections, while generating revenue from digital representations. In 2021, NFTs were also the object of the first exclusively dedicated online auction, at Christie's. That same year, a major flagship museum, the Uffizi Galleries, in Florence, Italy, organised the first sale of NFTs after its masterpiece by Michelangelo, the *Tondo Doni*, in its collection, to overcome financial problems due to the COVID pandemic. They were shortly followed by the Hermitage in Saint Petersburg, Russia, and several other major international museums. More recent developments include the British Museum partnering with international specialised technology companies, to create and auction off NFTs based on artworks from their collection (in collaboration with LaCollection), as well as interactive NFT experiences (in collaboration with Ethereum-based metaverse gaming platform The Sandbox) (Hirschmiller, 2023).

On a smaller scale, the Whitworth Art Gallery at Manchester University, UK, represents a unique best practice in terms of social, technological and environmental innovation in the uptake of NFTs and blockchain in its fundraising. In 2021, this museum, which is dedicated to using art for social change, teamed up with technological partner Vastari, and minted and sold an edition of 50 NFTs of William Blake's watercolour etching, *The Ancient of Days*. The proceeds were used to fund socially beneficial projects in education, health, environment, and social cohesion, which also fostered a sense of shared ownership and social responsibility, attracting a broader audience. The technological innovation was that the Whitworth used a spectrographic scan of artwork instead of a direct digital replica, which added a unique twist and maintained the integrity of the original artwork. In addition, the NFT was minted on the ecofriendly NFT marketplace Hic et Nunc (Bailey, 2021; Harris, 2021).

Despite their potential, NFTs face various challenges, such as regulatory uncertainty, environmental concerns due to energy consumption, and market volatility. Regulation on NFTs is lagging, as usually happens with fast-paced technological innovation. Moreover, regulatory frameworks lack international harmonisation. The use of NFTs in the heritage sector is particularly challenged by copyrights, and the possible re-definition of their perimeter. Moreover, OpenGLAM free licensing of artworks images introduced by flagship museums, has already been the subject of malicious use by the Global Art Museum (GAM) (Valeonti et al., 2021).

Other Models of Digital Financing

Overall, cultural and creative sectors experience difficulties in accessing forms of investment, even traditional ones, such as banks and venture capital (Di Novo et al., 2022). Whether this is also the case for museums depends on their financial structures. Running costs (including salaries, rents and other fixed costs) are usually prevalent in museums. Hence, museums can be less frequently the object of project funding, which is rather typical of startups and artists' projects, and emerging novel technology-driven financial instruments. Investment instruments, such as mini bonds and intellectual-property investment funds, are more common in social entrepreneurship (Loots et al., 2022).

We might question whether emergent instruments from entrepreneurial finance, typically designed to help young innovative firms (Block et al., 2018), including in the creative industries, could also be applied for the purpose of funding and financing museums, given certain characteristics of these tools. For instance, governmental venture capital funds are driven by social payoffs and positive externalities to the society. These motivations may also apply in the case of museums. Yet the source of these funds is public, as are more traditional and long-validated subsidies and grants to museums. Also, social venture funds are driven by non-financial goals, and their source is mainly private. However, these funds also aim at a reasonable financial return, delivered by for-profit, enterprises, which museums are usually not. For artworks still under copyrights, museums could use intellectual-property-backed debt funding, where copyrights could be exploited as a source of capital collateralised by the stream of revenues deriving from licensing or royalty agreements involving portfolios of copyrights. Although the trade-off is not straightforward, as this instrument is characterised by high structuring costs (Block et al., 2018), this may explain why it is still not practised by museums.

4 Conclusions

Notwithstanding museum's initial reluctancy to experiment and take risks in the uptake of innovative digital financial instruments, museum's idiosyncratic financial structure, and the COVID pandemic have fostered their venturing in this novel field in the last years. This chapter contributed an original mapping of examples of existing practices beyond flagship global museums, focusing instead on the context of smaller museums. Evidence points to an effective and efficient uptake of a variety of (yet) unestablished digital financial models, where digital funding is prevalent, compared to digital financing.

Financial support to museums and cultural heritage is confirmed to be especially motivated by reasons that substantially complement a monetary return, also in the case of digital financing, such as a sense of ownership, community involvement, interaction, co-creation, and playfulness. In this way, museums can reach out to new audiences and build the audience's loyalty. Noticeably, such reasons may support an effective adoption of innovative digital financial instruments also in other cultural sectors, especially by nonprofit cultural organisations, as it is already the case with, for example, crowdfunding. This chapter has also shown how some financial models can be virtually adopted by museums of any size and capacity, as it is the case of reward- and donation-based crowdfunding that is operated on available specialised platforms. Yet the implied entrepreneurial skills (Lazzaro & Noonan, 2021) increasingly demand partnerships with specialised technology providers, especially for more complex technologies, and their combinations, as it is the case of NFTs, impacting museums' business models.

Remarkably, the application of digital solutions in the cultural and creative sectors presents important challenges, such as possible revisions of national laws and regulations (Jung, 2025), and their harmonisation (Lazzaro & Noonan, 2020), as well as individuals' sensible data protection (Vuković et al., 2023), and ways of bridging the digital divide (Mihelj et al., 2019). An ethical and fair use of digital technologies calls for the respect of sensible data of museums' audiences, funders and investors, and inclusive digital systems, which are accessible to all, including those with disabilities (see, e.g., Rouhani, 2023). Moreover, the monetisation of digital content can conflict with the increased political and societal demands for museums to make their digital content openly available (Wiedemann et al., 2019). From an economic perspective, while novel technology-driven models of financing can reduce traditional transaction costs and lower asymmetries, they can generate new transaction costs and other costs, such as developing the required skills to operate such systems, and the initial investment in setting up the supporting systems and infrastructure technologies (Loots et al., 2022).

5 Competing Interests

The writing of this chapter was supported by a grant from the Research Council of Norway [301291].

Notes

1. Current platforms used also by museums are Fundriver (https://fundriver.com), and Endowment Solutions (http://www.endowmentsolutions.com).
2. Noticeably, the two groups do not necessarily overlap, as funders can be non-visitors, similarly to traditional "analogue" funding (see, e.g., Lazzaro & Voss, 2010).

References

Bailey, J. (2021, July 28). Why Museums Should Be Thinking Longer Term About NFTs. *Artnome*. https://www.artnome.com/news/2021/7/28/why-museums-should-be-thinking-longer-term-about-nfts

Belleflamme, P., Omrani, N., & Peitz, M. (2015). The economics of crowdfunding platforms. *Information Economics and Policy, 33*, 11–28.

Berg, I. U., & Larsen, H. (2024). Public art and private wealth: the controversial collaboration between the national museum in Norway and Fredriksen Family Art Company Ltd. *Museum Management and Curatorship*, 1–18.

Betzler, D., Loots, E., Prokůpek, M., Marques, L., & Grafenauer, P. (2021). COVID-19 and the arts and cultural sectors: Investigating countries' contextual factors and early policy measures. *International Journal of Cultural Policy, 27*(6), 796–814.

Block, J. H., Colombo, M. G., Cumming, D. J., & Vismara, S. (2018). New players in entrepreneurial finance and why they are there. *Small Business Economics, 50*(2), 239–250.

Borin, E., & Donato, F. (2023). Equity crowdfunding for cultural heritage: Some insights from a French case study. *International Journal of Entrepreneurship and Small Business, 48*(1), 10–26.

Boukis, A. (2024). The effect of tokenized rewards on customer loyalty programs. *Annals of Tourism Research, 109*, Article 103851.

Cadence (2019, March 20). What Is A Token Redemption? *Medium*. https://medium.com/@withcadence/what-is-a-token-redemption-df282fd92f88

Calderon, A. A. (2025). Digital Payments and their Role in Enhancing Financial Transactions Efficiency. *International Journal of Economics and Financial Issues, 15*(1), 182–189.

Camarero, C., Garrido, M. J., & Vicente, E. (2011). How cultural organizations' size and funding influence innovation and performance: The case of museums. *Journal of Cultural Economics, 35*, 247–266.

Carr, M. (2014, December 19). Transforming Crowdfunding Backers into Lifelong Museum Supporters. *MuseumNext*. https://www.museumnext.com/article/transforming-crowdfunding-backers-into-lifelong-museum-supporters/
Cristobal-Fransi, E., Ramón-Cardona, J., Daries, N., & Serra-Cantallops, A. (2021). Museums in the digital age: An analysis of online communication and the use of e-commerce. *Journal on Computing and Cultural Heritage, 14*(4), 1–21.
Csongrádi, G., Reicher, R., & Takács, I. (2018). Latest Trends and Technologies at the Field of Nonprofit Fundraising. *International Journal of Contemporary Management*, 17(4).
De Voldere, I., & Zeqo, K. (2017). *Crowdfunding: Reshaping the Crowd's Engagement in Culture*. European Commission.
Di Novo, S., Fazio, G., Sapsed, J., & Siepel, J. (2022). Starving the golden goose? Access to finance for innovators in the creative industries. *Journal of Cultural Economics, 46*(2), 345–386.
Digital Culture Network. (2020). *Introduction to ticketing for museums and galleries*. Arts Council England. https://digitalculturenetwork.org.uk/wp-content/uploads/2020/08/Introduction-to-ticketing-for-museums-and-galleries-08.07.20_0-1.pdf
Farmer, F., & Wallace, A. (2024). Making the Business Case for Open Access. *glam-e lab*. https://www.glamelab.org/files/making-the-business-case-for-open-access-report-white-paper.pdf
Fincham, D. (2019). Assessing the viability of blockchain to impact the antiquities trade. *Cardozo Arts & Entertainment Law Journal, 37*, 605.
Frey, B.S., & Meier, S. (2006). The Economics of Museums. In Ginsburgh, V.A., & Thorsby, D. (Eds), *Handbook of the Economics of Art and Culture* (Vol. 1, pp. 1017–1047). Elsevier.
Gebken, L., Drews, P., & Schirmer, I. (2021). Stakeholder and value orientation in digital social innovation: designing a digital donation concept to support homeless neighbors. *Proceedings of the 54th Hawaii International Conference on System Sciences*.
Giachino, C., Battisti, E., Rovera, C., & Stylianou, I. (2024). Young travelers: culture's lovers and crowdfunding supporters. *Management Research Review*.
Handke, C., & Dalla Chiesa, C. (2022). The art of crowdfunding arts and innovation: The cultural economic perspective. *Journal of Cultural Economics, 46*(2), 249–284.
Harris, G. (2021, July 23). The Whitworth Gallery in Manchester Mints a William Blake NFT in Aid of Community Causes. *The Art Newspaper*. https://www.theartnewspaper.com/2021/07/23/the-whitworth-gallery-in-manchester-mints-a-william-blake-nft-in-aid-of-community-causes

Hirschmiller, S. (2023, July 27). The British Museum Will Enter the Metaverse via 'The Sandbox'. *Decrypt*. Available on: https://decrypt.co/150405/british-museum-enter-metaverse-via-sandbox

International Council of Museums (ICOM). (2021). *Museums, Museum Professionals and COVID- 19: Third Survey*. ICOM. https://icom.museum/wp-content/uploads/2021/07/Museums-and-Covid-19_third-ICOM-report.pdf

Izzo, F. (2017). Stakeholders and Museum Crowdfunding. *Modern Economy, 8*(04), 518.

Jelinčić, D. A., & Šveb, M. (2021). Financial sustainability of cultural heritage: A review of crowdfunding in Europe. *Journal of Risk and Financial Management, 14*(3), 101.

Jung, Y. (2025). Do NFTs Merit a Change in the IP Legal Paradigm? An Application of the Theory of Punctuated Equilibrium. In Lazzaro, E., Moureau, N., & Turpin, A. (Eds), *Law and Finance in International Art Markets: Past and Present*. Routledge.

Koch, J.A., & Siering, M. (2015). Crowdfunding success factors: The characteristics of successfully funded projects on crowdfunding platforms, *Proceedings of the 23rd European Conference on Information Systems (ECIS 2015)*.

Kolbe, K. J., Velthuis, O., Aengenheyster, J., Rozenbaum, A. F., & Zhang, M. (2022). The global rise of private art museums a literature review. *Poetics, 95*, Article 101712.

Lazzaro, E., & Noonan, D. (2020). Cultural and creative crowdfunding: A comparative analysis of regulatory frameworks in Europe and the USA. *International Journal of Cultural Policy, 27*(5), 590–606.

Lazzaro, E., & Noonan, D. (2021). The contribution of crowdfunding regulation to cultural entrepreneurship in a supportive ecosystem. In *Cultural Initiatives for Sustainable Development: Management, Participation and Entrepreneurship in the Cultural and Creative Sector* (pp. 401–424). Springer, Book series: Contributions to Management Science

Lazzaro, E. & Nordgård, D. (2025). Crowdfunding visual artists: Alternative or complementary financing mode? In Lazzaro, E., Moureau, N., & Turpin, A. (Eds), *Law and Finance in International Art Markets: Past and Present*. Routledge.

Lazzaro, E., & Voss, Z. (2010). *Assessing Citizens and Visitors' Awareness*. Sharing of Meaning and Engagement in Dallas Public Art.

Li, J., Zheng, X., Watanabe, I., & Ochiai, Y. (2024). A systematic review of digital transformation technologies in museum exhibition. *Computers in Human Behavior*, 108407.

Loots, E., Betzler, D., Bille, T., Borowiecki, K.J., & Lee, B. (2022). New forms of finance and funding in the cultural and creative industries. Introduction to the special issue. *Journal of Cultural Economics*, 46(2), 205–230.

Loots, E., Piecyk, K., & Wijngaarden, Y. (2024). At the juncture of funding, policy, and technology: How promising is match-funding of arts and culture through crowdfunding platforms? *International Journal of Cultural Policy, 30*(1), 118–134.

Marchegiani, L. (2018). From Mecenatism to crowdfunding: Engagement and identification in cultural-creative projects. *Journal of Heritage Tourism, 13*(2), 143–151.

Medda, F., & Lipparini, F. (2021). Impact investment for urban cultural heritage. *City, Culture and Society, 26*, Article 100413.

Mihelj, S., Leguina, A., & Downey, J. (2019). Culture is digital: Cultural participation, diversity and the digital divide. *New Media & Society, 21*(7), 1465–1485.

Murphy, O. (2018). Coworking spaces, accelerators and incubators: Emerging forms of museum practice in an increasingly digital world. *Museum International, 70*(1–2), 62–75.

Museum Catharijne Convent. (2021). *Jaarverslag 2021.* https://www.catharijneconvent.nl/documents/298/Jaarverslag__Museum_Catharijneconvent_2021.pdf

Museum of Fine Arts Boston. (2022, June 23). MFA Boston and LaCollection.io Offer NFT Collection of Rarely Seen 19th-Century French Impressionist Pastels. Museum of Fine Arts Boston. https://www.mfa.org/press-release/mfa-boston-and-lacollectionio-offer-nft-collection

Najda-Janoszka, M., & Sawczuk, M. (2023). Exploring the barriers of multi-stakeholder value co-creation–the museum context. *Journal of Organizational Change Management, 36*(4), 603–620.

Najda-Janoszka, M., & Sawczuk, M. (2024). Crowdfunding in the museum context: Exploring alternative approaches to financial support. *Entrepreneurial Business and Economics Review, 12*, 83–97.

Nelson, G. (2024, June 5). A Tech Accelerator Helps Major Museums Develop Blockchain Projects to Stay Relevant to Younger Audiences. *ArtNews*. https://www.artnews.com/art-news/news/blockchain-we-are-museums-tech-accelerator-museums-1234708860/

Nikolaou, P. (2024). Museums and the Post-Digital: Revisiting Challenges in the Digital Transformation of Museums. *Heritage, 7*(3), 1784–1800.

Pahl-Wostl, C., Basurto, X., & Villamayor-Tomas, S. (2021). Comparative case study analysis. In R. Biggs, A. De Vos, R. Preiser, H. Clements, K. Maciejewski, & M. Schlüter (Eds.), *The Routledge handbook of research methods for social-ecological systems* (pp. 282–294). Routledge.

Prokůpek, M., Loots, E., & Betzler, D. (2023). Emergency or emerging financing strategies of art museums in the context of a pandemic? *Museum Management and Curatorship, 38*(5), 530–547.

Ramya, N., Sivasakthi, D., & Nandhini, M. (2017). Cashless transaction: Modes, advantages and disadvantages. *International Journal of Applied Research, 3*(1), 122–125.

Rouhani, B. (2023). Ethically Digital: Contested Cultural Heritage in Digital Context. *Studies in Digital Heritage, 7*(1), 1–16.

Rykkja, A., Maehle, N., Munim, Z. H., & Shneor, R. (2020). Crowdfunding in the cultural industries. In R. Shneor, L. Zhao, & B. T. Flåten (Eds.), *Advances in Crowdfunding* (pp. 423–440). Palgrave Macmillan.

Shaked, N. (2022). *Museums and wealth: The politics of contemporary art collections*. Bloomsbury Publishing.

Srinivasan, R., Boast, R., Furner, J., & Becvar, K. M. (2009). Digital museums and diverse cultural knowledges: Moving past the traditional catalog. *The Information Society, 25*(4), 265–278.

Temin, P. (1991). An economic history of American art museums. In M. Feldstein (Ed.), *The economics of art museums* (pp. 179–194). University of Chicago Press.

Turner, D. (2022, February 7). "Tap" into your Digital Fundraising Goals with Contactless Donations. MuseumNext. https://www.museumnext.com/article/tap-into-your-digital-fundraising-goals-with-contactless-donations/

Valeonti, F., Bikakis, A., Terras, M., Speed, C., Hudson-Smith, A., & Chalkias, K. (2021). Crypto collectibles, museum funding and OpenGLAM: Challenges, opportunities and the potential of Non-Fungible Tokens (NFTs). *Applied Sciences, 11*(21), 9931.

Vuković, M., & Štefanac, T. (2023). Digital Cultural Heritage, Cybersecurity, and the Human Factor. *Preservation, Digital Technology & Culture, 52*(4), 129–141.

Wang, L., Luo, X. R., & Lee, F. (2019). Unveiling the interplay between blockchain and loyalty program participation: A qualitative approach based on Bubichain. *International Journal of Information Management, 49*, 397–410.

Wang, Q., Li, R., Wang, Q., & Chen, S. (2021). Non-fungible token (NFT): Overview, evaluation, opportunities and challenges. *arXiv preprint* arXiv: 2105.07447.

Wiedemann, J., Schmitt, S., & Patzschke, E. (2019). Responding to open access: How German museums use digital content. *Museum and Society, 17*(2), 193–209.

Wilson, B. (2022). Innovation in Fundraising Technology: The Rise of Contactless Giving. *Culturehive*. https://www.culturehive.co.uk/digital-heritage-hub/resource/engagement/innovation-in-fundraising-technology-the-rise-of-contactless-giving/

Wright, M., & Walmsley, B. (2022). Using digital for creative fundraising. In M. Wright, B. Walmsley, & E. Simmons, (Eds.), *Fundraising in the Creative and Cultural Industries* (pp. 255–277). Routledge.

Open Access This chapter is licensed under the terms of the Creative Commons Attribution 4.0 International License (http://creativecommons.org/licenses/by/4.0/), which permits use, sharing, adaptation, distribution and reproduction in any medium or format, as long as you give appropriate credit to the original author(s) and the source, provide a link to the Creative Commons license and indicate if changes were made.

The images or other third party material in this chapter are included in the chapter's Creative Commons license, unless indicated otherwise in a credit line to the material. If material is not included in the chapter's Creative Commons license and your intended use is not permitted by statutory regulation or exceeds the permitted use, you will need to obtain permission directly from the copyright holder.

CHAPTER 14

Public–Private Partnerships: When Governance Tools Stimulate Alternative Funding of the Heritage Sector and Beyond

Aline Albertelli and Anna Mignosa

1 Introduction

Cultural policies, along with the organisation and financing of culture, have been constantly changing. A multitude of factors have influenced this scenario. Some examples include major financial needs, cultural developments, political landscapes as well as periods of economic crisis, such as the 2008's upheaval and the recent COVID-19 pandemic which, while shaking up the status quo, upheave the conditions of the Cultural and

A. Albertelli (✉)
Independent Researcher, Brussels, Turin, Belgium
e-mail: aline.albertelli@outlook.com

A. Mignosa
University of Catania, Catania, Italy

Erasmus University Rotterdam, Rotterdam, Netherlands

A. Mignosa
e-mail: mignosa@eshcc.eur.nl

© The Author(s) 2026
C. Dalla Chiesa and A. Rykkja (eds.), *Cultural Funding and Financing*, Cultural Economics & the Creative Economy,
https://doi.org/10.1007/978-3-031-96696-5_14

Creative Sector heightening the focus on its needs and on the ways to provide for the sector itself.

As a result, several changes have been taking place. In some cases, a reorganization of cultural organisations, either merging some of them or transforming their institutional setting (for instance, through the creation of foundations) took place. In general, a trend towards the reduction of the role of the central government and a consequent tendency to transfer decision-making power to lower levels of government has been noticed (Klamer et al., 2013). At the same time, more space has also been given to the private sector, whose participation in supporting culture has become increasingly essential. Next to "established" tools to get funds from the private sector through sponsorship and donations, new instruments to allow a participatory approaches have been introduced. Thus, individuals, communities, and non-profit-organisations (NPOs) are getting more involved in supporting the cultural sector through bottom-up processes that take place in various forms.[2]

In Belgium, the Brussels-Capital Region promotes the temporary use of abandoned buildings and has established a dedicated platform and a contact point for this purpose. The platform "temporary.brussels" meets this goal by connecting property owners with individuals or organisations seeking space for their projects (Guichet occupation temporaire, 2025). For instance, the Public Welfare Centre (CPAS in French and OCMW in Dutch) of Brussels has granted the temporary occupation of the Grand Hospice to a non-profit organisation "Pali Pali" (City of Brussels, 2023). The organisation manages the space with the support of the CPAS, developing projects related to different themes, including art & culture,[3] driven by a group of citizens with a common goal. In the Netherlands, in 2001, several craftspeople, artists, and students were looking for cheap rentals in Amsterdam. They created the "Kinetisch Noord Foundation" and received support from the municipality to settle in the NDSM (Nederlandsche Dok en Scheepsbouw Maatschappij), a cultural center emerged from an unused shipyard in the north of the city aimed at providing a space for creatives.[4] In Latvia, the Museum of the Occupation was created by a non-profit organisation not to burden the public budget (Museum of the Occupation of Latvia (n.d.). Initially, the Ministry of Culture only granted a space to host the museum, now the visit to the museum is part of the diplomatic protocol and the museum receives financial support also from the state.

The various forms of collaboration between public and private actors used for the management and governance of cultural spaces or projects can be also seen in the heritage sector, which is the focus of this chapter. We concentrate on a particular type of institutional arrangement where the collaboration is pursued by sharing resources and responsibilities to jointly manage public cultural projects or spaces through Public–Private-Partnerships—PPPs (National Council for Public–Private-Partnerships, 2017). PPPs are not new; in several countries, they have been in place for years. The Netherlands, for example, has a tradition of collaborative relationships among the public, private, and civil society sectors. This approach, known as the "Rhinelandic model", is characteristic of North-Western Europe (Koppenjan & De Jong, 2018). The difference here is that we concentrate on cases where these types of collaborations have been introduced in countries (normally) characterized by strong (centralized) public intervention for culture and where new, ad-hoc laws determine the rules and conditions necessary for these PPPs to exist. This diverges from other countries where public–private collaboration for culture is more diffused and where it is difficult to "standardize" these collaborations as they take a variety of forms[5] and follow no specific guidelines (Kobosilova, 2023).

We want to understand whether it is possible to create alternative ways to support culture by establishing different, more varied, governance models. Can we consider the examples of PPPs as alternative forms of financing culture? Are these governance tools an instrument for the public sector to attract private sources of financing for publicly owned cultural institutions or projects that remain unaddressed due to insufficient funding? In the case of heritage, is PPP a tool to guarantee the preservation and enhancement of lesser-known sites which, notwithstanding their relevance for a community, are often in a state of abandonment for the lack of public resources? To answer these questions, the next section will illustrate the changes in public administration that have laid the groundwork for the development of PPPs. Then, the focus will shift to the use of PPPs for culture. The following section will display some selected cases of PPPs. The last section will draw some concluding remarks.

2 Governance Shifts and PPPs

As a starting point, we deem it necessary to illustrate the governance shifts that contributed to the establishment of these new forms of participatory governance and PPPs, in particular. This background provides a lens to better understand the context and conditions in which these instruments are adopted and perceived across different countries, also in consideration of their distinct governance traditions.

Shift in Public Administration Models

Conceptual approaches to public administration can be categorised into three main archetypes: traditional Public Administration Management (PAM), New Public Management (NPM), and New Public Governance (NPG) (Osborne, 2006). The concept of an interventionist state that steps in to address market failures has been a defining feature of governmental arrangements or policy regimes, embraced by most Western nations from the late nineteenth century through the early 1980s (Osborne, 2006). This system is identified in PAM which is a highly centralized, hierarchical, and bureaucratic form of governance that peaked during the US New Deal of the 1930s (Gruening, 2001) and the post-World War II welfare state in the UK (Osborne, 2006), when the state was seen as responsible for meeting citizens' social and economic needs. However, from the early 1980s, Anglo-American countries witnessed a shift towards decentralization and market-oriented solutions, prompted by challenges to state efficiency and demands for more consumer-centric approaches (Homburg et al., 2007). This led to the emergence of NPM, characterized by a managerial approach to public services (Klijn, 2012; Osborne, 2006). NPM aimed to enhance efficiency by introducing market-like mechanisms and involving private actors in service delivery (Dickinson, 2016). In the early twenty-first century, NPG emerged. It represents a departure from hierarchical and market-driven approaches and promotes active collaboration among the actors involved through cooperative governance structures involving the public and private sectors (Osborne, 2006; Rhodes, 1996). Unlike NPM, NPG involves the co-designing and co-delivering of services by both the public and private sectors (Table 1).

Aligned with this transformation in governance, tools like PPPs have risen to prominence in the modernisation of public policy, indicating a move towards collaborative governance strategies (Ansell & Gash, 2008; Osborne, 2006). "Collaborative governance (CG) refers to a mode of policy and service delivery that shifts away from government- or market-centric settings to a setting in which public, private nonprofit, and private business actors are jointly involved in and accountable for policymaking and service delivery to create public value that could otherwise not be achieved" (Voets et al., 2021, pp.1). PPPs are examples of a possible implementation of this strategy.

Public–Private Partnerships (PPPs)

The concept of PPPs has been a subject of extensive debate in modern society (Klijn et al., 2007). Governments and international organisations increasingly view PPPs as crucial for modernising public policy, improving governance, and the financing of public services (OECD, 2013). Acknowledging the importance of PPPs, the European Investment Bank established the "European PPP Expertise Centre" to improve efficiency in service delivery and its economic impact. The World Bank created a Public–Private-Partnership Resource Centre with the aim of sharing information and guidance on PPPs (World Bank, n.d.a).

The emergence of PPPs gained scholarly attention during the 1970s–1980s, coinciding with the rise of the NPM reforms in the UK (Bovaird, 2010). Under NPM, PPPs were perceived as a means of privatization and outsourcing, with public actors retaining control and private entities assuming operational responsibilities (Osborne & Gaebler, 1993). In contrast, the NPG perspective views PPPs as part of a horizontal relationship between the public and private sectors, emphasizing cooperation in terms of sharing resources to realize shared objectives (Rhodes, 1996) and blending public and private skills to achieve common goals.

The National Council for Public–Private-Partnerships (2017) defines PPPs as "a contractual agreement between a public agency (federal, state, or local) and a private sector entity. Through this agreement, the skills and assets of each sector (public and private) are shared in delivering a service or facility for the use of the public. In addition to the sharing of resources, each party shares in the risks and rewards potential in the delivery of the service and/or facility". This definition underscores the importance of both ex-ante and ex-post interactions between the two parties, where responsibilities, skills, and strategies for the development of the project, as well as actual outcomes, including costs or revenues, are shared.

3 PPPs in the Cultural and Creative Sector

PPPs are increasingly emerging as a primary financing mechanism for public infrastructure projects across various economies (International Monetary Fund, 2024). According to the review of the European public–private partnership market, PPP transactions corresponded to an aggregate value of €13.6 billion in 2023, with transport being the main sector involved (European Investment Bank, 2024). Existing literature (Murwantara, 2023) identifies diverse motivations for government adoption of PPPs. Boardman and Vining (2010) delineate two principal categories: normative motives, such as technical efficiency and economies of scope or bundling activities; and positive motives, encompassing cost deferral, reduction of government debt, off-balance sheet financing, increased net cash flow, risk transfer, and mitigation of political risk. PPPs are often perceived as more efficient than traditional public procurement methods (Grimsey & Lewis, 2004; Hodge et al., 2010), facilitating timely project completion, adherence to budget constraints, and compliance with project specifications (Grimsey & Lewis, 2004).[6] Nonetheless, the success of PPP endeavours is not guaranteed, with many projects failing to deliver the anticipated benefits (Della Croce & Gatti, 2014).

Not all collaborations between the public sector and the private or third sector qualify as PPPs. There exist diverse interpretations of what constitutes a PPP, resulting in various typologies of PPPs. The World Bank Public–Private-Partnership Resource Centre refers to the types of contracts (World Bank, n.d.b). In principle, they all revolve around three core components: resources, responsibilities, and risks (Mcdonald & Cheong, 2014). Depending on how these components are managed and distributed, different forms of PPPs can emerge and, by achieving the appropriate balance among these elements, successful partnerships can be realized.

Data from the European Investment Bank (2024) on the aggregate value and the number of PPP projects in Europe show that, though PPPs are more frequently used in other sectors (transport, environment), they are also used for recreation and culture. And though the aggregate value is the lowest (€150 million), the number of projects is higher than in defence and similar to telecommunication.

We intend to illustrate how the use of PPPs can be beneficial for the heritage sector as an alternative source of financing. UNESCO (2013) underlines the "unexplored potential for partnerships" in the cultural sector, suggesting that their use could "bridge the funding gap of public entities [while at the same time providing for] interesting investment opportunities for the private sector". As a matter of fact, over the past two decades, Western countries have increasingly embraced the PPP model as an innovative approach to managing and governing heritage sites (Ferri & Zan, 2017). This shift can be associated with the gradual shrinking of government intervention in the cultural sector (among other sectors), in the process of désétatization,[7] which has given private organisations a more active role in heritage site governance and management (Dubini et al., 2012).

Various factors have contributed to this phenomenon next to the governance changes illustrated above. Public funding is insufficient to accommodate the growing amount of heritage, and the increasing range of activities that cultural institutions are expected to undertake: education, promotion, and enhancement next to the traditional ones, i.e., conservation, safeguarding and protection. The costs associated with managing cultural organisations, and cultural heritage, have risen (Mannino & Mignosa, 2017; Klamer et al., 2013; Dubini et al., 2012). Cultural developments have also influenced these changes; societies now expect cultural institutions to be active and drive change rather than being passive entities. Concepts such as sustainability, equity, inclusivity, and participation have gained importance in the cultural sector, as acknowledged and addressed by various cultural, social, political, and economic institutions, including the European Council (EC) through the Faro Convention,[8] the International Council of Museums (ICOM) with the new official definition of museums,[9] and the United Nations (UN) with the 2030 Agenda for Sustainable Development.[10] This shift contributes to the tendency to consider PPPs as models for the management and governance of cultural heritage.

PPPs are recognized as valuable to relieve pressure on public funds by using private resources, without losing public oversight to ensure the achievement of public objectives (Council of Europe, 2005; UNESCO, 2013). Additionally, PPPs address administrative and managerial challenges faced by the public sector by leveraging the competitive skills of private actors (UNESCO, 2013). In PPPs in the cultural sector, the parties involved can often be three: a public institution and a for-profit private entity, with a non-for-profit private entity acting as an intermediary or advisor in the partnership that intervenes as a third actor (Rypkema, 2008).

While the benefits for the public sector are often highlighted, PPPs can also be advantageous for private parties, which can contribute to social goals, enhancing their overall societal impact, i.e., their mission in the case of non-profit organisations. Often, PPPs improve the brand image of the private partner (Pignatti, 2022).

PPPs, however, are not without potential issues. Firstly, the benefits for the public partner emphasized in the literature hint at an imbalance of power, portraying the public sector as weak and reliant on private assistance. This imbalance can hinder the establishment of a truly collaborative and equitable relationship. Creating the right balance between public and private involvement through good governance is a challenge that requires negotiation skills and clear rules on the part of the public sector as well as appropriate incentives for the private partner (Dubini, 2012; McDonald & Cheong, 2014; Rypkema, 2008). Scholars argue that it is unlikely for risks to be evenly shared in PPPs, with the public sector assuming most of them (McDonald & Cheong, 2014).[11] Furthermore, in the context of cultural heritage, the implementation of PPPs is often hindered by unclear procedures and the resistance of public institutions (Mannino & Mignosa, 2017). A real common interest is a prerequisite of PPPs to avoid conflicting values between partners generating insurmountable differences.

If the relationship is not structured correctly, it can lead to an imbalanced and vertical arrangement that contrasts the potential benefits of such an agreement. However, if power dynamics are balanced, with shared commitments, responsibilities, and goals, and both parties contribute to the realization of the common objectives, the partnership is more likely to yield positive results. PPPs can thus bring together the best of both worlds (Mannino & Mignosa, 2017).

4 Case Studies

In what follows, we illustrate the potential role of this model in supporting the heritage sector by referring to cases from two different countries where, after the introduction of specific rules, PPPs have been used to run a municipality-owned monastery and a world heritage site owned by a public university in Italy, and several national museums in Brazil.

PPP in Italy

Italy's governance system reflects a tradition characterized by centralization, hierarchy, and uniformity (Kickert, 2007). This approach entails significant public intervention and bureaucratic structures (Kickert, 2007, p. 26). Following this framework, Italian cultural heritage governance combines extensive central control and local management. The Ministry of Culture oversees preservation efforts, while regional and municipal entities support enhancement activities. Over the years, different legislative measures, such as the Ronchey Law (1993),[12] the Cultural Heritage Code (2004), and the Franceschini reform (2014),[13] to name a few, have introduced different mechanisms for the involvement and engagement of the private sector in heritage preservation and enhancement.

In recent years, PPPs have emerged as an important tool in Italy. There is an increasing number of cases using PPPs as they can contribute to returning neglected heritage sites to "their" communities (Albertelli, 2022; Vitale, 2021). Even greater attention has been given to this form of governance through the National Recovery and Resilience Plan (NRRP), which seeks to advance infrastructure and utilities projects as a catalyst for Italy's economic recovery. In 2021, a significant initiative was introduced to rejuvenate lesser-known cultural heritage sites and bring them to life through public–private partnerships (PPPs) (MiC, 2021) by promoting the direct and active engagement of local communities and citizens, thus fostering inclusive participation in cultural and economic revitalization (Albertelli, 2022). "Special" PPPs (SPPPs), the first recognized form of horizontal PPPs in Italy, were specifically introduced for the cultural sector in 2023 with specific laws.[14] According to the law, the State, regions, and territorial entities are empowered to establish contracts free of charge to promote the enjoyment of the nation's cultural heritage and support scientific research for its protection and enhancement. These partnerships aim to facilitate the recovery, restoration, maintenance, management, public access, and enhancement of cultural assets.

SPPPs feature a streamlined private partner selection process under the principle of contractual autonomy, saving time and offering greater flexibility to private entities compared to vertical PPPs. Governed by the principle of cooperation, SPPPs are contracts "free of charge", unlike ordinary PPPs, which are defined by economic exchange. The collaborative framework of SPPPs, based on cooperation, co-planning, and co-designing of activities, should ensure a fair distribution of resources and responsibilities among the parties involved (Milella, 2018; Sciullo, 2021). Furthermore, SPPPs have a broader scope of action (Vitale, 2021). They include both enhancement and protection activities. Additionally, SPPPs have a much longer average duration (20–25 years) compared to the typical 2–5-year term of ordinary PPPs.

Discussions are underway to establish a national observatory to monitor the implementation and impact of PPPs for cultural heritage governance (ANCI, 2021). Recent legislative advancements and growing incentives suggest a positive trend in the adoption of PPPs. The analysis of the two Italian case studies intends to offer some insight to explain this trend. One case relates to the partnership between a nonprofit organisation, Officine Culturali (OC), and the University of Catania to enhance several heritage sites owned by the latter. The other case sees the collaboration between a theatre, Teatro Tascabile of Bergamo (TTB), and the municipality of the same town for the management and governance of an old Monastery in Bergamo Alta. In this case, what is remarkable is the synergy between heritage and the performing arts, where the former is the basis for the latter to thrive, and the latter makes sure that the former is truly enhanced.

The partnership between OC and the university, established prior to the introduction of SPPPs, has nevertheless embodied a horizontal partnership model from its inception. Similarly, TTB and the municipality initially established a contractual form of PPP and later transitioned to SPPPs, representing a structured form of collaborative partnership. As summarized in Table 2, both cases have consistently yielded favourable outcomes, enhancing organisational skills and the capacity to gather financial resources through mixed approaches. Additionally, they have developed culturally and socially impactful activities, underscoring the potential of PPPs for the governance of heritage sites, as well as their funding and the financing of related activities directly tied to the site (e.g., site visits) or connected to other cultural endeavours (e.g. theatre performances).

These are examples of a broader landscape, where numerous other case studies show the possibilities for improved governance and financing of cultural heritage.[15]

Table 1 Policy regimes

Paradigm	*Abbr*	*Characteristics*	*Emphasis*	*Governance Mechanism*	*Established*
Public Administration Management	PAM	Highly centralized, hierarchical, and bureaucratic form of governance	Implement policy	Hierarchy	1930s–50 s
New Public Management	NPM	Decentralized and market-oriented solutions	Economic Efficiency	Market through traditional contracts/ vertical partnerships	1980s
New Public Governance	NPG	Co-designing and co-delivering of public services in a networked structure	Cooperative governance structure for improved public service	Horizontal partnerships	1990s

Note Authors' elaboration from Osborne (2006; pp. 383); Dickinson (2016); Klijn (2012); Gruening, (2001); Homburg et al, (2007);Osborne and Gaebler, (1993)

PPP in Brazil: The Organizações Sociais in São Paulo

In Brazil, at the end of the 1990s, a process of policy reorganisation led to the introduction of hybrid models of governance that are examples of PPPs: the Organizações Sociais (OS—Social Organisations). These non-profit organisations were introduced to allow a more efficient and flexible management of public services—museums, theatres, hospitals, scientific institutes, etc. (Fiore et al., 2011). In this work, the focus is on those responsible for the management of museums.

The State can entrust OSs to provide public services using "management contracts.". The State can either finance the activity or concede the public assets, and the OS executes the necessary activities to provide the public service (Costin, 2008). The contract states the responsibilities of the parties, the goals of the OS, the number of public resources committed, the rules for the performance evaluation, and penalties in case of contract breach (Fiore et al., 2011). For the cultural OSs, the contract indicates the objectives connected to the earned income and admits the possibility of using fundraising and tax benefits (Alcoforado, 2005).

Table 2 Main characteristics of the PPPS of OC and TTB

Indicator	*OC*	*TTB*
Context	Municipal—regional	Municipal—Regional
Year of establishment	First agreement 2010 Renewed as a SPP in 2022	First Agreement in 1996 Renewed as a SPP in 2018
Adopted policy tool	SPPPs under Legislative Decree No. 50/2016	SPPPs under Legislative Decree No. 50/2016
Public contractor	University of Catania	Municipality of Bergamo
Private contractor	Associazione Impresa Sociale Officine Culturali	Teatro Tascabile of Bergamo
Other parties (if any)		Fitzcarraldo Foundation
Partnership length	20 years	20 years renewable
Objective	Enhance part of the heritage owned by the University and raise awareness about the social and cultural value it	Recover, restore, and re-functionalize the Carmine Complex while enhancing its cultural and economic value for the community
Governance model	Participatory Governance Model using a Technical Table	Participatory Governance Model using a Technical Table
Financing model	Ticket sales Revenues from cultural initiatives and commercial activities National and international projects	Grants from Public Administration Private contributions Revenues from cultural initiatives, commercial activities, donations & corporate partnerships
Division of responsibilities	Public: Responsible for the maintenance and governance of the sites under the technical supervision of the local branch of the regional office for culture (*Soprintendenza*) Private: Realization of all the activities necessary to enhance the sites, raise awareness on their importance, stimulate cultural participation and social inclusion	Public: Maintain an open dialogue with Lombardy Region's *Soprintendenza*, administrative offices, and the Ministry of Culture, while also ensuring the effective implementation of public policy instruments. Private: plan and execute preservation and enhancement activities, finding funds
Division of risks	Public: Maintenance of the heritage sites Private: Realization of all the activities	Public: Bureaucratic procedures Private: Realization of all the activities

(continued)

Table 2 (continued)

Indicator	*OC*	*TTB*
Economic results (until 2024)	Constant increase of the no. and variety of activities and thus of income In 2023: hiring of 4 new employees. In total, now 14 people have a fixed contract	Capacity of raising funds for interventions. Securing (2019–2023) more than € 3 million Since the end of 2020, TTB work team is composed of 3 employees and 20 collaborators
Cultural and social results (up until now)	Constant increase in the participation of the local community to the activities organised; involvement of youngster and people with physical and social difficulties to realize social inclusion through culture	Involvement of the Bergamo community. Cooperation with local businesses, theatres, and performance groups Participatory cultural activities for social inclusion and city regeneration
Comments		TTB's new structure for implementing SPPPs strengthened their financial and organisational capacity, enabling them to secure additional funding for theatre and performance activities and navigate crises like COVID-19

Note Date sourced from Officine Culturali (n.d.a; n.d.b); Teatro Tascabile ()

OSs are more efficient in the use of resources and can provide higher-quality cultural services as they do not need to follow bureaucratic procedures. They can also have access to external funding, thereby not having to rely solely on public funds. A further advantage is that OSs can manage the cultural service by involving civil society, for instance, including artists and cultural managers as board members (Fiore et al., 2011). Some authors (Costin, 2008; Fiore et al., 2011) worry about the risk that the State loses control over public policies, and others (Fiore et al., 2011; Martins, 2016) underline potential problems of (lack of) transparency. There are also doubts due to the lack of qualified OSs capable of managing cultural institutions and the consequent dependence on the already active ones.

A study on the role of OSs in the State of São Paulo (Mignosa & Mayer Tibeau, 2024) shows that they have been used as the primary model for cultural activities management, receiving 73% of the state cultural budget between 2010 and 2021 (Unidade de Monitoramento da Secretaria da Cultura do Estado de São Paulo, 2022). Among the four categories of cultural activities run by OSs—Libraries and Reading (Bibliotecas e Leitura); Cultural Dissemination (Difusão Cultural) related to performing arts; Cultural Education (Formação Cultural); and Museums (Museus), the latter is where contracts prevail. Mignosa and Mayer Tibeau (2024) analyse whether the OSs in the State of São Paulo reached the goals set in the contract with reference to attendance figures, dependence on public funding, and financial results. As for the first, visitors increased in all the OSs by 33% in the period 2009–2016, whereas, in the last year considered, there was a decrease attributable to the economic crisis connected to the impeachment of Brazil's president, and a fire in one of the museums.[16]

When it comes to the funding structure of the OSs and their dependence on public funding, these organisations proved to be more agile and flexible, not having to use public tenders to select companies for the provision of ancillary services. They also showed a tendency to reduce the dependence on public funding, having a more diversified operating income. A more balanced funding structure might lead to higher financial stability. However, the analysis also shows that OSs might adopt a strategy of deficit optimization to keep obtaining subsidies from the government, as organisations with surpluses might see a decrease in the public grants received (Frey Meer, 2006). This calls for more transparency and tools to control OSs, for instance, through public agencies monitoring the outcomes of the management contracts.

Comparison

The exploration of PPPs in Italy and Brazil demonstrates the valuable role these partnerships play as alternative financing models within the cultural and creative sectors. Though originally developed with different aims—Brazilian OSs as an explicit alternative to public governance, and Italian SPPPs to fulfil public interest goals by directing resources to heritage which is neglected but valuable for communities—both models reveal the potential for PPPs to enhance governance, efficiency, and financial sustainability.

These examples align with the motivations for government adoption of PPPs identified by Murwantara (2023), which include both normative motives, such as technical efficiency, and positive motives, such as cost deferral (Boardman & Vining, 2010). By leveraging private sector resources and expertise, these partnerships have facilitated more effective and sustainable cultural initiatives, echoing the efficiency observed in traditional infrastructure projects (Grimsey & Lewis, 2005; Hodge & Greve, 2010). Similarly, they also underscore how hybrid governance structures can enhance the organisational and financial capacities of cultural institutions. The flexible management of OSs, which bypasses bureaucratic constraints, aligns with the efficiencies that PPPs bring to public procurement, ensuring timely project completion and adherence to budget constraints (Grimsey & Lewis, 2004). The example also highlights the potential for PPPs to transform cultural governance and increase the financial sustainability of cultural organisations through the contribution of the private sector, providing a viable alternative to public financing. The over-mentioned effects of PPPs in Brazil and Italy are summarized in Table 3.

The Italian case studies demonstrate the potential of PPPs in delivering initiatives and activities across the entire cultural and creative sector. Both TTB and OC showcase improved management and enhancement of the heritage sites involved in the partnership, as well as the development of complementary cultural and creative activities. Moreover, the creation of jobs represents another important result, especially in an area (South of Italy) where unemployment is still very high.[17]

Despite their advantages, PPPs also present challenges related to power dynamics and transparency. The Italian legislative framework for SPPPs addresses these challenges by defining clear roles and responsibilities promoting a balanced and cooperative approach; its implementation, however, still presents some hiccups, slowing down the diffusion of this model. Issues of transparency and accountability remain, particularly in

Table 3 Comparison of the PPPS in Brazil and Italy

Country	*Increased efficiency*	*Reduction of public funds*	*Increased transparency*
Brazil	+	±	±
Italy	+	+	+

the Brazilian OS model, where the risk of deficit optimization and dependency on public subsidies necessitate robust monitoring and evaluation mechanisms (Della Croce & Gatti, 2014).

5 Concluding Remarks

While some may view PPPs as merely an alternative financial mechanism for managing and governing cultural heritage sites, numerous cases worldwide demonstrate a broader impact. For instance, TTB has a dedicated team that integrates its traditional activities with the strategic PPP framework for regenerating the Carmine Monastery (TTB, 2022). This initiative not only improves the efficiency of partnership management but also enhances the theatre's overall operations, ensuring greater financial sustainability for the company's activities. Similarly, in OC, a team of 15 professionals realize the various activities that guarantee the financial viability of the association. A comparable approach emerges in Brussels, where the "temporary.brussels" platform facilitates the adaptive reuse of vacant spaces, including recognized cultural heritage sites. The initiative enables various creative projects—such as artist studios, cultural events, and other artistic endeavours—to develop and thrive while breathing new life into underutilised heritage locations (Visit Brussels, 2024). Similarly, in NDSM, different cultural forms find their space through exhibitions, performances, talks and collaborative spaces. These cases show a reinterpretation of the role and value of cultural heritage in contemporary society; heritage sites are not static but evolve into dynamic spaces shaped by community-driven initiatives that foster new cultural and creative expressions and contribute to creating the heritage of the future. PPPs can play a role in achieving this goal (Council of Europe, 2020).

These partnerships offer a viable alternative to traditional public funding, addressing the growing financial needs of cultural institutions and directing resources toward neglected heritage sites and cultural events. The participatory and collaborative nature of PPPs fosters community involvement, enhances organisational capacity, and improves financial stability. This is a new approach to cultural governance where it is not about money but about acting and contributing with private resources to something which is deemed important for communities in a bottom-up approach. While challenges related to power dynamics and transparency exist, careful design and robust governance frameworks can mitigate these issues. The broader implications of PPPs highlight their versatility and adaptability, making them valuable tools for modernising public policy and governance and finally, financing tools.

As noted by McDonald and Cheong (2014), the success of PPPs depends on achieving a balance among resources, responsibilities, and risks. The success and functionality of PPPs are heavily influenced by the administrative and political settings in which they are introduced. Understanding contextual differences is crucial for adapting PPP models to various national and local settings, ensuring that they meet the unique needs and challenges of each context. Still, some common characteristics can be evidenced. Regular assessments of PPP performance are vital to introduce measures to improve the results or to avoid strategic behaviour, like the risk of deficit optimisation strategies for the Brazilian OS. A key element for the success of PPPs is a strong and ongoing horizontal collaboration between the public and private sectors. This entails open communication, regular meetings, and a willingness to work together towards shared goals. Equally important is the existence of a shared vision accompanied by the willingness to co-create and co-plan a strategy. Finally, a deep knowledge of the context and an understanding of the local community and its needs is essential. It is then possible to tailor PPPs to the specific administrative, cultural, and economic settings of each area to increase alignment with local objectives and community interests. Ultimately, cultural governance plays a pivotal role in shaping the financial landscape of the arts and heritage sectors. By fostering strategic partnerships and leveraging multi-stakeholder engagement, governance frameworks can ensure that cultural heritage remains a vibrant, accessible, and well-supported pillar of contemporary society. PPPs, when carefully designed and transparently managed, emerge as an alternative to traditional public funding capable to address the emerging needs of public cultural (and heritage) institutions by attracting private sources of funding and creating innovative pathways for cultural sustainability. As cultural policies continue to evolve in response to financial constraints and shifting societal needs, PPPs stand as a model for rethinking the intersection of governance, finance, and cultural heritage.

Notes

2. The Faro Convention (Council of Europe, 2005) proposes a shared approach to heritage, where its preservation and valorisation are shared responsibilities of communities.

3. The other themes concern: the community, sustainable development, and education & health.
4. Since 2009 a new foundation, Stichting NDSM-werf is in charge of the area (NDSM, n.d.).
5. For instance, PPPs are widely used for the management of World Heritage Sites in the Netherlands but there is not a unique model (Keuper, 2015).
6. In this work, we refer to efficiency as the ability to minimize costs or maximize outputs for given resources, and we use transparency as a synonym for accountability.
7. Désétatisation refers to the reduction of direct state control over cultural heritage management shifting responsibilities to private or mixed public–private entities.
8. The Faro Convention (Council of Europe, 2005) recognizes the importance of heritage as part of citizens' right to participate in cultural life. It emphasizes the need for collaboration among public institutions, and private actors.
9. ICOM, the International Council of Museums, is a non-governmental organisation representing museums and museum professionals worldwide. In 2017, ICOM established the Museum Definition, Prospects, and Potentials (MDPP) committee to address the need for a new definition of a museum that aligns with the demands of the twenty-first century.
10. The United Nations, through its specialized agency UNESCO, acknowledges the role of culture in pursuing the SDGs (Klamer and Mignosa, 2019).
11. However, this varies depending on the strength/weakness of the private partner.
12. Law 14.1.1993, N. 4.
13. Law Decree 31.05.2014, n.83.
14. Initially introduced by the Legislative Decree No. 50/2016, these partnerships are currently regulated by the Legislative Decree No. 36/2023, which took effect in July 2023.
15. The most reliable data currently available are the list of projects applying to the Call Viviamo Cultura. First launched in 2020, the Call Viviamo Cultura (2025) pioneered innovative PPP models in the cultural sphere.
16. The Museu da Língua Portuguesa.

17. In Sicily, it was 16% in 2023 according to the Italian Statistical Office (2025).

References

Albertelli, A. (2022). Public-private partnerships in the Italian cultural heritage – A case study (Master thesis). *Erasmus School of History, Culture and Communication.*

Alcoforado, F. C. G. (2005). Contratualização e eficiência no setor público: as organizações sociais. Available from: https://bresserpereira.org.br/documents/mare/OS/alcoforado_OS.pdf (Last Retrieved 31.05.2024)

ANCI. (2021). *Nasce l'Osservatorio ANCI, Forum Terzo Settore, Alleanza Coop per partenariati speciali.* Retrieved from https://www.anci.it/nasce-losservatorio-anci-forum-terzo-settore-alleanza-coop-per-partenariati-speciali/

Ansell, C., & Gash, A. (2008). Collaborative governance in theory and practice. *Journal of Public Administration Research and Theory, 18*(4), 543–571.

Boardman, A. E., & Vining, A. R. (2010). P3s in North America: Renting the money (in Canada), selling the roads (in the USA). In G. A. Hodge, C. Greve, & A. E. Boardman (Eds.), *International handbook on public–private partnerships* (pp. 354–398). Edward Elgar Publishing.

Bovaird, T. (2010). A brief intellectual history of the public–private partnership movement. In G. A. Hodge, C. Greve, & A. E. Boardman (Eds.), *International handbook on public–private partnerships* (pp. 43–67). Edward Elgar Publishing.

Costin, C. (2008). Organizações sociais como modelo para gestão de museus, orquestras e outras iniciativas culturais. *Revista Administração em Diálogo-RAD, 7*(1). Retrieved from https://revistas.pucsp.br/index.php/rad/article/viewFile/673/470

City of Brussels (2023). Grand Hospice: meeting place with 140 projects. https://www.brussels.be/grand-hospice-meeting-place-140-projects

Council of Europe. (2005). *Council of Europe framework convention on the value of cultural heritage for society Council of Europe Treaty Series - No. 199.* Retrieved from https://rm.coe.int/1680083746

Council of Europe. (2020). *The Faro Convention: The way forward with heritage.* Council of Europe Publishing. Retrieved from https://edoc.coe.int/en/cultural-heritage/8757-the-faro-convention-the-way-forward-with-heritage.html

Della Croce, R., & Gatti, S. (2014). Financing infrastructure – International trends. *OECD Journal: Financial Market Trends, 2011*(1), 123–159. Retrieved from https://www.oecd.org/content/dam/oecd/en/publications/reports/2014/10/oecd-journal-financial-market-trends-volume-2014-issue-1_g1g35f93/fmt-v2014-1-en.pdf

Dickinson, H. (2016). From new public management to new public governance: The implications for a 'new public service'. In *New Public Governance* (pp. 41–60). ANU Press.

Dubini, P., Leone, L., & Forti, L. (2012). Role distribution in public-private partnerships: The case of heritage management in Italy. *Managing Arts Organizations, 42*(2), 57–75.

European Investment Bank. (2024). *Market update: Review of the European public-private partnership market in 2023*. Retrieved from https://www.eib.org/attachments/lucalli/20240030_epec_market_update_2023_en.pdf

Ferri, P., & Zan, L. (2017). Partnerships for heritage conservation: Evidence from the archaeological site of Herculaneum. *Journal of Management & Governance, 21*(1), 1–25.

Fiore, D. C., Porta, R. H., & Duarte, T. S. B. (2011). Organizações sociais de cultura em São Paulo - desafios e perspectivas. Retrieved from https://docplayer.com.br/9627875-Organizacoes-sociais-de-cultura-em-sao-paulo-desafios-e-perspectivas-danilo-cesarfiore-rogerio-haucke-porta-tiago-silva-birkholz-duarte.html

Frey, B. S., & Meier, S. (2006). The economics of museums. In V. A. Ginsburgh & D. Throsby (Eds.), *Handbook of the economics of art and culture* (pp. 1017–1047). Elsevier North-Holland.

Grimsey, D., & Lewis, M. K. (2004). *PPP: The worldwide revolution in infrastructure provision and project finance*. Edward Elgar Publishing.

Grimsey, D., & Lewis, M. K. (2005). Are public-private partnerships value for money? Evaluating alternative approaches and comparing academic and practitioner views. *Accounting Forum, 29*(4), 345–378.

Gruening, G. (2001). Origin and theoretical basis of new public management. *International Public Management Journal, 4*(1), 1–25.

Guichet occupation temporaire. (2025). Le Guichet des Occupations Temporaires. https://temporary.brussels/?lang=fr

Hodge, G. A., Greve, C., & Boardman, A. E. (Eds.). (2010). *International handbook on public-private partnerships*. Edward Elgar Publishing.

Hodge, G., & Greve, C. (2005). *The challenge of public–private partnerships*. Edward Elgar Publishing.

Homburg, V., Pollitt, C., & van Thiel, S. (2007). Introduction. In V. Homburg, C. Pollitt, & S. van Thiel (Eds.), *New public management in Europe: Adaptation and alternatives* (pp. 1–9). Palgrave Macmillan.

International Monetary Fund. (2024). *IMF Committee on balance of payments statistics: 2023 annual report.*https://www.imf.org/en/Publications/Balance-of-Payments-Statistics/Issues/2024/02/22/IMF-Committee-on-Balance-of-Payments-Statistics-2023-Annual-Report-545151

Istituto Italiano di Statistica. (2025). Tasso di disoccupazione – dati regionali (Unemployment rate - by region). http://dati.istat.it/viewhtml.aspx?il=blank&vh=0000&vf=0&vcq=1100&graph=0&view-metadata=1&lang=it&QueryId=25419&metadata=DCCV_TAXDISOCCU1

Keuper, M. (2015). *Public-private partnerships in Dutch world heritage (Master thesis).* Culture and Communication, Erasmus University, Rotterdam.

Kickert, W. (2007). Public management reforms in countries with a Napoleonic state model: France, Italy, and Spain. In V. Homburg, C. Pollitt, & S. van Thiel (Eds.), *New public management in Europe: Adaptation and alternatives* (pp. 26–51). Palgrave Macmillan.

Klamer, A., Mignosa, A., & Petrova, L. (2013). Cultural heritage policies: A comparative perspective. In I. Rizzo & A. Mignosa (Eds.), *Handbook on the economics of cultural heritage* (pp. 37–86). Edward Elgar.

Klamer, A., & Mignosa, A. (2019). The financing of cultural heritage: A value-based approach. In: A. Jakubowski, K. Hausler, & F. Fiorentini, (Eds.), *Cultural heritage in the European Union: A critical inquiry into law and policy* (pp. 163–183). Brill Nijhoff.

Klijn, E. (2012). New public management and governance: A comparison. In D. Levi-Faur (Ed.), *The Oxford handbook of governance*. Oxford University Press.

Klijn, E. H., Edelenbos, J., Hughes, M., Pollitt, C. S., van Thiel, S., & Homburg, V. (2007). Public-private partnerships: A two-headed reform; a comparison of PPP in England and the Netherlands. In V. Homburg, C. Pollitt, & S. van Thiel (Eds.), *New public management in Europe: Adaptation and alternatives* (pp. 71–89). Palgrave Macmillan.

Kobosilova, T. (2023). *Partnership-led regeneration of heritage protection zones* (Master thesis).

Koppenjan, J., & de Jong, M. (2018). The introduction of public-private partnerships in the Netherlands as a case of institutional bricolage: The evolution of an Anglo-Saxon transplant in a Rhineland context. *Public Administration, 96*(1), 171–184.

Macdonald, S., & Cheong, C. (2014). *The role of public-private partnerships and the third sector in conserving heritage buildings, sites, and historic urban areas.* Getty Conservation Institute. http://hdl.handle.net/10020/gci_pubs/public_private_partnerships

Mannino, F., & Mignosa, A., et al. (2017). Public-private partnership for the enhancement of heritage: The case of the Benedictine monastery of Catania. In V. M. Ateca-Amestoy (Ed.), *Enhancing participation in the arts in the EU: Challenges and methods* (pp. 263–278). Springer.

Martins, L. D. J. (2016). *Transparência e responsabilização na contratualização de resultados com as organizações sociais de cultura no estado de São Paulo: Um estudo a partir da atuação do controle externo* (Master's thesis, Universidade de São Paulo). http://www.teses.usp.br/teses/disponiveis/100/100138/tde-30082016-155031/en.php

MiC. (2021). *Avviso pubblico progetti di rigenerazione culturale e sociale dei piccoli borghi storici PNRR M1C3 - Investimento 2.1 - Attrattività dei borghi – Linea B.* MiC. https://cultura.gov.it/borghi

Mignosa, A., & Tibeau, C. M. (2024). New governance models for museums: The case of Organizações Sociais in São Paulo, Brazil. In Babić, D. (Ed.) *International perspectives on museum management* (1st ed., pp. 11). Routledge. h

Milella, F. (2018). Si gioca, finalmente. *Il Giornale delle Fondazioni.* http://www.ilgiornaledellefondazioni.com/content/si-gioca-finalmente

Murwantara, R. (2023). *Government support for enhancing public-private partnerships (PPPs): Comparing, explaining, and studying the effects of variations across European countries* (Doctoral thesis, University of Antwerp, Faculty of Social Sciences). University of Antwerp. https://repository.uantwerpen.be/docstore/d:irua:16525

Museum of the Occupation of Latvia (n.d.) About the Museum. https://okupacijasmuzejs.lv/en/about-the-museum#about.

National Council for Public-Private Partnerships. (2017). *7 keys to successful public-private partnerships.* http://www.ncppp.org/ppp-basics/7-keys/

(NDSM, n.d.). NDSM - This is the place and the place is everything. https://www.ndsm.nl/en/over.

OECD. (2013). Public-private partnerships. In *Government at a glance 2013* (pp. 156–157). OECD Publishing.

Officine Culturali. (n.d.-a). *Cosa facciamo.* https://www.officineculturali.net/cosa-facciamo/

Officine Culturali. (n.d.-b). *Mission e obiettivi.* https://www.officineculturali.net/mission-e-obiettivi/

Osborne, S. P. (2006). The new public governance? *Public Management Review, 8*(3), 377–387.

Osborne, D., & Gaebler, T. (1993). *Reinventing government* (1st ed.). Penguin Books.

Pignatti, M. (2022). I modelli di partenariato pubblico-privato nella gestione e valorizzazione dei beni culturali come strumento per la creazione di ecosistemi innovativi e di sviluppo economico e sociale. *DPCE Online, 51*(1).

Rhodes, R. A. W. (1996). The new governance: Governing without government. *Political Studies, 44*(4), 652–667.

Rypkema, D. (2008). Heritage and development: The role of public-private partnerships. In M. Mälkki, R. Mäntysalo, & K. Schmidt-Thomé (Eds.), *Economics and built heritage: Towards new European initiatives* (pp. 131–150).

Sciullo, G. (2021). Il partenariato pubblico-privato in tema di patrimonio culturale dopo il Codice dei contratti. *Aedon (Bologna), 3*, 154–161. https://doi.org/10.7390/102982

Teatro Tascabile di Bergamo. (2023a). *Attività socio-culturali: Dossier di presentazione del primo quinquennio (2018–2023)*. https://carmine.teatrotascabile.org/wp-content/uploads/2023/11/QUINQUENNIO-ARTISTICO_Dossier-complessivo-dellandamento-complessivo-dal-2018-al-2023.pdf

Teatro Tascabile di Bergamo. (2023b). *Interventi sull'immobile: Dossier di presentazione del primo quinquennio (2018–2023)*. https://carmine.teatrotascabile.org/wp-content/uploads/2023/11/QUINQUENNIO_Dossier-complessivo-dellandamento-complessivo-dal-2018-al-2023.pdf

UNESCO. (2013). *Public-private partnership in the culture sector: Background note*. http://www.unesco.org/new/fileadmin/MULTIMEDIA/HQ/CLT/images/PublicPrivatePartnershipENG.pdf

Unidade de Monitoramento da Secretaria da Cultura do Estado de São Paulo. (2022). *Boletim UM – Orçamento da cultura no estado de São Paulo – SEC e Oss – 2010 à 2021* (UM publication No. 19). https://www.transparenciacultura.sp.gov.br/secretaria-da-cultura-boletins-unidade-monitoramento/

Vitale, C. (2021). Rigenerare per valorizzare. La rigenerazione urbana "gentile" e la riduzione delle diseguaglianze. *Aedon (Bologna), 2*, 82–93.

Visit Brussels. (2024). Cultural hotspots available for temporary occupation. https://www.visit.brussels/en/visitors/what-to-do/cultural-hotspots-available-for-temporary-occupation.

Viviamo Cultura. (2025). Call Viviamo Cultura – Il patrimonio di tutti. https://www.viviamocultura.com/

Voets, J., Brandsen, T., Koliba, C., & Verschuere, B. (2021). Collaborative governance. *Oxford Research Encyclopedia of Politics*. https://oxfordre.com/politics/view/https://doi.org/10.1093/acrefore/9780190228637.001.0001/acrefore-9780190228637-e-1419

World Bank. (n.d.-a). What are PPPs? Public-Private Partnership Resource Center. https://ppp.worldbank.org/public-private-partnership/about-us/about-public-private-partnerships

World Bank. (n.d.-b). PPP Contract Types and Terminology, Public-Private Partnership Resource Center. https://ppp.worldbank.org/public-private-partnership/applicable-all-sectors/ppp-contract-types-and-terminology

Open Access This chapter is licensed under the terms of the Creative Commons Attribution 4.0 International License (http://creativecommons.org/licenses/by/4.0/), which permits use, sharing, adaptation, distribution and reproduction in any medium or format, as long as you give appropriate credit to the original author(s) and the source, provide a link to the Creative Commons license and indicate if changes were made.

The images or other third party material in this chapter are included in the chapter's Creative Commons license, unless indicated otherwise in a credit line to the material. If material is not included in the chapter's Creative Commons license and your intended use is not permitted by statutory regulation or exceeds the permitted use, you will need to obtain permission directly from the copyright holder.

CHAPTER 15

Tainted Philanthropy in Arts Funding: The Case Study of National Portrait Gallery in London and the Sackler Trust

Marek Prokůpek

1 Introduction

Philanthropy has long been a cornerstone of financial support for cultural institutions, particularly in Western countries, where private donations often compensate for limited public funding (Toepler & Dewees, 2005). Arts organisations depend on charitable contributions to sustain their operations, preserve cultural heritage, and foster public engagement. However, as reliance on private funding grows (Alexander, 2019), so too does scrutiny over the ethical implications of accepting donations from certain sources. Increasingly, cultural institutions find themselves at the centre of debates over corporate social responsibility, with critics questioning whether financial necessity justifies partnerships with donors linked to controversial industries. In recent years, environmental activists and advocacy groups have pressured institutions to sever ties with fossil

M. Prokůpek (✉)
KEDGE Business School, Paris, France
e-mail: marek.prokupek@kedgebs.com

© The Author(s) 2026

C. Dalla Chiesa and A. Rykkja (eds.), *Cultural Funding and Financing*, Cultural Economics & the Creative Economy,
https://doi.org/10.1007/978-3-031-96696-5_15

fuel companies and arms manufacturers, arguing that cultural organisations should uphold ethical integrity in their fundraising practices.

One of the most prominent and contentious examples of this debate is the controversy surrounding the Sackler family, whose extensive philanthropic contributions to the arts have been overshadowed by their connection to the opioid crisis. As owners of Purdue Pharma, the pharmaceutical company responsible for a painkiller called OxyContin, the Sacklers have faced increasing condemnation for their role in a public health catastrophe that has claimed hundreds of thousands of lives in the United States (Warren & Rogers, 2020). What was once considered an act of cultural patronage has now been reframed as 'tainted philanthropy', raising critical concerns about the reputational risks associated with donor relationships. This ethical reckoning has been fuelled by the efforts of artist and activist Nan Goldin and her advocacy group P.A.I.N. (Prescription Addiction Intervention Now), which have led protests at major museums, demanding they sever ties with the Sackler Trust. The activism surrounding this issue has not only reshaped public discourse on philanthropic ethics but has also placed intense pressure on cultural institutions to take a stand.

Faced with this growing controversy, arts institutions have responded in different ways. Some, like the Louvre Museum, discreetly removed the Sackler name from their galleries, while others, including the Metropolitan Museum of Art, publicly announced that they would no longer accept Sackler funding. Against this backdrop, the National Portrait Gallery in London (NPG) became the first major cultural institution to formally decline a Sackler Trust donation. In 2019, after prolonged internal deliberations and external scrutiny, the NPG and the Sackler Trust announced a joint decision not to proceed with a planned £1.3 million donation. The NPG framed its decision as a mutual agreement, subtly reflecting the complexities of ethical philanthropy in the arts. This case highlights a critical turning point in the debate over cultural funding: while financial contributions remain vital, institutions must now navigate the increasing demand for ethical accountability in ways that balance financial sustainability, public trust, and reputational considerations.

While these controversies have sparked widespread public debate, academic scholarship on the ethics of philanthropy remains underexplored. The academic debate around philanthropy has been examined from various conceptual and empirical perspectives, resulting in a substantial body of academic literature. However, much of the existing research has primarily focused on understanding the motivations behind charitable giving, with analyses conducted from both individual (Bertacchini et al., 2011; Lindahl & Conley, 2002; Moir & Taffler, 2004; Shekhtman & Barabási, 2023) and corporate perspectives (Selma et al., 2020; Webb, 2004). Additionally, scholars have explored how external factors influence donation behaviour, including government subsidies (Borgonovi, 2006; Brooks, 1999) and financial incentives such as tax deductions (Donelli et al., 2022; Mulcahy, 1998; Pharoah, 2010). Recent studies have further expanded this discourse by examining the role of managerial practices in arts organisations and their impact on philanthropic success (Cobb, 2002; Donelli et al., 2023). Moreover, the broader societal implications of philanthropic contributions to the arts, particularly in relation to wellbeing, have garnered some scholarly attention (Addis & Rurale, 2024). Despite this growing scholarly interest in various aspects of art philanthropy, there is a notable scarcity of research critically examining philanthropy from an ethical perspective. More broadly, the ethical dimensions of fundraising have received limited attention from scholars and researchers across different sectors. When fundraising professionals engage with ethical concerns, their focus is often on resolving practical dilemmas rather than grounding their approaches in normative ethical frameworks (MacQuillin, 2023). While a few studies have addressed the theoretical foundations of fundraising ethics (Kelly, 1998; MacQuillin, 2023; MacQuillin & Sargeant, 2019; Prokůpek & Divíšková, 2023), there remains a pressing need for more comprehensive academic inquiry into the ethical implications of philanthropic practices in the arts sector.

This chapter critically examines the ethical tensions in arts philanthropy, focusing on the NPG's decision to reject Sackler Trust funding as a pivotal case. It first situates this controversy within the broader landscape of arts funding, exploring the sector's growing reliance on private donations and the ethical challenges that arise. Next, it analyses the implications of 'tainted philanthropy', considering transparency, reputational risks, and the influence of donor interests. The discussion then turns to institutional responses and activist interventions. Finally, the chapter proposes practical strategies for cultural institutions and other stakeholders to navigate funding ethics, balancing financial sustainability with accountability and social responsibility.

2 Current Landscape of Arts Funding

The challenge of securing and maintaining funding for arts organisations has long been a persistent issue, deeply rooted in historical patterns of philanthropy and arts advocacy (Upchurch, 2016). Over the past four decades, this challenge has grown more acute with the rise of neoliberal economic frameworks, which have shifted financial responsibility away from public funding and onto private donors and the organisations themselves (Alexander, 2018, 2019; Banks, 2020). This evolving financial environment highlights the tension arts organisations face as they strive to balance their financial needs with their cultural and social missions (Ashton, 2023).

In navigating this increasingly complex funding landscape (Prokůpek et al., 2023), arts organisations now rely on a diverse array of funding sources (Ashton, 2023). These sources are shaped by regional economic conditions, cultural policies, and societal contexts. Generally, funding for arts organisations is categorised into three main streams: public funding, private donations, and earned income (Lindqvist, 2012). In some regions, investment income also plays a significant role, as observed in the USA. The structure and emphasis of these funding streams, however, vary widely across different regions, reflecting distinct historical, cultural, and economic conditions.

For instance, in continental Europe, public funding has traditionally dominated the financial landscape. European museums often receive approximately 70% of their funding from government subsidies, with earned income accounting for 20% and private donations contributing around 10% (Pauget et al., 2021). In contrast, American museums operate under a far more diversified financial model. On average, U.S. museums rely on government support for just 19% of their funding, with 35% coming from private donations, 35% from earned income, and 11% from investment returns (American Alliance of Museums, 2020). These disparities not only reveal differing funding traditions but also reflect varying societal expectations about public responsibility in supporting the arts (Heilbrun & Gray, 2004; Katz, 2006).

The United Kingdom represents a hybrid approach, combining elements of both European and American funding models. As of 2023, government funding accounted for 31% of UK museums' income (down from 42% the previous year), while private contributions made up 13%, while self-generated revenue comprised 52%, reflecting a 10% increase over the previous year (UK Department for Digital, Culture, Media & Sport, 2023). These figures underscore a broader trend of declining public funding and increasing reliance on self-generated income across the sector.

This shifting landscape is not without its challenges. In the USA, cultural institutions have long faced limited government support, with the National Endowment for the Arts (NEA) frequently being subjected to budget cuts (Moraes et al., 2020). Similarly, austerity measures across Europe have placed significant financial strain on cultural organisations, further exacerbating the need for alternative funding sources.

In response to these pressures, many arts organisations have turned to private donors, philanthropists, and corporate sponsors to secure financial stability. However, the growing dependence on private funding has brought heightened scrutiny to donor relationships (Prokůpek, 2024a). Organisations often find themselves caught between financial necessity and ethical concerns, particularly in cases like the Sackler Trust controversy, where donations from contentious sources have sparked public backlash. These challenges force cultural institutions to carefully weigh the benefits of securing much-needed funding against potential reputational risks and ethical obligations, underscoring the delicate balance required to sustain their operations in a rapidly evolving funding environment.

3 Ethical Considerations in Arts Funding

Museums often face complex funding challenges, requiring them to strike a delicate balance between adopting innovative, entrepreneurial strategies and collaborating with private sector partners while upholding their ethical responsibilities (Prokůpek, 2024a). Defining what constitutes ethical behaviour is rarely straightforward, as these judgments are often nuanced and subjective. This complexity raises an essential question: how can museums enhance their decision-making frameworks to carefully evaluate and responsibly manage financial contributions from corporations and private donors? Addressing these challenges demands a robust ethical approach, critical to preserving the integrity of cultural institutions and maintaining public trust. Ethical considerations in arts funding extend beyond mere acceptance of financial support; they involve ensuring transparency, promoting equity, engaging stakeholders meaningfully, and safeguarding against undue influence that could compromise artistic freedom or shift organisational priorities. By embedding these principles into their funding strategies, museums can navigate the increasingly intricate financial landscape while remaining accountable to their mission and values.

Transparency and Influence

A central ethical challenge lies in the transparency of funding sources[2] and the potential for undue influence. When funding comes from private donors or corporations, there is a risk that these entities may impose their values or agendas on the funded projects.[3] This influence can compromise artistic integrity and autonomy, as organisations may feel pressured to align their work with the interests of their funders. To mitigate these risks, arts organisations must establish clear ethical guidelines and codes of conduct, promote accountability and ensure that funding relationships align with their core missions.

Ethical codes serve as frameworks that outline the values, principles, norms, and expected behaviour for participants within a specific system. They are designed to guide organisations facing ethical dilemmas, regulate conduct, and act as safeguards against unethical practices. However, a one-size-fits-all approach is impractical; each profession requires a tailored ethical code that reflects its unique characteristics and challenges. These codes must also be periodically reviewed and updated to remain relevant and address emerging issues. Today, having a well-defined code of ethics is often regarded as a competitive advantage, as it fosters trust and confidence among employees, customers, and other stakeholders (Prokůpek & Divíšková, 2023).

The acceptance of funding from controversial industries, such as fossil fuels, alcohol, or gambling, raises additional ethical concerns. Such partnerships can lead to the normalisation of harmful practices and erode public trust in arts institutions.[4] Museums and arts organisations must critically evaluate the alignment of these funding sources with their values and consider the long-term impact on their credibility. For instance, the reliance on corporate sponsorships in museums can sometimes result in funders exerting significant influence over exhibition content and organisational priorities[5] (Prokůpek, 2024a).

Managing Tainted Donations

Paul Dunn (2010) explores the risks associated with 'tainted donations', which arise when donor misconduct becomes publicly known. These situations can damage an institution's reputation, especially if the donor's actions conflict with the institution's values. Dunn identifies three key factors in managing such donations: stakeholder theory (the disproportionate influence of a single party), value incongruence (misalignment between donor and organisational values), and economic necessity (the pressure to prioritise financial benefits).

To navigate these challenges, Dunn (2010) outlines three strategies:

1. Acquiescence: Fully returning the donation.
2. Compromise: Making partial adjustments, such as renaming a building while retaining the funds.
3. Defiance: Retaining the donation despite public criticism.

Each approach carries implications for public trust, underscoring the need for proactive policies to handle such controversies. Additionally, boards must conduct thorough due diligence on financial gifts, ensuring that donations align with the institution's mission.

4 The Sackler Family and Their Philanthropic Legacy

The Sackler family, a billionaire American dynasty, has long been recognised for their substantial philanthropic contributions to arts, culture, and education. Institutions such as the Louvre Museum, the NPG in London, and the Solomon R. Guggenheim Museum benefited from their support. However, the family's philanthropic legacy has become a topic of intense ethical debate due to their association with Purdue Pharma, the pharmaceutical company responsible for producing OxyContin. Over the past decade, Purdue Pharma has faced widespread criticism for allegedly concealing the addictive nature of OxyContin, a key factor in the U.S. opioid crisis (Warren & Rogers, 2020).

Historically, the Sackler family has donated extensively to prestigious institutions, with their name prominently displayed in recognition of their generosity. Examples include the Sackler Wing at the Metropolitan Museum of Art in New York. However, as the opioid crisis has unfolded, these contributions have come under scrutiny, raising questions about the ethics of accepting funds tied to public health crises.

The concept of 'tainted money' has emerged as a central concern in this debate. Critics argue that accepting donations from the Sacklers implicates institutions in the harms caused by the opioid epidemic, which has led to widespread addiction and overdose deaths (Warren & Rogers, 2020). This raises significant questions about the moral responsibility of recipient institutions to vet their funding sources and consider the implications of aligning themselves with controversial donors.

The controversy surrounding the Sackler family's philanthropy highlights broader concerns about equity in philanthropic practices, particularly in the context of the opioid crisis. Given that this public health emergency has disproportionately impacted marginalised and underserved communities, there have been increasing calls for a more just allocation of philanthropic resources. Critics argue that instead of directing their wealth toward elite cultural institutions, the Sacklers should prioritise funding initiatives that address the root causes of addiction, support recovery programmes, and improve social determinants of health in affected communities (Bhati & Hansen, 2020). This shift in funding priorities could serve as a means of mitigating the harm associated with their wealth while fostering healing in the communities devastated by the opioid epidemic.

Such critiques align with the broader principles of social justice philanthropy, which seeks to redress systemic inequalities by redistributing resources and power to marginalised populations. Unlike traditional charity, which often focuses on alleviating immediate needs, social justice philanthropy aims to tackle the structural causes of social disparities by supporting initiatives that challenge existing power structures and advocate for policy reforms (Jensen, 2019). Research suggests that foundations committed to social justice are more likely to fund non-profit social action efforts, resulting in significant societal impact (Suárez, 2012). Furthermore, incorporating diversity, equity, inclusion, and justice (DEIJ) principles into grant-making processes has been shown to effectively advance health equity and broader social justice goals (Puntenney & Ruesga, 2010). By embracing these strategies, philanthropic efforts can transcend symbolic giving and instead contribute to lasting, transformative change, reinforcing the argument that philanthropy should prioritise systemic reform over institutional prestige.

5 Activist Response: The P.A.I.N. Activist Group

In recent years, public backlash against the Sackler family's donations has led numerous institutions to reconsider their associations with the family, largely driven by protests and media scrutiny. One of the most prominent figures in this movement is photographer Nan Goldin, who founded the advocacy group P.A.I.N. to highlight the Sackler family's role in the opioid epidemic. Founded in 2017, the group was born out of Goldin's personal experiences with addiction and her determination to expose the devastating consequences of the opioid crisis. P.A.I.N.'s activism extends beyond simply raising awareness; it actively pressures cultural and academic institutions to sever ties with the Sackler family, publicly acknowledge the harm caused by Purdue Pharma's products, and implement stronger ethical standards in donor acceptance. Moreover, the group advocates for broader systemic reforms, including expanded access to addiction treatment and recovery services (Jobey, 2019).

Goldin and fellow activists organised high-profile demonstrations at major cultural institutions, demanding the removal of the Sackler name from galleries and calling for greater accountability. Their efforts began to yield tangible results when, in 2019, the NPG in London became the first major institution to reject a £1.3 million donation from the family trust (Marshall, 2019). This decision set a precedent, prompting other institutions to reassess their affiliations. Later that year, the Louvre Museum in Paris removed the Sackler name from its galleries following public demonstrations, similarly, the Guggenheim Museum in New York, along with other prominent institutions, severed ties with the Sackler Trust.

The momentum continued beyond the art world, extending into academic institutions. Following the Louvre's decision, several universities took similar steps to distance themselves from the Sacklers. In December 2019, Tufts University announced the removal of the Sackler name from its medical school buildings and programmes after sustained pressure from students and faculty demanding more scrutiny of philanthropic funding sources (Seltzer, 2019). More recently, in 2023, the University of Oxford followed suit, eliminating the Sackler name from key academic and cultural buildings, including the Ashmolean Museum and the Bodleian Libraries, while opting to retain previously donated funds (Seymour, 2023). These developments underscore the far-reaching impact of activist pressure in reshaping institutional policies on donor affiliations.

These ongoing efforts also reflect a growing demand for transparency and ethical decision-making in philanthropy. Institutions are increasingly expected to adopt stringent guidelines for evaluating donors and their sources of wealth to ensure alignment with organisational values and societal expectations (Michon & Tandon, 2012). By prioritising accountability, cultural and academic institutions can help mitigate the risks of controversial funding while fostering a more equitable and responsible approach to philanthropy. The Sackler family's legacy serves as a pivotal case study in these ethical dilemmas, illustrating the complexities of modern philanthropy and the power of activism in driving meaningful change.

However, it is important to acknowledge that institutional responses to the Sackler controversy were not uniform across the cultural and educational sectors. While prominent institutions such as the NPG, Tate, and the Louvre chose to distance themselves from the Sackler family, other recipients adopted a more defiant stance. Evidence from the press reveals that, despite the public backlash, the Sackler Trust continued to distribute substantial grants in the UK even after announcing a pause in new giving in 2019. According to an article in The Guardian (Quinn, 2022), the Trust awarded over £14 million to UK public bodies in 2020, including £3.5 million in new commitments. These donations were not limited to elite national institutions but extended to smaller, regional, and educational bodies such as Newbury's Watermill Theatre (£500,000), the Oxford Philharmonic Orchestra (£280,000), and King's College London (£250,000).

The motivations and institutional responses to these donations varied. For some regional organisations, such as the Watermill Theatre, accepting Sackler funds was framed as a financial necessity to sustain vital cultural and community outreach activities. A spokesperson for the theatre emphasised that the decision to retain the funding had been carefully considered in line with ethical policies and regulatory guidance and would enable the theatre to deliver youth and rural engagement programmes. Similarly, King's College London defended the continuation of its Sackler funding as part of an ongoing research partnership supporting neurodevelopmental studies, stressing that the acceptance had been approved through its internal fundraising ethics review group (Quinn, 2022).

These examples illustrate that smaller or regionally embedded institutions may face different ethical pressures and public expectations compared to large, highly visible museums and galleries. For such organisations, the reputational risks associated with accepting contested donations may be less pronounced or outweighed by the immediate benefits to their beneficiaries and communities. Additionally, the case of King's College London suggests a more defiant or policy-based approach, whereby decisions to maintain Sackler funding were justified on procedural and scientific grounds rather than symbolic ethical considerations. This diversity of responses underscores the uneven landscape of ethical philanthropy, revealing how institutional size, mission, and stakeholder expectations shape different risk calculations in relation to tainted donations.

6 The National Portrait Gallery's Dilemma: Ethical Considerations in Philanthropy

The NPG in London operates as a non-departmental public body (NDPB), a status that grants it autonomy while maintaining accountability through its sponsoring department, the Department for Digital, Culture, Media, and Sport (DCMS, UK). Established under the Museums and Galleries Act in 1992, the NPG functions as an exempt charity, meaning it is not required to register with the Charity Commission but must adhere to charity regulations. This dual status ensures a balance between independent governance and public accountability, allowing the gallery to focus on its mission of preserving and promoting portraits of eminent British individuals while being partially funded by government resources (NPG, n.d.).

The governance of the NPG is overseen by a Board of Trustees, consisting of 15 members, two of whom are ex-officio appointments. The remaining trustees are appointed by the Prime Minister through a public appointment process. The board sets the strategic direction, determines policy, and oversees the gallery's operations, ensuring public funds are used effectively and aligning with the gallery's mission. Operational management of the NPG is delegated to the Director, who is responsible for the day-to-day administration and staffing of the gallery. Appointed by the Board with the Prime Minister's approval, the Director also ensuring financial accountability and overseeing the execution of the gallery's strategic plans (NPG, n.d.).

To supplement its government funding, the NPG must self-generate 70% of its operating budget through various income streams, including donations, retail shops, catering franchises, and venue hire. This diversification is achieved in part through the National Portrait Gallery Company, a fully owned trading subsidiary, which donates its profits to the gallery under the Gift Aid scheme. The company focuses on enhancing the visitor experience while maximising financial support for the gallery. This governance and operational framework ensure the NPG fulfils its public mission while maintaining financial sustainability and adapting to contemporary challenges in arts funding (NPG, n.d.).

The National Portrait Gallery's Income Structure (2018–2022)

The income structure of the NPG from 2018 to 2022 reflects a diverse range of funding sources, emphasising the importance of government support and self-generated income. Table 1 summarises the income figures for each year.

The National Portrait Gallery's income is supported by three primary streams: Government grant-in-aid, self-generated income, and investment income. Government grant-in-aid saw a significant increase in 2021–2022, reaching £15,498,000. This rise likely reflects an increased reliance on public funding during the COVID-19 pandemic, a period when disruptions to other revenue sources necessitated enhanced government support. Self-generated income, despite experiencing fluctuations, remained a major component of the gallery's funding, peaking at £19,628,000 in 2021–2022. This highlights the gallery's efforts to diversify its revenue through activities such as trading, fundraising, and charitable endeavours. Investment income, although relatively modest, demonstrated notable growth from £27,000 in 2020–2021 to £167,000 in 2021–2022, showcasing improved returns from financial assets and further contributing to the gallery's financial stability. Together, these

Table 1 Income structure of NPG between 2018 and 2022

Source of income	*2018–2019*	*2019–2020*	*2020–2021*	*2021–2022*
Government Grant-in-Aid	£7,634,000	£8,575,000	£9,410,000	£15,498,000
Self-Generated Income	£16,723,000	£14,815,000	£9,373,000	£19,628,000
Investment Income	0	£27,000	£27,000	£167,000
Total	24,357,000	23,357,000	18,810,000	35,293,000

Note Compiled by the author based on NPG (2023) annual report

Table 2 Self-generated income structure of the NPG between 2018 and 2022

Type of self-generated income	*2018–2019*	*2019–2020*	*2020–2021*	*2021–2022*
Donations and legacies	£8,411,000	£6,008,000	£6,008,000	£6,008,000
Other trading activities	£4,462,000	£4,759,000	£2,759,000	£4,759,000
Charitable activities	£3,850,000	£4,048,000	£606,000	£8,861,000

Note Compiled by the author based on NPG (2023) annual report

streams illustrate the gallery's adaptive approach to sustaining its operations during challenging times. Self-generated income is derived from three main categories, as detailed in Table 2

The NPG generates income through a variety of sources, categorised into donations and legacies, other trading activities, and charitable activities. Donations and legacies comprise contributions from individual donors, philanthropists, and major gifts, alongside grants from charitable foundations and trusts. Additionally, bequests and endowments from supporters, as well as fundraising campaigns tied to specific projects or initiatives, significantly bolster the gallery's resources. Other trading activities, managed by the National Portrait Gallery Company Limited, provide revenue through retail operations in gift shops and online stores, venue hires for private events and conferences, catering services within the gallery, and licensing income from royalties for the use of images from the gallery's collection. Charitable Activities, on the other hand, encompass admission fees for ticketed special exhibitions, income from educational programmes, workshops, and guided tours, and revenue generated through membership programmes and patrons' schemes. Furthermore, contributions from outreach and community engagement programmes play a vital role in supporting the gallery's mission and sustaining its operations. Together, these diverse revenue streams ensure the gallery's financial sustainability and its ability to fulfil its cultural and educational objectives (NPG, 2023).

The National Portrait Gallery's Dilemma: The Sackler Trust Donation

The NPG faced a pivotal moment in 2019 when it was offered a £1.3 million donation from the Sackler Trust, intended to support the NPG's Inspiring People project, a major initiative aimed at revitalising the gallery's programme, visitor engagement, and infrastructure. That year, Nan Goldin made a powerful statement by publicly declaring that she would refuse to organise or participate in an exhibition at the NPG if it accepted the Sackler donation. Her statement, coupled with her high-profile protests and relentless campaign against institutions associated with the Sackler name, placed pressure on the gallery's leadership to re-evaluate its funding decisions. Goldin's activism not only galvanised public opinion but also placed the ethical considerations of accepting 'tainted money' at the centre of the gallery's decision-making process (Marshall, 2019).

The controversy surrounding the Sackler name, long associated with prestigious philanthropic efforts, brought the NPG's decision-making process under intense scrutiny. For many critics, accepting the donation would undermine the gallery's mission and values, potentially alienating its audience and stakeholders. Goldin's personal opposition added weight to these concerns, with her pledge to boycott the gallery influencing public and internal discussions. The proposed donation thus became a focal point for broader debates about the role of ethics in arts funding and the responsibilities of cultural institutions.

The Decision-Making Process

The NPG's leadership faced a complex and highly visible decision-making process. Ultimately, the NPG and the Sackler Trust announced that they would not proceed with the donation. The joint statement of the NPG and the Sackler Trust stated: '*It has become evident that recent reporting of allegations made against Sackler family members may cause this new donation to deflect the National Portrait Gallery from its important work. The allegations against family members are vigorously denied, but to avoid being a distraction for the NPG, we have decided not to proceed at this time with the donation*' (Sackler Trust & NPG, n.d.). The Trust withdrew its pledge in March 2019. The decision not to proceed with the donation was jointly agreed by the NPG and the Trust.

Central to the NPG's deliberations was its Grants and Donations Policy, which guides the gallery's approach to philanthropic contributions. At the time of the Sackler discussions, the policy lacked explicit provisions addressing donor reputations or the ethical implications of funding sources, focusing instead on operational considerations such as naming rights and donor influence. This gap revealed the challenges institutions face in navigating increasingly complex funding environments.

Beyond the internal governance processes, the NPG's decision must also be understood in the broader context of stakeholder accountability. Although the NPG's Grants and Donations Policy at the time lacked explicit ethical guidelines, the institution was probably aware of the potential negative consequences its actions could have on its relationships with a wider network of stakeholders, including artists, audiences, public funders, advocacy groups, peer institutions, and the general public. In this sense, the NPG's decision can be seen as part of what FitzGibbon (2021) describes as the 'plate-spinning' act of accountability, whereby managers of arts organisations are required to constantly balance competing artistic, economic, and social responsibilities in response to the often-conflicting demands of diverse stakeholders.

The controversy surrounding the Sackler donation highlighted precisely this complexity. The NPG faced not only financial considerations but also reputational risks, ethical dilemmas, and pressure from both activist groups and its own artistic community. Accepting the donation could have alienated key stakeholders and undermining public trust and its relationships with future donors, artists, and audiences. A similar situation occurred at the Science Museum in London, which faced backlash from a group of prominent scientists, its key community, over its corporate sponsorship by Shell (Prokůpek, 2024b).

Moreover, the NPG's decision reflects what FitzGibbon (2021) calls the need for more flexible and nuanced approaches to accountability in the arts sector, ones that recognise the interdependence of stakeholder relationships and the ethical tensions inherent in philanthropic governance. By jointly agreeing with the Sackler Trust to decline the donation, the NPG not only responded to external pressures but also exercised an implicit, relational form of accountability, acknowledging that the acceptance of contested funding could damage the fragile ecosystem of trust and legitimacy on which it depends.

7 Implications for Arts Funding and Donation Policies

Short- and Long-Term Impacts on the NPG

In the short term, the NPG's end of the partnership with the Sackler posed financial challenges, as for the gallery, philanthropic contributions to support exhibitions, education programmes, and operational costs are an important source of income. Declining the £1.3 million donation could have necessitated finding alternative funding sources or scaling back initiatives. Additionally, the decision may have temporarily disrupted relationships with other potential donors wary of similar scrutiny.

However, the long-term benefits of the decision are significant. By prioritising ethical considerations, the NPG positioned itself as a leader in socially responsible fundraising, fostering trust and goodwill among patrons, visitors, and the broader public. This stance not only reinforced the gallery's commitment to its mission but also set a precedent for other institutions grappling with similar dilemmas. The decision encouraged a broader movement within the cultural sector to adopt stricter donation policies and align financial practices with institutional values and public trust.

Broader Implications for Arts Philanthropy

The NPG's decision to decline a £1.3 million donation from the Sackler Trust in 2019 marked a turning point in the cultural sector, as ethical concerns over philanthropy are receiving heightened scrutiny. This move set a precedent, prompting institutions like the Louvre Museum and the Guggenheim Museums to sever ties with the Sackler family due to their connection to the opioid crisis.

Beyond individual donors, institutions are also reconsidering corporate sponsorships. Tate Gallery and the Van Gogh Museum in Amsterdam have cut ties with fossil fuel companies, while the British Museum and Science Museum continue to face pressure to do the same. These shifts reflect a growing demand for transparency, ethical accountability, and alignment between funding sources and institutional missions.

Recognising this, the cultural sector has paid more attention to ethical funding principles. In March 2022, the ICOM expanded its Code of Ethics to include fundraising standards, emphasising that museums must establish clear policies on the legal and ethical aspects of donations, with governance bodies actively involved in their approval (ICOM, 2022).

To navigate these complexities, institutions are adopting structured frameworks for donation acceptance. These may include ethical review committees to assess donor alignment, stakeholder engagement models to incorporate community perspectives, transparent donor screening and disclosure policies, and funding diversification strategies to reduce reliance on controversial sources.

8 Conclusion

The case of the NPG is emblematic of a broader shift in arts philanthropy, one that grapples with ethical responsibility, donor scrutiny, and financial sustainability. However, beyond reputational concerns for arts institutions, the ethical dilemmas surrounding tainted philanthropy have profound consequences for marginalised communities that bear the brunt of the harms caused by certain donors. In the case of the Sacklers, the opioid crisis disproportionately affected low-income, rural, and minority communities, exacerbating systemic health and economic inequalities. Accepting funds from such donors raises critical ethical questions: Should institutions built on public trust and cultural heritage legitimise wealth derived from societal harm? And how can they ensure that their fundraising practices do not further disenfranchise the very communities most affected by these crises.

A social justice-oriented approach to philanthropy would demand that institutions consider not only the sources of their funding but also the redistribution of these resources in ways that acknowledge harm and foster equity. Ethically responsible philanthropy should prioritise initiatives that directly benefit the communities most impacted by corporate wrongdoing. In this context, cultural institutions should go beyond symbolic disassociation from controversial donors and actively engage in reparative justice efforts, such as directing resources toward addiction recovery programmes, community-led arts initiatives, and equitable access to cultural education.

To navigate the complexities of ethical philanthropy, different stakeholders, such as arts institutions, donors, policymakers, and activists, must take concerted actions to ensure funding aligns with principles of accountability and social equity. Arts institutions must implement robust donor ethics policies that go beyond reputational risk management. This includes adopting transparent screening processes, stakeholder consultation mechanisms, and ethical review committees to assess the alignment of funding sources with institutional values. Institutions should also actively engage in community-centred philanthropy, ensuring that funds contribute to reparative efforts for historically marginalised groups.

Funders should acknowledge the ethical responsibilities tied to their wealth. Instead of using cultural philanthropy as a means of reputational laundering, they should shift toward impact-driven giving, directing resources toward social programmes, addiction recovery efforts, and equitable arts funding that uplifts underrepresented communities.

Organisations such as the ICOM and policymakers must continue expanding and enforcing ethical fundraising standards. Policymakers should provide guidelines on donor transparency while ensuring that public funding mechanisms remain viable alternatives to ethically fraught private sponsorships.

Advocacy groups like P.A.I.N. have demonstrated the power of grassroots movements in holding institutions accountable. Continued public pressure is essential in pushing for long-term structural reforms in how arts organisations approach philanthropy. Furthermore, audience engagement through ethical consumer choices, such as supporting institutions that prioritise socially responsible fundraising, can reinforce these efforts.

The evolving debate over ethical philanthropy in the arts highlights a crucial turning point: financial necessity can no longer be used to justify complicity with harmful donors. Institutions must recognise that ethical funding is not just about avoiding controversy, it is about aligning cultural stewardship with broader societal responsibilities. By adopting transparent, inclusive, and justice-driven fundraising policies, the arts sector can lead by example, fostering a philanthropic landscape that prioritises equity, accountability, and long-term societal well-being. Cultural institutions must serve as platforms for ethical engagement, ensuring that the funding they accept does not perpetuate cycles of inequality but rather contributes to a more just and inclusive future.

Notes

1. The Tate Gallery and BP sponsorship controversy highlights transparency issues in arts funding. Their 26-year partnership faced criticism over ethical accountability, environmental concerns, and financial opacity. A key issue was Tate's reluctance to disclose BP's

funding amount, despite persistent demands from activist groups. In 2015, a Freedom of Information Act (FOIA) request forced Tate to reveal that BP's contributions ranged from £150,000 to £330,000 annually—just 0.2% of Tate's budget, far less than expected. Activists argued that Tate's secrecy aimed to obscure the partnership's modest financial benefit compared to its reputational damage (Khomami, 2016).

2. A notable example of this risk occurred at the Science Museum in London, which faced intense criticism over its sponsorship agreements with fossil fuel companies. In 2015, leaked emails revealed that Shell, one of the museum's corporate sponsors, had attempted to exert influence over the content of Atmosphere, an exhibition on climate science. The revelations sparked significant controversy, prompting a group of 30 prominent scientists to argue that partnerships with companies like Shell, BP, and Equinor compromised the museum's credibility as a scientific institution. Such controversies can have lasting consequences, eroding public trust, damaging institutional reputations, and diminishing confidence among professionals and peers (Prokůpek, 2024b).
3. A partnership that sparked reaction from environmental activist is The Van Gogh Museum in Amsterdam that maintained an 18-year sponsorship partnership with Royal Dutch Shell, focusing on funding technical research into Vincent van Gogh's later works. This collaboration became increasingly controversial due to growing public scrutiny over the ethical implications of cultural institutions accepting funding from fossil fuel companies. Activist groups, notably Fossil Free Culture NL, organised protests and performance art demonstrations to highlight concerns about 'artwashing', where corporations use cultural sponsorships to improve their public image despite environmentally harmful practices. In response to mounting pressure, the Van Gogh Museum decided in 2018 not to renew its sponsorship deal with Shell, signalling a shift towards more ethically conscious funding decisions in the arts sector (Prokůpek & Gombault, 2024).
4. An example of this issue occurred in 1999 when the Brooklyn Museum of Art hosted the exhibition Sensation: Young British Art from the Saatchi Collection. Originally presented at the Royal Academy of Arts in London in 1997, the exhibition featured works owned by Charles Saatchi, who was later revealed to be a major

financial sponsor of the show. Initially, the museum attempted to conceal this critical detail, which only intensified the controversy. Furthermore, a subsequent information leak exposed that Saatchi had also played a role in curating the exhibition, raising further ethical concerns (Prokůpek, 2024b).

References

Addis, M., & Rurale, A. (2024). Advancing arts philanthropy practices for well-being. *Journal of Philanthropy and Marketing, 29*(1).

Alexander, V. D. (2018). Enterprise culture and the arts: Neoliberal values and British art institutions. In V. D. Alexander, S. Hägg, S. Häyrynen, & E. Sevänen (Eds.), *Art and the challenge of markets* (Vol. 1, pp. 3–39). Palgrave Macmillan.

Alexander, V. D. (2019). Cultural policy effects on the marketing orientation in London art museums. In V. K. M. Ekström (Ed.), *Museum marketization* (pp. 81–97). Routledge.

American Alliance of Museums. (2020). *Trends watch: The future of financial sustainability*.

Ashton, D. (2023). Funding arts and culture: Everyday experiences and organisational portfolio precarity. *European Journal of Cultural Studies, 26*(3), 388–407.

Banks, M. (2020). The work of culture and C-19. *European Journal of Cultural Studies, 23*(4), 648–654.

Bekkers, R., & Wiepking, P. (2011). A literature review of empirical studies of philanthropy: Eight mechanisms that drive charitable giving. *Nonprofit and Voluntary Sector Quarterly, 40*(5), 924–973.

Bertacchini, E., Santagata, W., & Signorello, G. (2011). Individual giving to support cultural heritage. *International Journal of Arts Management, 13*(3), 41–55.

Bhati, A., & Hansen, R. (2020). A literature review of experimental studies in fundraising. *Journal of Behavioral Public Administration, 3*(1).

Borgonovi, F. (2006). Do public grants to American theatres crowd-out private donations? *Public Choice, 126*(3), 429–451.

Brooks, A. C. (1999). Do public subsidies leverage private philanthropy for the arts? Empirical evidence on symphony orchestras. *Nonprofit and Voluntary Sector Quarterly, 28*(1), 32–45.

Cobb, N. K. (2002). The new philanthropy: Its impact on funding arts and culture. *The Journal of Arts Management, Law, and Society, 32*(2), 125–143.

Donelli, C. C., Mozzoni, I., Badia, F., & Fanelli, S. (2022). Financing Sustainability in the Arts Sector: The Case of the Art Bonus Public Crowdfunding Campaign in Italy. *Sustainability, 14*(3), 1641.

Donelli, C. C., Rentschler, R., Fanelli, S., et al. (2023). Philanthropy patterns in major Australian performing arts organizations. *Journal of Management and Governance, 27*, 1367–1396. https://doi.org/10.1007/s10997-022-09657-2

Dunn, P. (2010, March 21). When a donor becomes tainted. *Nonprofit Quarterly*. https://nonprofitquarterly.org/2010/03/21/when-a-donor-becomes-tainted

FitzGibbon, A. (2021). Non-profit theatre managers as multi-stakeholder managers: The plate-spinning of accountability. *Financial Accountability & Management, 37*(4), 440–459.

Gardner, J. B. (2012). Ethical, entrepreneurial or inappropriate? Business practices in museums. In V. V. J. Marstine (Ed.), *The Routledge companion to museum ethics: Redefining ethics for the twenty-first-century museum* (pp. 304–316). Routledge.

Harvey, C., Gordon, J., & Maclean, M. (2021). The ethics of entrepreneurial philanthropy. *Journal of Business Ethics, 171*, 33–49.

Heilbrun, J., & Gray, C. M. (2004). *The economics of arts and culture: An American perspective* (2nd ed.). Cambridge University Press.

International Council of Museums (ICOM). (2022). *Standards on Fundraising of the International Council of Museums*. ICOM.

Jensen, C. (2019). The perfect pair or strange bedfellows? Neoliberal social change and social justice philanthropy. *Administrative Theory & Praxis, 41*(4), 368–387.

Jobey, L. (2019, November 8). Nan Goldin on art, addiction and her battle with the Sacklers over opioids. Financial Times. https://www.ft.com/content/d6500c16-002a-11ea-b7bc-f3fa4e77dd47

Katz, S. N. (2006). Philanthropy. In V. A. Ginsburgh & D. Throsby (Eds.), *Handbook of the economics of art and culture* (Vol. 1, pp. 1299–1321). Princeton University.

Kelly, K. S. (1998). Effective fund-raising management. Lawrence ErbaumAssociates

Kendall Adams, G. (2022, February 11). Tate becomes latest institution to drop Sackler name. Museum Journal. https://www.museumsassociation.org/museums-journal/news/2022/02/tate-becomes-latest-institution-to-drop-sackler-name/#

Khomami, N. (2016, March 11). BP to end Tate sponsorship after 26 years. *The Guardian*. https://www.theguardian.com/artanddesign/2016/mar/11/bp-to-end-tate-sponsorship-climate-protests

Lindahl, W. E., & Conley, A. T. (2002). Literature Review: Philanthropic Fundraising. *Nonprofit Management and Leadership, 13*(1), 91–112.

Lindqvist, K. (2012). Museum finances: Challenges beyond economic crises. *Museum Management and Curatorship, 27*(1), 1–15.

Marshall, A. (2019, July 17). Louvre removes Sackler family name from its walls. *The New York Times*. https://www.nytimes.com/2019/07/17/arts/design/sackler-family-louvre.html

MacQuillin, I. R., & Sargeant, A. (2019). Fundraising ethics: A rights-balancing approach. *Journal of Business Ethics, 160*(1), 239–250. https://doi.org/10.1007/s10551-018-3872-8

MacQuillin, I. (2023). Normative fundraising ethics: A review of the field. *Journal of Philanthropy and Marketing*, *28*(4),

Michon, R., & Tandon, A. (2012). Emerging philanthropy markets. *International Journal of Nonprofit and Voluntary Sector Marketing, 17*(4), 352–362.

Moir, L., & Taffler, R. (2004). Does corporate philanthropy exist? business giving to the arts in the UK. *Journal of Business Ethics, 54*, 149–161.

Moraes, C., Daskalopoulou, A., & Szmigin, I. (2020). Understanding individual voluntary giving as a practice: Implications for regional arts organisations in the UK. *Sociology, 54*(1), 70–88.

Mulcahy, K. V. (1998). Cultural Patronage in Comparative Perspective: Public Support for the Arts in France, Germany, Norway, and Canada. *The Journal of Arts Management Law and Society, 27*(4), 247–263.

National Portrait Gallery (NPG). (n.d.). *About us*. https://www.npg.org.uk/about/

National Portrait Gallery (NPG). (2023). *Annual report*. https://assets.publishing.service.gov.uk/media/66b25676ce1fd0da7b5933f4/The_National_Portrait_Gallery_Annual_Report_and_Accounts_2023_to_2024.pdf

Pauget, B., Tobelem, J. M., & Bootz, J. P. (2021). The future of French museums in 2030. *Technological Forecasting and Social Change, 162*, Article 120384.

Pharoah, C. (2010). Challenges for tax policy towards individual charitable giving: The experience of recent attempts to 'reform' the UK gift aid scheme. *Voluntary Sector Review, 1*(2), 259–267.

Prokůpek, M., Loots, E., & Betzler, D. (2023). Emergency or emerging financing strategies of art museums in the context of a pandemic? *Museum Management and Curatorship, 38*(5), 530–547.

Prokůpek, M., & Divíšková, B. (2023). Ethics in museum fundraising: Evidence from the Czech Republic. *The Journal of Arts Management, Law, and Society, 53*(1), 42–61.

Prokůpek, M., & Gombault, A. (2024). Museums and corporate partners: The case of Van Gogh Museum and Shell. *International Journal of Arts Management*, *27*(1).

Prokůpek, M. (2024a). Legal and ethical considerations. In Y. Jung, R. Shane, & J. Wells (Eds.), *Financial management in museums* (pp. 165–178). Routledge.

Prokůpek, M. (2024b). Ethical fundraising in museums. In D. Babic (Ed.), *International Perspectives on Museum Management* (pp. 184–197). Routledge.

Puntenney, D., & Ruesga, G. A. (2010). Social Justice Philanthropy Traditions. *DePaul University Publications*. https://resources.depaul.edu/abcd-institute/publications/Documents/PuntenneyRuesgaSocialJusticePhilanthropy.pdf

Quinn, B. (2022, January 9). Sackler Trust gave more than £14m to UK public bodies in 2020. *The Guardian*. https://www.theguardian.com/society/2022/jan/09/sackler-trust-gave-more-than-14m-to-uk-public-bodies-in-2020

Sackler Trust & National Portrait Gallery. (n.d.). *The Sackler Trust and the National Portrait Gallery have jointly agreed not to proceed at this time*. https://www.npg.org.uk/assets/files/pdf/press/2019/sackler_statement_final.pdf

Selma, M. B., Yan, W., & Hafsi, T. (2020). Board demographic diversity, institutional context and corporate philanthropic giving. *Journal of Management and Governance, 55*(8), 1–29.

Seltzer, R. (2019, December 6). *Tufts strikes sackler name from campus*. https://www.insidehighered.com/news/2019/12/06/tufts-will-remove-sackler-name-medical-campus-drawing-rebuke-purdue-pharmas-owners

Seymour, T. (2023, May 17). *After close ties revealed, University of Oxford drops Sackler name from museum and libraries—but keeps the money*. https://www.theartnewspaper.com/2023/05/17/after-close-ties-revealed-university-of-oxford-drops-sackler-name-from-museum-and-librariesbut-keeps-the-money

Shekhtman, L. M., & Barabási, A. L. (2023). Philanthropy in art: Locality, donor retention, and prestige. *Science and Reports, 13*, 12157.

Suárez, D. F. (2012). Grant making as advocacy: The emergence of social justice philanthropy. *Nonprofit Management and Leadership, 22*(3), 259–280.

Toepler, S., & Dewees, S. (2005). Are there limits to financing culture through the market? Evidence from the US Museum Field. *International Journal of Public Administration, 28*(1–2), 131–146. https://doi.org/10.1081/PAD-200044548

UK Department for Digital, Culture, Media & Sport. (2023). *Total income of DCMS-funded cultural organisations 2022/23*. https://www.gov.uk/government/statistics/total-income-of-dcms-funded-cultural-organisations-20222023/total-income-of-dcms-funded-cultural-organisations-202223-headline-release

Upchurch, A. R. (2016). *The origins of the Arts Council movement: Philanthropy and policy*. Springer.

Warren, K., & Rogers, T. N. (2020, March 23). The family behind OxyContin pocketed $10.7 billion from Purdue Pharma. Meet the Sacklers, who built their $13 billion fortune off the controversial opioid. *Business Insider*. https://www.businessinsider.com/who-are-the-sacklers-wealth-philanthropy-oxycontin-photos-2019-1

Webb, E. (2004). An examination of socially responsible firms' board structure. *Journal of Management and Governance, 8*(3), 255–277.

Open Access This chapter is licensed under the terms of the Creative Commons Attribution 4.0 International License (http://creativecommons.org/licenses/by/4.0/), which permits use, sharing, adaptation, distribution and reproduction in any medium or format, as long as you give appropriate credit to the original author(s) and the source, provide a link to the Creative Commons license and indicate if changes were made.

The images or other third party material in this chapter are included in the chapter's Creative Commons license, unless indicated otherwise in a credit line to the material. If material is not included in the chapter's Creative Commons license and your intended use is not permitted by statutory regulation or exceeds the permitted use, you will need to obtain permission directly from the copyright holder.

CHAPTER 16

Securing Funding for Independent Creative Firms: Insights from Video Game Monetisation

Manel González-Piñero and Anders Rykkja

1 Introduction

In recent decades, the rise of digital platforms has reshaped the mechanisms by which individual creators and independent firms interact with audiences and secure revenue for their works. These variegated forms of capturing revenue by creators[1] are in the literature on platforms and the digital creative economy conceptualised as monetisation (Poell et al., 2021).

There seems to be a consensus that 'monetisation', in the context of digital goods and services, refers to making money from apps (Salter, 2022) or indicates the phase of the cultural production cycle (cf.

M. González-Piñero (✉)
Universitat de Barcelona, Barcelona, Spain
e-mail: manel.gonzalez@ub.edu

A. Rykkja
Queen's University Belfast, Belfast, Northern Ireland
e-mail: a.rykkja@qub.ac.uk

© The Author(s) 2026

C. Dalla Chiesa and A. Rykkja (eds.), *Cultural Funding and Financing*, Cultural Economics & the Creative Economy,
https://doi.org/10.1007/978-3-031-96696-5_16

UNESCO, 2009) when content and creative works are commercially exploited through their dissemination to and consumption by audiences and consumers (Poell et al., 2021).

To understand processes of monetising and capturing revenue from online content, it is important to understand the different roles that platforms may have in the process. In some cases, platforms act as intermediaries by defining the parameters for possible choices and strategies. For example, some platforms, like the Apple App Store, limit creators to a choice between five different monetisation options: paid (a one-time payment), free (revenue from advertising), freemium (optional in-app purchases), subscription (recurring revenues), and 'paymium' (a hybrid of paid and freemium models) (Poell et al., 2021, p. 47). Other platforms define a set of rules for how users can contribute. These include the adoption of microdonations (e.g. Twitch) or recurring subscriptions (e.g. Patreon). For certain types of digital platforms, such as social media like Instagram, Facebook, or TikTok, their main value is the way in which they direct followers of creators on these platforms towards other sites or apps that monetise content (Dalla Chiesa & Rykkja, 2024).

These examples illustrate differences between platform internal and external forms of monetisation or revenue capture (Gaenssle, 2024). Internal revenue generation is monetisation that happens on or within the platform. The most common forms are purchases of a material good, access and subscription fees, advertising revenues, and micropayments (Ballon, 2009; Nieborg & Poell, 2018). External models enable the indirect monetisation of content by directing users to other platforms that sell tickets, merchandise, and ancillary products. The creator may also earn commissions on sales by promoting affiliate links or codes for products and services offered by third parties. Finally, external monetisation may result from cross-platform initiatives premised on co-creating or co-producing content with followers, which in some cases involves the use of crowdfunding (Dalla Chiesa & Rykkja, 2024) or crowdpatronage (Swords, 2017) whereby content is monetised through recurring subscription fees (Bonifacio et al., 2021).

To summarise, monetisation can be defined as a set of options for commercially exploiting content via platforms, which vary according to the type and infrastructure of these platforms and the strategies creators adopt to combine them to maximise revenue capture (Cunningham & Craig, 2019; Lobato, 2016; Nieborg & Poell, 2018). In other words, context matters when analysing monetisation. Different types of creators—such as influencers, musicians, fiction or non-fiction writers—will use different platforms and revenue capture models. For example, individual content creators may use Instagram or YouTube to generate internal revenue and direct followers to their Etsy or Patreon pages to secure external revenue from selling merchandise. Fiction writers, particularly those creating serialised fiction, for instance, may publish their work on Wattpad or similar platforms, where monetisation can occur via paid stories, advertising, or brand partnerships. Other factors to consider include whether the creator is an organisation or an individual and the type of content being monetised. The considerations mean that actual models will be characterised by hybridisation, where creators set up and manage proprietary assemblages that incorporate different platform-internal and external streams of income.

The focus of the chapter will be the monetisation strategies of independent video game development studios. This means that instead of focusing on how individual creators, as 'fans' (Cunningham et al., 2016) or influencers (Gaenssle, 2024), make a living from creating and distributing content via platforms, we will concentrate on how a specific type of organisation—the independent studio for video game development—uses online platforms to generate revenue from the games they have created as way to fund and sustain ongoing operation of the venture.

Being *independent* in the context of game development refers to producer organisations developing alternative models of creating, producing and distributing content through a direct relationship with potential end-users without any creative and financial interference from major corporations (Bowen et al., 2009). Independent game studios often stand out as experimental laboratories for innovative revenue capture strategies. In this context, innovation refers to the diversification and strategic combination of monetisation models, including internal options (e.g., in-game microtransactions, loot boxes, subscription or membership fees, and advertising revenues; Goh et al., 2023; González-Piñero, 2017; Ivanov et al., 2021) and external ones (e.g., crowdfunding, as discussed in Planells, 2017, or merchandise sales; Chang & Liu, 2025). Not all studios adopt this approach. As the case studies will show, some rely on more limited models, which allows for a critical reflection on when and how diversification contributes to innovation in practice.

To provide insights into how these combinations may look in practice, our chapter proposes a case study on the monetisation of independent game development based on the experiences of two Spanish (Catalan and Valencian) independent video game studios: Open House Games and Chibig Studio. The case analyses seek to contribute to the ongoing discourse on sustainable monetisation in cultural and creative industries (CCIs), raising critical questions about the viability of current funding models and their impact on the creative process. In this context, the notion of independence is not only defined by the absence of corporate ownership but also by a desire to maintain creative autonomy in decision-making. While external financing—such as venture capital or equity investment—can offer growth opportunities, it often entails trade-offs that may limit the freedom to pursue original or experimental content. Our question, therefore, is: 'How do independent creative studios leverage innovative monetisation strategies to sustain their operations while preserving their autonomy as creators'?

The remainder of the chapter is structured as follows. The next section introduces the methods, analysis techniques, and empirical data, alongside limitations of the study. Section 3 presents the findings of our case analysis while we return to a discussion of the theoretical and practical implications alongside possibilities for future research in the conclusion.

2 Methods and Data

Research Design and Selection of Cases

This study adopts a qualitative case study methodology to explore the monetisation strategies employed by two independent video game studios: Open House Games and Chibig Studio.

It has thus been designed as a single case study on monetisation strategies with the two firms serving as embedded units of analysis (Yin, 2018). By examining the particularities of these studios, this research aims to shed light on broader dynamics within the CCIs. Both embedded cases have been purposively sampled and represent relevant examples of successful monetisation strategies of independent creative organisations as content creators.

Open House Games and Chibig Studio provide fertile ground for this analysis. Open House Games, founded in Barcelona, has pursued a hybrid approach, combining traditional sales with strategic partnerships and limited crowdfunding initiatives. Its focus on narrative depth and artistic experimentation aligns with a broader trend in independent gaming, where storytelling becomes a vehicle for both artistic expression and market segmentation. The studio's flagship title has been lauded for its innovative gameplay mechanics and immersive world-building, yet its development journey highlights the financial hurdles that small studios often face (Goh et al., 2023).

Chibig Studio, by contrast, is known for its whimsical, community-driven games that the studio co-produces and creates with the input of a loyal fan base that actively participates in its creative process. While not originally founded through crowdfunding, Chibig has progressively adopted a monetisation strategy that relies significantly on platform-external sources. In particular, the studio has used crowdfunding in combination with community-building through platforms like Discord and the sale of game-related merchandise. As of 2025, Chibig has launched at least two major projects via Kickstarter, including *Summer in Mara* and *Koa and the Five Pirates of Mara*, which serve as key examples of this strategy. Each of these campaigns was carefully designed not only to secure the necessary funds for development but also to foster a sense of emotional investment and ownership among backers. This approach reflects broader trends in the European indie game industry, where crowdfunding has become an increasingly viable tool for financing and marketing (e.g., Betzler & Leuschen, 2021, on Switzerland; Planells, 2017).

Data Collection and Analysis

Data were collected through two primary methods: qualitative interviews with representatives of Open House Games and Chibig Studio and a review of documents. The interviews were central to the study, providing detailed insights into the monetisation strategies and community engagement practices employed by the studios. This phase involved examining industry reports, policy documents, and secondary data from market research firms and the presence of the two organisations on platforms that offer possibilities for platform internal (e.g., Discord) or external (e.g., Kickstarter) monetisation options in accordance with Gaenssle's (2024) taxonomy.

The objective of the document analysis was to provide a description of the broader ecosystem in which Open House Games and Chibig Studio operate, focusing on the country- and industry-specific factors that influence their monetisation strategies. Both studios are based in Spain, a country with a growing indie game development scene, as reported in the

Spanish Video Game Industry Annual Report (DEV, 2023), supported by initiatives like PlayStation Talents. The analysis also considered the global trends in the video game industry, such as the rise of crowdfunding platforms (e.g., Kickstarter) and the increasing importance of community engagement. Documents such as industry reports, policy documents, and secondary data helped to contextualise the insights gathered from the interviews. Furthermore, the study highlighted the impact of technological advancements, such as Artificial Intelligence (AI) and blockchain, on monetisation strategies, as well as the challenges posed by market saturation and evolving player expectations. This contextual analysis provided a comprehensive understanding of the opportunities and constraints faced by independent studios in the current gaming landscape.

The document analysis played a key role in informing the subsequent semi-structured interviews, guiding the development of themes and questions that were explored in more detail with key representatives from each of the studios. The interview with the Open House Games CEO, Joan Francesc Bañó, provided insights into the studio's hybrid monetisation model and the challenges associated with balancing artistic ambition with financial sustainability. The interview with Chibig Studio's Public Relations (PR) and Social Media Manager, Irina Moreno, focused on the studio's reliance on crowdfunding, the dynamics of community engagement, and their approach to managing audience expectations. In the write-up, we quote these interviews using in-text citations (i.e., Bañó for Open House Games and Moreno for Chibig Studio).

Each interview lasted approximately 1 hour and was conducted via videoconferencing. The semi-structured format allowed for flexibility, enabling the exploration of emergent themes while ensuring consistency in addressing core research questions. Interviews were recorded and transcribed for subsequent analysis.

We later analysed the data using thematic analysis, as described by Braun and Clarke (2006). This method involved identifying, analysing, and reporting patterns in the data. The analysis was iterative, with initial codes generated from interview transcripts and refined through constant comparison with literature and contextual data. Key themes included the role of crowdfunding in securing financial resources, the importance of community engagement in building player loyalty, and the tension between creative autonomy and financial sustainability. The analysis also highlighted the differences in monetisation strategies between Open House Games, which relies on publisher partnerships, and Chibig Studio, which emphasises crowdfunding and community-driven development. By triangulating data from multiple sources, including interviews and documents, the study ensured a robust and comprehensive understanding of the monetisation strategies employed by these independent studios.

Reliability and Validity

The research design of our study was chosen to help us describe and explain how independent creative firms can capture revenue through monetisation of their output to help fund and sustain an independent venture. This approach implies that our focus is the firm and not the individual level. In terms of findings and contributions, our focus is on understanding what the game developing studio does to monetise their production. Our analysis has little to say about how the efforts of individual video bloggers producing and monetising content for YouTube or streaming gameplay via Twitch support the monetisation efforts of our embedded case organisations. This is simply because none of the firms we analyse made exhaustive use of these strategies, so we are unable to describe or explain the potential or impact of adopting these strategies. A limitation of the study is therefore that our focus on the firm level means that findings and contributions are limited to transferable examples (Flyvbjerg, 2006) of possible ways independent game studios can deploy platform-external and internal monetisation strategies while saying little about what other stakeholders, e.g., individual gamers and content creators, do to monetise content based on the productions of these studios.

3 Case Studies

Open House Games

Background

Open House Games, founded in 2019 in Barcelona, exemplifies the adaptability required in today's indie gaming sector. The studio operates with a lean core team of four members—a model that emphasises agility and cost-efficiency. A dynamic network of freelancers and subcontractors supports this core team, bringing them in based on project needs. According to Bañó[2] (personal interview, October 7, 2024), the flexible structure not only allows Open House Games to allocate resources efficiently but also helps maintain the quality and creative vision of the overall artistic projects and ambitions of the studio. As Bañó (personal interview, October 7, 2024) explains, 'We try to keep a very lean core team and bring in freelancers or other studios based on project needs. This way, we can adapt quickly without growing too big too fast'.

Its debut title, A Tale of Paper, emerged as a standout project through the PlayStation Talents programme, which supports emerging studios by providing resources, mentorship, and visibility. Winning the PlayStation Talents award was a pivotal moment for the studio, as it secured a publishing deal with Digerati Games. This partnership enabled A Tale of Paper to expand its reach across major platforms, including PlayStation 5, Xbox, and Nintendo Switch, establishing Open House Games as a notable player in the indie scene.

Beyond its original IPs, Open House Games has diversified its portfolio by engaging in third-party projects. Notably, the studio has developed mobile games based on a Catalan animated series inspired by the works of Joan Miró. These projects showcase the studio's versatility and ability to adapt to different creative and market demands. This diversification strategy stabilises revenue streams and allows the studio to explore new genres and platforms, broadening its expertise and market presence.

In addition to its development work, Open House Games places a strong emphasis on innovation and collaboration within the gaming community. The studio regularly participates in industry events, such as the Game Developers Conference (GDC) and regional showcases, to stay updated on the latest trends and technologies. By fostering connections with gamers and industry stakeholders, Open House Games ensures it remains at the forefront of indie game development. This proactive approach has helped the studio navigate the challenges of a rapidly evolving market while continuing to deliver engaging and visually compelling games.

Challenges and Barriers

Financial stability is a persistent challenge for Open House Games. As Bañó (personal interview, October 7, 2024) points out, the tightening of investment streams, particularly post-pandemic, has increased competition for limited resources. For Open House Games, this often means making frequent adjustments to project scopes and timelines to align with the available funding. While the *work for hire* model provides a financial buffer, balancing client-driven projects with internal creative ambitions places significant strain on the small core team. This pressure can hinder innovation and reduce the studio's ability to deliver ambitious projects.

One of the most significant hurdles is achieving visibility in an over-saturated market Platforms like Steam, PlayStation, and Xbox collectively host thousands of new game releases each year, making it difficult for smaller titles to stand out. While publishers improve visibility, the lack of direct access to player data limits the studio's ability to foster long-term engagement and loyalty. As Bañó noted, relying on publishers limits the studio's control over how their games are positioned in the market, reducing their ability to engage directly with players. This disconnection hampers the studio's capacity to gather actionable insights, which are critical for fostering long-term player engagement and brand loyalty that translate into revenue capture and monetisation. As Bañó (personal interview, October 7, 2024) notes, 'The real problem is that we don't have direct access to our players. We can't build the kind of direct relationships that would allow us to better understand and engage our audience'.

Another barrier involves the fragmented nature of the indie development ecosystem. According to Bañó (personal interview, October 7, 2024), access to advanced development tools, robust infrastructure, and cross-disciplinary collaboration networks is often limited for smaller studios. For Open House Games, keeping up with these technological advancements while managing day-to-day operations requires a delicate balance. The studio's lean structure means that any effort to integrate new technologies can strain resources, slowing production timelines and complicating project management. The rapid evolution of game engines and AI-driven tools further intensifies this challenge. Moreover, as Bañó has emphasised, audience expectations are evolving rapidly. Players increasingly demand not only high-quality content but also alignment with emerging trends such as sustainability, diversity in storytelling, and ongoing post-launch support.

The studio's strategies to deal with these issues and attempt to stabilise monetisation are to expand into new genres and platforms and seek to better integrate player feedback dynamically. Open House Games does this by, on the one hand, leveraging their experience in narrative-driven games and, on the other, aligning with user expectations and market demands to maximise revenue and access to funding while preserving their creative identity.

Table 1 Overview of the monetisation strategies of open house games

Monetisation strategy	Name of platforms
Platform internal	Steam, PlayStation, Xbox, Epic Games, YouTube, BlueSky
Platform external	None

Monetisation Strategies

We detail the platforms in Open House Games use for monetisation, as suggested by Bañó (personal interview, October 7, 2024), in Table 1. The studio primarily relies on platform internal monetisation, with most of their revenue capture coming from premium game sales through their publishing partnerships with Digerati Games that provides essential support in marketing and distribution, helping the studio reach global audiences.

Moreover, the *work for hire* model provides consistent revenue, which is essential for sustaining operations in a volatile market. This approach aligns with broader industry trends, where studios balance client-driven projects with internal creative ventures to ensure financial sustainability (Betzler & Leuschen, 2021). As Bañó (personal interview, October 7, 2024) emphasised, diversifying income through work-for-hire projects and considering crowdfunding could ensure creative independence, it does not guarantee long-term financial sustainability on its own. Crowdfunding can provide a temporary boost in income, but true sustainability emerges from stabilising and growing demand coupled with ongoing community engagement and benefits. This balance would allow the studio to maintain their creative autonomy while securing the financial foundation necessary for long-term success.

Chibig

Background

Chibig Studio, founded in 2016 in Valencia, was born from the desire to create games that evoke a sense of adventure, emotional connection, and environmental awareness. Led by Abraham Cózar, the studio quickly established its identity within the cosy game niche by blending exploration, farming mechanics, and narrative depth.

A notable aspect of Chibig's approach is its commitment to creating a cohesive universe where every game enriches the overall lore. This strategic choice fosters a strong sense of continuity and encourages players to explore other titles within the universe and has proven to be a powerful tool for long-term engagement with players. As an example, the studio's first major release, *Deiland*, was conceived as a small project but started to gain traction through positive reception on platforms like Steam. The monetisation through Steam subsequently enabled partnerships with major distributors and an expansion of its universe through the follow-up title *Summer in Mara*, efficiently solidifying Chibig's reputation among players and industry stakeholders.

To support its ambitious projects, Chibig operates with a flexible structure. The core team collaborates with freelancers and external specialists across various disciplines, including animation, localisation, and sound design. This strategy allows the studio to access a diverse pool of talent while optimising costs. Additionally, Chibig has invested in developing strong ties with its fan community through platforms like Discord and Kickstarter, where they provide regular updates and invite players to contribute feedback, vote on design choices, and participate in beta testing. This open communication fosters a sense of co-creation, with players often suggesting features or improvements that are incorporated into the final product. Such involvement not only strengthens the bond between the studio and its fans but also ensures that the games evolve in ways that reflect the community's desires and expectations. As Irina Moreno,[3] PR and Social Media Manager at Chibig, emphasises, one of the key factors to their success is 'getting new people to trust the project and support it financially' (personal interview, October 7, 2025). This approach has become a cornerstone of their development philosophy, ensuring that their games resonate with their audience from concept to release.

Challenges and Barriers

Despite its successes, Chibig Studio faces several challenges that test its operational capacity and hence operational resilience.

A first challenge is financial stability. Chibig Studio has used crowdfunding as a primary source of funding for the development of new titles. However, while these campaigns provide an initial base of funding, this source of income does not represent sufficient funds to cover the full costs of production or guarantee consistent revenue throughout the game lifecycle. As a result, Chibig often needs to adjust its project timelines and scope to align with available resources, while also balancing the need to meet the expectations set during crowdfunding campaigns. This is particularly difficult when stretch goals are involved, as these can place additional pressure on the team, sometimes leading to delays or resource strain. As Irina Moreno, PR and Social Media Manager at Chibig, explains, after five crowdfunding projects, the studio has developed different strategies to secure the necessary funds for their games: 'What you have to do, somehow, is get new people to trust the project and support it financially' (personal interview, October 7, 2025).

The rapid growth of the studio's shared universe represents the second challenge. Ensuring narrative and thematic consistency across multiple titles requires meticulous planning and collaboration. This challenge is compounded as the studio explores new platforms and genres, which demand different design and narrative approaches.

Thirdly, Chibig is exploring opportunities in new markets, including mobile and Virtual Reality (VR) platforms such as Oculus Rift and PlayStation VR. These initiatives aim to diversify their portfolio and reach new demographics, ensuring sustained growth. According to Moreno (2024), this strategic diversification positions Chibig Studio as a pioneer in blending narrative depth with accessible and innovative gameplay that integrates immersive environments and interactivity. By leveraging the unique capabilities of VR, such as first-person perspectives and spatial interaction, Chibig creates experiences that allow players to engage with the story in a more dynamic and participatory manner, pushing the boundaries of traditional storytelling in games.

Monetisation Strategies

A key pillar of Chibig Studio's financial strategy is crowdfunding, which they have used effectively to fund multiple projects. Their campaigns for *Summer in Mara* and *Ankora: Lost Days* on Kickstarter not only raised over €250,000 but also laid the foundation for a loyal community. As Irina Moreno, PR and Social Media Manager at Chibig Studio, emphasised, 'Our Kickstarter backers are not just donors; they're part of the family. They support us because they believe in our vision' (personal interview, October 10, 2024). This community engagement goes beyond mere financial support; it fosters a sense of ownership among backers, who often become brand ambassadors, promoting the studio's games within their networks. As Moreno further noted, 'We see a direct impact from our backers sharing our updates and talking about our games to their own networks' (personal interview, October 10, 2024).

Table 2 Overview of the monetisation strategies of Chibig studio

Monetisation strategy	Name of platform
Platform Internal	Steam, Playstation, Nintendo, Epic Games, YouTube, Twitch, X, Instagram
Platform External	Kickstarter, Undigital Atelier

Crowdfunding also serves as a valuable marketing tool By generating excitement during the campaign phase, Chibig can build anticipation for their games well before release. According to Moreno (2024), these campaigns provide an essential platform for gathering early feedback, enabling the studio to refine their games in response to player suggestions. This feedback loop strengthens the bond between the studio and its community, leading to higher retention and repeat engagement.

Table 2 exhibits the monetisation strategies of Chibig. In addition to crowdfunding, monetisation and revenue capture happen through platform internal monetisation via Steam, Nintendo Switch, and PlayStation combined with platform external monetisation through crowdfunding (Kickstarter) and the sales of merchandise and physical game products via a partner site (Undigital Atelier).

Comparative Analysis

This section compares the revenue capture and monetisation strategies of Open House Games and Chibig Studio. While both studios operate within the indie game sector, their approaches to securing funding and engaging with their communities reveal distinct strategic priorities and challenges.

Crowdfunding as a Central or Supporting Tool

A key distinction between the two studios lies in their use of platform-based external strategies for monetisation, such as crowdfunding. For Chibig Studio, crowdfunding and the development of ancillary revenue streams from merchandise and physical products through platform external monetisation have become a central pillar of their business model This methodology enables them to finance multiple projects while building a loyal and engaged community. Their successful Kickstarter campaigns for *Summer in Mara* and *Ankora: Lost Days* have demonstrated how crowdfunding can simultaneously provide early financial backing, validate game concepts, and serve as a marketing tool, which fosters a sense of co-ownership among their backers.

In contrast, Open House Games views crowdfunding and platform external monetisation as potential avenues to explore. Their strategy relies heavily on partnerships with publishers like Digerati Games, which provide crucial support in marketing and distribution. While this model ensures stable income and broad platform reach, it limits direct engagement with their player base during the early stages of development. Open House's intentions to explore crowdfunding in the future could help bridge this gap by enhancing community involvement and diversifying revenue streams.

Community Engagement and Market Visibility

Community engagement plays a pivotal role in both studios' strategies, albeit with different emphases. Chibig Studio's crowdfunding campaigns serve as a platform for ongoing dialogue with their players, primarily during the active campaign period. This dialogue fosters a deep sense of community and involvement in the creative process among early supporters and backers. Although this form of engagement is often limited to pre-buyers or donors and may be temporary in nature, it plays a crucial role in generating early emotional investment and a sense of co-ownership. This participatory model strengthens player loyalty and provides valuable feedback that shapes game development.

Open House Games, on the other hand, relies more on external partnerships to reach wider audiences, which can dilute their direct interaction with players. However, their participation in programs like PlayStation Talent and industry events has helped them gain visibility and establish credibility within the gaming community. As they consider integrating crowdfunding into their strategy, they can enhance their community engagement, potentially improving player loyalty and long-term support.

Navigating Challenges and Future Directions

Both Open House Games and Chibig Studio face significant challenges in sustaining visibility and financial stability in an increasingly competitive market. However, their strategic responses highlight innovative approaches to monetisation and community engagement. Open House Games is exploring the integration of emerging technologies such as AI to streamline development processes, including procedural level generation and user testing. This aligns with the broader trend of leveraging AI to enhance creativity and efficiency in game development (Filipović, 2023). Additionally, the studio is considering the potential of blockchain technology[4] (Baber, 2020) to increase transparency in funding processes, particularly in crowdfunding campaigns.

Moreover, Open House Games could benefit from adopting network effect strategies (Liebowitz & Margolis, 1994) to enhance user engagement and efficiency in terms of monetisation and revenue capture. As highlighted in the attached article, network effects play a crucial role in two-sided markets (Evans & Schmalensee, 2016) where the value of the platform increases as more users join (Katz & Shapiro, 1985). By fostering a community-driven ecosystem where players can interact, share content, and collaborate on game development, Open House Games could amplify the positive network effects within its player base. This approach strengthens user loyalty and creates a self-sustaining cycle of engagement, as seen in successful platforms like online dating services and social networks (Voigt & Hinz, 2015).

Chibig Studio, on the other hand, is focusing on deepening its community engagement through innovative crowdfunding models. By involving players in the creative process and leveraging platform-external strategies through the combined use of Discord and Kickstarter, the studio is building a loyal fan base that actively participates in game development. This approach resonates with the concept of co-production (Gamble, 2018), where users become co-producers of value, as discussed by Poell et al. (2021). Furthermore, Chibig's exploration of new markets, such as mobile and VR platforms, reflects a commitment to diversifying its portfolio and reaching new demographics. These strategies not only enhance the studio's financial sustainability by expanding on the possibilities for revenue capture but also position it as a leader in narrative-driven indie games.

Chibig Studio could further enhance its monetisation strategies by leveraging platform internal strategies, for example, by combining freemium models and paymium. Recent research by Tyrväinen and Karjaluoto (2024) highlights that the willingness to pay for additional content in freemium games varies significantly depending on the perceived value of premium features and the user's engagement level. While Chibig's engaged user base may align with early adopters and high-value customers, as identified by Voigt and Hinz (2016), their specific monetisation strategy would benefit from these insights into how user engagement and network effects create opportunities for sustained retention. This suggests that, by leveraging the right retention strategies, Chibig can cater more effectively to its community's needs and enhance long-term player loyalty.

To end this section, both cases exhibit that a key to the financial success of these monetisation efforts is the entrepreneurial efforts of the studios in terms of using digitalisation tools to build creative and commercial projects with internal and external platform use. With a platform external strategy, they may try to reach new social networks, generate community benefits which potentially help in the *attention competition* (Lanham, 2006) propelled by digitalisation. With platform internal, firms can build actual monetisation of the product while consuming it. This is something that crowdfunding does not allow, for example, because of its platform-external way of raising funds before the product reaches the market. Elaborating on both strategies, can thus support entrepreneurs to harness the potential of (digital) monetisation in the CCIs.

4 Conclusion

This chapter has explored how independent video game studios navigate the evolving landscape of monetisation within the creative industries. Through the cases of Open House Games and Chibig Studio, we have addressed the guiding research question: How do independent creative studios leverage innovative monetisation strategies to sustain their operations while maintaining creative autonomy? The findings highlight the importance of emerging technologies, community-driven engagement, and adaptive monetisation models, such as freemium and blockchain-based transparency. These strategies not only enhance financial sustainability but also foster creative autonomy, offering a roadmap for other indie studios facing similar challenges.

Both case studies reveal the critical role of monetisation strategies in shaping the trajectory of independent studios. Open House Games exemplifies the standard model of seeking to maximise platform-internal revenue and monetisation through a strategic partnership with a publisher. In contrast, Chibig Studio operates within a fully integrated platform external model of monetisation where crowdfunding and ancillary revenue from merchandise help fund projects and foster community engagement. While this strategy enables greater financial independence, it also demands significant resources to manage audience expectations and deliver on promises.

A key finding across both cases is the importance of community engagement as a dual mechanism for efficient monetisation (Dalla Chiesa & Rykkja, 2024). However, this model introduces new challenges, including the risk of over-reliance on backers and the pressures of constant transparency and accountability. Moreover, the success of these strategies is deeply intertwined with the studios' ability to craft compelling narratives and maintain consistent communication, which serves to solidify trust and enhance brand loyalty.

From a theoretical perspective, this study contributes to the emerging research into platform internal and external strategies among independent video game development studios. It highlights the dynamic nature of monetisation strategies, emphasising their role as both enablers and constraints of creative production (González-Piñero, 2021) and developing proprietary combinations of strategic use of different types of platforms to succeed (Gaenssle, 2024). It also stresses the need for interdisciplinary efforts that bring research on platforms and monetisation video games (Goh et al., 2023) into a dialogue with the literature on cultural entrepreneurship (Hausmann & Heinze, 2016) and innovation ecosystems (Beaudry et al., 2022) as a way to do empirical study into how and in what way monetisation and revenue capture need to adapt to the unique needs of any creative enterprise. This is timely as cultural entrepreneurship post-digitalisation is widely focused on securing sustainable funding in attempts to reconcile the paradox of balancing a need for some form of creative independence with sustainable monetisation strategies (Loots, 2023).

For practitioners, this study offers several actionable insights. First, the success of both Open House Games and Chibig Studio underscores the importance of aligning monetisation strategies with the studio's creative and operational goals. Studios must critically assess their funding options, balancing short-term financial gains with long-term sustainability and creative autonomy. Second, the embedded cases highlight the value of building and nurturing a community of engaged supporters. For studios considering platform external monetisation options such as crowdfunding, it is essential to invest in transparent communication and continuous engagement with backers. Such collaboration not only secures financial support but also fosters a sense of co-ownership and loyalty, which can be leveraged for future projects. Lastly, the regional context plays a significant role in shaping the opportunities and constraints faced by independent studios. For instance, Barcelona's vibrant cultural ecosystem, coupled with supportive policies and access to talent, has been instrumental in fostering the growth of both case study studios. Policymakers and industry stakeholders should consider how to create and sustain such ecosystems while emphasising the importance of cultural funding and international collaboration.

While this study provides valuable insights into monetisation strategies within independent video game studios, several areas merit further exploration. One key recommendation is the diversification of monetisation models. Future research could examine the long-term sustainability of community-driven funding models. Crowdfunding campaigns often rely heavily on initial momentum and community enthusiasm, but a more diversified approach –incorporating a mix of crowdfunding, microtransactions, and subscription models- could offer studios a more resilient financial strategy over time. Moreover, the integration of emerging technologies, such as blockchain, could revolutionise transparency and accountability in monetisation processes and revenue capture. Blockchain enables immutable records of financial transactions, which could address some of the trust issues inherent in crowdfunding. For instance, studios could leverage smart contracts to ensure that backer funds are only released upon meeting specific milestones, thereby increasing confidence among supporters and fostering long-term community trust.

Another promising avenue involves comparative analyses across different cultural and regulatory contexts. While this chapter focuses on studios operating in Barcelona and Valencia, examining studios in regions with distinct funding landscapes—such as North America or Asia—could offer a more global perspective. A cross-cultural approach could reveal how government support, cultural attitudes toward crowdfunding, and local market conditions influence the viability and success of different monetisation strategies.

Lastly, interdisciplinary research involving fields like behavioural economics and digital marketing could provide further insights into optimising platform-based monetisation strategies. For example, understanding how consumer behaviour adjusts to different pricing models in games (e.g., microtransactions versus subscription services) could inform more effective revenue generation approaches.

In sum, the future of platform-based monetisation strategies will likely hinge on a blend of technological innovation, community-driven co-creation, and regional adaptability. Diversifying funding models, leveraging emerging technologies, and embracing a more global view of the regulatory and cultural landscape will be key for independent studios in staying competitive and sustainable in an evolving market. Addressing these areas can advance both academic understanding and practical implementation, ensuring that independent creative firms continue to thrive.

5 Competing Interests

The writing of this chapter was supported by a grant from the Research Council of Norway [301291].

Notes

1. In this chapter, we use the concept of a 'creator' as a portmanteau term to signify any individual artist and cultural entrepreneur or organisation that produces creative goods and services such as music, books, games, visual art, performances, blogs, vlogs, etc.
2. Joan Francesc Bañó, CEO at Open House Games, personal interview, October 7, 2024, Barcelona (in-person interview).
3. Irina Moreno, PR and Social Media Manager at Chibig, personal interview, October 10, 2024, conducted via Zoom.
4. It is beyond this chapter to discuss the integration of blockchain with crowdfunding. We refer those who are curious to learn more to Baber (2020). Baber points out that the biggest benefit of using blockchain technology in reward-based crowdfunding is that the money raised and kept in a bank can be swapped for tokens that represent ownership in the project, and these digital currencies can also be sold later as cryptographic shares. Blockchain thus increases security and confidence by providing transparency and removes the bank as a passive stakeholder in the transaction.

References

Baber, H. (2020). Blockchain-Based Crowdfunding. In R. Rosa Righi, A. Alberti & M. Singh (Eds.), *Blockchain Technology for Industry 4.0. Blockchain Technologies*. Springer.

Ballon, P. (2009). Control and Value in Mobile Communications: A Political Economy of the Reconfiguration of Business Models in the European Mobile Industry. Available at SSRN 1331439.

Beaudry, C., Burger-Helmchen, T., & Cohendet, P. (2022). Introduction: Innovation Policies and Practices Within Innovation Ecosystems. In *Innovation Policies and Practices Within Innovation Ecosystems* (pp. 1–9). Routledge.

Betzler, D., & Leuschen, L. (2021). Digitised Value Chains in the Creative Industries: Is There a Convergence of Swiss Film and Game Production? *Creative Industries Journal, 14*(3), 226–244.

Bonifacio, R., Hair, L., & Wohn, D. Y. (2021). Beyond Fans: The Relational Labor and Communication Practices of Creators on Patreon. *New Media & Society,* 14614448211027961.

Bowen, M., Martin, C. B., & Deuze, M. (2009). The New Gatekeepers: The Occupational Ideologies of Independent Video Game Producers. *New Media & Society, 11*(3), 295–318. https://doi.org/10.1177/146144480810 0203

Braun, V., & Clarke, V. (2006). Using Thematic Analysis in Psychology. *Qualitative Research in Psychology, 3*(2), 77–101.

Chang, T.-S., & Liu, W.-C. (2025). Decoding the Gamer's Code: A Dive into Game Merchandise Consumption Through the Lens of Consumer Culture Theory. *Asia Pacific Journal of Marketing and Logistics, 37*(1), 132–149.

Cunningham, S., Craig, D., & Silver, J. (2016). YouTube, Multichannel Networks and the Accelerated Evolution of the New Screen Ecology. *Convergence, 22*(4), 376–391.

Cunningham, S., & Craig, D. (2019). *Social Media Entertainment: The New Intersection of Hollywood and Silicon Valley*. NYU Press.

Dalla Chiesa, C., & Rykkja, A. (2024). Bridging the Urban-digital Divide: Crowdfunding as an Online Middleground Space. *City, Culture and Society, 37*(1), Article 100580.

DEV. (2023). Libro blanco del desarrollo español de videojuegos 2023. Asociación Española de Empresas Productoras y Desarrolladoras de Videojuegos y Software de Entretenimiento (DEV).

Evans, D. S., & Schmalensee, R. (2016). *Matchmakers: The New Economics of Multisided Platforms*. Harvard Business Review Press.

Filipović, A. (2023). The Role of Artificial Intelligence in Video Game Development. *Kultura Polisa, 20*(3), 50–67.

Flyvbjerg, B. (2006). Five Misunderstandings About Case-study Research. *Qualitative Inquiry, 12*(2), 219–245.

Gaenssle, S. (2024). Income Distribution and Nudity on Social Media: Attention Economics of Instagram Stars. *Kyklos, 77*(1), 184–212.

Gamble, J. R. (2018). With a Little Help from My Fans: The Transformative Role of the Consumer in Music Co-production. *Production Planning & Control, 29*(10), 826–844.

Goh, E., Al-Tabbaa, O., & Khan, Z. (2023). Unravelling the Complexity of the Video Game Industry: An Integrative Framework and Future Research Directions. *Telematics and Informatics Reports, 12*, Article 100100.

González-Piñero, M. (2017). Redefining the Value Chain of the Video Games Industry. *Memory, 36*(4), 75–90.

González-Piñero, M. (2021). La Innovación en la gestión de la cultura: reflexiones y experiencias. In L. Bonet & M. González-Piñero (Eds.), *La innovación en la gestión de la cultura: Reflexiones y experiencias*. Edicions de la Universitat de Barcelona.

Hausmann, A., & Heinze, A. (2016). Entrepreneurship in the Cultural and Creative Industries: Insights from an Emergent Field. *Artivate, 5*(2), 7–22.

Ivanov, M., Wittenzellner, H., & Wardaszko, M. (2021, 2021//). Video Game Monetization Mechanisms in Triple A (AAA) Video Games. Simulation Gaming Through Times and Disciplines.

Katz, M. L., & Shapiro, C. (1985). Network Externalities, Competition, and Compatibility. *The American Economic Review, 75*(3), 424–440.

Lanham, R. A. (2006). *The Economics of Attention: Style and Substance in the Age of Information*. University of Chicago Press.

Liebowitz, S. J., & Margolis, S. E. (1994). Network Externality: An Uncommon Tragedy. *Journal of Economic Perspectives, 8*(2), 133–150.

Lobato, R. (2016). The Cultural Logic of Digital Intermediaries: YouTube Multichannel Networks. *Convergence, 22*(4), 348–360.

Loots, E. (2023). Entrepreneurship Research in Cultural and Creative Industries: Identifying Key Ingredients of a 'Hodgepodge.' In I. Hill, S. R. S. T. A. Elias, S. Dobson, & P. Jones (Eds.), *Creative (and Cultural) Industry Entrepreneurship in the 21st Century* (pp. 17–30). Emerald Publishing Limited.

Nieborg, D. B., & Poell, T. (2018). The Platformization of Cultural Production: Theorizing the Contingent Cultural Commodity. *New Media & Society, 20*(11), 4275–4292.

Planells, A. J. (2017). Video Games and the Crowdfunding Ideology: From the Gamer-buyer to the Prosumer-investor. *Journal of Consumer Culture, 17*(3), 620–638.

Poell, T., Nieborg, D. B., & Duffy, B. E. (2021). *Platforms and Cultural Production*. Polity Press.

Salter, T. (2022). Monetization. In *Technological and Business Fundamentals for Mobile App Development* (pp. 133–157). Springer International Publishing.

Swords, J. (2017). Crowd-patronage-Intermediaries, Geographies and Relationships in Patronage Networks. *Poetics, 64*, 63–73.

Tyrväinen, O., & Karjaluoto, H. (2024). Willingness to Pay for Freemium Services: Addressing the Differences Between Monetization Strategies. *International Journal of Information Management, 77*, Article 102787.

UNESCO. (2009). *2009 UNESCO Framework for Cultural Statistics*. U. I. f. Statistics. https://www.uis.unesco.org/sites/default/files/documents/unesco-framework-for-cultural-statistics-2009-en_0.pdf

Voigt, S., & Hinz, O. (2015). Network Effects in Two-sided Markets: Why a 50/50 User Split is Not Necessarily Revenue Optimal. *Business Research, 8*(1), 139–170.

Voigt, S., & Hinz, O. (2016). Making Digital Freemium Business Models a Success: Predicting Customers' Lifetime Value via Initial Purchase Information. *Business & Information Systems Engineering, 58*(2), 107–118.

Yin, R. K. (2018). *Case Study Research and Applications* (6th ed.). Sage publications.

Open Access This chapter is licensed under the terms of the Creative Commons Attribution 4.0 International License (http://creativecommons.org/licenses/by/4.0/), which permits use, sharing, adaptation, distribution and reproduction in any medium or format, as long as you give appropriate credit to the original author(s) and the source, provide a link to the Creative Commons license and indicate if changes were made.

The images or other third party material in this chapter are included in the chapter's Creative Commons license, unless indicated otherwise in a credit line to the material. If material is not included in the chapter's Creative Commons license and your intended use is not permitted by statutory regulation or exceeds the permitted use, you will need to obtain permission directly from the copyright holder.

CHAPTER 17

(Co-)Creating from 'Nothing', (Co-) Producing Digitally: The Art of Funding Cultural Projects Through Bottom-Up Collaboration and Co-Creation

Alice Demattos Guimarães and Natalia Maehle

1 Introduction

Digitalization has enabled many communities to come together to share, create, produce, diffuse, and consume arts and culture. Virtual platforms serve as spaces of encounter, reinventing traditional formats of interaction in the art-culture circuits, where groups of people with similar interests and shared values collectively (and digitally) provide inputs for the benefit

A. D. Guimarães (✉) · N. Maehle
Western Norway University of Applied Sciences, Bergen, Norway
e-mail: alice.demattos.guimaraes@hvl.no

N. Maehle
e-mail: natalia.mehle@hvl.no

A. D. Guimarães
Department of Business, Humanities, and Law, Copenhagen Business School, Copenhagen, Denmark

© The Author(s) 2026

C. Dalla Chiesa and A. Rykkja (eds.), *Cultural Funding and Financing*, Cultural Economics & the Creative Economy,
https://doi.org/10.1007/978-3-031-96696-5_17

of the diverse projects. Community engagement enables the realization of projects or ventures based on the (co-)production of value(s) and efforts to turn a proposition into a reality. Regardless of whether they are managed by established cultural organizations or emerging artists, various cultural and socially engaged projects come to life because of the bonds and common beliefs between the individuals in the network behind them. In this sense, the current chapter aims to illustrate how to produce arts and culture starting with 'nothing' through crowdfunding and co-creation. As we show, the category of 'nothing' challenges the idea of the void in socio-economically disadvantaged communities since agents there often rely on rich social networks, friendships, and communal bonds. Bearing this in mind, we believe that exploring web-enabled collaborative models as a contemporary way to initiate artistic endeavours in a digital future is timely and can inform practitioners, academics, and policymakers. In particular, we aim to answer the following research question: Under what circumstances does digital funding allow or give room for co-creation?.

The empirical case chosen for this investigation lies at the intersection of a classical art form and social engagement, using a combination of alternative funding to support the continued existence of a unique artistic venture. Located in Brazil, in the city of Belo Horizonte (Minas Gerais State), the OVO—Formation and Transformation Orchestra[1] was created in 2019 with the purpose of giving dozens of young music students an orchestral experience of excellence. With an online centre to share knowledge, a work team focused on entrepreneurship in the musical scene, and concerts in a proper opera house, OVO has been extensively operating its funding and financing through a crowdfunding platform, Évoe. This platform, specifically dedicated to creative initiatives, allows both subscription and reward-based crowdfunding, besides having arrangements to enable tax income benefits. OVO adopts all the possible channels, expanding its performance as a non-profit association (Citizen Education Centre NEC), accompanying its growth amid professionalization and, thus, increasing operating costs. With a monthly income goal (subscription) combined with specific campaigns for concerts or socio-educational activities (reward), OVO has been successfully supporting its existence through the digital collaborative network.

By combining observatory participation, social media analysis, and in-depth interviews with the different OVO stakeholders, we investigate the resilience of collective finance from the perspectives of the project creators, project participants, backers, and the platform itself. OVO demonstrates lessons of resilience per se by employing a funding strategy concentrated in one single digital space and a high level of network coordination. The innovative practices of OVO boost the comprehension of the potential of co-production of and for artistic ventures filled with co-creation (of shared and diverse) values and diffusion, ultimately improving socioeconomic realities.

Next, we present our theoretical background on the digitally enabled cultural projects development departing from financing mechanism but in a broader-than-raising money perspective; rather a (digital) space for and of co-production and co-creation. Then, we describe our case study, OVO, followed by our methodological approach. To conclude, we illustrate the findings alongside a refined discussion and final remarks.

2 Theoretical Background: Exploring Co-Creation with Alternative Funding

The digital transformation has been deeply affecting production, distribution, consumption, and financing in the cultural-creative industries (CCIs). Digitalization has been redefining and reshaping old dynamics, and the emergence of digital platforms where creators can share, exchange, and co-create across geographical boundaries has boosted collaboration through unprecedented levels of connectedness. This so-called platformization also challenges the role of CCI's traditional intermediaries (Benghozi & Paris, 2016; Poell et al., 2021). Yet, there is a lack of both understanding and exploiting the digitally enabled collaborative practices from an academic discourse, an institutional/policymaking perspective, and a practical or managerial standpoint (Demattos et al., 2024; Loots et al., 2023). Especially in the field of digital finance, where crowdfunding is a great example, there is an unrealized and unpacked potential linked to aspects of co-production and co-creation (Dalla Chiesa, 2020; Rykkja & Hauge, 2021). Although we acknowledge the diversity of novel digital collaboration forms, our theoretical background focuses on co-production and co-creation frameworks within cultural-creative crowdfunding. The main reason for that is twofold: the everlasting financial struggles of the culture sector, with not only limited public budgets and austerity policies but also increasing competition for private donors and investors (Lazzaro & Noonan, 2021); and the pioneering role of artists in crowdfunding which also shares similarities with 'classical' arts practices of busking and patronage (Dalla Chiesa, 2020; Demattos, 2024; Rykkja, 2023).

Cultural-Creative Crowdfunding and the Potential for Co-Production and Co-Creation

In short, cultural-creative crowdfunding (hereafter CCCF) is 'a method of financing projects, initiatives, or ventures within the culture sectors and its CCIs through soliciting contributions/funds and support from the crowd/community of supporters via online platforms' (Demattos et al., 2024, p. 2). Crowdfunding has exhibited a fast-paced worldwide expansion in several industries and sectors of the global economy (Ziegler et al., 2020). It exists in two main logics; (1) investment with the models of equity and lending, and (2) non-investment, being reward- and donation-based (Ibid.). As previous studies have pointed out, CCIs have been predominantly adopting the second logic (Cicchiello et al., 2022; Mollick, 2014; Rykkja et al., 2024), where backers either gain some sort of non-monetary benefits or act out of philanthropy and altruism (Bretschneider & Leimeister, 2017; Cicchiello et al., 2022). Nevertheless, scholars have argued that while crowdfunding has grown exponentially in various industries, the clash between its commercial aspect and its artistic values seems to generate slow development within the culture sector (Handke & Dalla Chiesa, 2021). Accordingly, following recent works on CCCF (see, for instance, Demattos et al., 2024), broadening up the perspective of CCCF as an umbrella of collaborative practices might make it more attractive for CCIs. From this viewpoint, we further elaborate on theories of co-production of cultural projects and co-creation of values.

First, it is relevant to highlight that at times it is difficult to distinguish between co-production and co-creation. In a certain way, they denote similar practices (Brandsen & Honingh, 2018). Yet, seeking a distinction, Brandsen and Honingh (2018, p.13) define co-production as 'generally associated with services citizens receive during the implementation phase of the production cycle, whereas co-creation concerns services at a strategic level'. This means that when individuals are engaged in the planning of something, there is co-creation; and when they shape the service (or product) in the later phases, there is co-production (Ibid.). Nevertheless, studies on both co-production and co-creation have mostly focused on their drivers rather than outcomes (Verschuere et al., 2012;

Voorberg et al., 2015). Noteworthy, a great number of papers address both concepts in relation to the public sector and government actions (ibid.). In the present study, we rather want to draw on how co-creation and co-production make funding different. More specifically, in which cases crowdfunding can be an arena for co-creation and co-production in the context of the cultural sector.

Following the argument that collective action can facilitate co-production (Pestoff, 2014), which in turn can boost co-creation of value(-in-context) (Luonila & Jyrämä, 2020; Minkiewicz et al., 2016; Thyne & Hede, 2016), we suggest that CCCF offers a meta-level of co-creation and co-production (see also Quero et al., 2017). Even though the cultural sector often appears to be similar to public goods, we focus on the active participation of backers (rather than citizens) in the development of a creative project (rather than the provision of public services) alongside the interconnection and intermediation of the crowdfunding platform (rather than the state). We outline that both co-production and co-creation emphasize collaboration, shared responsibility, and mutual engagement between backers, project creators, and platforms. Through interactions and co-production, value is being co-created, which leads to favourable outcomes for all the involved parties. Accordingly, CCCF not only involves backer participation in funding projects but also enables them to shape cultural products and services, creating a broader platform for engagement that can also be considered a digital middleground (see Dalla Chiesa & Rykkja, 2024).

In summary, we propose that CCCF acts as a higher-level mechanism where the principles of collective action, co-production, and co-creation converge, providing a fertile ground for deeper involvement in both the financial and creative aspects of cultural production. Figure 1 illustrates it and further shows how CCCF fosters both financial and creative collaboration within a crowdfunding platform, thus amplifying collective action and resulting in co-creation of diverse values. Through CCCF, citizens are not just passive donors; they actively engage in shaping the outcomes by contributing to a dynamic process of co-production and co-creation (see also Quero et al., 2017). According to Quero et al. (2017), there are different types of co-creation, i.e. co-evaluation, co-ideation, co-design, co-testing, co-launch, co-consumption and co-financing. Arguably, some of those co-creation types are also co-production, at the implementation phase of the production cycle (Brandsen & Honingh, 2018). Thereby, Fig. 1 shows the intersection of co-creation and co-production in CCCF.

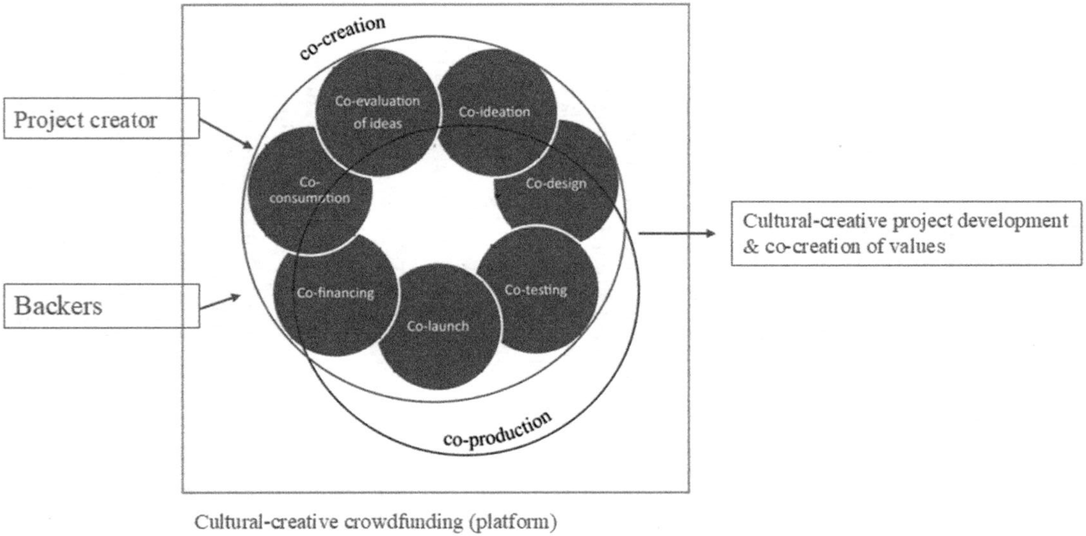

Fig. 1 The intersection of co-creation and co-production in CCCF (*Note* Elaborated by the authors and partially adapted from Quero et al. [2017])

A Note on the Perspective of 'Nothing' in the Culture Sector

While this chapter does not aim to provide exhaustive definitions of the culture sector and CCIs (see, for instance, Throsby, 2001, 2008), it is relevant to briefly distinguish them due to their implications for co-creation practices. The core cultural sector traditionally refers to commercial and non-commercial activities centred on heritage, the arts, and cultural institutions, often reliant on public funding or philanthropic support. In contrast, the CCIs encompass a broader range of commercial and non-commercial activities that leverage creativity for economic purposes, including sectors like design, media, fashion, and digital games. This distinction matters because co-creation manifests differently across these domains: in the cultural sector, it often focuses on participatory engagement and community-driven content, while in CCIs, co-creation can be tied to market-driven innovation and collaborative value creation (Handke & Dalla Chiesa, 2021; Throsby, 2001, 2008). Yet, the current study highlights their functioning as networks of agents and agencies fostering innovation through social interactions, thriving on horizontal dynamics and collaborative production processes (Poell et al., 2021; Potts et al., 2008). As digitalization transforms these sectors and crowdfunding emerges as a significant tool that not only facilitates funding but also enhances value co-creation in the intersection of co-creating and co-producing, it challenges the traditional notions of socio-economic disadvantage that often overlook the importance of rich social networks. This chapter, then, aims to analyse how crowdfunding can enable the harnessing of non-financial resources and facilitate the construction of reciprocity among stakeholders, revealing the potential for remarkable outcomes when collaborative practices are leveraged within the cultural sector in the context of the digital realm. While this discussion can seem abstract and subjective, an empirical case can help illustrate these ideas. Accordingly, the next section introduces this study's methodology before proceeding to our case study embedded in arts, creativity, and culture—surely amid digitalization.

3 Methodological Approach

This chapter adopts an exploratory case study approach (Yin, 2014) to better understand the abstract and subjective dynamics of value co-creation and reciprocity within crowdfunding practices. Examining a real-world example provides tangible illustrations of how non-financial resources are leveraged in the culture sector and shows that alternative funding and co-creation co-exist. As mentioned in the Introduction, our case study is the OVO—Formation and Transformation Orchestra, from the city of Belo Horizonte, Brazil. The main reason for choosing OVO is the fact that it represents a 'core cultural activity' (Throsby, 2008) closely related to the main ideals of artistic value and the paradigm of excellence (Bonet & Négrier, 2018), and yet it supports its existence and continuous operation via alternative funding through digital platforms.

To collect the data, we performed participatory observation of OVO actively interacting with them during a crowdfunding event; we also followed OVO's campaign via a subscription channel and on social media. In brief, participatory observation involves the researchers immersing themselves in the culture or community they are studying, actively participating in the daily activities while also observing and documenting their behaviours, beliefs, and practices (see Goldenberg, 2011; Haguette, 2001). Although we were not fully immersed in either the OVO or their crowdfunding platform Évoe over a long period of time, we did have a shared day of exchanges and discussion during the crowdfunding event in Brazil.[2] Later on, we followed up their crowdfunding campaign process through direct contact, giving some feedback, and monitoring their social media activities. During the event, we took field notes, photographs, and audio and video recordings, which were transcribed afterwards.

In addition, we conducted five in-depth interviews with the participants involved in the project as well as with the platform operators for this single case study. In particular, we conducted three interviews with the founder and conductor of OVO—two before the event in 2022 and another one in the process of writing this chapter; one interview with the managers of Évoe platform in 2022; and one interview with a premium OVO backer. The interviews followed a semi-structured approach and included questions regarding motivation towards crowdfunding, the perception of such funding mechanisms, the role of digitalization in cultural production and consumption, and aspects of co-creation and co-production such as engagement, shared beliefs, and collaboration. All interviews were recorded and transcribed in its original language and included in this chapter after translation to English.

Further, we used social media analysis as OVO is rather active on Instagram and YouTube, in addition to its channel on Évoe platform. In the context of exploring digitalization in the culture sector, social media analysis is an appropriate methodological approach that involves examining and interpreting data generated from social media platforms to understand patterns of communication, behaviour, and interactions within online communities (Lai & To, 2015). Our main focus was on qualitative data like sentiment, topics, and user-generated content. In the context of crowdfunding and the culture sector, social media analysis can uncover how campaigns gain traction, how supporters form their networks, and how co-creation (and co-production) processes(es) unfold in digital spaces. This method complemented our participatory observation by offering valuable insights into how communities form, engage, collaborate, and mobilize resources beyond financial transactions. It has also allowed us to integrate the opinions of other stakeholders, e.g., participating musicians who talked about OVO in a reel or backers who left an open message or comment.

Both authors analysed all the collected data using CAQDAS (Computer-assisted qualitative data analysis software, i.e. NVivo) to identify patterns, themes, and insights related to the research questions. Beyond the technical use of CAQDAS, we employed a reflexive thematic analysis approach as outlined by Braun and Clarke (2006). This involved familiarization with the data through repeated readings, generating initial codes, and iteratively reviewing these codes to identify meaningful patterns and themes. We then refined these themes by considering their relevance to the research questions and the theoretical framework, ensuring they reflected both the explicit content and underlying assumptions within the data. This process allowed for a nuanced interpretation, where themes were not only descriptive but also analytical, capturing the complexity of alternative funding mechanisms in the arts and their intersection with co-creation.[3] The reflexive nature of this method encouraged continuous critical engagement with the data, allowing us to question our assumptions and remain open to emergent insights throughout the analysis (Braun & Clarke, 2006). Before proceeding to the findings, we present the OVO case.

4 The Formation and Transformation Orchestra (OVO): A Case Study

The Formation and Transformation Orchestra (OVO) aims to give dozens of young musicians an orchestral experience of excellence. The orchestra consists of music students who have already mastered their instruments but have little experience in orchestras. Most of the members are undergraduate music students from public universities, either from the Federal University of Minas Gerais or the State University of Minas Gerais. They come from diverse socioeconomic backgrounds, yet predominantly from disadvantaged ones in the peripherical places. Moreover, several musicians from the Minas Gerais Philharmonic Orchestra participate in OVO to accompany the rehearsals and performances with the purpose of helping and instructing these talented students technically and artistically.

The idea behind OVO's emergence was planted in 2018 when the current conductor was invited to join as a conductor for another youth orchestra in Brazil. In September 2019, there was the last concert of the year for this youth orchestra. Then, looking at the time until the next practice started again, the co-ideation of OVO officially started, fuelled by the enthusiasm and passion of playing together. Philharmonic musician Werner Silveira, who is OVO's founder, artistic director, and conductor, got the project running with the support of his network, including fellow philharmonic musicians and business partners. Through private sponsorship and non-financial support, e.g., musicians monitoring the training, the Voluntary Orchestra, or Orquestra Voluntária, in Portuguese, had its debut in December 2019, playing Beethoven in the Minas Gerais opera house. As the orchestra expanded, the name was rebranded as OVO—Orquestra de Formação e Transformação or Formation and Transformation Orchestra. Noteworthy that the acronym OVO is a word in Portuguese, 'ovo', which means 'egg'.

OVO has early on begun to extensively operate its funding and financing through crowdfunding mechanisms, mainly adopting a subscription model, which is a continuous monthly support of the project. To begin with, the campaign, or the subscription channel, was launched by a financial service company, not a crowdfunding platform per se. The migration to a specialized platform happened when Évoe—the crowdfunding platform dedicated to creative initiatives—contacted OVO and invited them to join their space. Évoe became the main financing channel of OVO, with a great mission of understanding and practising crowdfunding not only as an alternative finance tool but rather as a channel for cultural project development. Briefly, this platform allows both subscription and reward-based crowdfunding, in addition to the arrangements enabling tax benefits. OVO's subscription channel on the platform has three options with different amounts to donate monthly and respective different rewards. Back to the egg-analogy, when you become an OVO backer, you join the 'Granja', the farm or grange; and the subscription options are all related to eggs, for instance, the bumpkin, the organic, and the premium omelette.[4]

As of 2024, OVO has become a non-profit association—Citizen Education Centre (NEC), which reflects its growth amid professionalization and, thus, increasing operating costs. Those fixed costs are covered by the monthly subscription income gathered through 'Évoe's' platform. In the next sections of Findings and Discussion, we will discuss more about OVO's characteristics and features as an online centre to share knowledge focused on entrepreneurship in the musical scene and how co-production and co-creation contribute to its functioning. Still, as illustrated above, OVO orchestrates elements that allow us to investigate the resilience of collective finance, as it represents a co-ideation project that incorporates perspectives of the project creators, project participants, backers, and the platform itself.

5 Findings

Our findings are presented thematically under three distinct headings: (1) Digitalization and CCIs, (2) Funding and Financing, and (3) Co-creation following the thematic analysis of our qualitative data

Digitalization and CCI

The co-ideation of OVO did not start digitally; however, its existence heavily relies on the understanding of how digitalization transforms the culture sector and offers new possibilities to succeed. After the first concert and receiving a positive co-evaluation of the idea from the private sponsors, collaborators, and participating musicians, OVO employed digital tools to ensure its continuity as not only a one-off project but as an orchestra (OVO Director, Interview, 2024). Recognizing that the project was enthusiastically accepted by the public and receiving encouraging feedback to keep going, OVO started building in its digital presence because, in the conductor's words:

> The public wants to be closer to the artists. (Werner Silveira, Interview 2024)

As illustrated above, OVO's director envisioned that to create a sense of community, the audience wishes to feel proximity to the artists, and this is certainly something that digitalization can offer. Accordingly, OVO first invested in its visual identity, then it established a presence in social media channels (Facebook and Instagram) and later on the subscription channel, followed by the YouTube channel (OVO manager, Interview, 2024). When exploring those digital platforms and intermediary spaces, we observe that the main aim of OVO is education—education of musicians, of the audience, and, more broadly, of society. The content mostly offers knowledge, e.g., explaining the instruments that are part of the different orchestra sections or presenting the great composers. The digital performances of OVO, either in its social media or in the 'granja', focus on being a platform to share knowledge, with the belief in the transformative power of the arts (OVO, 2024).

> I want to be able to live working with music, but I want to be a dream booster. (OVO musician, documentary 2021)

OVO has also made a documentary featuring musicians participating in the project. The sentence above is from one of them and demonstrates that the musicians see OVO as a space that gives opportunities and encourages dreams. Such dreams can be passed forward through community engagement. OVO, as its name says, is an orchestra of formation and transformation. The digitalization embedded in OVO's core is to assure that even at the centre of cultural expressions and artistic values of excellence, digital spaces offer proximity between creators and consumers, breaking elitist (invisible) barriers that place orchestra as a space of few privileged ones. Furthermore, the proximity of musicians and audiences in the digital realm allows co-consumption, alongside co-production and co-creation. It is in this configuration that the main motivation for co-financing lays; backers decide to support OVO especially because they see artistic excellence inside a specific socioeconomic context, giving opportunity and transforming lives (event round table, 2024).

Funding and Financing

OVO has almost 20 thousand followers on Instagram, more than 500 subscribers on YouTube, yet no more than 50 backers on their subscription channel. Most of them know Werner Silveira personally, and believe in his work, ambition, and dreams. They do not necessarily decide what will be in the concert repertoire, but they join the pre-concert lectures to learn more about the music history and the story behind different compositions, contextualizing the music to be played. Nonetheless, musicians, collaborators, and the audience, although actively interacting in the digital realm, are truly eager to participate in the in-person attendance to have the experience (and feelings) that only an orchestra concert can provide (CrowdCul event recording, 2022). For this, OVO has to secure financial resources.

Even if not more than 50 backers are co-financing OVO, the monthly income is around U$600,00 (OVO Director, Interview, 2024), which covers the main costs, e.g., 12% to the platform, 50% for educational activities, 30% for fixed costs—management and marketing, and 8% to projects to be submitted to public calls for financing culture (Leis de Incentivo a Cultura) (Évoe, n.d.). '*Grain by grain, the hen fills its crop*' (OVO Instagram, n.d.) is the motor behind this operationalization. Before tapping into the fact that a small proportion of the income goes to the projects aiming to get public money, it is relevant to recall the role of Évoe.

Évoe is one platform with multiple voices. It connects institutions, sponsors, creators and supporters/backers (Évoe, n.d.). As mentioned in the case study description, it was Évoe team who approached OVO to invite the orchestra to their platform (OVO director, Interview, 2024). They did that because they saw OVO as not only an artistic initiative of excellence but a socially engaged cultural project. A project that was not a one-off initiative but a long-term vision. Évoe perceives crowdfunding as more than just an alternative source of finance. It has to be a channel, or opportunity, of and for cultural project development (CrowdCul event recording, 2022). As the platform's representative discusses:

> Cultural-creative crowdfunding, rather than a collective finance for cultural-creative production, is about project development. (Évoe, round table, 2022)

A cultural project of a youth orchestra, including young music students who do not necessarily have access to orchestral experience and come from socioeconomically disadvantaged communities, was a project that Évoe wanted to host on the platform. As stated in OVO's Instagram page:

> Recalling a great Brazilian composer, Heitor Villa-Lobos, 'Music is as useful as bread and water. It is an essential element in the education of the character of youth.' (OVO's Instagram, n.d.)

This statement corresponds well with Évoe's beliefs that a crowdfunding platform committed to the core values of the cultural sector has an active role in promoting spaces of exchange, sharing, and collaboration. Ultimately, crowdfunding is seen as project development: 'management is simplified, and the community grows, everyone wins, because we can bring culture to more people' (Évoe, n.d.; event recordings, 2022). Évoe is committed to proposing new solutions and is willing to listen to suggestions in a flexible manner, supporting the continued existence of cultural (and socially engaged) projects. By seeing the relative success of OVO's granja, enabling them to cover the basic costs forOVO's existence, the participants state:

> Dream that is dreamed together is reality. (OVO musician, documentary, 2021)

It is noteworthy that all the revenue that OVO makes from the concert ticket sales is shared among all the musicians. Back to the revenue dedicated to preparing projects to get public funds, this illustrates co-creation and co-production, as using the alternative funding enables co-launch, co-testing and co-design. Without discussing the Brazilian cultural policy and its mechanisms of funding and financing, the fact is that at the intersection of digitalization and alternative finance, co-production and co-creation are happening, aiming to expand OVO's financial portfolio. In other words, it was because of the 'granja' (farm, in English) and the digital community that OVO started up-scaling its activities and reached the 'formal' level, unlocking public grants for culture. Werner Silveira says that he envisions a diversified portfolio of investments for OVO, and he does have innovative ideas for novel instruments—but this is an issue for future research (or practical experimentation).

Co-Creation

The aspects of co-creation are undoubtedly the most challenging to grasp, as they are by far the most intangible ones. Co-creation is often rather a theoretical analytical tool than a practice that creators and consumers are actively engaging with. However, even with this being the case, there are some empirical illustrations of the co-creation aspects as presented in Fig. 2.

Following Dalla Chiesa and Rykkja (2024)'s approach to digital platforms as mediators of creativity, where actors can outreach community ties, our findings on co-creation aspects point out precisely the existence of this 'digital middleground' where the scope of creativity is digitally dispersed in different forms of exchange. By integrating Fig. 1, namely, the intersection of co-creation and co-production in CCCF, with Dalla Chiesa and Rykkja (2024)'s framework, we see how OVO, through its engagement with a subscription-based crowdfunding campaign closely connected to its active online media presence, not only involves backer participation in funding projects but also enables them to shape the development of a cultural-artistic project.

It might be the case that within the principles of collective action, co-production, and co-creation, the involvement on the financial side is deeper than the creative aspects of cultural production. However, the digital space still provides a fertile ground for all the elements with the prefix 'co-'. Most relevant, community engagement results in the co-creation of diverse values, which are connected to the many values of culture (see Throsby, 2001). The exercise here is, therefore, to perceive the abstraction of co-creation aspects in terms of social tactility, especially in the sense of the capacity to engage with the subtle dimension of co-producing a project. Making OVO existence possible, digital involvement, including the financing support, is crucial, but it also gives room to tactile value—the concert itself—to reflect the tangible aspects of social bonds that are felt and experienced. The tangible aspects come together with intangible aspects of social cohesion, enhancing value through experiences that are tactile in nature, even in digital contexts, but also non-tactile when the dimension of opportunity plays a role. From this perspective, OVO team acknowledges that backers support their continued existence because it is about '*artistic excellence embedded in specific context*' (Werner Silveira, Interview, 2024).

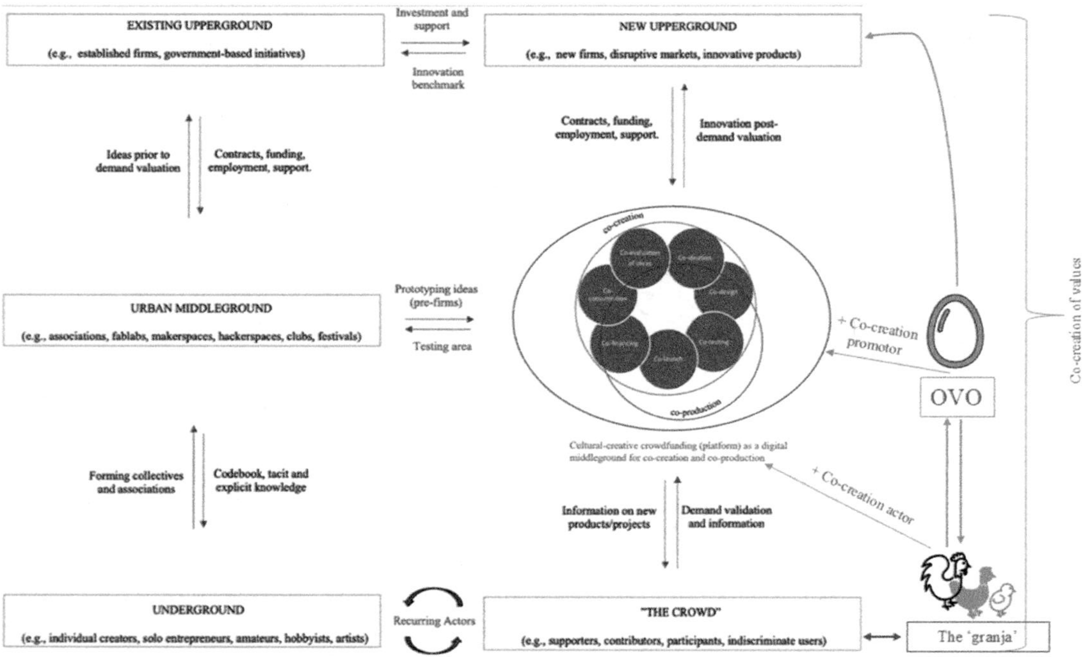

Fig. 2 (Co-)creating from 'grains', (co-)producing by shared beliefs, making it happen digitally (*Note* Adapted from Dalla Chiesa & Rykkja [2024])

In other words, A cultural project of orchestral experience for young musicians from disadvantaged communities is something that this of people believe in and want to realize. It is the co-production and co-creation for project development, and the continuation of OVO's existence makes co-creation of values (-in-context) a reality. In this sense, the tangibility of a live connection that shapes a valuable social experience, especially in community-driven or collaborative spaces, is the core of digital co-creation. Artistic excellence embedded in a specific context thrives on co-production and co-creation, where communities' ability to engage plays a pivotal role. This form of excellence, in the means of becoming a renowned orchestra, is not just about skills but also about creating tactile value, a value that is experienced and shared within a community. OVO gives an opportunity, thus allowing dreams, and those dreams become a new form of creativity that is digitally dispersed.

In this process, OVO is evolving, musicians are being formed, and the public engaging in the digital realm also experiences the in-person feelings that only a concert can offer. Yet, the digital involvement through OVO's social media content, crowdfunding rewards, and audience behaviour, demonstrates another aspect of co-creation; there is a co-education practice embedded in all of it. To conclude, OVO co-created its existence through community ties and expanded its co-production by understanding the connectivity of bottom-up digital collaborations. Bearing this in mind, the following section advances this discussion by bringing it closer to the existing literature and contributing with lessons for the practitioners.

6 Discussion and Final Remarks

This discussion part aims to summarize the chapter's main contributions to theory and practice, highlighting both the empirical and theoretical insights gained from the study. By employing a combination of participatory observation, social media analysis and interviews, we take a rich, immersive approach to examining the resilience of collective finance through the case of OVO. This approach allows us to explore the nuances of digital collaborative practices—particularly co-production and co-creation—and the ways digital platforms act as intermediaries to enhance these processes. However, it remains challenging to precisely measure co-creation, especially in the context of funding strategies, as it requires complex observations and robust data collection. Thus, we acknowledge that, despite its contributions, the study has some limitations, notably due to the abstract and, to some extent, intangible nature of the concepts and the single-case design, suggesting that future research should apply these theoretical propositions more broadly across the culture sector vis-à-vis the CCIs.

Yet, in response to the research question, 'Under what circumstances does digital funding allow or give room for co-creation?, our findings indicate that digital funding facilitates co-creation when three key circumstances align: the design of the digital platform as a participatory space, the alignment of artistic values with community engagement, and the transparency of the funding process. Platforms that enable active interaction between creators and supporters—not merely transactional exchanges—foster an environment where co-creation thrives. OVO, an orchestra, represents a core cultural expression closely tied to the ideals of artistic value and excellence, aligning these with digital platforms and alternative funding strategies. As a unique case, OVO shows how crowdfunding intersects with artistic excellence (see Demattos et al., 2024), also by embedding practices within a digital space that fosters co-creation and co-production through blending with grassroots participation. This process respects local cultural and social nuances, adding depth and authenticity to the artistic work and embedding context-specific values that enhance the relevance of art within its community, thus allowing for authentic engagement that extends beyond financial contributions. OVO's innovative practices underscore the potential for co-production in artistic ventures; they foster co-creation of shared and diverse values, promote wide diffusion, and ultimately enhance socioeconomic realities.

However, co-creation in digital funding remains contingent on the willingness of both artists and audiences to engage beyond traditional roles. It signals that while digital tools offer co-creation potential, the success of co-creative funding models depends on intentional design and reciprocal commitment.

To further develop the discussion around our findings and their theoretical contributions, we categorise them according to three themes emerging from the analysis: Digitalization, Funding, and Co-Creation.

Digitalization and CCIs. OVO leverages digitalization to bring artists and audiences closer together, in line with the literature indicating that digitalization redefines CCI dynamics and fosters unprecedented levels of connectedness (Benghozi & Paris, 2016; Poell et al., 2021). OVO recognizes that community-building requires audiences to feel a sense of proximity to the artists, which is achieved through a digital presence. This commitment to engagement also brings a new layer of *co-education* to OVO's activities, as their crowdfunding rewards are tied to educational and audience-building experiences. This points to a previously underexplored potential in CCCF for integrating co-production and co-creation, demonstrating how digital finance shapes new pathways for audience engagement and project sustainability (Dalla Chiesa, 2020; Rykkja & Hauge, 2021). Furthermore, although OVO initially relied on its network to fund its first concert, it quickly incorporated aspects of traditional art practices like busking and patronage while also strategically embracing digital finance to secure its future.

Funding and Financing. Starting with a single digital platform, OVO has diversified its funding sources and developed robust resource management and network coordination strategies. This highlights how platformization, specifically crowdfunding, challenges the role of traditional intermediaries in CCIs (Benghozi & Paris, 2016; Poell et al., 2021). OVO's digital funding strategy has allowed it to access public grants, effectively bridging traditional mechanisms with non-traditional ones. This digital *middleground* (Dalla Chiesa & Rykkja, 2024) is evident in OVO's journey from crowdfunding to formal cultural incentives, demonstrating how CCCF not only supports project funding but also enables backers to participate actively in shaping project development. Here, co-creation plays a transformative role; the collaborative, non-hierarchical exchanges between agents often reshape funding strategies, creating distinct expectations and a more community-driven funding model that differs significantly from conventional approaches. By integrating socially engaged practices into the funding process, OVO illustrates the profound impact co-creation can have on transforming realities, both economically and socially.

Co-Creation. Returning to our theoretical foundation, CCCF operates as a higher-level mechanism in which collective action, co-production, and co-creation converge. This convergence supports a contemporary, open, and non-hierarchical form of creativity aligned with culture sector dynamics (Dalla Chiesa & Rykkja, 2024; Poell et al., 2021; Potts et al., 2008). OVO exemplifies how creativity can flourish within digital communities, where social networks and shared values drive co-creation. In such networks, OVO taps into non-financial resources, reciprocity, and social engagement, emphasizing that successful co-creation relies on a robust network. OVO's case demonstrates that a platform can play an active role in shaping socially engaged practices, revealing the deep impact co-creation can have on community resilience and cultural innovation. This socially-engaged aspect also highlights the importance of crowdfunding, not only as a financial tool but as a means for backers to engage in project development, ultimately shaping cultural production in profound ways.

In sum, this chapter provides a foundation for future research on co-creation in the CCIs by using case studies to explore its mechanisms and reflexivity, helping researchers to better understand how co-creation unfolds in the practices of a socio-cultural project aimed at disadvantaged social groups who can largely benefit from grassroots funding actions.

For practitioners, the findings suggest that socially engaged co-creation models can enrich funding strategies and foster sustainable cultural projects. OVO's case also underscores the potential to further explore the role of non-financial contributions and community dynamics in fostering successful crowdfunding, particularly where alternative funding and participatory models may have distinct impacts on the culture sector. OVO's practices demonstrate that co-creation requires a networked approach, with digital platforms actively facilitating engagement and encouraging socially driven initiatives. This chapter argues for a nuanced understanding of co-creation within cultural projects, as these practices provide a way to embed values-in-context, bringing broader, context-specific meaning to cultural production while fostering resilience, economic impact, and social transformation.

7 Competing Interests

The writing of this chapter was supported by a grant from the Research Council of Norway [301291].

Notes

1. The name OVO—Formation and Transformation Orchestra, or OVO—Orquestra de Formação e Transformação, in Portuguese, is the new name of the initiative, effective from 2022. When it was created, OVO was an acronym for the Voluntary Orchestra, or Orquestra Voluntária in Portuguese. In a later section of this chapter, there is more about the story of OVO. For now, as a note of curiosity, in Portuguese, OVO means egg.

2. The international research project CrowdCul (Crowdfunding in the Culture Sector), funded by the Research Council of Norway (Project Grant Number: 301291), organized an event in Belo Horizonte, Brazil, in July 2022. This event gathered artists, cultural managers and producers, cultural workers, crowdfunding platforms, creative entrepreneurs, students, researchers, and anyone interested in understanding and exploring the various aspects of crowdfunding in arts and culture. The CrowdCul event in Brazil included the participation of Werner Silveira, founder and conductor of OVO, and representatives of the crowdfunding platform, Évoe, in which OVO has its subscription channel. After the event, the researchers kept in contact with them, also following up on the crowdfunding process. This allowed the participatory observation in our case study.
3. The following seven main themes emerged from iterative coding, grounded in both the data and theoretical frameworks related to co-creation, platformization and digital tools, and alternative funding: (1) Digital Platforms as Enablers of Co-Creation, (2) Narratives of Resource Scarcity and Creative Autonomy, (3) Mechanisms of Bottom-Up Collaboration, (4) Trust, Transparency, and Community Building in Crowdfunding, (5) Redefining Value: Beyond Financial Metrics, (6) Tensions Between Commercialization and Artistic Integrity, and (7) Sustainability and Long-Term Impact of Alternative Funding Models. The authors are available upon request for further explanation of the thematic analysis.
4. The packages and respective rewards are the following: (1) Bumpkin (Basic)—less than U$ 10,00 per month, exclusive videos of the orchestra, one pair of tickets to watch the concert at the end of the year, one lottery ticket for a dinner with the conductor paid for by the Orchestra. (2) Organic (Intermediary), around U$15 per month, exclusive videos of the orchestra, one pair of tickets to watch the concert at the end of the year, two lottery tickets for a dinner with the conductor paid for by the Orchestra, and access to an exclusive lecture about the concert taught by Werner Silveira (in person or online). (3) Premium Omelet—around U$20 per month, exclusive videos of the orchestra, one pair of tickets in the VIP section to watch the concert at the end of the year, four lottery tickets for a dinner with the conductor paid for by the Orchestra, access to an exclusive lecture about the concert taught by Werner Silveira (in person or online), watching the dress rehearsal on stage from chairs

alongside the musicians and after-the-rehearsal talk with the musicians and conductor about the experience, a special gift from the OVO orchestra.

References

Benghozi, P.-J., & Paris, T. (2016). The Cultural Economy in the Digital Age: A Revolution in Intermediation? *City, Culture and Society, 7*(2), 75–80.

Bonet, L., & Négrier, E. (2018). The Participative Turn in Cultural Policy: Paradigms, Models, Contexts. *Poetics, 66*, 64–73.

Brandsen, T., & Honingh, M. (2018). Definitions of Co-Production and Co-Creation. In T. Brandsen, B. Verschuere, & T. Steen (Eds.), *Co-Production and Co-Creation* (pp. 9–17). Routledge.

Braun, V., & Clarke, V. (2006). Using Thematic Analysis in Psychology. *Qualitative Research in Psychology, 3*(2), 77–101.

Bretschneider, U., & Leimeister, J. M. (2017). Not Just an Ego-trip: Exploring Backers' Motivation for Funding in Incentive-based Crowdfunding. *The Journal of Strategic Information Systems, 26*(4), 246–260.

Cicchiello, A. F., Gallo, S., & Monferrà, S. (2022). Mapping Crowdfunding in Cultural and Creative Industries: A Conceptual and Empirical Overview. *European Management Review, 19*(1), 22–37.

Dalla Chiesa, C. (2020). Crowdfunding the Queer Museum: A Polycentric Identity Quarrel. In E. Dekker & P. Kuchar (Eds.), *Governing Markets as Knowledge Commons* (pp. 238–235). Cambridge University Press.

Dalla Chiesa, C., & Rykkja, A. (2024). Bridging the Urban-digital divide: Crowdfunding as an Online Middleground Space. *City, Culture and Society, 37*, Article 100580.

Demattos Guimarães, A., Maehle, M., & Bonet, L. (2024). The Relational Forms of Cultural-creative Crowdfunding: A Typology of Practices Through Mapping Platforms in Europe and Latin America. *Poetics, 105*, Article 101913.

Demattos Guimarães, A. (2024). *The Equilibrist Hope: Perspectives & prospectives on cultural-creative crowdfunding*. Western Norway University of Applied Science [PhD Dissertation].

Évoe. (2024). Clube de assinaturas da Orquestra OVO. https://www.evoe.cc/parceiro/orquestra-ovo/bem-vindo

Goldenberg, M. (2011). *A arte de pesquisar: como fazer pesquisa qualitativa em Ciências Sociais*, 8ª ed. Record.

Haguette, T. M. F. (2001). *Qualitative Methodologies in Sociology*. Vozes.

Handke, C., & Dalla Chiesa, C. (2021). The Art of Crowdfunding Arts and Innovation: The Cultural Economic Perspective. *Journal of Cultural Economics, 46*, 249–284.

Lai, L. S. L., & Ming To, W. (2015). Content Analysis of Social Media: A Grounded Theory Approach. *Journal of Electronic Commerce Research, 16*(2), 138.

Lazzaro, E., & Noonan, D. (2021). A Comparative Analysis of US and EU Regulatory Frameworks of Crowdfunding for the Cultural and Creative Industries. *International Journal of Cultural Policy, 27*(5), 590–606.

Loots, E., Piecyk, K., & Wijngaarden, Y. (2023). At the Juncture of Funding, Policy, and Technology: How Promising is Match-funding of Arts and Culture Through Crowdfunding Platforms? *International Journal of Cultural Policy, 30*(1), 118–134.

Luonila, M., & Jyrämä, A. (2020). Does Co-production Build on Co-creation or Does Co-creation Result in Co-producing? *Arts and the Market, 10*(1), 1–17.

Minkiewicz, J., Bridson, K., & Evans, J. (2016). Co-production of Service Experiences: Insights from the Cultural Sector. *Journal of Services Marketing, 30*(7), 749–761.

Mollick, E. (2014). The Dynamics of Crowdfunding: An Exploratory Study. *Journal of Business Venturing, 29*(1), 1–16.

Pestoff, V. (2014). Collective Action and the Sustainability of Co-Production. *Public Management Review, 16*(3), 383–401.

Poell, T., Nieborg, D. B., & Duffy, B. E. (2021). *Platforms and Cultural Production*. John Wiley & Sons.

Potts, J., Cunningham, S., Hartley, J., & Ormerod, P. (2008). Social network markets: A new definition of the creative industries. *Journal of cultural economics, 32*(3), 167–185.

Quero, M. J., Ventura, R., & Kelleher, C. (2017). Value-in-context in Crowdfunding Ecosystems: How Context Frames Value Co-creation. *Service Business, 11*, 405–425.

Rykkja, A., Shneor, R., Maehle, N., & Munim, Z. H. (2024). Cultural Crowdfunding: Does Experience Matter? *Beta, 37*(1), 1–18.

Rykkja, A. (2023). *Take a Chance on Me: cultural Crowdfunding as a Necessary, Complementary, or Substitutive Business Model in the Nordic Countries and in Spain*. Inland Norway University of Applied Science [PhD dissertation].

Rykkja, A., & Hauge, A. (2021). Crowdfunding and Co-creation of Value: The Case of the Fashion Brand Linjer. In B. J. Hracs, T. Brydges, T. Haisch, A. Hauge, J. Jansson & J. Sjoholm (Eds.), *Culture, Creativity and Economy: Collaborative Practices, Value Creation and Spaces of Creativity*. Routledge.

Throsby, D. (2001). *Economics and Culture*. Cambridge University Press.

Throsby, D. (2008). Modelling the Cultural Industries. *International Journal of Cultural Policy, 14*(3), 217–232.
Thyne, M., & Hede, A.-M. (2016). Approaches to Managing Co-production for the Co-creation of Value in a Museum Setting: When Authenticity Matters. *Journal of Marketing Management, 32*(15–16), 1478–1493.
Verschuere, B., Brandsen, T., & Pestoff, V. (2012). Co-Production: The State of the Art in Research and the Future Agenda. VOLUNTAS: *International Journal of Voluntary and Nonprofit Organizations, 23*, 1083–1101.
Voorberg, W. H., Bekkers, V. J. J. M., & Tummers, L. G. (2015). A Systematic Review of Co-creation and Co-production: Embarking on the Social Innovation Journey. *Public Management Review, 17*(9), 1333–1357.
Yin, R. K. (2014). *Case Study Design and Research Methods* (5th ed.). Sage.
Ziegler, T., Shneor, R. Wenzlaff, K., Wang, B.W., Kim, J., Odorovi´c, A., Camargo Paes, F. F., Suresh, K., Zhang, B. Z., Johanson, D., Lopez, C., Mammadova, L., Adams, N., & Luo, D. (2020). *The Global Alternative Finance Market Benchmarking Report*. Cambridge Centre for Alternative Finance.

Open Access This chapter is licensed under the terms of the Creative Commons Attribution 4.0 International License (http://creativecommons.org/licenses/by/4.0/), which permits use, sharing, adaptation, distribution and reproduction in any medium or format, as long as you give appropriate credit to the original author(s) and the source, provide a link to the Creative Commons license and indicate if changes were made.

The images or other third party material in this chapter are included in the chapter's Creative Commons license, unless indicated otherwise in a credit line to the material. If material is not included in the chapter's Creative Commons license and your intended use is not permitted by statutory regulation or exceeds the permitted use, you will need to obtain permission directly from the copyright holder.

CHAPTER 18

Conclusions

Carolina Dalla Chiesa and *Anders Rykkja*

1 Some Final Thoughts and Future Directions

Let us end this volume by sharing some thoughts on developing a future research agenda for funding and financing of the arts and culture.

As we explained in the introduction, the main objective of editing the volume was to explore traditional as well as newer funding and financing tools/methods or models for cultural production in the era post-digitalisation. Despite contemporary developments in the field of arts funding, grosso modo, the making and distribution of arts and culture is to a great extent enabled by a combination of public support, private funding, private financing, or earned income (cf. Srakar & Čopič, 2012). Our interest lies in the relationships and interplay between these alternatives and the impact of digitalisation on their contemporary use as models for funding and financing arts and culture.

C. Dalla Chiesa (✉)
Erasmus University Rotterdam, Rotterdam, Netherlands
e-mail: c.dallachiesa@eshcc.eur.nl

A. Rykkja
Queen's University Belfast, Belfast, Northern Ireland
e-mail: a.rykkja@qub.ac.uk

© The Author(s) 2026
C. Dalla Chiesa and A. Rykkja (eds.), *Cultural Funding and Financing*, Cultural Economics & the Creative Economy,
https://doi.org/10.1007/978-3-031-96696-5_18

As such, an initial idea for future research lies in the development of analyses regarding these models' contemporary adoption patterns, individually as well as combined around the globe. This ties in with a need for research looking into how much of the provision of cultural goods and services is facilitated by public or private sources, or how the proportions of self-funding impact cultural ventures. Moreover, there is the issue of declining cultural public budgets in Europe and the globe (cf. Chapter "Introduction"). Is this a sustained scenario extending to regions beyond the EU and other major economies? Can we observe any intra-regional similarities or differences? What causes them? While these questions are, in a way, basic, they are also timeless. Returning to the basics of understanding the dynamics of sources of funding and finance remains an everlasting concern in the arts and culture. The global state of public funding of arts and culture necessitates more robust comparative analyses.

A second line of research, in part related to the former proposal, is trying to understand how the use of funding and financing models is conditioned by differences in the institutional context and the make-up of local ecosystems in the different cultural and creative sectors (CCS). This type of research could explore whether there is a tendency for models to converge and overlap as a rule or whether overlap and convergence is triggered by specific conditions. The suggestion is also an opportunity to advance research into a fundamental question in cultural economics, that is, the extent to which government support crowds-out private investment. It is, however, important to emphasise that future research into this topic should strive to go beyond establishing whether crowding-in or out is taking place. A complementary objective would be to examine how forms of monetary support encompass various symbols, and motivations beyond a price signal. If the premise guiding this type of research is that different funding and financing sources can and do join efforts rather than force one another out, we can suppose that agents minimally trust each other in specific institutional settings. This would imply that the presence of multiple tools working together could yield better credibility signals for the cultural sectors compared with contexts in which they work separately, hence adding to our understanding of the variables that may or may not produce variance in funding and finance usage across countries, institutions, and sectoral affiliations.

A third concern is the plurality of value(s) of culture, a concern that elicits strong interest among scholars across a broad range of disciplines, notably in cultural economics, cultural management, entrepreneurship, sociology and cultural studies more broadly. Ascertaining the value of cultural and creative goods is a complex issue. The value and worth of CCS-related products extend beyond their price (Dekker, 2015), and they are often characterised by their singularity (Karpik, 2021), incommensurability (Espeland & Stevens, 1998), and infinite surprises (Hutter, 2015). Some forms of creativity are not meant to be traded on or constitute market transactions, as they are artistic creations and productive work motivated by exercising creative capabilities (Sen, 1999). Therefore a market is just one out of many viable ways to gain access to production resources. If we, however, insist that this is the (only) way to exist, a number of creators, artists, and producers' risk being denied access to means of production owing to personal preference or inability to meet the formal standards of a market economy. In this sense, inquiring about "unseen" cultural production, hobbyists, amateurs, and early-stage career professionals may give us a better view into value creation processes.

The choice may not be as pressing compared to enduring concerns about precarious working conditions and changes to patterns of multiple job holding. Yet, we believe it is worth shedding more light on the fringes of cultural production that emerge from hobbyist activities and amateurism (Prior, 2018). Indeed, these forms of cultural labour and artistic work may constitute valuable expressions, just like those deemed to have commercial potential or considered excellent according to peer- or merit-based criteria. The recent and ongoing surge in amateur cultural production in households therefore necessitates further investigation to better understand the extent to which cultural labour, outputs and productions are channelled through markets, made available via public interventions, or independently as a result of different practices that vary in terms of their levels of professionalisation.

Fourth, a look at careers can help scholars develop a longitudinal view of the CCS centred on human potential and motivation. When careers advance, just like in the story of our aspiring musician in the introduction, different paths towards what we label 'hybridisation' of financing mechanisms reveal themselves as options. Hybridisation would involve combining funding (a grant, a lump sum, or a donation) and financing (earned income, debt, and equity financing when possible) sources into a model that works for a given person in a given context. Thus far, we have limited knowledge of how hybridisation plays out: if, when and how funding and financing models become substitutes? Since we can expect more hybridisation and new platform-based models of funding to emerge, with others disappearing or fading in importance, a focus on better understanding hybrid combinations will be important going forward. Current academic literature fails to adequately cover many of these developments, particularly as we are currently experiencing dramatic technological changes. The development of generative artificial intelligence (Gen-AI) technology can bring an array of new avenues for researchers interested in how the CCS shares and reorganises its value in a world where machines create, displace labour, and potentially upend what it is to make and distribute creative products.

This ties in with a fifth and final concern, which is the need to reform or rethink public funding structures for the twenty-first century. The rationale, based on the case of Europe, is that the current levels of allocations are insufficient to meet the needs and demands of a growing cultural workforce (Mangset, 2020; Mangset et al., 2018). The critical view (cf. Chapter "Introduction") convincingly argues that innovation and development of public funding models have been limited in recent decades. An agenda has recently been launched in response, advocating for more research into how models of public intervention can better support production, consumption, and access to arts and culture (Mazzucato et al., 2025). However, implementing changes requires either new ideas or a greater adoption of existing concepts that have been discussed for some time. Examples of the latter (not so new) 'innovations', notably match funding or public–private partnerships, involve transferring power from some of the present holders and wielders (e.g., civil servants, experts, and members of Arts Councils) in favour of audiences and consumers. Some more so-called "alternatives" like crowdfunding, are not new anymore, although their mechanisms can innovatively allow institutions to harness the benefits of demand revealing at early-stage creation stages and reveal (or not) the audience's approval next to more traditional marks of appreciation such as governmental support and private investment by firms. If we were to operationalise these challenges into research questions, we would establish to what extent it is (will be) possible to implement models premised on both novel forms of co-creation and bottom-up community-driven support within traditional models and structures for allocating grants without artists and creators necessarily having to forego a decent disposable income, which, in many cases, is already minimal. These are also questions that tie in with thinking around concepts such as inequality, democracy, quality, excellence and market formation: topics dear to both cultural economists and sociologists alike.

Some questions and concerns unanswered. Thinking around others has advanced and become clearer thanks to the many contributors in this volume-to whom we are truly grateful. This edited volume encapsulates our belief about the role of academic publishing in opening new research projects. We sought to open avenues for discussion and foster a hope that, after this long and laborious process, some topics would gain sufficient critical mass to inspire a search for new answers or perhaps new questions worth asking globally.

With these final thoughts, we close this volume, certain that the individual contributions provide ideas that will help develop new research and improve our knowledge and understanding of the way in which the funding and financing of cultural production continues to evolve its combined use of traditional and novel models.

References

Dekker, E. (2015). Two Approaches to Study the Value of Art and Culture, and the Emergence of a Third. *Journal of Cultural Economics, 39*(4), 309–326.

Espeland, W. N., & Stevens, M. L. (1998). Commensuration as a Social Process. *Annual Review of Sociology, 24*, 313–343.

Hutter, M. (2015). Infinite Surprises: On the Stabilization of Value in the Creative Industries. In J. Beckert & P. Aspers (Eds.), *The Worth of Goods: Valuation and Pricing in the Economy* (pp. 201–220). Oxford Academic.

Karpik, L. (2021). *Valuing the Unique: The Economics of Singularities*. Princeton University Press.

Mangset, P. (2020). The End of Cultural Policy? *International Journal of Cultural Policy, 26*(3), 398–411.

Mangset, P., Heian, M. T., Kleppe, B., & Løyland, K. (2018). Why are Artists Getting Poorer? About the Reproduction of Low Income Among Artists. *International Journal of Cultural Policy, 24*(4), 539–558.

Mazzucato, M., O'Connor, J., & Bennett, T. (2025). The Art of the Public: Cultural Economy and Cultural Policy. *Journal of Cultural Economy,* 1–14.

Prior, N. (2018). *New Amateurs Revisited: Popular Music, Digital Technology, and the Fate of Cultural Production*. Routledge.

Sen, A. (1999). *Development as Freedom*. Oxford University Press.

Srakar, A., & Čopič, V. (2012). Private Investments, Public Values: A Value-based Approach to Argumenting for Public Support to the Arts. *Cultural Trends, 21*(3), 227–237.

Open Access This chapter is licensed under the terms of the Creative Commons Attribution 4.0 International License (http://creativecommons.org/licenses/by/4.0/), which permits use, sharing, adaptation, distribution and reproduction in any medium or format, as long as you give appropriate credit to the original author(s) and the source, provide a link to the Creative Commons license and indicate if changes were made.

The images or other third party material in this chapter are included in the chapter's Creative Commons license, unless indicated otherwise in a credit line to the material. If material is not included in the chapter's Creative Commons license and your intended use is not permitted by statutory regulation or exceeds the permitted use, you will need to obtain permission directly from the copyright holder.

Index

© The Editor(s) (if applicable) and The Author(s) 2026
C. Dalla Chiesa and A. Rykkja (eds.), *Cultural Funding and Financing*, Cultural Economics & the Creative Economy,
https://doi.org/10.1007/978-3-031-96696-5

Q

GPSR Compliance

The European Union's (EU) General Product Safety Regulation (GPSR) is a set of rules that requires consumer products to be safe and our obligations to ensure this.

If you have any concerns about our products, you can contact us on ProductSafety@springernature.com

In case Publisher is established outside the EU, the EU authorized representative is:

Springer Nature Customer Service Center GmbH
Europaplatz 3
69115 Heidelberg, Germany

Batch number: 10844637

Printed by Printforce, the Netherlands